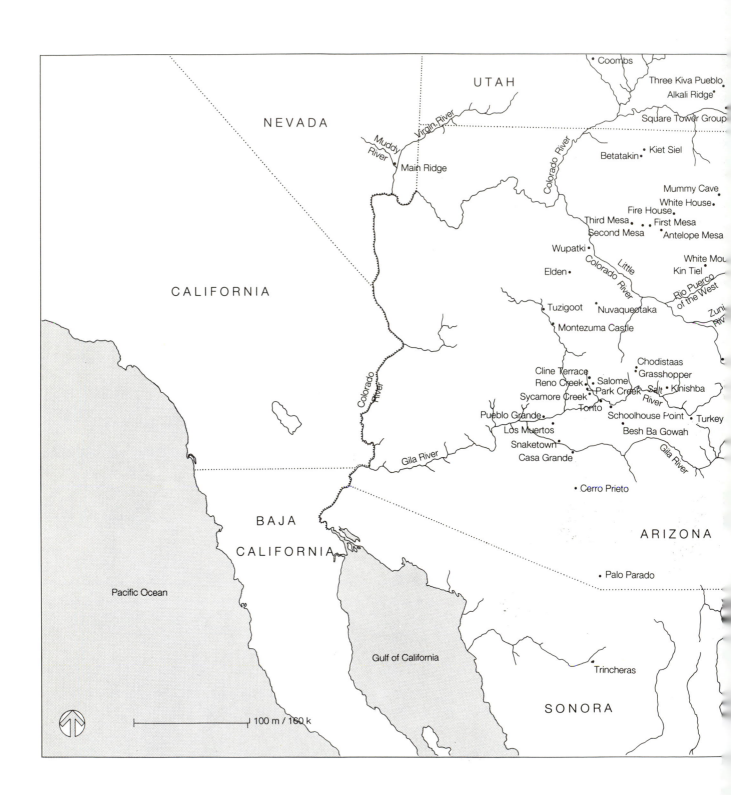

Coombs

Three Kiva Pueblo
Alkali Ridge

UTAH

Square Tower Group

NEVADA

Kiet Siel

Betatakin

Virgin River

Muddy
River

Colorado River

Mummy Cave
White House
Fire House
Third Mesa   First Mesa
Second Mesa   Antelope Mesa

Main Ridge

Wupatki

White Mou
Kin Tiel

Colorado River

Little

CALIFORNIA

Elden

Rio Puerco
of the West

Zuni
Riv

Tuzigoot   Nuvaqueotaka

Montezuma Castle

Chodistaas
Cline Terrace   Grasshopper
Reno Creek   Salome   Kinishba
Park Creek   Salt
Sycamore Creek   River
Tonto
Pueblo Grande   Schoolhouse Point   Turkey
Los Muertos   Besh Ba Gowah
Snaketown
Casa Grande

Colorado   River

Gila River

Cerro Prieto

ARIZONA

BAJA

CALIFORNIA

Palo Parado

Pacific Ocean

Gulf of California

Trincheras

SONORA

100 m / 160 k

ANCIENT ARCHITECTURE OF THE SOUTHWEST

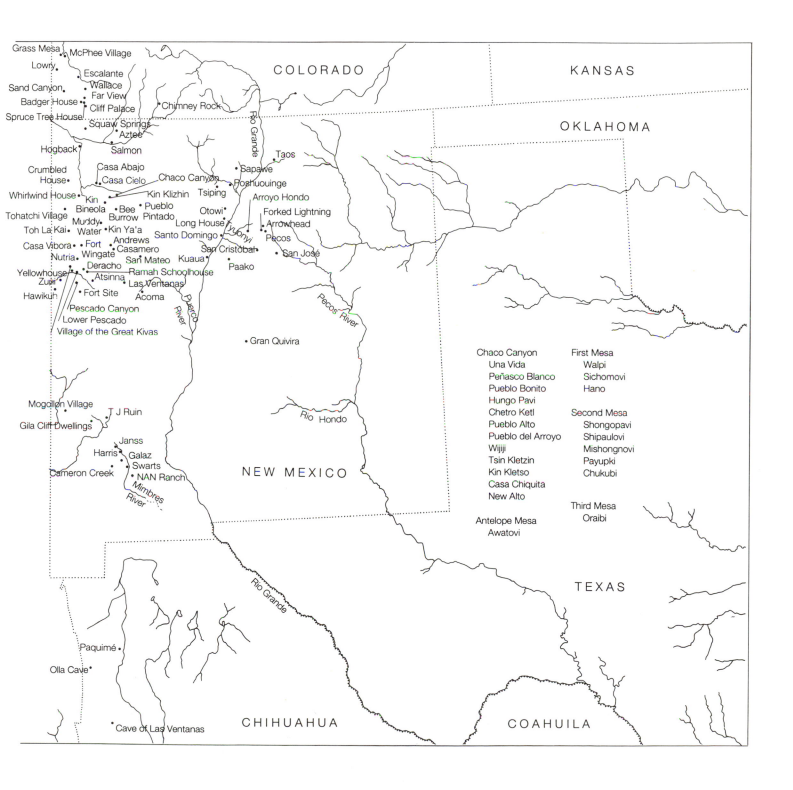

COLORADO

KANSAS

OKLAHOMA

Grass Mesa
McPhee Village
Lowry
Escalante
Wallace
Sand Canyon
Far View
Badger House
Cliff Palace
Chimney Rock
Spruce Tree House
Squaw Springs
Aztec
Hogback
Salmon
Taos
Crumbled House
Casa Abajo
Sapawe
Casa Cielo
Chaco Canyon
Poshuouinge
Whirlwind House
Kin Klizhin
Tsiping
Kin
Arroyo Hondo
Tohatchi Village
Bineola
Bee
Pueblo
Otowi
Forked Lightning
Muddy
Burrow
Pintado
Long House
Arrowhead
Toh La Kai
Water
Kin Ya'a
Tyuonyi
Pecos
Santo Domingo
Casa Vibora
Andrews
Fort
Casamero
San Cristóbal
Nutria
Wingate
Kuaua
San José
San Mateo
Deracho
Paako
Yellowhouse
Atsinna
Ramah Schoolhouse
Zuni
Las Ventanas
Hawikuh
Fort Site
Acoma
Pescado Canyon
Lower Pescado
Village of the Great Kivas

Puerco River

Pecos River

Gran Quivira

Mogollon Village
T J Ruin
Gila Cliff Dwellings
Rio Hondo
Janss
Harris
Galaz
Swarts
Cameron Creek
NAN Ranch
Mimbres River

NEW MEXICO

TEXAS

Paquimé
Olla Cave

Rio Grande

CHIHUAHUA
Cave of Las Ventanas
COAHUILA

Chaco Canyon
  Una Vida
  Peñasco Blanco
  Pueblo Bonito
  Hungo Pavi
  Chetro Ketl
  Pueblo Alto
  Pueblo del Arroyo
  Wijiji
  Tsin Kletzin
  Kin Kletso
  Casa Chiquita
  New Alto

Antelope Mesa
  Awatovi

First Mesa
  Walpi
  Sichomovi
  Hano

Second Mesa
  Shongopavi
  Shipaulovi
  Mishongnovi
  Payupki
  Chukubi

Third Mesa
  Oraibi

ANCIENT ARCHITECTURE OF THE SOUTHWEST

By WILLIAM N. MORGAN

Foreword by Rina Swentzell

 **University of Texas Press**
Austin

Research for this project was
supported in part by a grant from the
National Endowment for the Arts,
a federal agency

Library of Congress
Cataloging-in-Publication Data

Morgan, William N.
    Ancient architecture of the
Southwest / by William N. Morgan ;
foreword by Rina Swentzell. — 1st ed.
            p.   cm.
    Includes bibliographical references
and index.
    ISBN 0-292-75159-1
    1. Indians of North America—
Southwest, New—Architecture.
I. Title.
E78.S7M756   1994
720'.979—dc20   93-21256

CONTENTS

The relationship between people and the natural environment is of rising importance in our times. As a descendant of the people of the ancient Southwest, I believe that that relationship was the primary focus for my ancestors, who defined an intimate reciprocity with the earth and sky, mountains and clouds, and plants and animals. We, the descendants of "those gone before us," are left with a faint memory of their way of knowing, thinking, and being on this land. "Those gone before us" understood that humans are not distinct, separate beings from the natural environment but that every act and thought of any human being affects the cosmos. They moved through the land with a sensibility that allowed nuances of the wind, sun, and ground to affect their decision making. These sensibilities are visible in the exquisite ruins dotting the landscape of the Southwest and northern Mexico.

The numerous sites recorded here are but a sampling of ruins found on the hillsides, plateaus, and valleys of the region. The vast numbers of sites indicate, to me, the continuous movement of the people on the land rather than uncountable numbers of people. The scattered house units and unified village forms were places through which the people moved. They did not settle in one place for a long period of time but rather emulated the movement of the seasons, wind, clouds, and life cycles by moving frequently. They responded to the movement of floods, droughts, and social tensions. The movement of the clouds in the sky told them how they should move on the ground. Their sense of home, or place, was in the space between the earth and the sky and not within a specific human-built structure.

Structures, then, were generally not built to last forever but rather to meet immediate needs. Beliefs and values were clearly expressed in those structures. With adaptive flexibility and constant modification of structures, "those gone before us" left their legacy of people working within human scale creating aesthetically functional structures using accessible, simple materials, such as mud, wood, and stone. The unity of these forms is impressive and speaks about the concept of an inherent oneness of human beings with the land and the sky. Yet, the variety of the built forms is remarkable. The myriad expressions of house clusterings, village forms, enclosures, and plaza spaces are endless and, at the same time, give an overwhelming sense of wholeness as if one spirit pervaded them all.

I grew up in a modern Pueblo Indian community and spent much time within and around the ruins of the Pajarito Plateau of northern New Mexico. They continue to be a source of strength and power because I can breathe the breath of "those gone before us" in such places. Pueblo tradition tells us that we leave our sweat and breath wherever we go. The place never forgets us. Even more, the structures that we build also have breath. They are alive and participate in their own cycles of life and death and of those who have lived within them. The memory of "those gone before us" is, then, visually and psychically there to empower our present thoughts and lives.

William Morgan, in recording the limitless variety of architectural village plans in the Southwest, reinforces and validates a way of perceiving—a way of life. A way of life that looks to spiritual fulfillment rather than material acquisition or possession. A way that affirms that all life expressions are of one spirit or breath. The infusion of the spirit into the built form is evident in the aesthetic quality of the forms and sense of unity between the land and the village. It confirms for me the feeling that interrelations as expressed by the connected house units of that old world are necessary for our continued existence as one species of organism dependent like all others upon the breath, or spirit, that informs the whole universe.

Rina Swentzell
Santa Clara Pueblo

Conducted over a period of several years during the latter 1980s and early 1990s, this study took place both in the Southwest and elsewhere in the United States. The survey follows along the lines of two earlier inquiries into ancient architecture, *Prehistoric Architecture in the Eastern United States* and *Prehistoric Architecture in Micronesia*. Like its predecessors, the exploration of ancient architecture of the Southwest was encouraged and supported from the outset by two advisors who deserve special appreciation: Professor Eduard F. Sekler of the Harvard Graduate School of Design and Professor Stephen Williams of the Peabody Museum of Harvard University.

Several advisors within the Smithsonian Institution also merit special mention: Roger Kennedy, Director of the National Museum of American History, supported the research effort as it unfolded and made several suggestions for improvement; W. Richard West, Jr., Director of the National Museum of the American Indian, and David Warren, Deputy Director, have encouraged the project and offered several additional sources of information; Bruce D. Smith and Karen Dohn of the National Museum of Natural History were exceptionally helpful in assembling data and facilitating access to the National Anthropological Archives' extensive resources, including particularly the original field notes prepared by Victor Mindeleff for his *Study of Pueblo Architecture in Tusayan and Cibola*.

Without the generous support of a USA Fellowship from the National Endowment of the Arts this study would not have been possible. Special thanks are due to Randolph McAusland and Mina Berryman of the Design Arts Program, who patiently assisted in the application process and reinforced the goals for the final study. The fellowship made possible extensive travel and site visitations in the Southwest that provided valuable insights into the region's ancient architecture.

Anthropologist and author Joseph J. Snyder of Harpers Ferry, West Virginia, offered valuable suggestions in the organization and breadth of the study from its inception. John B. Carlson, Director of the Center of Archaeoastronomy in College Park, Maryland, provided helpful insights on pre-Columbian astronomy and architecture in the early phases of the research.

No single individual has been of greater assistance to this study than Stephen H. Lekson, President of the Crow Canyon Archaeological Center in Cortez, Colorado, formerly Curator of Archaeology in the Laboratory of Anthropology for the Museum of New Mexico in Santa Fe. His eminent qualifications include years of field experience on Anasazi, Mogollon, and Hohokam sites, personal knowledge of leading authorities in southwestern archaeology, and specific interest in the area of the development and evolution of ancient architecture. Stephen Lekson's contribution to the work has been prodigious.

Also of great assistance in the Laboratory of Anthropology have been Librarian Laura Holt, who spent countless hours gathering and reproducing requested information, and Rosemary Talley, Directory of Archaeological Site

Records, who retrieved data on many dozens of unpublished sites from the laboratory's extensive computer bank.

Special thanks are due to Rina Swentzell, an architectural consultant in Santa Fe, an articulate writer, and an exceptionally perceptive observer. A native of Santa Clara Pueblo in the Rio Grande Valley, she is particularly sensitive to the space, form, and mythology of Pueblo architecture. Fortunately, she also has great patience with people interested in learning about Pueblo mythology and architecture, and she has produced a number of insightful studies on Pueblo architecture in general and that of Santa Clara Pueblo in particular. She generously has contributed the Foreword to this volume.

Archaeologist Cathy Cameron of the School of American Research in Santa Fe assisted with the review of Oraibi and other Hopi sites. Acknowledgment is due to John Stein for his review and corrections of the work on Chaco communities of the San Juan Basin and particularly for his new data on the Crumbled House site. Appreciation also is extended to Chief Park Archaeologist Jack E. Smith of Mesa Verde National Park for his assistance and for the informative seminar on Anasazi architecture he hosted in the spring of 1991.

For the base map of Aztec Ruin, including a concept plan of the East Ruin Complexes, I am indebted to Peter J. McKenna of the Santa Fe office of the National Park Service. Keith M. Anderson, Chief of the Division of Archaeology in the Tucson office of the National Park Service, generously provided site plans for Montezuma Castle, Tuzigoot, and Tonto. I wish to acknowledge the help of John M. Andresen of the Casa Grande Ruins National Monument for the plans and descriptions of the recorded compounds and ball court at Casa Grande.

Arthur H. Rohn (Ferguson & Rohn, 1987) of Wichita State University's Department of Anthropology furnished a number of Anasazi site plans and related information, particularly on Montezuma Valley ruins. City of Phoenix Archaeologist Todd W. Bostwick provided a reconstructed perspective and other valuable data on Pueblo Grande, and Christian E. Downum of the Department of Anthropology of the University of Arizona supplied a definitive drawing depicting the platform mound between A.D. 1300 and 1350. Dr. Downum also called attention to Cerro Prieto and other *trincheras* sites of southern Arizona and northern Sonora.

Glenn E. Rice and Charles Redman of Arizona State University and J. Scott Wood of the Tonto National Forest staff generously assisted studies of Cline Terrace, Schoolhouse Point, and other Salado sites of the Tonto Basin. Appreciation goes to Jeffrey S. Dean of the University of Arizona's Laboratory of Tree-Ring Research not only for information and site plans for Betatakin, Kiet Siel, and Paquimé but also for his thoughtful suggestions for improving the research.

Special thanks are due to Steve Germick of the Tonto National Forest staff for his field tour of Salado sites and for extensive research information on upland Salado sites as well as on Besh Ba Gowah. I also thank Joe Crary for his insights and suggestions during Salado site visitations, particularly for his composite site map incorporating Adolf Bandelier's 1883 plan of Besh Ba Gowah with the survey of existing conditions.

George J. Gumerman of the Center of Archaeological Investigations at Southern Illinois University in Carbondale assisted the research with a thorough bibliography developed in connection with his work on Black Mesa and elsewhere in the Southwest. I extend my appreciation to Patricia A. Gilman of the University of Oklahoma's Department of Anthropology for her advice on Mimbres sites, particularly Mogollon Village, and for her dissertation on the transition from pit houses to pueblos on Black Mesa. Of special assistance regarding Galaz and other Mimbres sites has been Steven A. LeBlanc of Questor Systems in Pasadena, California.

The presentation of Chimney Rock Pueblo was assisted greatly by Frank W. Eddy of the Department of Anthropology of the University of Colorado at Boulder. John Hohman of Louis Berger and Associates in Phoenix generously furnished a recent archaeological report on the Casa Malpais site prepared for the City of Springerville, Arizona. Paul E. Minnis of the University of Oklahoma's Department of Anthropology provided helpful suggestions about Mimbres sites in New Mexico, Paquimé and Cuaranta Casas in Chihuahua, and Trincheras in Sonora.

I am grateful to Peter Pilles and Ann Baldwin of the Coconino National Forest for precise information on Elden Pueblo and other Sinagua sites. To J. Jefferson Reid of the Department of Anthropology of the University of Arizona I am indebted for information on Grasshopper, Chodistaas, and other Mogollon sites. Robert C. Savi of the University of Arizona's School of Architecture provided detailed information on Hohokam sites and a thorough list of research sources for ancient southwestern architecture.

The presentation of Arroyo Hondo is based primarily on fieldwork directed by Douglas W. Schwartz, President of the School of American Research in Santa Fe. Archaeologist William Whatley furnished information on the large Anasazi pueblo of Kwastiyukwa in the Jemez Mountains west of the Rio Grande. Mark Michel, President of the Archaeological Conservancy, supplied site plans and data on Mud Springs, Las Ventanas, Pueblo San Marcos, and a number of other important sites. Park Ranger Eric Finkelstein of the Gila National Forest conducted an informative tour of snow-covered T J Ruin high in the Mogollon Mountains.

I am especially grateful to David R. Wilcox of the Museum of Northern Arizona in Flagstaff for his advice and information on Snaketown, Palo Parado, White Mound, Grass Mesa, Coombs, and other sites. Margaret Lyneis of the Department of Anthropology in the University of Nevada at Las Vegas made possible the presentation of the Virgin Anasazi community of Main Ridge in the Lost City area near Overton, Nevada. Thanks also go to Wirt H.

Willis, Director of the Archaeology Field School of the University of New Mexico, for information on several large Anasazi sites west of the Rio Grande.

A special word of appreciation is due to George Anselevicius, Dean of the School of Architecture and Planning at the University of New Mexico, for his encouragement of the research and his unfailing enthusiasm for architecture. I also wish to acknowledge the general advice and specific information on the Sand Canyon site provided by Bruce Bradley and Ian Thompson of the Crow Canyon Archaeological Center in Cortez, Colorado. The publications, lectures, and seminars of Alfonso Ortiz (1979; Erdoes & Ortiz 1984) have broadened my awareness of the myths and realities of the Southwest.

Finally, I owe special thanks to my staff, particularly architects Ronald L. Scalisi, Karen H. Rutter, and Jack P. Jenkins, for their seemingly endless patience in the preparation of their highly disciplined drawings, and to Bunny Morgan for her unfailing assistance in reviewing, coordinating, and producing the final study.

We have lived upon this land from days beyond history's records. . . . The story of my people and the story of this place are one single story.
— *a Taos Pueblo man*
(Henry et al. 1970:35)

This study explores the diverse and remarkable architecture created by Native American people living in the arid southwestern United States and northwestern Mexico between the early centuries of the Christian era and the present day. Their extraordinary achievements range from the cliff dwellings of Canyon de Chelly and Mesa Verde to walled compounds on the desert floor of the Salt and Gila Basin, from the stone monuments of Chaco Canyon to the adobe pueblos of the Rio Grande Valley, and from the solitary towers of Hovenweep to the grand trading center of Paquimé in Chihuahua. The volume analyzes and compares 132 ancient sites suggesting the breadth and variety of our architectural legacy in the Southwest.

Physical Setting

The geographical area of the survey encompasses some 300,000 square miles (770,000 square kilometers), a territory more than 20 percent larger in size than the combined areas of Spain and Portugal. The territory extends from Coombs Village, Utah, in the north to the Cave of Las Ventanas, Chihuahua, in the south and from Main Ridge, Nevada, to the San José site in eastern New Mexico. The distances are roughly equivalent to those from Cleveland south to Atlanta and from Detroit east to Boston.

Much of the land within the study area is situated more than 5,000 feet (1,524 meters) above sea level. Some peaks in the southern Rocky Mountains reach altitudes of more than 14,000 feet (4,267 meters), while the terrain descends through low-lying desert plains to sea level along the shores of the Gulf of California. Temperatures range from well below freezing during winter months in the mountains and upland plateaus to well above 100 degrees Fahrenheit (38 degrees Celsius) on the Sonora Desert floor during summer months.

Dry climate characterizes the entire Southwest where water is the most critical resource. Rain and snow fall mostly in the uplands and mountainous interiors where warm, moisture-laden clouds release precipitation as they cool and rise. Numerous upland sources form the headwaters of the great rivers of the Southwest: the Rio Grande and its tributaries, which flow into the Gulf of Mexico, and the San Juan, Little Colorado, and Gila, which join the Colorado and discharge into the Gulf of California.

Early Migrations

People of Asian origin probably entered the Western Hemisphere by way of a land bridge across the Bering Strait caused by the formation of glaciers, which lowered the sea level. Several opportunities to walk from Siberia to Alaska occurred between 23,000 and 8,000 B.C., and other opportunities occurred even earlier. The early migrants quite likely were hunters who followed wandering herds of mammoths and other large animals into North America.

The early hunters and gatherers are known as Paleo Indians. Some of their earliest remains are found at the Folsom site in northeastern New Mexico and Sandía Cave 15 miles (24 kilometers) northeast of Albuquerque. Distinctively fashioned projectile points, knives, scrapers, and other tools of stone and bone are associated with Paleo Indian sites where mammoth, camelid, giant sloth, and extinct forms of bison were killed and processed. Radiocarbon data for Clovis projectile points used by Paleo Indians yield dates between 9,500 and 9,000 B.C.

Camp sites of hunters and gatherers are very difficult to identify only a few years after they are abandoned. A high degree of mobility is characteristic of Paleo Indian groups, who presumably moved more or less constantly in search of their prey. By perhaps 5500 B.C. mammoths were extinct and other species of large animals were disappearing from the Southwest. These events necessitated the adoption of new strategies for subsistence.

The division of time between 5500 B.C. and A.D. 100 in the Southwest is called the Archaic Period. Hunting and gathering continued during the Archaic Period, but emphasis shifted to smaller game within limited ranges and the gathering of locally available foods. The cultivation of corn probably was borrowed from neighbors to the south sometime around 1500 B.C. (Corn, beans, and squash were domesticated in Mesoamerica sometime between 7000 and 3000 B.C.) With the introduction of cultivated crops in the Southwest, the Archaic people became more sedentary, storage practices were initiated, and the population over time may have begun to expand.

Broadly varying water management strategies were devised in highly diverse physical settings. For example, in some places small stone dams across drainageways formed holding ponds to retain storm water runoff, while in other locations agricultural terraces and gridded gardens were developed. Irrigation canals required a substantial investment of labor, favorable terrain, and frequent maintenance.

Prehistoric Cultures

Agriculture sets the peoples of the Southwest apart from the roving bison hunters of the Great Plains to the east and the hunters and gatherers of California to the west and the Great Basin to the north. Although hunting and gathering continued to be important, agriculture began to promote sedentariness to the extent required for the eventual development of a distinctive type of architecture, an attainment unequaled by neighboring groups.

The ancient peoples employed digging sticks for cultivation, used grinding stones called *metates* and hand stones known as *manos*, and manufactured ceramics using the coil method rather than the wheel. Pit houses traditionally were built and used from very early times throughout most of the

Southwest. Eventually, rectangular surface structures with multiple rooms appeared both in aggregated villages and in dispersed settlements, and occasionally more sophisticated towns arose with unique forms of public architecture.

The ancient peoples of the Southwest appear to be heterogeneous in language and culture. Nonetheless, they lacked state-level societies, well-developed systems of writing and notation, and large urban centers with public architecture on the scale of such Mesoamerican centers as Teotihuacán, Monte Albán, or Tikal. In addition to food crops, the ancient peoples may have borrowed from Mesoamerica the knowledge of pottery making, certain irrigation techniques, and possibly some religious beliefs (Cordell 1984).

Throughout their prehistories the ancient people moved constantly between sedentariness and mobility, between regionally integrated centers with widespread economic and social systems and widely dispersed farmsteads and hamlets. Perhaps for this reason they did not develop an architecture that endured more than a season or so without maintenance. Their buildings may be viewed less as permanent structures than as byproducts of nature constantly in the process of returning to nature.

The four major cultural traditions usually associated with the ancient Southwest are the Patayan, Hohokam, Mogollon, and Anasazi traditions. To these a number of minor ones could be added. The Patayan people inhabited the lower Colorado River Valley from the Grand Canyon to its confluence with the Gulf of California, an area poorly known except for occasional farmsteads or hamlets widely dispersed in the arid landscape. The other three traditions, however, are better known and are associated with more or less distinctive architectural characteristics.

Hohokam The Hohokam tradition was centered in the Sonoran Desert of southern Arizona and the adjacent area of Sonora, Mexico. Characteristic Hohokam settlements were called *rancherias*, each of which consisted of a small group of detached houses occupied by members of the same family. A reversal of the general architectural rule occurred during the thirteenth and fourteenth centuries when compact, multistory great houses were built on the flood plain of the Salt and Gila rivers in the vicinity of Phoenix and Tucson.

The Spanish translation of great houses is *casas grandes*, an alternative name for the famous trading center of Paquimé in Chihuahua. Examples of Hohokam great houses in this study are Los Muertos, Casa Grande, and Pueblo Grande. The descendants of the Hohokam may be the present-day Tohono O'odham and Papago Indians, some of whom early observers found living near Casa Grande.

Mogollon The Mogollon cultural tradition occupied a vast area of southeastern Arizona and southern New Mexico and adjacent areas of Sonora and Chihuahua in northwestern Mexico. Early Mogollon settlements were *rancheria* communities composed of pit houses, such as Mogollon Village and the Harris site in this study. After A.D. 1000 villages of compact surface room blocks replaced earlier pit house settlements in such areas as the Mimbres Valley of New Mexico and the uplands of central Arizona.

Early Mogollon settlements presented in this study include Cameron Creek, Galaz, Swarts, NAN Ranch, and T J Ruin. Later Mogollon villages and centers are represented by Turkey Creek, Kinishba, Grasshopper, Casa Malpais, Paquimé, and others. Mogollon settlements generally were abandoned before the Spanish *entrada* in 1540. Their descendants may have joined Hopi, Zuni, Acoma, Laguna, or other pueblos in the Rio Grande Valley.

Anasazi The remains of early Anasazi hamlets and farmsteads are found in northern New Mexico and Arizona, southwestern Colorado, and southern Utah and Nevada. Examples in this study include White Mound Village, Grass Mesa Village, Coombs, Badger House, Tohatchi Village, Alkali Ridge, and others. In time the Anasazi became the first group in the Southwest to develop compact villages having one or more multiroom surface blocks. Later room blocks often were several stories high and usually were grouped closely around one or more plazas, which frequently were rectangular in shape.

Some of the best known Anasazi sites in this study are situated in and around Chaco Canyon, Mesa Verde, Canyon de Chelly, the Hopi mesas, Zuni Pueblo, and the Rio Grande Valley. The northern and western Anasazi areas largely were abandoned during prehistoric times. The modern Pueblo Indians probably are descended from the Anasazi.

Obviously, no records exist to explain prehistoric beliefs systems, languages, or other cultural characteristics of the ancient peoples. Nevertheless, information gathered from present-day American Indians may yield valuable insights into the cultural traditions of their ancestors.

Contemporary Southern Peoples The vast territory of southern Arizona and northwestern Mexico includes fertile valleys, mountainous uplands, and inhospitable deserts. The American Indians who presently live in this area are agriculturalists who speak Uto-Aztecan languages and for the most part live in *rancherias*. Their settlement patterns quite likely resemble those of their ancient ancestors. In river valleys, houses are clustered more closely together and form larger communities than do settlements in the mountains or deserts.

Riverine communities successfully practice flood-plain irrigation as they have for many generations. The architecture of houses and other structures varies considerably. For example, a Tarahumara *rancheria* might consist of several one-room log houses with adjacent grain-storage cabins, while a typical Papago residence is a dome-shaped brush structure with a slightly excavated floor and a nearby *ramada* shading an exterior work area.

Traditional Yaqui houses have flat roofs that bear on rectangular walls built of wattle and daub. A high cane fence typically encloses the area around each house, including its nearby *ramadas* and outdoor cooking areas. *Ranche-*

rias seldom are self-sufficient; family members often participate with others in communal work projects. Political organizations beyond the village level are rare for most groups, except in unusual circumstances involving regional interaction.

Contemporary Northern Peoples The present-day Pueblo Indians speak diverse languages but generally share a common culture. Most Hopi speak Uto-Aztecan languages, while the Zuni language seems to be related to the language spoken by some California peoples. The residents of pueblos in the Rio Grande Valley speak various dialects of unrelated Kersean and Tanoan languages. Other ancient languages have been lost in historic times.

Contemporary Pueblo Indians traditionally live in compact villages rather than *rancherias*. Built of both stone and adobe, the villages often consist of multistory room blocks usually fronting on a plaza or street. Lower floors of multistory pueblos customarily are used for storage, and rooftops frequently serve as additional work areas.

All traditional pueblos have at least one ceremonial room, known as a kiva, and most of them have several. The kivas of the Eastern Pueblo, which is to say those of the Rio Grande Valley, usually are round in plan and often are freestanding, partially subterranean chambers. The kivas of Acoma, Zuni, and the Hopi mesas customarily are rectangular in plan and frequently are incorporated into surface room blocks.

The basic unit of social organization in a Western Pueblo is a matriarchal household, which in turn belongs to a matrilineal clan. Clans control land and resources and are responsible for educational, ceremonial, religious, and other activities of the group. In prehistoric times the Western Anasazi typically lived in *rancherias* rather than compact communities.

By contrast the Tanoan-speaking pueblos of the Rio Grande traditionally are organized in extended families, which are associated with one of the pueblo's dual social divisions called a moiety. Children usually belong to their father's moiety, which in turn is responsible for coordinating the activities of the group. Members of the Keresan-speaking pueblos of the Rio Grande mostly have social organizations that bridge between Eastern and Western Pueblos.

The Navajo and Apache who live today in the Southwest are descended from Athapaskan-speaking Indians who arrived perhaps during the sixteenth century shortly before the Spanish *entrada*. Athapaskan languages also are spoken by American Indians who live in the inland valleys of central Alaska and northwestern Canada. Due to their relatively late arrival their contributions to the ancient architecture of the Southwest were limited.

Presentation

The study is divided into five chronological periods, which again are subdivided into several geographical areas. The periods are:

> Early settlements to A.D. 900
> Regional developments, 900 to 1140
> Unrest and adjustment, 1140 to 1300
> Migration and consolidation, 1300 to 1540
> Historic pueblos, 1540 to present

The chronological periods are intended to assist the reader in understanding the general character of architectural developments; they clearly are not intended to suggest a rigid separation of ideas devoid of continuity.

Such sites as Acoma and Oraibi probably were founded and occupied in the study's second chronological period and continue to be occupied today. To avoid repetition, the sites are discussed in only one period where clear reference is made to their full chronologies. The morphologies of other sites, for example, of Cameron Creek, changed significantly in time; their variations are noted in the texts accompanying their plans.

The sites in this discussion usually are associated with either Mogollon, Hohokam, or Anasazi cultural groups. The categories should not be viewed too narrowly since many sites have characteristics associated with more than one group. For example, thirteenth-century Mogollon sites in central Arizona sometimes show Hohokam influences from the south or Anasazi influences from the north, or both, and Chacoan outliers, such as the Village of the Great Kivas and Las Ventanas, seem to anticipate later architectural developments in Zuni sites.

General introductions precede each of the five chronological sections with the view of summarizing major architectural ideas. Each introduction closes with references to contemporary architectural developments elsewhere in North America and other places in the world. The study continues well into the historic period in order to examine the diverse architectural strategies the people of the Southwest adopted in coping with foreign ideas after 1540.

Methodology

The sites presented in this survey illustrate chronological, geographical, and architectural diversity with the view of exploring the overall character of ancient southwestern architecture. Chronologically, the sites range from early *rancheria* settlements composed of pit houses to nineteenth-century Zuni farming communities. Some settlements are modest in scale and humble in character, while other sites demonstrate exceptionally high levels of architectural achievement. Texts accompanying the sites suggest, where possible, architectural ideas preceding or succeeding those under discussion.

Each site appears on a background grid 100 feet (30.5 meters) square. North is oriented consistently toward the top of the page. Shadows generally are cast at forty-five-degree angles toward the northwest, or within fifteen degrees of northwest where required for enhanced graphic clarity. The reader may discern the heights of buildings by the length of the shadows; for example, one-story structures cast roughly 10-foot- (3-meter-) long shadows, two-story structures cast about 20-foot (6-meter) shadows, and so forth.

Key plans accompany a number of sites in order to indicate the extent of architectural developments beyond the gridded format. The scales of key plans vary, but the direction of north is consistently oriented toward the top of the page. Small grids within the key plans refer to the areas within the plan presented on the study's standard grid. Sites presented on two adjoining pages generally show the plans of adjacent architectural elements. In the case of Palo Parado, however, the north and south halves of the gridded plan slightly overlap.

References

The accompanying bibliography lists additional sources of information on subjects of interest to students of ancient southwestern architecture. Subjects on which much has been written include the morphology of pit houses and kivas, wood frame structural systems of the prehistoric Southwest, masonry styles and techniques of the Anasazi, ball courts and earth platforms of the Hohokam, dendrochronology and other dating techniques, theories of abandonment, and other matters.

Adolph Bandelier's classic *The Delight Makers* vividly reconstructs the life and times of a prehistoric community in the upper Rio Grande area. Although the account is fictional, it is the most nearly authentic portrayal of its type available. Willa Cather's *Death Comes for the Archbishop*, also a novel, imaginatively depicts the lives and aspirations of Americans, Mexicans, Europeans, and American Indians living in the Southwest during the nineteenth century.

Linda Cordell's *Prehistory of the Southwest* gives a comprehensive overview of the subject from the point of view of a distinguished anthropologist. The Smithsonian Institution's *Handbook of North American Indians*, Volume 9, edited by Alfonso Ortiz, contains a wealth of historical and anthropological information. Victor Mindeleff's *A Study of Pueblo Architecture in Tusayan and Cibola* remains a classic study of traditional Hopi and Zuni architecture.

Anasazi Ruins of the Southwest in Color, by William M. Ferguson and Arthur H. Rohn, is a well-illustrated and highly informative volume on the subject. Another excellent study of Anasazi architecture is Stephen H. Lekson's *Great Pueblo Architecture of Chaco Canyon.* The late Charles C. Di Peso's series entitled *Casas Grandes: A Fallen Trading Center of the Gran Chichimeca,* Volumes 1–3, remains the most comprehensive study available on the fascinating subject of Paquimé and its environs.

    Pueblo Style and Regional Architecture, edited by Nicholas Markovitch, et al., presents a number of instructive essays on the subject by knowledgeable architects and educators. The National Park Service, Bureau of Land Management, and U.S. Forest Services often publish descriptions of ancient ruins within their jurisdictions; the descriptions generally are concise and accurate and often contain information of interest to students of ancient architecture.

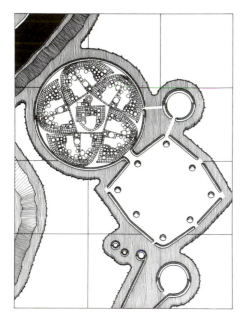

Comparative Scales

One of the most pronounced differences between the prehistoric architecture of the Eastern United States and that of the Southwest is scale. For example, the relative sizes of the well-documented monuments of Chaco Canyon are very small in comparison with ancient monuments of the Ohio Valley. To illustrate the relative scales, a diagram is presented here showing the plans of Pueblo Bonito and Pueblo del Arroyo superimposed at the same scale on the plan of High Bank (Morgan 1980:17), a prehistoric earthwork near Chillicothe, Ohio.

    The circular enclosure of High Bank has a diameter of some 1,050 feet (320 meters). In plan D-shaped Pueblo Bonito measures overall about 310 by 505 feet (95 by 154 meters). The diagram shows the plans of five buildings the size of Pueblo Bonito placed within High Bank's circular enclosure, with space remaining in the middle for Pueblo del Arroyo. The High Bank background is a grid 656 feet (200 meters) square, not to be confused with the standard 100-foot (30.5-meter) square grid used elsewhere in this study.

PHOTOGRAPHS

Two keyhole-shaped kivas are closely associated with Far View Tower, a cylindrical stone structure superimposed on the remains of an earlier room block in Far View Community. Mesa Verde, A.D. 1100–1150.

Four portals interconnect a gentle arc of storage rooms formed by massive walls of carefully fitted tabular sandstones in Pueblo Bonito, one of the finest examples of ancient architecture in the Southwest.

Chaco Canyon, A.D. 930–1130.

A horizontal band of dark green stones forms a strong visual contrast with neatly laid
courses of thick sandstone blocks alternating with thin tabular slabs in the west wall of
Aztec West Ruin.   Northern San Juan, A.D. 1100–1200.

One of seven room blocks forming a greater community, partially reconstructed Kinishba suggests the appearance of a once prosperous Mogollon pueblo containing almost four hundred rooms arranged around a central plaza. Upper Salt River Valley, A.D. 1300–1450.

One of several solitary masonry towers found at broadly dispersed intervals in Hovenweep National Monument, rectangular Holly Tower stands on top of an enormous sandstone boulder like a timeless sentinel at the head of Keely Canyon.   Montezuma Valley, A.D. 1200–1300.

The spectacular Sinagua cliff dwelling of Montezuma Castle peers out from the face
of a sheer limestone cliff across a fertile valley watered by a tributary of the Verde River
in central Arizona.   Verde Valley, A.D. 1200–1300.

Originally four or five stories high, the D-shaped great house of Pueblo Bonito once contained perhaps eight hundred rooms and thirty-seven kivas at the base of a canyon wall 100 feet (130 meters) high.

Chaco Canyon, A.D. 920–1130.

Reasons for building cliff dwellings in the walls of Canyon de Chelly may have included conserving limited available land for food production, avoiding occasional floods on the canyon floor, and taking advantage of the protective overhangs of natural caves.   Canyon de Chelly, A.D. 1000–1300.

Dramatic White House derives its name from the once white plastered walls of a cliff dwelling recessed above the remains of a room block at the base of an overhanging cliff some 500 feet (150 meters) high.
Canyon de Chelly, A.D. 1060–1275.

The eroded remains of extensive room blocks surround an open plaza containing a restored subterranean kiva in the coursed adobe pueblo of Kuaua, an aggregated community once containing more than twelve hundred rooms.   Rio Grande Valley, A.D. 1300–1700.

Open-sided ramadas shade outdoor work areas on the south side of North House in the adobe pueblo of Taos, a traditional settlement situated in a well-watered valley west of the Sangre de Cristo Mountains.   Rio Grande Valley, A.D. 1450 to present.

Privacy fences near the east end of North House screen rooftop entries into three of the traditional kivas of Taos, the only underground chambers presently known to be used in the Rio Grande Valley.   Rio Grande Valley, A.D. 1450 to present.

A circular sandstone bench supports pilasters engaging the curving walls of a subterranean kiva in Aztec, the largest Anasazi great house located outside of Chaco Canyon.

Northern San Juan, A.D. 1100–1200.

Extensive remains of caliche walls outline the apartments, courtyards, and colonnades of multi-story buildings overlooking the public market place of once magnificent Paquimé, the grand trading center of the Chichimeca.

Chihuahua, A.D. 1275–1500.

The snow-covered ruins of historic Mound Seven at Gran Quivira are built on top of an earlier circular pueblo which once contained more than two hundred rooms surrounding a central open space. Estancia Valley, A.D. 1300–1672.

NEVADA

U T A H

C O L O R A D O

Grass Mesa• •McPhee Village

Alkali Ridge •

Dolores
River

San Juan
River

•Badger House

Muddy
River

Virgin
River

Colorado
River

Chinle
Wash

Animas
River

Rio
Grande

Chaco
Wash

Rio
Chama

•Tohatchi Village

Little Colorado
River

White Mound •

Rio Puerco
of the West

Galisteo
Creek

Pecos
River

Verde
River

Zuni
River

Puerco River

CALIFORNIA

A R I Z O N A

N E W   M E X I C O

Colorado
River

Tonto
Creek

Salt
River

•Mogollon Village

Rio
Hondo

Gila
River

Gila
River

Harris •

Mimbres
River

T E X A S

Rio
Grande

GULF
OF
CALIFORNIA

S O N O R A

C H I H U A H U A

100 m/160 k

In the arid deserts and mountains of the southwestern United States and northwestern Mexico there exists the most complete record of the origins and evolution of architecture in North America. Here in the early centuries of the Christian era people continued to develop increasingly successful methods of providing food and shelter in an often adverse environment. In time seasonal shelters and permanent dwellings appeared, sometimes in small clusters.

The most typical settlements throughout the Southwest from very early times have been farmsteads or hamlets often located at widely dispersed intervals in the landscape. Villages having more than one hundred residents were not characteristic of the period preceding A.D. 900. The Harris site, for example, may have begun as a hamlet consisting of five concurrently occupied dwellings where perhaps twenty-five persons lived. Although the word "village" is associated with the names for such settlements as Mogollon Village, Tohatchi Village, White Mound Village, and others, these sites more accurately would be termed "hamlets."

Pit Houses

The earliest permanent dwellings constructed in the Southwest most likely were pit houses. The structures were excavated into the earth and enclosed by roofs of wood and brush covered with mantles of earth or mud plaster. Pit houses are a generic type of structure built in many parts of the world from very early times.

Dwellings excavated into the earth came into use in eastern Europe about thirty-seven thousand years ago (Musgrove 1987:198) and in time were found widely throughout Europe and northern Asia. Pit houses continued to be built in Europe during the nineteenth century; an example may be seen in the open-air museum at Arnhem, Holland (Eduard Sekler, personal communication).

The tradition of building pit houses may have been brought from Siberia to North America by the ancestors of the American Indians. The remains of prehistoric pit houses are found at various sites in Alaska, Canada, and many areas of the United States, including the Southwest and the East. For example, aerial photographs of Marksville, Louisiana (Morgan 1980:158–159), show the remains of numerous pit houses outside the perimeter embankment enclosing the prehistoric ceremonial center. The earliest occupation and construction at Marksville may have occurred between A.D. 100 and 300.

Pit houses were built and used in the Southwest from very early times until recently. Eventually, in some areas the building type evolved into a type of kiva. For example, the Eastern Anasazi developed highly specialized round chambers, often at least partly underground, for clan or community gatherings and other uses. A close parallel exists between this type of kiva in the Southwest and the circular, semisubterranean earth lodges or winter council houses that were constructed and used in the Eastern United States during prehistoric times.

An example of a kiva-like structure in the Eastern United States is the ancient winter council house that has been reconstructed in Ocmulgee National Monument near Macon, Georgia. The earth lodge measures inside 42 feet (12.8 meters) in diameter and is entered by way of a tunnel-like extension to the east. A low roof of heavy logs covered with sod encloses the chamber. A continuous clay bench about 6 inches (15 centimeters) high engages the base of the perimeter wall, and an opening in the roof admits light and emits smoke from the fire in the central hearth.

The reasons for building pit houses instead of other structures may be severalfold. The amount of labor required to build a pit house is relatively small, an earth-encased room is exceptionally well insulated against extreme temperatures, no special skills or sophisticated tools are required for construction, and the needed materials are readily available in most habitable locations.

Mogollon Groups of pit houses probably began to appear in the Mogollon Mountains of southwestern New Mexico in the early centuries of the Christian era. Our discussion of ancient architecture in the Southwest begins with Mogollon Village, a large group of pit houses built between possibly A.D. 400 and 900 on a mesa top near the continental divide. The sunken rooms are of various sizes and shapes. They appear to be entered by means of extended ramps generally oriented toward the east.

The Harris site, another early Mogollon pit house settlement in New Mexico, is situated on a bench in the Mimbres Valley southeast of Mogollon Village. Here the number and density of pit houses in the community increase, and two very large underground chambers are found. The large structures may be great kivas, which are places where the community as a whole may gather on special occasions.

Chaco Anasazi The modest hamlet called White Mound Village is characteristic of settlement patterns in the Southwest during early as well as later periods of development. Tohatchi Village crowds a mesa top in the Chuska Mountains west of Chaco Canyon. In addition to its remarkably large kiva, the Tohatchi site is noteworthy because of the appearance of numerous surface store rooms relatively early in the evolution of ancient architecture in the Southwest.

Northern San Juan Anasazi The Badger House community in southwestern Colorado provides a further elaboration of architectural ideas associated with White Mound and Tohatchi Village. Here parallel rows of small storage rooms and large dwellings are built side by side in surface blocks northwest of their respective kivas. In time the functions of the subterranean chambers seem to change from private dwellings to kiva-like places for the assembly of small groups, perhaps extended families or clans.

The Dolores River Valley north of Badger House is the location of McPhee Village, an exceptionally large community extending over an area of perhaps 60 acres (24.2 hectares). The settlement contains some twenty-two room blocks oriented toward the southeast, where subterranean chambers are situated. Smaller kivas may have served only a single clan or small group, while the larger kivas appear to be capable of accommodating much larger segments of the community as a whole.

A neighbor of McPhee village in the Dolores River Valley, Grass Mesa Village is a good example of the development and demise of early northern Anasazi settlements. A great kiva and scattered pit houses with surface rooms in time are replaced by numerous clan kivas and six orderly surface room blocks. Changes in temperature in the late ninth century may have caused consecutive crop failures, thus encouraging a renewed emphasis on hunting and gathering, which preceded the eventual abandonment of the once-burgeoning community.

Alkali Ridge in southeastern Utah provides a valuable architectural record of the transition from pit houses to pueblos in the Southwest. The site serves as a summary of the ideas developed in the preceding discussion. Mogollon Village and Harris contain modest numbers of pit houses facing east, White Mound and Tohatchi Village introduce surface room blocks oriented toward the south and east, while Badger House, McPhee Village, and Grass Mesa illustrate more sophisticated combinations of surface and subsurface structures in larger-scale communities.

Contemporary Architecture beyond the Southwest

Eastern United States The period of the A.D. second through the ninth centuries was a time of transition in the Eastern United States, but the transition was very different from that in the Southwest. The second century of the Christian era marked the beginning of a decline in the spectacular artistic and architectural achievements of the Adena and Hopewell people living in the Ohio River Valley. Their cultural influence seems to have spread over the vast geographical area extending from lower Canada to the Gulf of Mexico and from the Atlantic Ocean to the Great Plains.

The Ohio Valley people created numerous large-scale ceremonial centers, some with conical earth mounds and huge earthen embankments forming squares, circles, octagons, and other geometric figures. Remains of the ancient earthworks are found at Newark, Marietta, High Bank, Oldtown, Seal, and other sites along the banks of the Ohio River and its tributaries.

Elsewhere in the Eastern United States during the early Christian era, D-shaped earthen enclosures with outer moats were constructed on riverbanks in Marksville, Louisiana, and at Spanish Fort near Holly Bluff, Mississippi. About the same time ideas from the Ohio Valley spread to such distant places as Fort Center in South Florida. Here a ceremonial center and a large circular field with a perimeter moat and embankment were built near Lake Okeechobee.

After a period of limited architectural activity between A.D. 200 and 800, new ideas began to emerge in the central Mississippi Valley. Perhaps in the ninth century rectangular earth mounds with flat tops started to appear around orthogonal plazas. The practice of building truncated platforms and plazas spread widely and quickly through much of the Eastern United States and continued in many areas until a century or so before Europeans arrived in North America (Morgan 1980).

Mesoamerica In Mesoamerica during the early Christian era the impressive ceremonial city of Teotihuacán was the dominant force in Central Mexico until its destruction in the eighth century. Lowland Mayan ceremonial centers, such as Tikal and Copán, flourished in the jungles of Guatemala and Honduras, respectively, until they were abandoned for unknown reasons in the ninth century. By then the majestic Zapotec capital of Monte Albán had reached essentially its final form in the Valley of Oaxaca with the completion of its major stone platforms, ball court, carved reliefs, and painted tombs (Heyden & Gendrop 1973).

Micronesia The first millennium of the Christian era largely was a period of architectural development rather than transition in Micronesia. Unlike the peoples of the Americas, who had arrived in their new lands tens of thousands of years earlier, the Micronesians for the most part had settled in their islands only recently, and some islands remained unpopulated until several centuries after the time of Christ.

Before the end of the ninth century, sculpted earth terraces began to appear on the steep hillsides overlooking Ngchemiangel Bay on the west coast of Babeldoab Island in the Palau archipelago. During the eighth and ninth centuries construction proceeded on the stone platform of Usendau, one of the ninety-two artificial islets forming the unique ceremonial center of Nan Madol on the east coast of Pohnpei.

In the Mariana Islands toward the end of the first millennium, buildings elevated on distinctive stone piers called *latte* were erected on the banks of the Talofofo River on Guam, at Mochong on the north coast of Rota, and in other locations. However, the most remarkable architectural achievements of Micronesia, like those of the Southwest, remained for the future (Morgan 1988).

MOGOLLON VILLAGE

Mogollon Village is located on the east bank of the San Francisco River about 170 miles (272 kilometers) southwest of Albuquerque. Although the site is called a "village," the term "hamlet" may describe the small settlement more accurately. Probably occupied by Mogollon people from A.D. 400 or earlier until 900, the hamlet is built on a mesa top measuring at most 330 by 525 feet (100 by 160 meters).

The site is situated on an isolated knoll some 200 feet (60 meters) above the valley floor at an elevation of 5,140 feet (1,567 meters) above sea level. The name Mogollon is derived from the mountains in which this and other prehistoric sites are found. The mountains in turn are named for an early Spanish colonial governor of New Mexico.

In 1933 and 1934 Emil Haury (1936) located and mapped nineteen pit houses in Mogollon Village. Investigations by Patricia Gilman (1991) and Raymond Mauldin in 1989 and 1991 revealed many more pit houses across the entire mesa top. The structures range from 16 to 26 feet (5 to 8 meters) in diameter, but unfortunately a new site plan is not available. For this reason the reconstruction presented here is based on Haury's 1936 map.

Of the nineteen pit houses that Haury located, nine were excavated; the remaining structures are represented by circles with dashed lines. Six of the excavated houses are roughly rectangular in plan with rounded corners, two are circular, and one seems to have an oval shape. Comparatively large, circular or oval floor plans are characteristic of earlier Mogollon pit houses; in time smaller,

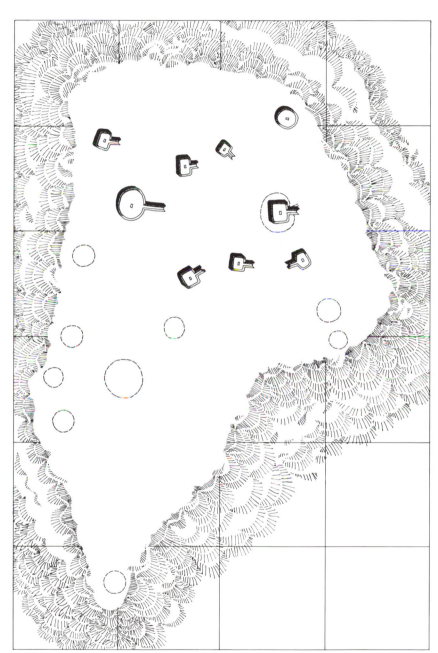

MOGOLLON VILLAGE

rectangular structures became more common.

Mogollon pit houses were partly subterranean chambers covered over with brush and mud roofs. Entry ramps provided access to the residences from ground level. With a single exception the ramps of Mogollon Village were oriented toward the east. The reconstructed plan presented here shows pit house floors at a depth of 4 feet (1.2 meters) below grade.

The bean-shaped house shown in the northeast area of the site is a typical early Mogollon structure. Measuring perhaps 20 by 40 feet (9 by 12 meters), the earlier residence was more than twice as long and wide as its later more rectangular successor. The more recent ramp was at least as long as its predecessor and both were oriented to the east.

Inherently cool in the summer, the pit houses could be adequately heated by relatively small fires in the winter. Also found at this site were a number of stone-lined storage pits, several burials in and near the houses, and the remains of a cremation. Inhumation was the usual burial practice of the Mogollon people, just as cremation was of the Hohokam.

Like other earlier pit house communities, Mogollon Village seems to lack an orderly arrangement of elements in an overall plan. In time new pit houses were constructed, sometimes on top of earlier ones. Probably not all of the houses were occupied at the same time. At least one of the village's circular structures most likely was a kiva, a large chamber set aside for community uses, such as council meetings, daily tasks, or ceremonies.

The large number of projectile points recovered from the site suggests that hunting may have been the major focus of subsistence with agriculture contributing only to a limited extent. Fire pits yield the remains of eighteen different animals and birds ranging from bison to ducks.

Later Mogollon settlements like those in the Mimbres Valley usually are situated along river terraces close to water and arable land. In time agriculture seems to have become more important than hunting as a basis of subsistence. Mogollon Village most likely was occupied seasonally during the winter, while the sedentary communities of the Mimbres Valley remained occupied throughout the year.

HARRIS

Located in the Mimbres Valley high in the mountains of southwestern New Mexico, the Harris site probably was occupied by Mogollon people between A.D. 550 and 1000. According to Emil Haury (1936) the site contained at most some thirty-four pit houses, of which twenty-five are shown in the reconstruction presented here. The circular figure drawn with dashed lines represents an unexcavated depression. Not shown are seven additional pit houses; these were superimposed on the structures shown during various stages of development.

Like other Mogollon sites occupied over extended periods of time, Harris was situated on the first terrace above a river. The plan of the hamlet seems to be a random grouping of elements within an area extending about 400 feet (122 meters) from east to west by 250 feet (76 meters) from north to south. In this presentation the pit houses are shown with level floors sunken about 4 feet (1.2 meters) below grade. In plan the structures range from almost round to kidney shaped or lobed to nearly rectangular.

Most of the pit houses probably were habitations, but one or two most likely served as kivas or communal structures. Sloping ramps typically provided access into Mogollon houses. Like the hamlet plan as a whole, the compass orientations of entry ramps appear to be arbitrary, although entry from a generally easterly direction seems to be preferred.

During the first century of its existence the Harris site apparently was a hamlet having no more than five pit houses. This would suggest a maximum population of perhaps twenty-five residents, assuming five persons per family and single family occupancy of each pit house. An alternative interpretation would be that an extended family with a number of relatives occupied each residence; if so, a somewhat larger population reasonably could be assumed for the hamlet.

Between 550 and 650 the average size of Mogollon pit houses in the vicinity of Harris may have been about 154 square feet (14.3 square meters). While corn, beans, squash, and cotton were cultivated, the inhabitants continued to hunt deer, rabbits, rodents, and birds and to gather wild grasses, acorns, piñons, and wild succulents.

From 650 and until perhaps 850 typical Mogollon hamlets increased in size to between fifteen and twenty

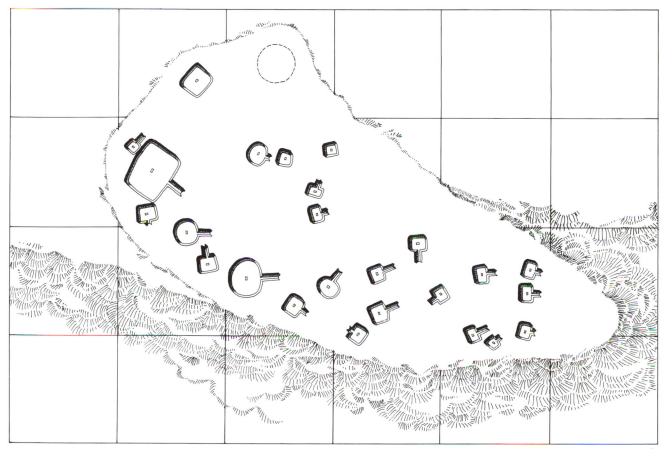

HARRIS

pit houses, and the average size of dwellings grew to some 170 square feet (15.8 square meters). Probably not all of the pit houses were occupied concurrently. The unusually large rectangular structure toward the west end of Harris measures about 31 by 43 feet (9.4 by 13.1 meters), an area of roughly 1,330 square feet (123 square meters).

During this time period the plan of Mogollon residences characteristically became more decidedly rectangular while communal structures had distinctly curved walls. Although

some houses lacked hearths, their interiors apparently were more carefully finished, and extended ramps became more common. New varieties of beans and squash came into use, the cultivation of cotton increased, and the population grew though not dramatically.

The final phase of occupation at Harris spanned from 850 to possibly 975 or 1000. During that time the average size of pit houses declined to perhaps 140 square feet (13 square meters). Typical residences became more nearly rectangular in plan, their

perimeter walls below grade often were faced with stone cobbles, and their floors were excavated less deeply into the ground.

The population grew substantially, suggesting a possible increase in the number of families who in turn lived in more though smaller houses. Haury's work at Harris and other Mogollon sites enabled him to identify distinctive characteristics of the Mogollon people and their unique architecture (Cordell 1984). Unlike Hohokam pit houses, Mogollon residences evolved in plan from round to rectangular, and sloping ramps were developed for entries instead of short steps down.

The Mogollon also developed large ceremonial structures for communal uses, which the Hohokam lacked. Although Mogollon ceremonial chambers resemble somewhat their Anasazi counterparts in the San Juan Basin, the former lacked such architectural features as perimeter benches, draft deflectors for fire pits, or floor holes of spiritual significance called *sipapus*.

WHITE MOUND

WHITE MOUND VILLAGE

White Mound Village is actually a modest hamlet situated on a rounded hilltop about a mile (1.6 kilometers) east of Houck in eastern Arizona, roughly halfway between Flagstaff and Albuquerque. The community is located some 400 yards (366 meters) north of the Rio Puerco of the West whose level valley once provided an ideal environment for agriculture. The water course is not to be confused with the Puerco River of the Rio Grande Valley to the east. The ruins of many other early hamlets and farmsteads are found in the vicinity.

Rolling hills extend westward from the site, while to the north the land rises toward ridges and plateaus covered with piñon and juniper. The White Mound hamlet consists of six pit houses and eighteen surface store rooms in three groups together with

a large number of *ramadas*, or sunscreens, storage cists, pits, platforms, outdoor cooking areas, and other structures. Two of the six dwellings are known to have been abandoned while the others remained in use. The reconstruction presented here is based on information published by Harold S. Gladwin in 1945.

The pit houses vary in plan configuration from circular to square with rounded corners. The floors of the dwellings are excavated to a depth of 7 feet (2 meters) or so. Their maximum diameters are approximately 16 feet (5 meters), and their areas seem to range from 140 to 230 square feet (13 to 21 square meters). The pit houses have central fire pits with draft deflectors, *sipapus*, or spirit holes, and ventilator tunnels and shafts oriented toward the southeast. A low wall typically separates the southeast part of each floor from the rest of the room.

The floors of White Mound's pit houses are excavated more deeply into the earth than are those of Mogollon Village, Harris, or Badger

House. The method of entering a dwelling in White Mound probably was by means of a ladder descending through a roof opening above the hearth in the center of the room. By contrast Mogollon pit houses typically were entered by way of extended ramps; Hohokam dwellings, by means of short entry stairs; and Badger House pit houses, by way of anterooms and entry tunnels, which also served as ventilation systems for the fireplaces.

The rectangular surface store rooms of White Mound Village measure about 7 feet (2 meters) in width and range in length from perhaps 7 to 10 feet (2 to 3 meters). They are arranged in rows of three to ten contiguous rooms, which probably are accessible by means of doors rather than roof hatches. The floors of two store rooms are excavated to a depth of 26 inches (65 centimeters) below grade, presumably for the purpose of increasing the volume of space available for storage.

The absence of hearths in an area where temperatures often drop to zero degrees Fahrenheit (minus 18 degrees Celsius) clearly indicates that the surface rooms were not built for use as dwellings. Bearing walls of adobe on stone base courses enclosed the store rooms and quite likely supported flat timber roofs.

Of all the sites presented in this section, none is more characteristic of southwestern architecture before A.D. 900 than White Mound Village. The small hamlet probably was constructed and used sometime during the seventh and eighth centuries. The appearance of contiguous surface room blocks signals the beginning of new directions in the evolution of ancient architecture in the Southwest.

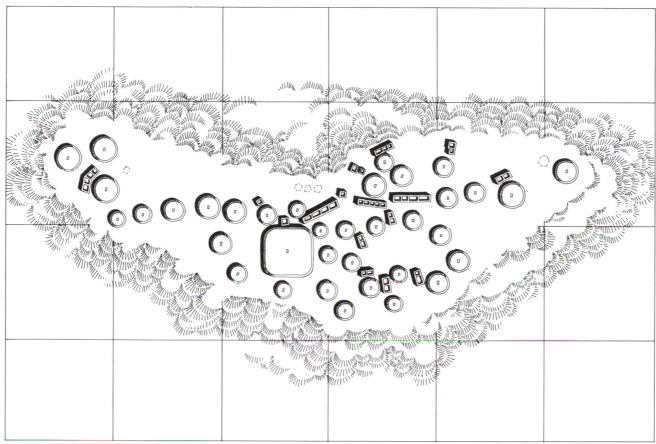

TOHATCHI VILLAGE

TOHATCHI VILLAGE

An isolated mesa top some 6,460 feet (2,713 meters) above sea level is the site of Tohatchi Village. Located in the southern Chuska Valley of New Mexico, the community apparently was occupied between A.D. 500 and 750. The largely unexcavated village seems to have contained at least thirty-five circular pit houses, one large kiva, forty-one rectangular surface rooms or granaries, and five slab-lined cists (Stuart & Gauthier 1988). Probably not all of the dwellings were occupied at the same time.

Structures crowd almost the entire mesa top. The promontory extends in a curving arc from east to west some 530 feet (162 meters) and measures at most 180 feet (55 meters) from north to south. In the absence of excavations the method of entering the dwellings is assumed to have been by means of roof hatches like those used at the White Mound site 50 miles (80 kilometers) or so to the southwest. This presentation assumes the floor levels of all subterranean structures to be about 4 feet (1.2 meters) below grade.

An unusual feature of Tohatchi Village is the comparatively large kiva located near the center of the settlement. The unexcavated chamber is defined by a depression 10 to 20 inches (25 to 50 centimeters) deep with a rubble perimeter suggesting the remains of subterranean walls. Rather than being circular in plan the walls appear to describe a rectangle about 49 by 52 feet (15 by 16 meters) with rounded corners. This arrangement recalls Mogollon influences although Tohatchi Village was affiliated culturally with the San Juan Anasazi.

During the time of occupation at Tohatchi Village, people began to use bows and arrows instead of *atlatls,* a device used by ancient bison and deer hunters to give added leverage and impetus to the throw of their spears (Frazier 1986:89). Thus the configuration of their stone projectile points changed markedly. Pottery in use at this time was rare and, by later standards, crude.

The reconstruction proposed here is based on S. L. Peckham's plan published in 1969. Particularly noteworthy in the village plan is the appearance of rectangular store rooms or granaries above grade in addition to the below-grade cists often associated with pit houses. The rooms may have been used to store corn or other commodities.

The surface structures range in number from one to five in a row and always are found near pit houses. The volume of storage space per typical residence seems to represent an increase, perhaps to accommodate larger quantities of food or other domestic supplies.

Although the elements of Tohatchi Village appear to be arranged somewhat randomly, the overall composition seems to anticipate future communities in the Southwest with more orderly plans. As time went on the numbers of above-grade rooms in typical settlements often increased while those of subterranean chambers decreased. Eventually, multistory pueblos appeared, often accompanied by subterranean kivas and plazas within a disciplined overall plan.

BADGER HOUSE

Occupied intermittently for more than six centuries, Badger House community consists of four prehistoric ruins on a 7-acre (2.8-hectare) site in Mesa Verde National Park. The ruins are situated at an elevation of 7,100 feet (2,164 meters) on the sloping top of Wetherill Mesa, one of a series of narrow sandstone uplifts in southwestern Colorado. The estimated 148 rooms of the settlement provide a valuable insight into the development of Anasazi architecture from pit houses to pueblos between the sixth and thirteenth centuries.

Navajo workers excavating the site in the early 1960s named the place for a badger they found living in the ruins. About 1,300 feet (400 meters) to the southwest the mesa edge descends abruptly some 650 feet (200 meters) into a deep narrow canyon, which drains into the Mancos River to the south. The moderately heavy stand of juniper and piñon covering most of Wetherill Mesa grows more openly in the immediate vicinity of Badger House community.

The plateaus and valleys in the immediate vicinity of Wetherill Mesa for centuries have been the habitats for mule deer, bighorn sheep, turkeys, and smaller game. Also within the range of prehistoric hunters were bison, antelope, and possibly elk. The combination of fertile soils and an average of more than 18 inches (45 centimeters) of precipitation per annum are ideal for dry farming.

Typically, 158 days per year are frost free on Wetherill Mesa, a climate favorable for raising such crops as corn and beans. The variety of corn grown by the Hopi requires 100 days to mature, and at Zuni common beans ripen in 135 days. Other site re-sources available to the residents of Badger House community were constant sources of water in nearby streams and springs and several natural outcrops of sandstones suitable for construction.

The reconstruction presented here is based primarily on data published by Alden C. Hayes and James A. Lancaster (1975:figs. 2, 12, 13), who mapped the site and excavated about half of the ruins in the 1960s. Not shown are a group of eight surface rooms, three kivas and a tower about 140 feet (43 kilometers) to the east, and two pit houses with five surface rooms a short distance to the northwest. Not all of the structures shown in the site plan were in use at the same time.

One of the most informative structures in Badger House community is the pit house shown farthest to the south on the site plan. Here perhaps as early as the A.D. 580s a bean-shaped excavation about 2.7 feet (82 centimeters) deep was dug into the mesa top. Oriented along a northwest-to-southeast axis, the sunken floor's plan measures about 12.3 by 14.6 feet (3.7 by 4.4 meters).

The features of the south pit house are very similar to those in later structures in Badger House community. A continuous bench about 1.9 feet high and 2.2 feet wide (58 and 67 centimeters) lines three sides of the room. Posts in the four corners support a timber roof, and partitions enclose storage bins in the east and south corners. Near the middle of the floor is a fire pit perhaps 2 feet (60 centimeters) in diameter and 7 inches (18 centimeters) deep. Originally, a rectangular roof hatch likely was centered above the fire pit.

A tunnel-like passageway approxi-

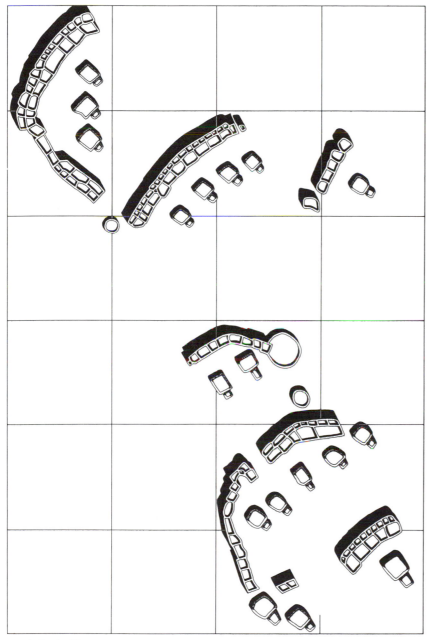

BADGER HOUSE

mately 1.6 feet (50 centimeters) wide leads some 4 feet (1.2 meters) southeast into the antechamber of the pit house. The floor levels of the main room and the antechamber are about the same. Partitions form storage bins in the north and west corners of the chamber.

The south pit house probably continued to be occupied into the 630s when the roof burned and collapsed and the structure was abandoned. About the same time construction seems to have begun on the pit house roughly 120 feet (37 meters) to the east. The builders of the new structure may have been the former occupants of the abandoned house. The new dwelling is about 20 feet (6 meters) square and has rounded corners with benches on all four sides.

Similar in many respects to its predecessor, the new pit house was excavated to a depth of 3.3 feet (1 meter) below grade. The sunken room had two fire pits and eight shallow storage cavities recessed into its floor, and a 7-by-9-foot (2.1-by-2.7-meter) antechamber to the southeast. A single family seems to have occupied the dwelling. Possibly around 710 construction began on new storage spaces above grade 20 feet (6 meters) or so to the northwest.

Two small storage rooms, each about 7 feet (2.1 meters) square, were built of jacal construction (adobe applied to both sides of vertical poles placed close together) side by side with portals facing southeast. At first a 15-foot (4.6-meter) square *ramada* likely was located on the southeast side of the storage spaces for use in the summer. In time the *ramada* appears to have been enclosed to serve as the living room for a three-room apartment on ground level.

Around 750 another change appeared in the architecture of Badger House community. Four additional three-room apartments were added to the original one, forming a rectangular, single-story room block 70 feet (21 meters) long facing the pit house to the southeast. In effect the surface building was a pueblo containing fifteen rooms in five dwelling units. At this time the former pit house probably was modified to serve as a kiva for five families.

Gradually all of the apartments except the original one were abandoned. Around 800 the structures burned and thereafter fell into disuse. Neighboring residences continued to be occupied until between 860 and 900, when the remaining houses burned and the people relocated.

Sometime after 900 work began a short distance to the east on a surface structure with stone walls and several kivas. These were used until about 1080 and during a brief period of reoccupation after 1250. Visitors to the ruins today can see a number of the excavated and preserved architectural features of Badger House community.

McPHEE VILLAGE

Situated on the west bank of the Dolores River in southwestern Colorado, McPhee Village consists of twenty-two surface room blocks with associated plazas and pit houses or kivas. The village measures at most about

KEY PLAN OF MCPHEE VILLAGE

1,450 by 1,800 feet (440 by 550 meters) and occupies an area of roughly 60 acres (24.2 hectares). Located approximately 40 miles (64 kilometers) north of Badger House on Wetherill Mesa, McPhee Village is the center of a larger community containing dozens of smaller residences, field houses, agricultural plots, and other prehistoric remains.

The earliest Anasazi occupants of McPhee Village may have been hunters and gatherers who arrived in the area during the seventh century, remained at most two or three decades, and then moved on. Around A.D. 800 an agricultural village seems to have been established. The settlements apparently flourished until sometime in the late ninth or early tenth century when agricultural productivity declined and the village first was abandoned.

McPhee Village provides a valuable insight into the architectural evolution of pueblos. The site lies above the seasonal flood plain of the river on terrain sloping down to the southeast from an elevation of 6,850 to

6,835 feet (2,088 to 2,083 meters). The reconstruction presented here is based on information compiled by A. E. Kane and C. K. Robinson (1988: figs. 1.1, 1.5, 1.8).

Conditions favoring the development of the site include access to both upland and riverine plants and animals, arable land with good-quality soils, a constant source of water, and the availability of stones suitable for construction within the village limits. A disadvantage of the site, however, was the relatively high risk of potential frost damage due to natural variations in annual temperatures. Sustained crop failures probably were a contributing factor in the eventual abandonment of McPhee Village.

The typical surface dwelling unit in the settlement seems to consist of a living room with two smaller storage rooms oriented toward the southeast and associated with one or more pit structures. The same arrangement of architectural elements is found at Badger House and other northern Anasazi villages during and after the eighth century. The reconstruction presented here shows a group of two large and four small room blocks at the study's comparative scale (Kane & Robinson 1988).

The overall length of the C-shaped room block is about 330 feet (100 meters) measured along the curving centerline of the structure. The pueblo contains a total of fifty rooms; possibly seventeen represent dwellings and the balance served for storage. The average dwelling measures roughly 10 by 16 feet (3 by 5 meters) and contains perhaps 160 square feet (15 square meters). Store rooms appear to be about half the size of those used for living.

In the plaza to the southeast are

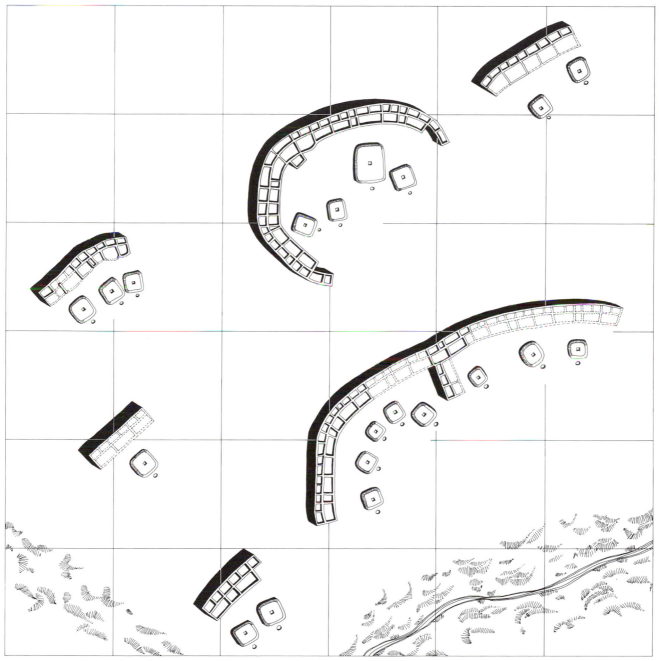

NORTH-CENTRAL MCPHEE VILLAGE

four subterranean structures oriented toward the southeast. Unlike the pit houses at Badger House, the kivas in McPhee Village lack antechambers but have traditional ventilators and draft deflectors southeast of their fire pits. Access into a typical kiva most likely was gained by descending a ladder through the roof hatch above the fire pit.

Each of the three smaller kivas may have served as the focus of activities for five or six families living in the pueblo. Each chamber measures perhaps 20 feet (6 meters) square and has rounded corners. Storage bins are located behind partitions in the south and east corners, but perimeter benches are missing. The large kiva measures approximately 30 by 36 feet (9 by 11 meters) and has a perimeter bench on three sides and floor pits in several locations.

The large kiva apparently served all the occupants of the room block. At McPhee Village each room block with fewer than twenty rooms is associated with one to three small kivas but lacks a large kiva. The clustered pueblos generally are spaced 165 feet (50 meters) or so apart, but in one place two room blocks adjoin each other end to end, and several others almost touch.

Most of the walls and partitions at McPhee Village are built of single courses of stones covered with adobe plaster on both sides. A limited number of interior walls are of jacal construction. Roofs as a rule are of timbers bearing on wood posts, usually located in room corners. The posts form bays at most 10 feet (3 meters) square. The use of wood posts to support roofs appears to be a carry-over from building pit houses; masonry bearing walls invariably support

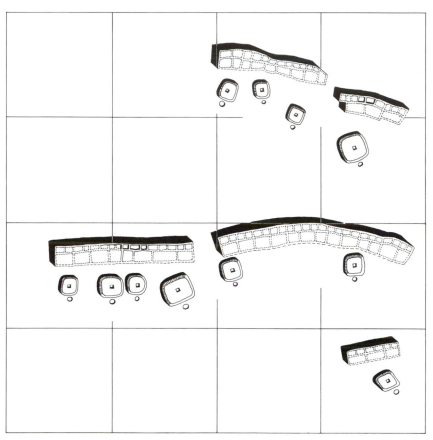

GRASS MESA, WEST PORTION

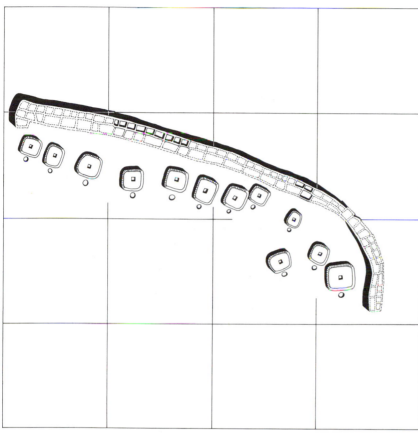

GRASS MESA, EAST PORTION

floors and roofs in pueblos built later.

Warm temperatures generally prevailed in the Dolores River Valley from 800 to 860 and agricultural production was favorable for an increasing population. However, between 880 and 920 annual temperatures often were too cool for crops to mature and a large population could not be supported. Emigration and partial abandonment probably ensued. Shortly after 975 McPhee Village was entirely abandoned.

GRASS MESA VILLAGE

Grass Mesa Village is a good example of the establishment, growth, and eventual abandonment of a typical northern Anasazi community early in the evolution of architecture in the Southwest. The site lies in the Dolores River Valley of southwestern Colorado not far from the contemporary settlement of McPhee Village. The reconstruction presented here is based on information published by William D. Lipe, James N. Morris, and Timothy A. Kohler in 1988. The reconstruction suggests the appearance of the community during the second of three successive chronological periods.

Between A.D. 700 and 840 During the eighth century early settlers established a number of farming settlements on the banks of the constantly flowing Dolores River. In time Grass

Mesa Village extended over an area measuring roughly 345 by 820 feet (105 by 250 meters) and contained perhaps twenty-seven pit structures and a number of surface rooms randomly dispersed in the landscape. Not all of the pit structures were occupied at the same time, but all except one were dwellings containing hearths for heating and cooking.

The exceptional early pit structure at Grass Mesa Village was a great kiva measuring possibly 69 feet (21 meters) in diameter. Located in the northwest quadrant of the site, the large, circular chamber contained an area of some 3,740 square feet (347 square meters), more than ten times the size of a typical dwelling. The great kiva is a community room where all or most of the residents could gather on special occasions.

In addition to the pit structures associated with the early phase of development, Grass Mesa Village had an estimated thirty-nine surface rooms that most likely were used for storage. The store rooms were found in scattered locations both singly and in clusters generally in the north and west areas of the site. The nine easternmost dwellings had no nearby store rooms at all. Although all of the dwellings were oriented more or less toward the south, the community plan lacked the orderly coherence of Grass Mesa's succeeding phase of development.

Between 840 and 880 During this period warm temperatures combined with the constant water supply of the Dolores River to provide optimum conditions for agricultural production in the fertile valley. The population of Grass Mesa Village may have reached its maximum around this time. Increased agricultural production and population suggest provisions for additional storage and housing, both affecting the burgeoning community's physical plan.

The accompanying reconstruction of Grass Mesa Village shows a relatively well-organized site consisting of possibly 180 surface rooms and twenty-three pit structures, which together demonstrate a new pattern in community planning. The reconstruction omits three additional pit structures because they were built partially on top of the structures shown. For comparison purposes only, dashed lines in the reconstruction indicate the location of the earlier great kiva, although the circular chamber had been abandoned prior to the current phase of development.

The community is more compact than during the former phase; the plan occupies a more or less 330-by-720-foot (100-by-220-meter) area representing a 16 percent reduction in size compared to the earlier plan. The surface rooms now are grouped in six linear room blocks ranging in length from 50 to 435 feet (15 to 133 meters) and generally extending from east to west. The typical room block is composed of rows of contiguous large dwelling rooms, each interconnected with two small adjacent store rooms, which form the north wall of the room block.

The dwellings open toward the south onto porches or *ramadas* in the direction of nearby pit structures. The underground chambers probably no longer function as residences. More likely they now serve as kivas where small groups or clans could gather, recalling the similar chambers of McPhee Village, Badger House, Alkali Ridge, and other early northern Anasazi settlements.

Although Grass Mesa's earlier great kiva no longer is used, twenty-three clan kivas may serve somewhat parallel functions in the new community. Perhaps sixty of the larger surface rooms are dwellings; the remaining 120 or so smaller rooms may be used for storage. Most of the kivas seem to be associated with two or three nearby dwellings having possibly six to nine adjacent store rooms.

Grass Mesa's clan kivas are relatively evenly distributed in the community. The underground chambers are approximately square in plan and have rounded corners; for the most part they range in size from 300 to 400 square feet (28 to 37 square meters). None of the clan kivas approaches the size of the earlier great kiva.

Between 880 and 910 During the late ninth and early tenth centuries annual temperatures on the average were too cool for crops to mature in the Dolores Valley. Consequently, agriculture no longer could be relied on to sustain the large population of Grass Mesa Village. Presumably, the residents began to rely on a subsistence system based more heavily on hunting and gathering, and the population may have begun to disperse in small groups. The decline in agricultural activity reduced the need for store rooms, and large sections of the former room blocks fell into disuse.

The disciplined architectural organization of the earlier era was eroded further by the building of new pit structures beyond the previous limits of Grass Mesa Village, particularly to the north and west. The sprawling new settlement occupied more than 20 percent more land than during the preceding phase. Most of the pit structures apparently reverted to their original functions as dwellings.

In all, fifty-nine pit structures and forty-eight assorted surface store rooms are identified with the third phase of occupancy in the settlement. The largest of the pit structures is circular in plan and has a diameter of around 26 feet (8 meters); this feature may represent a kiva used for the gathering of limited numbers of people. During the early tenth century, emigration most likely continued, and Grass Mesa Village effectively was abandoned.

ALKALI RIDGE

Most likely occupied intermittently over a period of several centuries, the prehistoric Anasazi village on Alkali Ridge records the transition from pit houses to pueblos in southeastern Utah. The site is located near Lowry, Three Kiva Pueblo, and Hovenweep National Monument. Alkali Ridge represents a major change in settlement size and architectural plan in the Northern San Juan area beginning perhaps sometime around A.D. 700.

The reconstruction presented here is based primarily on documentation by John Otis Brew (1946: fig. 27) of Harvard University's Peabody Museum recording his excavations in 1932 and 1933. The community basically is made up of four arching rows of surface rooms, which flank the north and west sides of plazas containing pit houses. The last structures built at the site appear to be the two-story pueblo facing a subterranean kiva to the north and a three-room

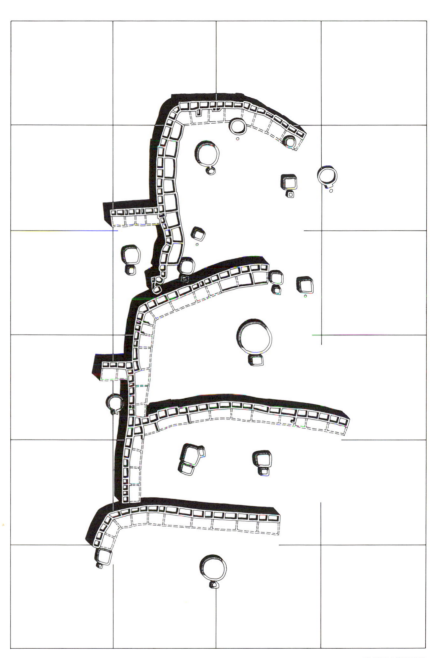

ALKALI RIDGE

house of coursed masonry construction. The latter features are not shown because they are not original structures.

Overall, the ruins measure approximately 240 by 520 feet (73 by 158 meters), an area of possibly 2.87 acres (1.6 hectares). The site slopes down perhaps 10 feet (3 meters) from north to south. The L-shaped room blocks form an almost continuous wall more than 400 feet (122 meters) long on the west side of the village.

In all, Alkali Ridge once may have contained up to 185 surface rooms, at least fourteen pit houses, two or more kivas, a two-story pueblo, and other surface structures. Not all of the structures existed or were occupied at the same time. The surface structures were divided into four groups, each containing some thirty to sixty-seven living and storage rooms.

The earliest structures built at Alkali Ridge probably were the large, round pit houses with antechambers facing south. Ranging from about 21 to 31 feet (6.4 to 9.4 meters) in diameter, the structures are located near the centers of the north, north central, and south plazas. The pit houses may have been constructed sometime around A.D. 700, although very similar structures appeared at Badger House on Wetherill Mesa at least a century earlier.

Next in the construction sequence quite likely were one-story surface rooms of jacal construction. The basic residential module appears to be a three-room apartment composed of two small storage rooms opening into a much larger living room facing toward the south or east. The living rooms originally may have been open-sided *ramadas* where domestic chores could be performed in warm weather.

The newer pit houses associated with surface room blocks are smaller in diameter and have more deeply sunken floors than their predecessors. Of the eight transitional pit houses found by Brew, five have antechambers connected by tunnels to their main rooms, two have ventilator shafts like those at McPhee Village, and the configuration of the last is uncertain. Almost completely subterranean, some of the structures are recessed as deeply as 3 feet (1 meter) into the bedrock underlying the topsoil.

The main rooms of the pit houses usually are divided into two areas of unequal sizes. Low jacal partitions or wing walls about 3 feet (1 meter) high screen off small storage areas near the antechambers or ventilators to the south of the main living space. Each pit house appears to serve as the focus of activities for a number of families living in the room block close-by to the northwest.

The last subterranean structures added to the community on Alkali Ridge are small, deep, Mesa Verde–type kivas. The two-story pueblo and the coursed masonry house mentioned previously are the products of a later reoccupation. The extensive ceramic collection gathered at the site records intermittent occupation of Alkali Ridge over a period of several centuries.

Coombs

U T A H

NEVADA

Three Kiva Pueblo   Lowry   Escalante

Wallace
Far View

COLORADO

Chimney Rock

Muddy
River   Virgin
River

Main Ridge

San Juan
River

Chinle
Wash

Colorado
River

Rio
Grande

Squaw Springs
Salmon   Aztec

Hogback

Casa Abajo
Casa Cielo   Chaco Canyon

Rio
Chama

White House
Whirlwind House

Kin Klizhin

Kin Bineola   Pueblo Pintado
Bee Burrow

Toh La Kai   Muddy Water

Kin Ya'a
Fort Wingate   Casamero
Andrews   San Mateo

Galisteo
Creek

Pecos
River

Las Ventanas

Little Colorado
River

Zuni
River

Rio
Puerco

CALIFORNIA

Verde
River

A R I Z O N A

N E W   M E X I C O

Chaco Canyon

Una Vida
Peñasco Blanco
Pueblo Bonito
Hungo Pavi
Chetro Ketl
Pueblo Alto
Pueblo del Arroyo
Wijiji
Tsin Kletzin
Kin Kletso
Casa Chiquita
New Alto

Tonto
Creek

Salt
River

T J Ruin

Colorado
River

Gila
River

Snaketown

Gila
River

T E X A S

Galaz   Swarts
Cameron Creek   NAN Ranch

Mimbres
River

Rio
Grande

GULF
OF
CALIFORNIA

S O N O R A

C H I H U A H U A

100 m/160 k

<big>D</big>uring the tenth and eleventh centuries distinctive architectural characteristics emerged in the Mogollon, Hohokam, and Anasazi cultural areas of the Southwest. Pit houses similar to those in use in preceding centuries continued to serve as dwellings in many settlements, but kivas developed specialized features in some places, and dramatic strides occurred in the architecture of surface room blocks. The reconstructed plans of forty-four sites presented in this section are intended to suggest the general character of architectural developments in the ancient Southwest between A.D. 900 and 1140.

Mogollon

The Mogollon area is represented by five communities in the Mimbres and Gila River valleys of mountainous southwestern New Mexico. Cameron Creek illustrates the settlement's character as a pit house hamlet, initially, and later as a group of surface room blocks. The remains of pit houses frequently are found below ancient surface structures in the Southwest.

The Galaz and Swarts sites present variations of typical single-story Mogollon pueblos grouped around irregular plazas. Like Cameron Creek, the Swarts Ruin is composed of room blocks organized generally into north and south divisions, while the structures of the larger Galaz site are grouped around a sizable community plaza. Two large room blocks and several smaller features form the orderly pueblo of the nearby NAN Ranch on the east bank of the Mimbres River.

The largest Classic Mimbres (A.D. 1000–1150) site in this discussion, T J Ruin, may contain the remains of as many as 280 rooms in at least five room blocks. Free-standing circular kivas and possibly multistory construction suggest Anasazi influences from the north. The unexcavated pueblo occupies a dramatic cliff edge overlooking a fertile valley near the headwaters of the Gila River in southwestern New Mexico.

Hohokam

The comparatively large community of Snaketown illustrates Hohokam architectural developments in the Gila and Salt River Basin of south-central Arizona. By the tenth century the desert farmers had successfully completed the construction of extensive irrigation networks involving many miles of canals serving numerous farm plots. Snaketown's impressive ball courts, central plaza, platform mound, and canal works suggest Mesoamerican influences.

Chaco Canyon Anasazi

The architectural monuments created in Chaco Canyon during the tenth and eleventh centuries are among the foremost achievements of the ancient Southwest. Here in the relatively brief span of time between perhaps 1050 and 1130 the Chaco Phenomenon occurred, an imperfectly understood event that is the subject of continuing study. Characteristics of the phenomenon seem to include the development of highly disciplined architecture, construction of an extensive road system, establishment of numerous settlements, and participation in a widespread trade network extending into northern Mexico and to the Pacific and Texas coasts.

Una Vida, Peñasco Blanco, and Pueblo Bonito are three early Chacoan pueblos, often called great houses, on which construction began between perhaps 860 and 920. All three are exceptionally large, multistory masonry room blocks to which wall-enclosed plazas subsequently were added. The plazas were oriented generally toward the south and each contained a number of kivas. The largest and perhaps best known of all Chacoan structures is Pueblo Bonito, once a five-story building more than 500 feet (152 meters) long and including possibly as many as eight hundred rooms.

Hungo Pavi, Chetro Ketl, and Pueblo Alto illustrate a second generation of Chacoan great houses; they were begun late in the tenth century or early in the eleventh. All three pueblos have later additions in the form of curving south walls enclosing large plazas with one or more subterranean kivas, and all have large room blocks with numerous storage rooms but few dwellings. The Chacoan great houses appear to have been used more for storage and perhaps ceremonial functions than for residential purposes.

Pueblo del Arroyo and Wijiji are the last two great houses built in Chaco Canyon with distinctive Chacoan masonry. During the early twelfth century a new type of masonry called McElmo appeared, and the last four major structures were erected in Chaco Canyon. Tsin Kletzin, Kin Kletso, Casa Chiquita, and New Alto are built with stone blocks of the McElmo style; all four are relatively small, compact pueblos with limited numbers of kivas, and only Tsin Kletzin has a formal plaza.

San Juan Basin Anasazi

Anasazi communities in the San Juan Basin related to the activities of Chaco Canyon often are referred to as Chacoan outliers. Small communities built on the basin floor within twenty miles of Pueblo Bonito typically had small, orderly plans containing nine to twenty rooms with one or more wall-enclosed surface kivas. Chaco outliers often are found near the remains of ancient roads, which once may have linked them to Chaco Canyon.

Examples of outliers on the basin floor more than 6,000 feet (1,800 meters) above sea level are Bee Burrow, Casa Cielo, Casa Abajo, Kin Klizhin, and Whirlwind House. An exceptionally large outlier on the basin floor is Kin Bineola, an E-shaped room block containing some two hundred rooms up to three stories high. The large pueblo has a great kiva and two plazas oriented toward the southeast.

The easternmost Chacoan outlier on the San Juan Basin floor is Pueblo Pintado. Somewhat similar in plan to Una Vida, Pueblo Pintado occupies an isolated site approximately 17 miles (27 kilometers) east of Pueblo Bonito. The large outlier contains perhaps 135 rooms up to three stories high, five surface kivas, a curving wall enclosing a plaza oriented to the southeast, and a great kiva.

Chaco outliers in the Red Mesa Valley are situated some 42 to 70 miles (67 to 112 kilometers) south of Chaco Canyon at elevations of 6,700 to 7,200 feet (2,042 to 2,195 meters) above sea level. Typical sites are Andrews, Casamero, Fort Wingate, Las Ventanas, and San Mateo. All five are orderly rectangular room blocks containing between perhaps 14 and 112 rooms each; all are associated with one or more great kivas, and most belong to larger neighboring communities.

Kin Ya'a, Muddy Water, and Toh La Kai are examples of Chaco outliers on the South Chaco Slope. The orderly rectangular pueblos lie 26 to 48 miles (42 to 77 kilometers) south of Pueblo Bonito, and each contains between twenty-five and thirty-nine or so rooms. Unusual architectural features of the group are Kin Ya'a's four-story tower, Toh La Kai's unusual orientation to the north, and the huge residential community surrounding Muddy Water.

The final example of Chaco outliers on the San Juan Basin floor is Hogback, a small pueblo located on the south bank of the San Juan River about 54 miles (87 kilometers) north of Chaco Canyon. The northernmost of the outliers in this section, Hogback contains some fifteen rooms and a wall-enclosed kiva. The pueblo is located favorably for trade between the populous communities north of the San Juan River and Chaco Canyon to the south.

Immediately west of the San Juan Basin in northeastern Arizona is spectacular Canyon de Chelly where construction of the Chacoan outlier called White House began in 1060. The sixty-room masonry structure contains four kivas and is built at the base of a sheer cliff some 500 feet (120 meters) high. Later occupants of White House constructed a unique twenty-room dwelling in a natural cave directly above the original room block.

Northern San Juan Anasazi

Far View House and Pipe Shrine House on Mesa Verde and Lowry Pueblo in southwestern Colorado are components of extensive Anasazi towns active during the tenth and eleventh centuries. Far View Community was an important mesa-top complex until the twelfth century when the Mesa Verdeans began to move down into cliff dwellings in the walls of the mesa. Lowry is situated in rich farmland in the Montezuma Valley where an Anasazi complex with possibly twenty-four sites once flourished.

Aztec, the largest Chacoan great house outside Chaco Canyon, and nearby Salmon are two large Chacoan outliers in the Northern San Juan area. The three-story West Ruin at Aztec contained perhaps more than 480 rooms, and East Ruin counted possibly 290 more. Somewhat smaller Salmon has 140 ground-floor rooms and a remarkable tower kiva.

Located in the Four Corners area, Squaw Springs and Wallace have perhaps twenty-three and one hundred rooms, respectively. The small pueblo of Escalante is situated on a beautiful hillcrest overlooking the Dolores River in southwestern Colorado. Three Kiva Pueblo, a structure of modest size located in southeast Utah, contains fourteen rooms, a small kiva, and probably a turkey pen.

This study's final example of Eastern Anasazi architecture in the Northern San Juan Region between 900 and 1140 was constructed toward the very end of the time period under consideration. Remarkable Chimney Rock Pueblo occupies a spectacular ridge crest 7,600 feet (2,316 meters) high in south-central Colorado. The exceptional structure is constructed at one of the highest altitudes in this study.

Virgin and Kayenta Anasazi

The Main Ridge community in southern Nevada is the westernmost Anasazi settlement in this discussion. The construction of pit houses on the site began perhaps as early as A.D. 500. In time the pit houses were replaced by surface store rooms and dwellings with adobe walls. During the period of peak activity between perhaps 1050 and 1100, dozens of crescent-shaped rows or rooms faced southward on irregular sites in the hilly terrain. By the middle of the twelfth century Main Ridge was abandoned entirely for unknown reasons.

The largest Anasazi community west of the Colorado River, Coombs Village demonstrates primarily Kayentan architectural characteristics but also shows influences of the Fremont people to the north, the Virgin Anasazi to the west, and Mesa Verde ideas from the east. The cultural crossroad not surprisingly contains both masonry and jacal construction and also a number of pit houses excavated into a sandy deposit along the south edge of the hilltop site. Probably established around 1075, Coombs was abandoned about 1275.

Contemporary Architecture beyond the Southwest

During the tenth and eleventh centuries in the Eastern United States, construction continued on multiterraced Monks Mound at Cahokia near St. Louis, the largest truncated earthwork in North America. Probably around A.D. 1000 the Caddo culture appeared at Spiro in eastern Oklahoma; here residential areas were built between earlier ceremonial and mortuary groups containing truncated rectangular and conical mounds. A short while later work began at one of the northernmost prehistoric sites in the Eastern United States, Aztalan in southeastern Wisconsin. One or more palisades enclosed the medium-size settlement and its three truncated earth mounds all modest in scale (Morgan 1980).

During the same time period in Mesoamerica, work proceeded on the complex of distinguished buildings at Uxmal. These include one of the foremost examples of Maya architecture, the Governor's Palace, which is elevated on several impressive platforms. Meanwhile, on a beautiful hilltop near the south edge of the Central Plateau of Mexico, Toltec builders erected Xochicalco with its ball court and platforms embellished by ornately carved stelle and bas reliefs. To the north Maya influences appeared in the grand colonnades, palace, temples, and ball courts of Tula, a Toltec city strategically located to discourage Chichimec incursions from the north (Heyden & Gendrop 1973).

About the same time in Micronesia, *latte* building continued to evolve in the Mariana Islands where stone columns and capstones maintained the traditional practice of elevating houses on stilts in Island Southeast Asia. Around the year 1000 the scale of terrace building activities increased on the island of Babeldaob in the Palau archipelago where major activity continued until perhaps 1400. Meanwhile in Pohnpei construction advanced on the artificial islets that eventually would form Nan Madol, "The Venice of the Pacific" (Morgan 1988).

CAMERON CREEK
Mogollon

Some 15 miles (24 kilometers) southwest of the Harris site lies Cameron Creek, a Classic Mimbres pueblo built on the remains of an earlier Mogollon pit house settlement. The site occupies a gentle rise oriented more or less from the northeast to the southwest about 5 miles (8 kilometers) west of San Vicente Arroyo, a tributary of the Mimbres River. Cameron Creek is located roughly 190 miles (306 kilometers) southwest of Albuquerque.

The earlier pit house community consists of two clusters of subterranean structures. Between the two clusters a large kiva is flanked by perhaps thirty-one dwellings to the southwest and possibly twenty-eight to the northeast. South of the kiva is Cameron Creek's central plaza, a major element in the architectural organization and most likely the focus of community-wide activities.

Not all of the sixty semisubterranean structures shown in the reconstruction were contemporaries; some were built adjoining or on top of their abandoned predecessors (Stuart & Gauthier 1988). Ramp orientations vary, but a generally southeasterly direction appears frequently in more recent structures. Near the center of each residence was a roof hatch for ventilation and illumination.

Cameron Creek's large kiva contains an area of roughly 950 square feet (88 square meters), about four times the size of typical habitations in the community. Characteristic of Mogollon great kivas, the structure is quadrilateral and has a large, extended entry ramp oriented to the southeast. Even larger community chambers are found in other Mogollon settlements.

The second reconstructed plan shown here represents Cameron Creek during the Classic Mimbres period between perhaps A.D. 1000 and 1150. Other well-known Classic Mimbres sites in this discussion are NAN Ranch (Shafer 1990), Swarts (Cosgrove & Cosgrove 1932), Galaz (Anyon & LeBlanc 1984), and T J Ruin (McKenna & Bradford 1989). During this period Cameron Creek consisted of five single-story room blocks, each with an aggregation of from four to forty-one contiguous surface rooms.

The latter community seems to contain at most ninety-seven rooms, some of which may be divided internally into smaller spaces. Residential units most likely were entered by means of roof hatches. Like the plan of the preceding pit house community, Cameron Creek during Classic Mimbres times is organized into northeast and southwest sections flanking a central plaza.

The settlement's architectural features, functions, and details are similar for the most part to those described for the Galaz site in this study. Unlike Galaz, however, Cameron Creek is somewhat smaller in size, has a more linear arrangement of room blocks, and presents greater variations in room sizes, proportions, and orientations. Ceramicists at both sites produced exceptionally beautiful black-on-white pottery, a distinctive characteristic of the Mimbres people.

Like the Mesa Verdeans in southwest Colorado, the people in the Mimbres region of New Mexico lived in relatively large aggregated villages between 900 and 1150. Mogollon traits found at Cameron Creek in-

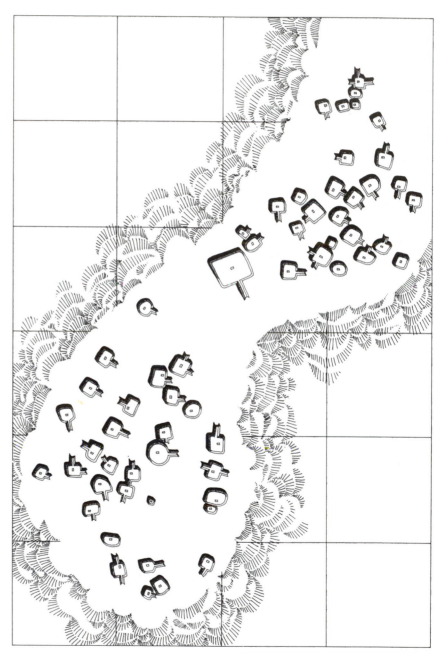

CAMERON CREEK, PIT HOUSE COMMUNITY

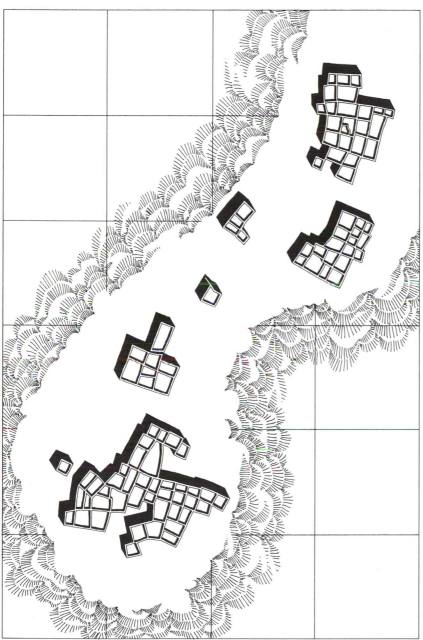

CAMERON CREEK, SURFACE ROOM BLOCKS

clude standardized architectural construction, public architecture in the form of a great kiva, and craft specialization. For subsistence the people depended on agriculture supplemented by hunting and gathering. The architecture and planning of the Mimbres people retained a high degree of adaptive flexibility through time.

GALAZ
Mogollon

Galaz is one of the largest, longest occupied, and best known of the Mimbres settlements. The ruin is located on the west bank of the Mimbres River approximately 170 miles (272 kilometers) southwest of Albuquerque. Other well-known Mimbres pueblos in this study are Swarts and NAN Ranch situated roughly 10 miles (16 kilometers) to the south, Cameron Creek about 14 miles (22 kilometers) to the southwest, and T J Ruin some 35 miles (56 kilometers) to the west. All four sites have earlier pit house components.

Founded probably around A.D. 550, Galaz continued to be occupied for the next eight centuries, an exceptional length of occupancy for a prehistoric southwestern site. The earliest pit houses constructed at Galaz, as at other Mimbres communities, were circular or oval in plan; they later became rectangular. By the end of the tenth century forty-five or more

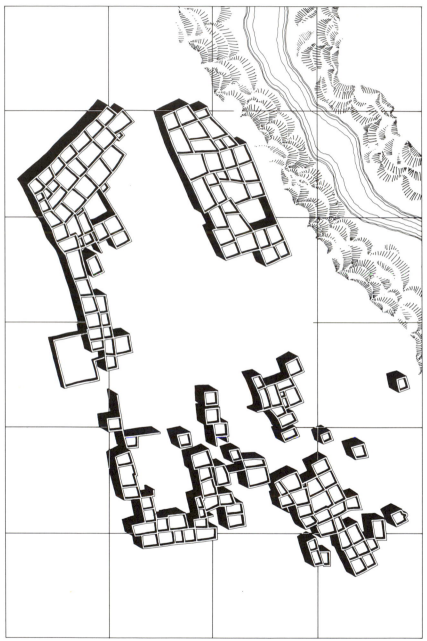

GALAZ

pit houses apparently were in use on the site.

Between 1000 and 1150, the Classic Mimbres period, Galaz underwent an architectural transformation. One-room pit houses were replaced by above-ground room clusters built with walls of cobble set in adobe. The reconstruction presented here shows the community as it may have appeared at its peak of development with an estimated 142 single-story surface rooms (Anyon & LeBlanc 1984: figs. 3.2, 3.5).

During the Classic Mimbres period the population increased by possibly two and one-half times, agriculture intensified, and new settlements appeared in the Mimbres Valley. In time the community grew by accretion into one small and four large room clusters arranged loosely around a central plaza. In plan Galaz extends some 440 feet (134 meters) along the riverbank and 300 feet (90 meters) to the west.

The room clusters are agglomerations of room groups, clearly not room blocks with predetermined plans. The room clusters generally consist of many dwellings, very few store rooms, and several communal spaces. Each cluster contains between eleven and forty-three rooms. The rooms seem to be arranged in groups, all apparently entered from the exterior by means of ladders and roof hatches.

Living and store rooms can be identified in room groups alongside semi-subterranean kivas, special purpose rooms, and courtyards (Anyon & LeBlanc 1984). Roof tops, patios, and courtyards most likely accommodated outside activities except during inclement weather. Living rooms usually contained 85 to 280 square feet (8 to 26 square meters). Spaces smaller than dwellings presumably were used for storage, and larger rooms are assumed to have served communal functions.

Living rooms typically have hearths, cobblestone floors, grinding stones called *metates*, and rows of roof posts along their centerlines. The seven large communal surface rooms found in Galaz range in size from 305 to 510 square feet (28.4 to 47 square meters). Distributed throughout the room clusters, the large communal rooms most likely served the entire population of Galaz.

Semisubterranean kivas seem to be smaller communal or ceremonial facilities serving only limited segments of the community. The small kivas often have ventilation shafts and never have ramps suggesting access by means of roof hatches. Some kivas may be remodeled pit houses; they frequently are found on the outer edges of room clusters.

The most remarkable architectural feature of Galaz is the extraordinarily large, semisubterranean community chamber located near the south end of the northwest room block. The rectangular structure measures 36 by 46 feet (11 by 14 meters) or so and contains an area as large as 1,656 square feet (154 square meters).

Three wood posts 24 to 28 inches (60 to 70 centimeters) in diameter support the large chamber's main roof beam. The roof structure seems to consist of two bays, each about 18 feet (5.5 meters) wide. These are exceptionally long spans for roof joists in ancient southwestern architecture.

A ramp some 10 feet (3 meters) wide leads from the sunken chamber up toward the plaza to the east, widening slightly as it rises. The rooms shown in the reconstruction at the east end of the ramp may not have existed when the kiva was in use. The smooth adobe floor of the chamber is recessed about 5.5 feet (1.7 meters) into the gravel subsurface of the site.

Walls 12 to 24 inches (30 to 60 centimeters) thick enclose the large room. Recessed into the gravel under the floor are a hearth measuring possibly 37 by 44 by 7 inches (94 by 112 by 18 centimeters) deep, a *sipapu*, or spirit hole, at most 3 inches (7 centimeters) in diameter, and three roof postholes each about 6.8 feet (2.06 meters) deep. The sunken structure may have served public functions similar to those of semisubterranean great kivas during earlier periods.

Subfloor compartments in the chamber contained such ceremonial objects as a carved shell effigy, beads, crystals, a shell bracelet, and beads and pendants of turquoise, shell, and stone. One of the community rooms at Galaz yielded a macaw skeleton wrapped with strings of turquoise, shell, and stone beads and other exotic goods suggesting widespread trade.

Although Mimbres pottery represents one of the foremost artistic achievements of the ancient Southwest, the same cannot be said for Mimbres architecture. The construction of Classic Mimbres buildings appears to be inherently unsound. The relatively thin walls typically lack conventional foundations and consist of unshaped river stones laid in abundant mud mortar. Multistory construction seems highly unlikely. Bearing walls and one to four internal posts usually support roofs.

The plazas of Galaz probably served community-wide activities and functions as they do among contemporary Pueblo people. Like the residents of other Classic Mimbres communities, the people of Galaz apparently lived in a relatively egalitarian society with rich artistic and ceremonial traditions. Fortunately, before the site was looted and bulldozed in 1976, Galaz yielded more than eight hundred Mimbres bowls and a wealth of information about ancient architecture and community planning in the Mimbres Valley.

SWARTS
Mogollon

A Classic Mimbres site in southwestern New Mexico, the Swarts Ruin lies in the Mimbres Valley approximately 180 miles (290 kilometers) south-southeast of Albuquerque. Probably constructed sometime between A.D. 975 and 1150, the stone pueblo consists basically of two room blocks. The north house contains sixty-eight more or less rectangular chambers while the south block has forty-nine (Cosgrove & Cosgrove 1932).

One or more ceremonial rooms serving functions similar to those of kivas may have been situated within each room block. The frequent misalignment of walls, geometric inconsistencies in plan, and wide variations in room proportions and sizes suggest construction by random accretion rather than according to a predetermined plan.

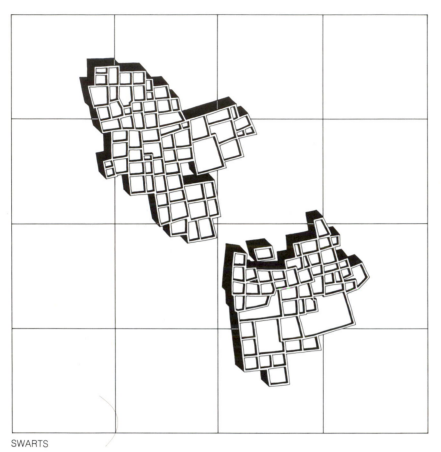

SWARTS

ments have no more than twenty rooms. Thus, with a total of 117 rooms, the Swarts Ruin is an exceptionally large Mimbres pueblo.

The appearance of surface masonry room blocks represents a distinct break architecturally from earlier Mogollon sites where a maximum of seventy to eighty pit houses are found. Communities with two or more room blocks commonly are found after about A.D. 1000. The pueblos typically have walls constructed of cobble masonry laid in beds of adobe mortar.

Most Mogollon pit houses averaged about 170 square feet in area (15.8 square meters) during the ninth century. However, the typical size of rooms in Mimbres pueblos during the same time period declined to 130 square feet (12 square meters) or less. Like other Mimbres sites, the Swarts Ruin was built on top of earlier pit houses and associated structures.

The population most likely increased substantially during Classic Mimbres times. The highest level of construction activity in the Mimbres Valley probably occurred between 1060 and 1080. This also was a time of major building in Chaco Canyon some 230 miles (370 kilometers) north of the Swarts Ruin.

The distinctive Mimbres culture is perhaps best known for its exceptionally beautiful black-on-white pottery often incorporating extraordinary geometric and zoomorphic designs. The continuing influence of Mimbres pottery can be seen in ceramic wares being produced today in the Southwest (Ortiz 1979). A branch of the broader Mogollon culture, the Mimbres people in time were absorbed by the expanding and closely related Pueblo people to the north.

Unlike the roughly contemporary monuments in Chaco Canyon, Classic Mimbres sites had large numbers of burials in room floors and in the immediate vicinity of house blocks. An average of five burials per room is common in major sites of the Mimbres Valley. Grave offerings indicate trade over a widespread geographical area; these include shell from the Gulf of California, turquoise, and macaw feathers (Stuart & Gauthier 1988:199–205).

Hundreds of Mimbres sites have been found varying in size from two to two hundred or more rooms. The overwhelming majority of settle-

NAN RANCH
Mogollon

The Classic Mimbres pueblo called the NAN Ranch ruin overlooks the Mimbres River from a low alluvial terrace about a mile and a half (2.5 kilometers) southeast of the Swarts site in southwestern New Mexico. The remains are elevated some 13 feet (4 meters) above the river plain, which lies 160 feet (50 meters) or so southwest of the site. The basis of this reconstruction is a village plan reflecting more than a decade of investigations in the ruins by Harry J. Shafer (1990: fig. 2) and others.

Like the contemporary Mimbres Valley settlements to the north, the NAN Ranch pueblo lies on top of an earlier village consisting of at least sixteen pit houses built probably between A.D. 850 and 1000. The surface structures of the community include the large East Room Block having perhaps forty-nine rooms, the compact South Room Block with ten rooms closer to the river, the largely unexplored West Room Block comprising probably more than fifty rooms, and two rooms built on a midden to the southeast. By no means did all one hundred or more rooms exist at the same time.

In plan the NAN Ranch ruin measures overall approximately 275 feet (84 meters) square. Ongoing investigations at NAN Ranch suggest that additional rooms may lie below the silted surface; these would confirm the pueblo as one of the larger Classic Mimbres villages. The community plan closely resembles the Swarts site except for NAN Ruin's South Room Block.

The earliest tree-ring date for the pueblo is the year 1008 provided by a

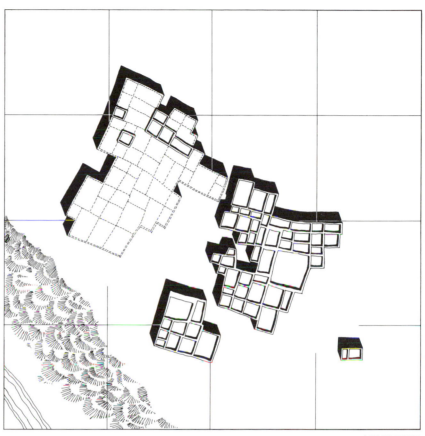

NAN RANCH

roof beam in the northeast room of the East Room Block. More than two dozen other tree-ring dates record the continuation of construction until at least 1128, the latest tree-cutting date known for a Classic Mimbres structure. The community quite likely was occupied until sometime between 1130 and 1150 when Classic Mimbres activities ceased and the Mimbres Valley was abandoned.

An unusual feature of the East Room Block is the exceptionally large room centered along the east side fronting the East Plaza. Much disturbed by pothunters, the remarkable chamber measures very nearly 31 by 33 feet (9.5 by 10 meters) and contains an estimated 1,023 square feet (95 square meters), one of the largest rooms reported in the Mimbres Valley. Although it may have served for storage or utility, the great space more likely was a communal room following the Mogollon tradition of a great kiva where the community as a whole could assemble.

Construction of the large communal room may have occurred around 1110 when earlier structures were razed and the rooms to the west and north were completed. A row of possibly three juniper posts along the centerline divides the roof structure into two 16-foot- (5-meter-) wide bays. An indication of the chamber's importance may be found in the sturdiness of its surrounding double walls; other walls were left to deteriorate after their purposes had been served.

The East Room Block seems to have expanded by accretion and internal subdivision during the eleventh century. The rooms of the pueblo probably were used for living, storage, granaries, or the assembly of small groups or the community as a whole. Living rooms generally have slab-lined hearths and often *metates*; they typically contain areas of 205 square feet (19 square meters).

Store rooms usually lack floor features and often are more or less 124 square feet (11.5 square meters) in size. A suite of adjacent rooms interconnected by doorways seems to represent a typical family's functional requirements for living and store rooms. The only access to the family suite normally is a roof hatch and ladder leading into the living room.

The South Room Block includes ten well-constructed rooms containing the most concentrated cemeteries and wealthiest graves in the NAN Ranch Ruin. The first of several phases of construction began with the central room and the adjoining space to the south. Burials in the floor of the central room yielded the remains of at least forty and perhaps more than fifty individuals, the largest number of burials in a single room reported in the Mimbres Valley.

Built perhaps between 1066 and 1114, the South Room Block contains in its northwest corner what probably was a small community room. The chamber measures about 20 feet (6 meters) square, an area of 400 square

feet (36 square meters). Four roof support posts form a square in the center of the room and divide the ceiling into three equal bays. The massive north wall consists of an original two-course wall to which a three-course wall was added later; this is the most conservative construction in the NAN Ranch pueblo.

The large room on the east side of the South Room Block was the final addition to the compact group. Double-coursed stone walls enclose the 422-square-foot (39.2-square-meter) space, which most likely was a large storage room. Built between 1096 and 1114 on top of an earlier pit house, the surface room may have had a row of two or three roof support posts along its longitudinal centerline. Three adobe-lined fire pits are situated along the south wall outside the South Room Block.

The two rooms southeast of the main group have an extensive midden, two pit houses, two exterior fire pits, and ten burials. The partially excavated East Plaza yields evidence of many adobe-lined cooking basins, at least one pit house, a number of *ramadas*, or sunshades, associated with outside work areas, numerous burials, including some in middens, and a cremation area likely dating to the late 900s.

Bird burials have been found in the East Room Block and elsewhere in the NAN Ranch ruin. The remains of hawks, turkeys, or eagles are found in graves covered with stone slabs like many human burials at the site. The special treatment of birds in death suggests that they played an important role in the Mimbres belief system.

Early in the twelfth century a shift toward lower quality in building con-

struction became apparent, perhaps anticipating a decline in Classic Mimbres activities. Slabs of rhyolite, a granite-like igneous rock associated with lava, began to appear in wall construction where formerly only river or upland cobbles were used. Adobe made of earth and midden mud began to replace traditional and more durable adobe made of clay, and room plans became more irregular in shape.

During his last visit to the site during the winter of 1882–83, Adolph Bandelier noted a shallow depression possibly 5 feet (1.5 meters) deep surrounded by a low earth retaining wall some 120 feet (36.5 meters) north of the NAN Ranch ruins. No longer visible, the feature suggests the possibility of a reservoir related to nearby farm plots. Some of the walls proposed in the reconstruction also are no longer visible; a number of rooms are assumed to have existed in extensively disturbed areas of the ancient pueblo.

T J RUIN
Mogollon

By far the largest Classic Mimbres (1000–1150) pueblo in this study, T J Ruin occupies a dramatic cliff edge overlooking the West Fork of the Gila River approximately 42 miles (67 kilometers) north of Silver City in southwestern New Mexico. Although the remains have not been excavated

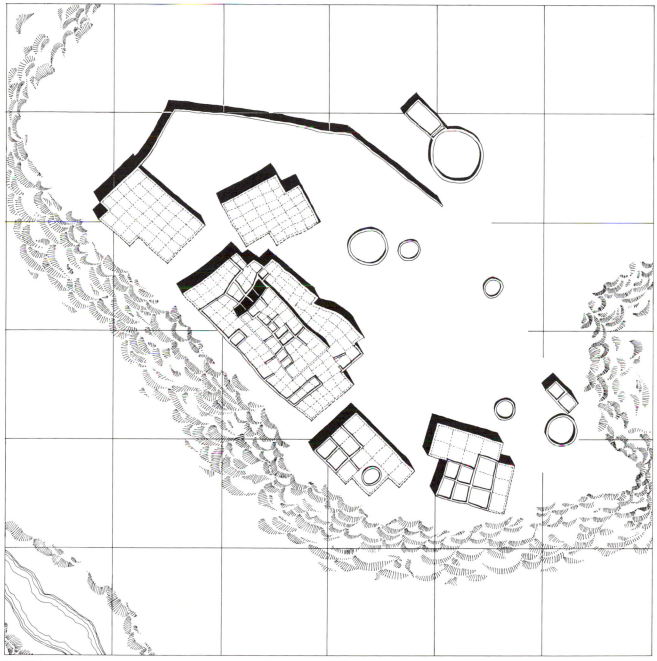

T J RUIN

or trenched, the architecture, community plan, and ceramics collected on the surface of the ruins suggest construction and occupation sometime between A.D. 900 and 1150. The tentative reconstruction proposed here is based on an accurate survey showing surviving wall alignments, mounds containing collapsed structures, circular depressions, topographic contours, and other observable surface features (McKenna & Bradford 1989: fig. 4).

Now under the protection of the U.S. Forest Service, the ruins formerly were part of the T J Ranch, whose owners fortunately protected them from pothunting and other disturbances. The relatively level area northeast of the site recently served as a polo field. Situated well more than a mile (1.6 kilometers) above sea level, the extensive remains of T J Ruin await future investigation. Although the site is in ruins, I observed the general outlines of several room blocks and wall alignments under a light blanket of snow in January 1992.

Overall, the site appears to contain at least five masonry room blocks, seven kivas, and a large central plaza partially enclosed by a distinctive masonry wall on its north side. Four room blocks extend about 500 feet (152 meters) along the southwest edge of the mesa, from which they command a spectacular view of the surrounding Mogollon Mountains and the Gila River Valley below. The residents of T J Ruin were Mogollon farmers who raised corn, beans, and squash on the fertile flood plain of the river and hunted and gathered food in the nearby alpine wilderness.

Unlike Swarts, Cameron Creek, Galaz, and other Classic Mimbres sites, T J Ruin is situated on a dramatic cliff edge rather than on the first terrace above the river's flood plain. The site clearly is oriented with respect to the mesa's edge, not to the cardinal points of the compass. The siting of the room blocks along the cliff edge is highly impressive from the floor of the river valley.

The plaza's enclosing wall extends perhaps 345 feet (105 meters) eastward from the northwest room block. At its easterly terminus the wall defines an entry portal or gateway some 18 feet (5.5 meters) wide. The remains of what probably was a great kiva about 52 feet (16 meters) in diameter flank the entry to the northeast.

The stone slab and adobe walls of the central and southeastern room blocks and the plaza's enclosing wall rest on foundations called *cimientos*. The foundations consist of rows of large upright cobble stones set close together, some as big as basketballs. The reason for using *cimientos* seems to be to retard the erosion of wall bases, a particularly severe problem for adobe walls or stone structures employing ample mortar joints.

The largest three circular depressions range from 26 to 52 feet (8 to 16 meters) in diameter. Most likely great kivas, the structures appear to have associated surface structures, such as the unusually large rectangular room extending northwest from the north great kiva. The remaining four kivas measure 16 to 18 feet (5 to 5.5 meters) in diameter; they probably served smaller groups, possibly members of a clan or an extended family.

Unlike the free-standing circular kivas of T J Ruin, the ceremonial rooms of Swarts, Cameron Creek, NAN Ranch, and Galaz are rectangular and are incorporated into room blocks. Free-standing circular kivas are characteristic of Anasazi architecture, not of Classic Mimbres or Mogollon architecture after A.D. 1000. Other pit houses may be located outside T J Ruin along the mesa edge to the southeast and northwest.

The unexcavated central mound presently rises about 6 feet (2 meters) above the plaza level. The structure quite likely had at least a partial second floor. Of the thirty-three rooms whose walls can be identified with some confidence, only ten are well enough defined to provide dimensions. The southern two room blocks have relatively large rooms, each containing an average area of 215 square feet (20 square meters), which is a typical size for a later Mimbres room.

The central room block has smaller rooms; each contains an area of about 137 square feet (12.7 square meters), roughly the same size as a typical room in Swarts, for example. The walls supporting second stories probably are thicker and their alignments most likely are more regular than those of single-story room blocks. The room sizes in the northern two room blocks cannot be determined from surface observations; they are assumed to be similar in size to the rooms of the central room block.

The reconstructed plan of the T J Ruin proposes a total of 245 ground-floor rooms and thirty-six second-floor rooms, a total of 280 rooms in five room blocks. If so, the pueblo would have possibly twice as many rooms as Galaz, the second-largest Classic Mimbres site in this discussion. Masonry room blocks were only one of the types of housing used in the Mimbres region; at least some Mogollon families probably continued to occupy pit houses long after the introduction of surface structures.

SNAKETOWN
Hohokam

The large Hohokam settlement of Snaketown is situated on the north terrace of the Gila River about 23 miles (37 kilometers) southeast of Phoenix. Here early in the Christian era settlers began to establish communities on the floor of the Sonoran Desert, a region naturally productive of food plants. Probably beginning sometime after A.D. 600 (Cable & Doyel 1987), the Hohokam developed canal systems to provide water for their villages and farms. Centuries ago the Gila River flowed more constantly than it does today; it once supported fish and shellfish and provided havens for game and waterfowl.

Parts of Snaketown have been thoroughly excavated and studied (Gladwin et al. 1937; Haury 1976), and architectural plans exist for the excavated portions of the extensive ruins. Today the site has been filled in and the remains lie buried below the desert floor. The reconstruction presented here is based on diagrams and information published by Wilcox, McGuire, and Sternberg (1981: figs. 2, 40).

Sometime between A.D. 900 and 1100, the plan of Snaketown probably consisted of a central plaza area roughly 450 feet (137 meters) in diameter, surrounded by inner and outer residential zones. Eight low earth mounds formed a circle more or less 1,150 feet (350 meters) in diameter, separating the inner and outer zones. Snaketown's outer diameter quite likely was around 3,000 feet (915 meters).

The outer residential zone apparently was not densely populated but contained two ball courts. The key plan for Snaketown presented here

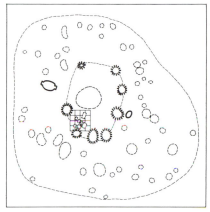

KEY PLAN OF SNAKETOWN

shows the ball courts as elliptical figures with bold outlines, and mounds as circular figures with radial perimeter lines. Important examples of public architecture, the ball courts lie east and west of the central plaza.

The larger west ball court is an elongated oval in plan; it measures about 63 by 203 feet (19 by 62 meters) and is flanked by 12-foot-(3.7-meter-) high walls of compacted earth. Three stone markers were found on the field, one at each end and one in the center. Other ball courts discussed in this study are found at Casa Grande, Paquimé, and Wupatki.

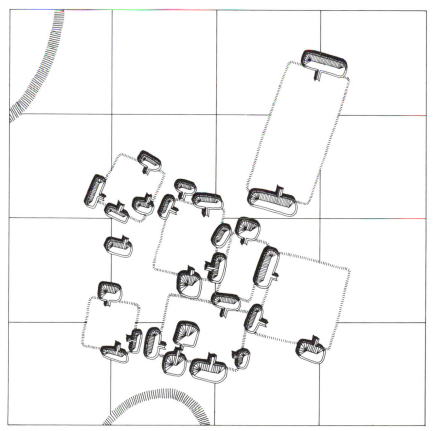

SNAKETOWN, INNER ZONE RESIDENCES

Other important examples of public architecture in Hohokam settlements are platform mounds. The earth mound due north of Snaketown's plaza clearly was a platform mound. The structure was capped by one or more layers of caliche and surrounded by a palisade of posts. Later in Hohokam prehistory, platform mounds evolved into elevated, rectangular enclosures containing one or more houses. Examples of later settlements with platform mounds are Los Muertos, Pueblo Grande, Casa Grande, and Paquimé.

The cluster of pit houses shown in this reconstruction is located in the residential quadrant southwest of Snaketown's central plaza. Earth mounds appear south and northwest of the cluster. A total of twenty-six pit houses are shown in the cluster. They are grouped around seven possible courtyards, each having two to six dwellings.

Compared with the plan of Snaketown, the community plans of Harris, Mogollon Village, and early Cameron Creek appear to be somewhat randomly arranged. The pit houses of Snaketown are placed orthogonally with respect to their courtyards in orderly groups. The cluster plan seems to anticipate the disciplined, axially organized, rectangular compounds of later Hohokam settlements.

The two large pit houses to the northeast face each other across a rectangular open space measuring perhaps 59 by 125 feet (18 by 38 meters). A broad access corridor may have extended through the middle of the courtyard. The avenue seems to have proceeded from the mound shown to the northwest through the courtyard, continuing to the east some 820 feet (250 meters). The corridor's centerline would have been perpendicular to the courtyard's longitudinal axis.

The sizes of individual pit houses in Snaketown's southwest quadrant range from 171 to 646 square feet (15.9 to 59.1 square meters). Unlike contemporary Mogollon pit houses, Hohokam dwellings appear to be built like houses in a pit (Jennings 1974:286). In a typical Hohokam house the posts supporting the roof perimeter rest on the surface of the sunken floor, not on the surrounding ground level; the edges of the pit are not incorporated into the house walls.

Also unlike the plans of typical Mogollon houses, those at Snaketown between 900 and 1100 resemble extended rectangles with rounded ends. A typical roof frame consists of possibly three posts supporting a continuous ridge beam aligned with the longitudinal axis of the house (Sayles 1937). Thus, a 16-foot- (5-meter-) wide roof would be divided into two equal bays, both 8 feet (2.5 meters) wide.

Perimeter posts and beams seem to support the roof edges of typical Snaketown dwellings. By contrast, Mogollon pit houses usually have flat roofs with short walls filling in the space between roof edges and the surrounding ground. Four corner posts in a roughly square plan support the roofs of typical Mogollon pit houses.

A typical dwelling at Snaketown is entered below a short roof extending from the main structure, usually located near the middle of the house. Steps lead down to the sunken floor level. Fire pits are situated near the entry, perhaps to minimize the accumulation of smoke inside the house. By contrast Mogollon dwellings have extended ramps descending through tunnel-like entryways, and centrally located fire pits beneath smoke holes.

The marked disparity in the sizes of Snaketown's houses indicates that some families had almost four times as much space as did others, assuming the houses were occupied by single families. This suggests a social hierarchy in which some persons, families, or groups occupied a higher status in the community than did others. Social hierarchies, ball courts, platform mounds, buildings flanking plazas, distinctive trade items, and extensive canal systems raise the possibilities of influences from Mesoamerica.

One of the reasons the Hohokam people appear to have preferred living in pit houses may be related to the thermal properties of the structures. Readily available in the desert environment, earth and adobe are efficient thermal insulators. Rooms within pit houses inherently tend to be cooler than the surrounding desert during the heat of the day and to be warmer during the cool of the night. Pit houses also require relatively little labor for construction and minimal maintenance in dry regions where rainfall is comparatively low.

Pit houses continued to be used by the Hohokam people for the millennia or more they occupied their desert homeland, successfully adapting to the harsh environment. They developed a well-ordered society capable of constructing and maintaining extensive canal networks, platform mounds, and ball courts. Evidence of their widespread trade networks includes items carved from marine shell, copper bells, macaws, and pottery from distant sources.

The maximum population of Snaketown between 900 and 1100 is

estimated to have been around five hundred people. This is a minor fraction of the population of many Hopi, Zuni, or Rio Grande pueblos late in southwestern prehistory (Fish 1989). The Hohokam tradition seems to have ceased to exist at least a century before the Spanish *entrada*. The descendants of the Hohokam quite likely are the present-day Tohono O'odham and Papago Indians. The Tohono O'odham word "hohokam" means "those who came before" or "been all used up" (Haury 1976).

The following twelve pueblos are among the most magnificent examples of ancient architecture to be found in the Southwest. Constructed during the tenth, eleventh, and early twelfth centuries, the pueblos are situated within 9 miles (14 kilometers) of each other in Chaco Canyon, which is located about 100 miles (160 kilometers) northwest of Albuquerque. The ancient ruins lie at altitudes of 6,100 to 6,500 feet (1,860 to 1,980 meters) above sea level a few miles west of the continental divide.

Eight of the monuments are situated on the valley floor near the base of the cliff forming the north wall of Chaco Canyon. The other four ruins are found on the tops of mesas located on both sides of the valley. Chaco Canyon is carved into the desert floor by Chaco Wash, which flows to the west and north where it joins the San Juan, a tributary of the Colorado River.

Persons planning to visit Chaco Canyon may be well advised to verify in advance the condition of the unpaved access roads; they sometimes become impassable during rainy weather.

UNA VIDA
Chaco Canyon Anasazi

Perhaps one of the first Anasazi great houses begun in Chaco Canyon, Una Vida is located about 3.5 miles (5.6 kilometers) southeast of Pueblo Bonito and approximately 100 miles (160 kilometers) northwest of Albuquerque. Tree-ring dates suggest that construction may have commenced on the site around A.D. 860, and the last masonry walls were added possibly 235 years later. Una Vida's construction spans roughly the same pe-

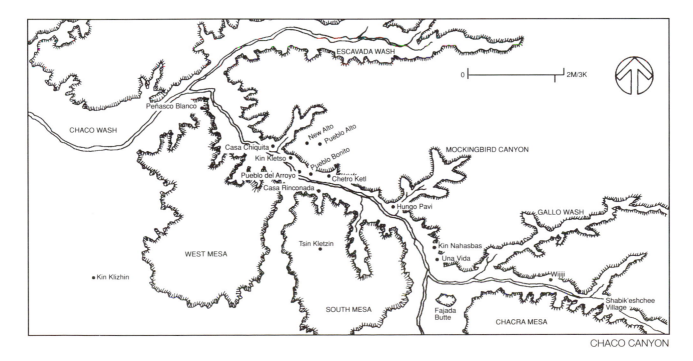

CHACO CANYON

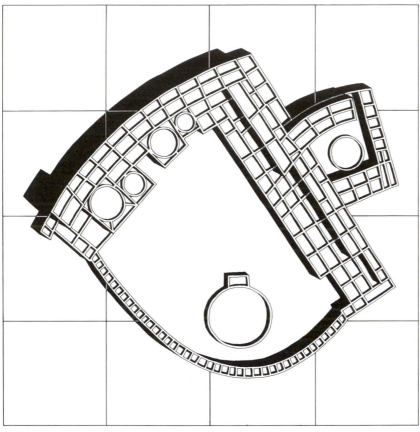

UNA VIDA

third-floor rooms, probably six kivas, and a curving row containing some forty-four small storage rooms. The first structure built appears to be the two-story block with six rooms per floor, which forms a slight arc and extends east from the east wing.

The curving arc most likely was constructed between 860 and 865. Each of the dozen rooms forming the early block contains about 194 square feet (18 square meters). A depression in the courtyard to the south suggests a kiva perhaps 30 feet (9 meters) in diameter. The curved room block seems to represent one of the earliest multistory structures to be built in Chaco Canyon.

Between 930 and 950 the block forming the north wall of the west wing probably was built; it consisted of a curving tier two rooms wide and two stories high. One or two third-story rooms were added to the west end of the block forming a unique tower. A two-story room block connected the west wing to the earlier structure, adding a total of forty-six multistory rooms to Una Vida. A large free-standing kiva some 58 feet (17.7 meters) in diameter may be part of this construction phase.

During the next decade apparently nineteen ground-floor rooms were added to the south side of the west wing and on both sides of the connecting room block. The new rooms are consistently around 11 feet (3.4 meters) wide but their lengths vary; their areas range from 118 to 210 square feet (11 to 19.5 square meters). Following this phase of construction a building hiatus of some ninety years seems to have occurred.

Construction may have resumed at Una Vida around 1050 and continued into the 1090s. Additions during this

riod of time as do its larger contemporaries, Pueblo Bonito and Peñasco Blanco.

Meaning "one life" in Spanish, Una Vida is situated on the canyon floor near the base of the north cliff and a short distance east of Kin Nahasbas, the smaller of Chaco Canyon's two semisubterranean great kivas. The larger of the isolated chambers, Casa Rinconada, has an inside diameter slightly exceeding 63 feet (19.2 meters) and is situated on the south side of Chaco Canyon opposite Pueblo Bonito.

Overall, the mostly unexcavated structure measures some 315 by 345 feet (96 by 105 meters). In plan the pueblo resembles an inverted letter V with its apex pointing to the north. The orderly structure is more or less symmetrical about its north-south axis and has east and west wings of roughly similar sizes.

The reconstruction proposed here is based primarily on information published by Stephen H. Lekson (1987:79–94) and William B. Gillespie. Una Vida contains an estimated one hundred ground-floor rooms, presumably fifty second-floor rooms, a tower-like mass with one or two

period include several wall-enclosed kivas ranging in diameter from roughly 16 to 31 feet (5 to 9.4 meters), several rooms enclosing the small east courtyard, and most of the east wing. Soon after 1090 the curving south wall enclosing the main plaza was completed, bringing Una Vida essentially to its final form.

Two of the single-story, almost square rooms in the plaza's north corner appear to be special-purpose rooms, not dwellings like many of the plaza-front rooms. They lack doors, implying access by roof hatches, and their walls have thickly colored layers of plaster. Large central fire pits, wall niches, subfloor ventilators, and other special features suggest some form of ceremonialism.

Another unusual architectural feature of Una Vida is a door leading out of a second-story room in the east wing. The absence of a rooftop or terrace outside the portal raises the possibility of an exterior balcony. Some of the last rooms added to the east wing are the largest in Una Vida: they range in area from 160 to 375 square feet (15 to 35 square meters).

The remains of Una Vida lie very near the present-day National Park Service Visitors Center. The ancient site is accessible for visits but little of the plan is recognizable other than a remnant of the distinctive tower and depressions indicating the probable locations of kivas.

PEÑASCO BLANCO
Chaco Canyon Anasazi

Construction probably began on the elliptical pueblo of Peñasco Blanco earlier than on many of the other large structures of Chaco Canyon. The extensive ruins are situated on top of West Mesa at an elevation of some 330 feet (100 meters) above the canyon floor. Located on the south side of the canyon approximately 2.7 miles (4.3 kilometers) west of Pueblo Bonito, Peñasco Blanco commands a clear view of Escavada Wash and Chaco Wash to the north.

Meaning "white cliff" in Spanish, Peñasco Blanco is named for a conspicuous light-colored sandstone bluff about 1,000 feet (300 meters) south of the ruin. The reconstruction proposed here is based primarily on information published by Stephen H. Lekson (1987:94–109). The plan presents a total of 160 ground-floor rooms, three great kivas, eight smaller kivas, and a small outlying room block.

Peñasco Blanco is composed of a curving 560-foot- (170-meter-) long room block five rooms deep and up to three stories high with a one-room-deep arc enclosing an oval plaza. Oriented toward the southeast, the room block terraces down from three stories along its northwest side to one story around the plaza. Tree-ring dates indicate that the large pueblo was constructed over a period of 225 years between perhaps A.D. 900 and 1125.

The site includes a great kiva to the northwest beyond the edge of the reconstructed drawing, a large artificial terrace serving as a podium for the room block to the northeast, prehistoric roads, retaining walls, and other ancient features. The great kiva south

of the ruin measures possibly 62 feet (19 meters) in diameter and has an alcove on its north side. The two great kivas inside the oval plaza have diameters of perhaps 40 and 48 feet (12 and 14.6 meters).

During his visit to Peñasco Blanco in the 1880s Victor Mindeleff (1989:150) found original roofs consisting of narrow wood planks laid across main beams. By the turn of the century, however, no roofs remained intact in the ancient pueblo. Although most of the ruins have not been excavated, a relatively large number of tree-ring dates have been obtained from numerous remaining wood fragments. Today the site is in poor condition due largely to extensive vandalism prior to stabilization by the National Park Service.

Construction began on Peñasco Blanco with the erection of a curving multistory room block establishing the basic form to which subsequent additions conform. The curved structure is roughly 400 feet (120 meters) long, two to three rooms deep and mostly two stories high. Small store rooms in the room block outnumber large dwellings by a ratio of four to one.

The pueblo's store rooms typically are two stories high; each contains about 137 square feet (12.7 square meters). Tree-ring dates indicate little or no construction on Peñasco Blanco between 915 and 1050, a time period roughly corresponding to the building hiatus of neighboring Una Vida pueblo.

Construction resumed on Peñasco Blanco between 1050 and 1065 with the extension of the room block some 100 feet (30 meters) to the northeast. The extension added twenty rooms in two stories to the original arc. Around

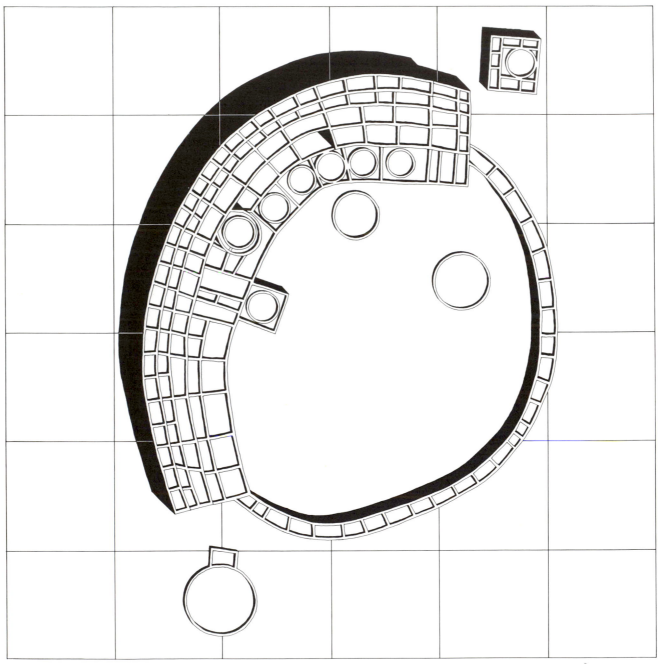

PEÑASCO BLANCO

the same time the large one-story rooms facing the plaza were constructed, including the wall-enclosed kiva projecting from the center of the room block.

The row of three-story rooms forming the northwest wall of Peñasco Blanco was erected shortly after 1085. About the same time final additions were made to the southwest and northeast ends of the room block, and four kivas were built inside single-story rooms previously constructed along the plaza front. The single-story arc of forty-four storage rooms enclosing the plaza and a second-story kiva with double walls were completed before 1125.

The small room block with seven rooms and a subterranean kiva northeast of the elliptical pueblo is called the "McElmo Ruin" because of its massive style of masonry. The structure is situated on a platform or podium contained by a massive retaining wall more than 66 feet (20 meters) long on each side and at most 6 feet (1.75 meters) high downslope. The stages of masonry development in the walls of Peñasco Blanco range from early slab walls, through banded coursing, to rubble-cored veneer recalling the stonework of Pueblo Bonito and Chetro Ketl.

PUEBLO BONITO
Chaco Canyon Anasazi

One of the most spectacular examples of ancient architecture in the Southwest is Pueblo Bonito. The well-known D-shaped building is located in Chaco Canyon approximately 100 miles (160 kilometers) northwest of Albuquerque. Meaning "beautiful town" in Spanish, Pueblo Bonito lies on the north side of the canyon at the base of a 100-foot (30-meter) cliff.

When it was completed early in the twelfth century, Pueblo Bonito contained perhaps as many as eight hundred rooms, although many have collapsed since the structure was abandoned. A number of lower-floor rooms were filled with debris suggesting that probably at most 650 rooms may have been in use at the same time. Thirty-seven kivas have been identified, and others may have been reconfigured or built over during one of the pueblo's numerous modifications.

In January of 1941 a huge sandstone monolith named Threatening Rock fell from the cliff face, leveling a number of rooms in the northeast section of the room block. The reconstruction presented here shows Pueblo Bonito as it appeared before the catastrophe, based on an accurate survey recorded by Neil M. Judd (1964) in the 1920s. The orderly plan measures overall about 310 by 505 feet (94.5 by 154 meters) and has two large rectangular platforms to the south.

People probably were living in Chaco Canyon in such settlements as Shabik'eshchee Village as early as the sixth century of the Christian era. During the ninth century an Anasazi pit house settlement occupied the

site of Pueblo Bonito. The following description of the development of the great house is based on a recent study by Stephen H. Lekson (1987) incorporating tree-ring dates, stratigraphy, masonry styles, wall abutments, and related information.

Major construction most likely began on Pueblo Bonito around 920, some forty years after work had commenced on Una Vida and possibly twenty years after Peñasco Blanco was started. Pueblo Bonito's initial structure was a semicircular arc of one hundred ground-floor rooms one, two, and three stories high. The early room block formed an open plaza oriented toward the south where four to six kivas were situated.

The initial structure established a small-scale version of the general character Pueblo Bonito was to develop over the next two centuries. The final architectural form results from a number of phases of construction, however, not from a predetermined plan. Like Peñasco Blanco, Pueblo Bonito has a curving north room block containing numerous small storage rooms and a terraced roof, which steps down to a single story around the plaza.

The original room block consists of four small segments added one after another forming an arc opening to the south. The average sizes of rooms in the various segments ranged from 87 to 145 square feet (8.1 to 13.5 square meters). Each larger room seems to be associated with two or more smaller rooms.

The initial phase of construction at Pueblo Bonito concluded around the year 935. Apparently no further construction was undertaken for more than a century, recalling a similar building hiatus about the same time

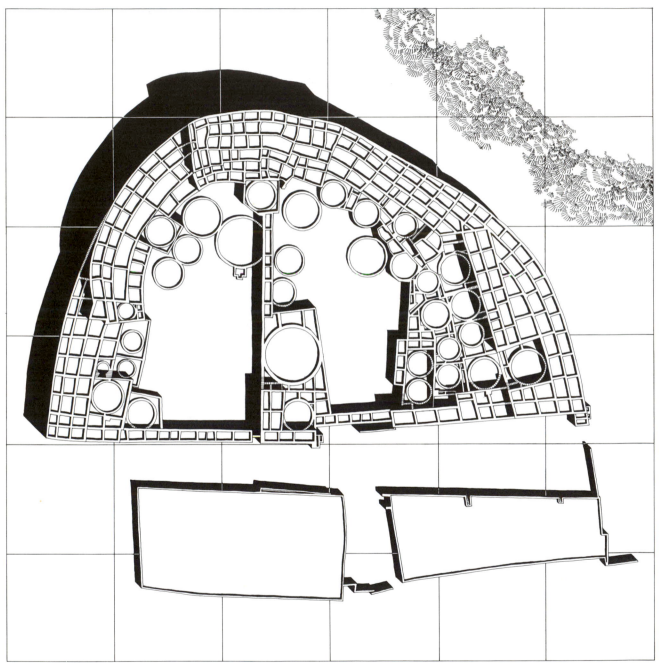

PUEBLO BONITO

at Una Vida and Peñasco Blanco. Between 1040 and 1050 a new phase of construction began using a distinctive new type of coursed masonry, which employed carefully fitted stones laid with very little mortar.

At this time a single row of two-story rooms was added along the curving outer wall of Pueblo Bonito. The new addition was built on top of 7 feet (2 meters) or so of silt, which had accumulated against the north wall during the long pause in construction. Consequently, the new roofs were level with the third-story roof of the earlier structure. The new rooms were interconnected to each other by doors and to the rooms of the original building by roof hatches.

Next, several sections of wall were erected along the south side of the central open space forming a small D-shaped plaza. Finally, a number of second-story rooms were added to earlier structures fronting on the plaza, four small kivas were built, and a fifth kiva roughly 45 feet (13.7 meters) in diameter was placed in the center of the plaza. The new additions brought order and clarity to the original plan.

Construction proceeded shortly after 1050 with the erection of a 60-by-115-foot (18-by-35-meter) block containing twenty-six rooms and three kivas at the east end of the pueblo, and a 35-by-100-foot (10-by-30-meter) block containing ten rooms on the west end. The earlier south wall was razed, and a new double-walled enclosure was built some distance to the south. Foundations were laid for a nine-room extension to the west, but this structure never was finished.

Between 1060 and 1075 a number of rooms in the northeast section of Pueblo Bonito were razed and rebuilt, and an ambitious scheme was undertaken to extend a linear arrangement of walls and rooms fully 500 feet (150 meters) to the east. Foundations were placed but the scheme was abandoned before major construction began above grade. The scheme would have altered radically the pueblo's essentially symmetrical plan.

During the following decade Pueblo Bonito reached essentially its final form with the major additions of 115 rooms with two kivas to the east end of the curving arc and sixty-three rooms with one small kiva to the west. Sometime after 1085 the great kiva near the center of the plaza was constructed over an earlier great kiva and the single row of rooms forming the south wall of the plaza was erected. The final additions appear to be a number of kivas with associated rooms and the north-south row of rooms dividing the plaza into east and west sections.

The two large platforms situated approximatley 50 feet (15 meters) south of Pueblo Bonito consist of perimeter walls more than 6.6 feet (2 meters) high retaining rubble, trash, and sand fill with level surfaces. The east platform measures at most 80 by 195 feet (24 by 59 meters); the west, 100 by 192 feet (30 by 58 meters). Ceramic samples taken from the mostly unexcavated platforms yield dates between 1050 and 1130.

Recent investigations (Lekson et al. 1988) at Pueblo Bonito reveal the presence of only a limited number of household suites of rooms, probably representing a smaller permanent population than previously estimated. More than half of the total area of the pueblo is composed of suites of large rooms suitable for storing substantial quantities of trade materials. Nearby roadways radiate in several directions from Chaco Canyon, suggesting an extensive regional trade network during the eleventh and twelfth centuries.

Large suites of storage rooms also have been found in Pueblo Alto, Chetro Ketl, and probably Peñasco Blanco. Exotic trade items associated with Pueblo Bonito and other great houses of Chaco Canyon include turquoise from the Santa Fe area 115 miles (184 kilometers) to the east, ornamental shells from the Gulf of California, and copper bells and macaw feathers from northern Mexico.

The relatively small population estimated for Pueblo Bonito may explain the paucity of burials in and near the great house. The large proportion of kivas seems to imply a major emphasis on ceremonialism, and the distinct layers of trash in refuse mounds may be indications of relatively large numbers of people for brief periods of occupancy. These interpretations suggest that Pueblo Bonito may have been a major storage facility perhaps visited briefly by large groups of people, possibly on ceremonial occasions.

When the structure was completed early in the twelfth century Pueblo Bonito quite likely was in places up to five stories high. The partially excavated ruins contain some of the finest masonry in the ancient Southwest. Unquestionably one of the most magnificent examples of ancient architecture in this discussion, the well-known monument is part of the Chaco Culture National Historic Park and is open daily to the public.

HUNGO PAVI
Chaco Canyon Anasazi

The medium-size Anasazi pueblo of Hungo Pavi is located in Chaco Canyon at its junction with Mockingbird Canyon approximately 2 miles (3.2 kilometers) east of Pueblo Bonito. The unexcavated ruins lie on the canyon floor at the base of the cliff north of Chaco Wash. The meaning of the name Hungo Pavi is unknown; the words have no translation in English, Spanish, Navajo, or Pueblo languages.

The remarkably symmetrical plan of Hungo Pavi is composed of an E-shaped room block with a curving arc of rooms to the south enclosing a plaza. The overall dimensions of the pueblo are about 220 by 320 feet (67 by 98 meters). The plaza contains a great kiva some 45 feet (13.7 meters) in diameter. A second kiva perhaps 26 feet (8 meters) in diameter is elevated above a filled second-floor room near the center of the north room block.

In the 1870s a number of the rooms in the three-story pueblo remained in place with roofs and floors supported by heavy pine beams. By the 1920s, however, most of the beams had vanished, many walls had collapsed, and the pueblo was in an advanced state of deterioration. The reconstruction proposed here is based primarily on information published by Steven H. Lekson (1987:144–152).

The north block of rooms in Hungo Pavi consists of one-, two-, and three-story rows of rooms stepping down from the north wall to the plaza. Room sizes in the pueblo vary considerably, the average being roughly 190 square feet (17.5 square meters). The average area of the north row of rooms is only 102 square feet (9.5 square meters), while typical rooms facing the

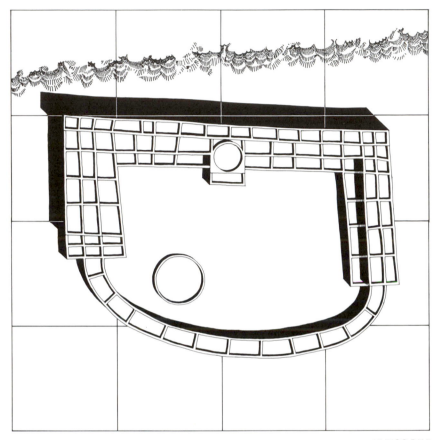

HUNGO PAVI

plaza in the east and west wings each contain more or less 320 square feet (30 square meters).

The limited number of tree-ring dates for Hungo Pavi suggests that the pueblo probably was constructed in two building phases between A.D. 990 and 1080 or so. The walls of the room blocks are surprisingly homogeneous in appearance; they all display the same masonry style consisting of small, carefully fitted sandstone blocks and slabs with very little mortar.

The first phase of construction at Hungo Pavi probably occurred between 990 and 1014. The initial structure most likely was an elongated rectangle two tiers wide forming the north wall; it contained possibly twenty-eight ground-floor rooms. Two beams in the ceiling of the ground-floor room at the northwest corner of the pueblo yielded tree-ring dates of 942 and 943, but it seems likely they were taken from a structure built earlier and reused.

The second cluster of tree-ring dates for Hungo Pavi lies between 1060 and 1080 when major additions were made and the pueblo was completed. During this period an estimated total of 131 rooms were added, including the second and third stories of the north room block, the east and west wings, a row of single-story rooms on the north side of the plaza, and the two kivas.

The curving arc of twelve rooms enclosing the plaza apparently was the last structure completed at Hungo Pavi. This addition brought the total number of rooms in the pueblo to 143. Much in ruins today, the site is part of the Chaco Culture National Historic Park in northwest New Mexico.

CHETRO KETL
Chaco Canyon Anasazi

The second-largest pueblo in Chaco Canyon, magnificent Chetro Ketl is rivaled in size only by Pueblo Bonito, which lies about half a mile (800 meters) to the west. In plan E-shaped like the contemporary pueblo of Hungo Pavi, Chetro Ketl contains well over five hundred rooms, at least a dozen kivas including a rare tower kiva, a unique colonnade, and a great kiva with a diameter exceeding 60 feet (18 meters). The meaning of the name Chetro Ketl is unknown.

Overall, the great house measures at most approximately 290 by 510 feet (88 by 155 meters) and rises at least four stories in height. Construction appears to have begun on Chetro Ketl around 1010, possibly ninety years after the commencement of Pueblo Bonito, and continued for almost a century. Three hundred and eighty tree-ring dates make possible a relatively accurate chronology of building phases for Chetro Ketl.

The reconstruction presented here is based on information published by Stephen M. Lekson (1983: fig. I:2; 1987:152–192) and a map provided by the National Park Service. The northeast corner of the extensive ruin and most of the west wing never have been excavated. Unfortunately, a disastrous flood in 1947 caused extensive damage to the remains before an accurate plan was recorded; the reconstruction consequently contains assumptions in several areas.

One of the noteworthy architectural elements in Chetro Ketl is the great kiva sunken some 14 feet (4.3 meters) below present grade in the west end of the plaza. Here early in the 1930s excavators under the direc-

tion of Edgar Lee Hewett found several original wall niches that had been sealed long ago during a remodeling of the circular chamber. One of the niches contained a string of more than seventeen thousand shell beads and turquoise pendants.

The fire pit in the center of the great kiva is flanked by two masonry floor vaults and four circular pits. Circular foundation stones in the pits receive columns that support the roof. In plan the columns form an almost perfect square measuring 26 feet (8 meters) on each side. A stone bench encircles the base of the perimeter wall, and an antechamber is situated on the chamber's north side recalling similar features in the reconstructed great kiva of Aztec near Farmington.

The 470-foot- (143-meter-) long north wall of Chetro Ketl is one of the finest examples of stone masonry in the ancient Southwest. The long straight wall consists of horizontal courses of carefully fitted sandstone blocks alternating with several courses of thin tabular slabs, which form veneers on both sides of a rubble core. The wall diminishes in thickness as it rises.

Construction of Chetro Ketl most likely began sometime after 1010 when twenty-two rooms or more and two small kivas were built near the center of the north room block. The two rows of early single-story rooms no longer are visible; their remains lie buried below structures built subsequently. The masonry style bears a striking resemblance to the stonework of Pueblo Alto, a great house under construction about the same time on the mesa top north of Chetro Ketl.

The large pueblo's early rooms generally are small in size; they have an

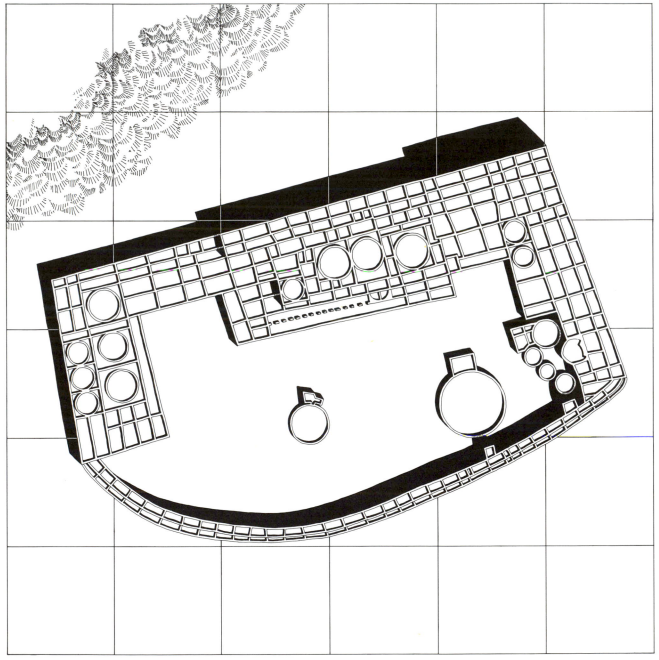

CHETRO KETL

average area of roughly 124 square feet (11.5 square meters). A remarkable diagonal door, the earliest recorded in Chaco Canyon, interconnects the adjoining corners of two rooms. South-facing *ramadas* or rooms presumably were constructed between the early room rows and the circular chambers.

Around 1045 a single row of one-story rooms was added on the north side of Chetro Ketl. The row likely had at least eighteen rooms and measured possibly 360 feet (110 meters) in length. The addition had an unusual double wall on its south side to avoid bearing on the earlier wall. Reasons for the double wall may have been to improve the structure's lateral support, to reduce the span of beams between walls, or to provide large wall niches for each room (Lekson 1987:185).

Double walls and niches are unusual features in Chacoan architecture. The north rooms were relatively uniform in size; they have an average floor area of 121 square feet (11.2 square meters) while smaller rooms to the north were typically only half that size. About the same time most of the ground-floor rooms forming the east wing were built, temporarily forming an asymmetrical, L-shaped building.

A short time later three ground-floor rows of six rooms each and a single row on the second floor probably were added to the west wing, restoring symmetry to the ground-floor plan. About the same time the first of several pairs of curving walls began to enclose the plaza to the south. In succeeding years a new row of rooms was added along the north side of the plaza and on the southeast corner of the pueblo, third-story rooms ap-peared along the north wall, and a second floor was constructed on the east wing.

Next, several elevated round rooms were built near the center of the north room block, and a row of fourth-story rooms was added on the pueblo's north side near the east corner. A curving roofed passageway about 2 feet (60 centimeters) wide and 6.6 feet (2 meters) high enclosed the plaza, and several wall-enclosed kivas were constructed in the west and north room blocks. In the decade succeeding 1095 a dozen rooms and two elevated kivas were added on the second- and third-floor levels of the central room block.

The small elevated kiva toward the west end of the central block became the only tower kiva located in Chaco Canyon. The unusual kiva retained its original bench, fire pit, and other features on the ground-floor level while its circular perimeter wall extended upward. Fewer than half a dozen Chacoan tower kivas are known to exist; examples are found at such outliers as Kin Ya'a and Salmon Ruin.

Sometime around 1105 Chetro Ketl attained essentially its final form with the completion of a colonnade and an addition to the plaza's south wall. The 100-foot- (30-meter-) long colonnade is located on the south wall of the central room block and consists of at least thirteen square columns resting on a stone wall about 32 inches (80 centimeters) high. The columns are spaced 4.25 feet (1.3 meters) or so apart.

A curving row of single-story rooms was added to the north side of the roofed passageway enclosing the plaza. Each room has a door facing the plaza and at least four rooms have fire pits and mealing bins, compartments equipped with slabs of stone for grinding corn or other commodities. The average size of rooms in the curving arc is more or less 125 square feet (11.6 square meters).

Well after the completion of Chetro Ketl an irregular row of poorly constructed rooms was built south of the colonnade and the spaces between the columns were filled with masonry. Three small kivas and assorted rooms were placed randomly in the east end of the plaza. The late structures may have been added by newcomers who briefly occupied Chetro Ketl after the original builders had departed.

Like Pueblo Bonito, Chetro Ketl is an excellent example of ancient architecture in the Southwest. Today the splendid remains are part of Chaco Culture National Historic Park and are open to the public daily.

PUEBLO ALTO
Chaco Canyon Anasazi

The mesa-top ruins of Pueblo Alto lie about 3,500 feet (1.1 kilometers) north of Pueblo Bonito and Chetro Ketl in Chaco Canyon. Resembling somewhat Hungo Pavi and Chetro Ketl, Pueblo Alto is unique among the great houses of Chaco Canyon in being only one story high. The U-shaped, rectangular pueblo measures overall approximately 285 by 380 feet (87 by 116 meters). The building is

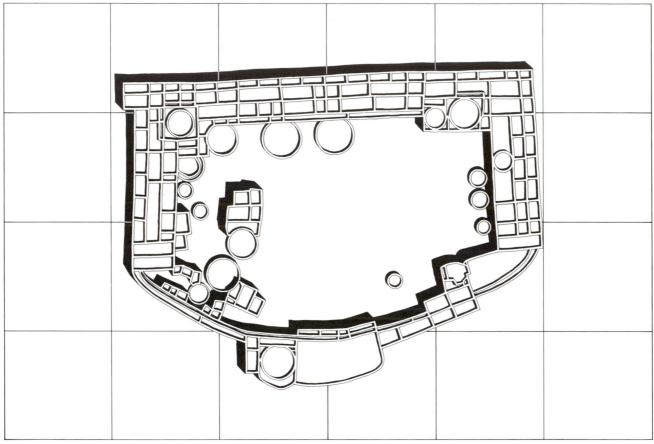

PUEBLO ALTO

noted for its unusually high walls and exceptionally large rooms.

Situated on the mesa top near Pueblo Alto are the smaller structures of New Alto, East Ruin, and Rabbit Ruin. Seven prehistoric roads radiate from Pueblo Alto, including the Great North Road, which has been traced some 44 miles (70 kilometers) north to the vicinity of Salmon. Construction probably began on Pueblo Alto about A.D. 1020, possibly ten years after building commenced on Chetro Ketl and some thirty years after work started on Hungo Pavi.

When completed around 1140, Pueblo Alto likely contained as many as 110 rooms and eleven kivas. The reconstruction proposed here shows seventeen circular rooms, but presumably not all were in use at the same time. The reconstruction is based primarily on information published by Thomas C. Windes (in Lekson 1987:192–209), who supervised most of the fieldwork during excavations between 1976 and 1978.

The initial phase of construction on Pueblo Alto consists of an elongated, rectangular room block with two ki-

vas to the south closely resembling the early structures of Chetro Ketl. The building measures about 25 by 213 feet (7.7 by 65 meters) and contains a row of twelve small rooms to the north next to a row of seven large rooms facing south. Room areas range from 83 to 408 square feet (7.7 to 38 square meters).

Both kivas have diameters of approximately 33 feet (10 meters). Doors interconnect all of the rooms from north to south, and all of the suites have doors leading to the plaza. Subsequently, a row of seven large rooms with average areas of possibly 405 square feet (37.6 square meters) was constructed along the south side of the room block, and a kiva with a diameter of roughly 28 feet (8.6 meters) was added west of the original two circular chambers.

About the same time a small masonry block composed of two adjoining rooms was built in what was to become the curving south wall of the plaza. The small structure measured perhaps 12 by 25 feet (3.7 by 7.6 meters). A prehistoric road from the direction of Pueblo Bonito entered the plaza along the west side of the small room block. The structure seems to be associated with a kiva possibly 30 feet (9 meters) in diameter built on its east side.

Sometime before 1040 a block of eleven rooms was added to the east end of the main building. The extension measures more or less 43 by 82 feet (13 by 25 meters). The six larger rooms have average areas of 364 square feet (33.8 square meters) or so while the smaller five were little more than one-third that size. Three of the large rooms later were remodeled to become part of two wall-enclosed kivas.

Next, the west wing appears to have been constructed. A block of nineteen rooms measuring possibly 41 by 171 feet (12.5 by 52 meters) was added to the west end of the central room block. At this time the plan of Pueblo Alto was L-shaped and probably resembled the configuration of Una Vida or Pueblo Pintado. Concurrently, two kivas at most 30.5 feet (9.3 meters) in diameter were built in the plaza's west end.

Most likely between 1040 and 1060, Pueblo Alto's east wing was constructed, restoring symmetry to the plan. Similar in size and proportion to the west wing, the east addition was built in a later style of masonry. The new wing contained twenty rectangular rooms and a circular structure only 15.6 feet (4.75 meters) in diameter, which may represent a tower kiva.

During the same phase of construction at Pueblo Alto a block containing four rooms was built on the south side of the plaza. Measuring an estimated 27 by 46 feet (8 by 14 meters) the small structure appears to be located on the east side of the prehistoric road entering the plaza from the direction of Chetro Ketl to the south. Shortly after 1080 three wall-enclosed kivas were built in remodeled sections of the room block's northeast and northwest corners.

By 1100 the main building of Pueblo Alto had attained essentially its final form. During the next four decades curving double and triple walls enclosed the plaza to the south, eight small kivas appeared in the east and west ends of the plaza, and a number of small rooms were built primarily in the south and west portions of the plaza. Construction ceased completely by 1140, and within a decade thereafter Pueblo Alto apparently was abandoned.

One of the important activities undertaken at Pueblo Alto was the processing of turquoise into finished ornaments. Chaco Canyon seems to have exerted control over an important source of turquoise in the ancient Southwest, a mine near Cerillos more than 100 miles (160 kilometers) to the east. Turquoise became a valuable item of exchange for the people of Chaco Canyon, who lacked the resources of most of the neighbors with whom they traded.

The population of Pueblo Alto seems to have been intermittent or seasonal, or at most a very small number of permanent residents. The mesa-top pueblo seems likely to have functioned more as a warehouse for the storage of trade materials than as a center of population. Now part of the Chaco Culture National Historic Park, Pueblo Alto is open daily to the public and affords visitors spectacular views of Pueblo Bonito, Chetro Ketl, Pueblo del Arroyo, and other monuments in the canyon below.

PUEBLO DEL ARROYO
Chaco Canyon Anasazi

One of the last great houses built in Chaco Canyon, Pueblo del Arroyo is located on the northeast bank of Chaco Wash about a quarter of a mile (440 meters) west of Pueblo Bonito. Unlike other major Chacoan structures, Pueblo del Arroyo faces toward the east, not the south, and is situated in the middle of the canyon floor, not near the cliff base or on a mesa top. The compact D-shaped pueblo contained at its zenith an estimated 284 rooms up to four stories high and possibly twenty-three kivas, although probably not more than half of them were used at the same time.

Meaning "town of the gully" in Spanish, Pueblo del Arroyo's name in Navajo means "house beside water's edge." Both translations refer to the

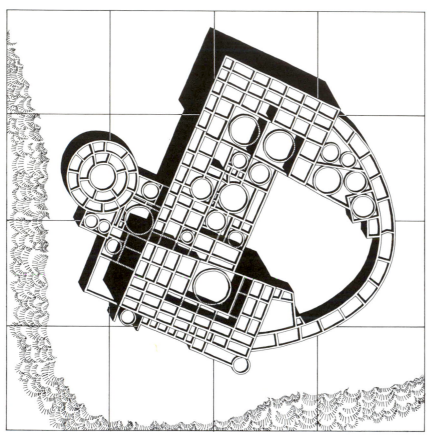

PUEBLO DEL ARROYO

pueblo's proximity to Chaco Wash. The original building measured approximately 224 by 260 feet (68 by 79 meters) and most likely was built between 1065 and 1110. The circular structure west of the main room block is called a tri-wall; it is the largest of several elements added to Pueblo del Arroyo sometime after 1110 by people other than the original builders.

Construction began on Pueblo del Arroyo perhaps fifty-five years after work started on Chetro Ketl and almost a century and a half after building began on Pueblo Bonito. Between 1025 and 1075 the population of Chaco Canyon appears to have doubled. Pueblo del Arroyo seems to have been occupied primarily during the latter half of the period of Chacoan prosperity when the population was at or near its maximum.

The reconstruction presented here suggests the appearance of Pueblo del Arroyo after the addition of the tri-wall. The plan is based on information published by Stephen H. Lekson (1987:209–223). Construction apparently began between 1065 and 1075 with a room block measuring roughly 41 by 112 feet (12.5 by 34 meters) along the west side of the pueblo.

The original block consisted of some forty rooms in three rows of one- and two-story rectangular rooms. Room areas ranged from around 108 to 344 square feet (10 to 32 square meters). Circular rooms or kivas were built in the room block later by reconfiguring the rectangular rooms. Constant modifications and additions are basic characteristics of ancient architecture in the Southwest.

The second period of construction was the largest in the history of

Pueblo del Arroyo. In the decade following 1095 compact multistory wings were added north and south of the central room block. The south room block measures at most 73 by 132 feet (22 by 40 meters) and contains 124 rooms and a second-floor kiva with a diameter of 33 feet (10 meters) or so.

The rooms of the south wing range from two to four stories in height. The wing has an unusual massing arrangement: the rooms do not step down as usual toward the plaza to the east. Instead, four-story rooms flank the east, south, and west walls of the south wing and step down toward the second-story kiva to the north.

The north wing has more or less the same ground-floor area and dimensions as the south wings but contains only seventy-six rooms. Its massing arrangement mirrors the south wings: three-story rooms flank the east, north, and west sides of the north wing and step down to the south. The spatial focus of the north wing is a block of two wall-enclosed kivas, neither exceeding 27 feet (8.2 meters) in diameter. One is situated on ground level, and the other is on the second floor.

At this point Pueblo del Arroyo consisted of two C-shaped multistory room blocks facing each other across the original two-story central room block. The orderly, symmetrical pueblo likely contained in all some 240 rooms and three kivas. Balconies perhaps 5 to 6 feet (1.5 to 1.8 meters) wide probably projected from the third floor of the north wall and from the second floor of the south wall.

Cantilevered floor beams apparently supported the balconies and a limited number of doors probably provided access. Shortly after 1105 a single-story block measuring not more than 46 by 85 feet (14 to 26 meters) was added in the plaza on the east side of the central room block. The addition contained several rectangular rooms and six kivas ranging in diameter from possibly 14 to 25 feet (4.3 to 7.6 meters).

About the same time a curving, single-story row of thirteen rooms was built along the east side of the plaza. The average room size was approximately 264 square feet (24.5 square meters). During this phase of development Pueblo del Arroyo may have corresponded in plan to a small-scale version of Pueblo Alto or even Hungo Pavi. This was the concluding phase of Chacoan construction in Pueblo del Arroyo.

Sometime after 1110 and likely before 1140, builders manifesting Mesa Verdean characteristics made several additions, none enhancing the architectural integrity of the original pueblo. A maze of irregularly shaped rooms and five small kivas were constructed in the north and south corners of the plaza, and a row composed of eight rectangular and two circular rooms was added along the south side of the room block. The major addition, however, was the tri-wall to the west.

By the time work began on the tri-wall, an estimated 6 feet (1.8 meters) of soil was deposited against the west wall of Pueblo del Arroyo. Overall, the building has an outer diameter of around 70 feet (21 meters) and a center room or court 27 feet (8.2 meters) or so in diameter. The outer walls contain ten curved rooms; the inner walls, six. Doors with raised sills interconnected the rooms of each row.

Sandstone slabs partially pave the center room in the tri-wall. Between the tri-wall and the west wall of the room block are several single-story, rectangular rooms and five kivas at most 26 feet (8 meters) in diameter. Tri-wall structures also are found on Chacra Mesa south of Chaco Canyon, near Aztec Ruins, and in a number of sites in the Montezuma Valley area north of the San Juan River.

A relatively small number of hearths are found in Pueblo del Arroyo; all are in ground-floor rooms facing the plaza. The dearth of hearths suggests a comparatively small population. The functional emphasis appears to be on warehousing and perhaps ceremonialism in view of the numerous kivas. The closely fitted tablet-size stones in Pueblo del Arroyo are among the finest examples of masonry to be found in Chaco Canyon.

Like Una Vida, Pueblo Bonito, Kin Kletso, and several other sites in Chaco Canyon, Pueblo del Arroyo had a turquoise workshop. The precious stone became a valuable trade item for the Chacoans as early as the tenth century. Other indications of trade are the skeletons of three macaws found in the long room on the west side of the plaza. Chaco Canyon's closest source of macaws probably was northern Mexico, hundreds of miles to the south.

Today many of Pueblo del Arroyo's original walls remain standing to the second-story height, and the lower walls and foundations of many rooms and kivas are clearly visible. An interpretive trail guides visitors through the ruins. The stabilized remains are part of Chaco Culture National Historic Park and are open daily to visitors.

WIJIJI

Chaco Canyon Anasazi

One of the most symmetrical buildings in this study, Wijiji appeared toward the end of building development in Chaco Canyon. The disciplined pueblo probably was erected in a single phase of construction between 1110 and 1115, about the time Pueblo del Arroyo was reaching completion. Located near the base of the cliff north of Chaco Wash, the remains of Wijiji lie approximately 5.5 miles (8.8 kilometers) east of Pueblo Bonito.

A rough translation of the name Wijiji in Navajo is "black greasewood" (Franstead & Werner 1974). The reconstruction presented here is based primarily on information published by Stephen H. Lekson (1987:224–231). At most three stories high, Wijiji measures in plan perhaps 110 by 175 feet (33.5 by 53.5 meters).

A row of sixteen three-story rooms forms the north wall of the carefully composed pueblo. To the south one hundred two-story rooms form a C-shaped block oriented slightly east of due south. Eighteen single-story rooms line the north, east, and west sides of the plaza, and two wall-enclosed kivas, both some 26 feet (8 meters) in diameter, are situated in the northeast and northwest corners of the room block.

Wijiji has a total of 206 rooms; of these 104 occupy the ground floor. The relatively small rooms are remarkably uniform in size; their average floor area is more or less 58 square feet (5.4 square meters). Doors interconnecting the rooms generally provide access toward the plaza. Wijiji lacks the curving arc of rooms enclosing its plaza found in its contempo-

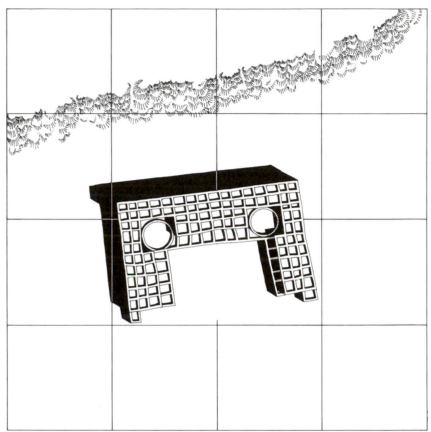

WIJIJI

raries Tsin Kletsin and Pueblo del Arroyo.

Unfortunately, the unstable foundation conditions of Wijiji are causing the poorly bonded walls to collapse. A layer of expansive clay possibly 5 feet (1.5 meters) thick underlies the site. Fluctuations in ground water cause the clay to expand and contract alternately; this results in the disruption of the masonry walls, which bear on the unstable deposit.

The masonry of Wijiji is uniform in appearance and excellent in craftsmanship. Walls typically consist of horizontal courses of sandstone blocks alternating with several courses of skillfully fitted, thin tabular slabs. Among the most sophisticated stonework in the ancient Southwest, the banded masonry of Wijiji is highly refined compared to the coarse though substantial stonework of the Mesa Verde style.

The uniformly dark stones of Wijiji are taken from the weathered top of the sandstone cliff north of the ruin. Although many of the handsome walls have collapsed, some remain standing to the second-story level. Today the ruins are part of the Chaco Culture National Historic Park and are accessible by way of a two-mile foot trail from the Visitors Center.

TSIN KLETZIN
Chaco Canyon Anasazi

Located on the windswept top of South Mesa, Tsin Kletzin lies about a mile and a half (2.4 kilometers) south of Pueblo Bonito in Chaco Canyon. Three tree-ring dates from the ruins suggest that the east kiva and its associated rooms may have been constructed between 1110 and 1115, about the same time Wijiji was being built. Similarities in the masonry style of the walls of Tsin Kletzin indicate that all of the walls most likely were erected in the early twelfth century.

Translations of the name Tsin Kletzin vary; the local Navajo call the pueblo "house on top." The site's unusual location may be due to the convergence of six sight lines on the east kiva, the pueblo's highest part. From this vantage point observers can see Pueblo Alto, Peñasco Blanco, Kin Kletso, Kin Klizhin, and Bis sa'ani roughly 10 miles (16 kilometers) to the east and Kin Ya'a some 26 miles (42 kilometers) to the south. Even a slight shift in position would block the sight line to one or more sites.

Around half a mile (800 meters) northwest of Tsin Kletzin a massive dam just below the mesa top retains storm water runoff after summer showers. This reservoir may have been the primary source of domestic water for the residents of the pueblo much of the year. The dam is 130 feet (40 meters) long, 5.5 feet (1.7 meters) thick, and 8 feet (2.4 meters) high (Frazier 1986:101).

The reconstruction proposed here is based primarily on information published by Stephen H. Lekson (1987:231–238). At most two stories high, Tsin Kletzin originally contained an estimated total of eighty-one rooms, three kivas, a plaza to the south, and an enclosure to the north. The plan of the asymmetrical pueblo measures overall approximately 150 by 190 feet (46 by 58 meters).

The first structure erected at Tsin Kletzin appears to be the east kiva and its associated rooms forming a roughly 60-foot- (18-meter-) square block. The structure contains fifteen ground-floor and seven second-floor rooms. Elevated to the second-floor level, the kiva measures 27 feet (8.2 meters) or so in diameter. The rectangular rooms range in floor areas from perhaps 97 to 118 square feet (9 to 11 square meters).

The next phase of construction probably was an extension of the main room block westward, adding possibly twenty-two ground-floor rooms, twelve second-floor rooms, and a kiva on the upper floor with a diameter of 20 feet (6 meters) more or less. Subsequently, the curving arc of fifteen rooms was added, enclosing the plaza to the south. Each of the curving rooms has an average size in the range of 67 square feet (6.2 square meters).

A 3-foot (1-meter) wide entry portal provides access into the plaza from the south. The final addition to the main room block seems to be the ground-floor kiva to the southwest and its associated rooms. The low wall forming the north enclosure could have been added at any time after the initial phase of construction. Doorways interconnecting ground-floor rooms with the plaza range in width from 21 to 24 inches (53 to 61 centimeters).

The masonry style of Tsin Kletzin is called McElmo, a style distinguished by the predominant use of

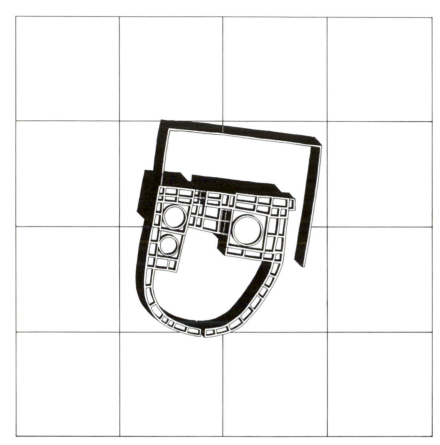

TSIN KLETZIN

large sandstone blocks with relatively few small tabular slabs. Compared with the stonework of contemporary Wijiji pueblo, Tsin Kletzin's is less refined but sturdy nonetheless. Now part of the Chaco Culture National Historic Park, the largely unexcavated and much reduced ruins of Tsin Kletzin are not readily accessible to visitors.

KIN KLETSO
Chaco Canyon Anasazi

The compact rectangular pueblo of Kin Kletso is the largest structure erected during the later phases of major construction in Chaco Canyon. Meaning "yellow house" in Navajo, the name Kin Kletso refers to the pueblo's buff-colored sandstone masonry. Most of the homogeneous, 2-foot- (60-centimeter-) thick walls are McElmo-type masonry consisting of thick sandstone block facings on both sides of a thin core filled with small stones and mortar.

The cliff-side pueblo lies on the canyon floor approximately half a mile (800 meters) west of Pueblo Bonito at a point where Chaco Wash comes close to the canyon's north wall. In plan Kin Kletso measures overall some 80 by 160 feet (24 by 49 meters) and contains a total of 132 rooms up to three stories high, four kivas, a tower kiva, and a compartmentalized south wall like Casa Chi-

quita's. The reconstruction proposed here is based on a report provided by the National Park Service (Vivian & Mathews 1965) and information published by Stephen H. Lekson (1987: 238–246).

Kin Kletso seems to have been constructed mainly between 1125 and 1130. The initial building stage consisted of a roughly 75-by-80-foot (23-by-14.4-meter) room block containing perhaps sixty-nine rooms and two kivas. The early pueblo's plan resembles New Alto's: both room blocks are more or less square in plan, and both are laid out on a grid with six rooms in both directions.

Three-story rooms form the north and west sides of the initial-stage building. All the remaining rooms are two stories high except the kiva. Kin Kletso's west kiva is a remarkable three-story tower kiva incorporating a huge sandstone boulder into its lowest floor. A T-shaped door leads into the kiva's elevated floor with a central fireplace and cylindrical walls possibly 15 feet (4.6 meters) high.

The 18-foot- (5.5-meter-) diameter tower kiva rises above the single-story kiva situated 22 feet (6.7 meters) to the east. Most of the ground-floor rooms surrounding the tower kiva are filled solidly with adobe. The average room size in the initial-stage pueblo is around 92 square feet (8.55 square meters), a relatively small area compared to the room sizes of most Chacoan great houses.

The second stage of construction at Kin Kletso appears to have followed immediately after the initial building was completed. A mirror of the earlier structure, the addition formed a probably 65-by-80-foot (20-by-24.4-meter) room block extending to the east and added most likely sixty-one rooms and a central kiva. Room sizes in the addition increased 10 percent or so above the initial sizes, but they still were small in comparison with Chacoan standards.

The new addition brought Kin Kletso essentially to its final architectural form. Also built at this time was the unusual low south wall located about 2 feet (60 centimeters) from the room block's multistory wall. Low perpendicular walls interconnect the parallel walls forming compartments, which measured an estimated 2 by 4 feet (60 by 120 centimeters). The purpose of the compartmented wall is obscure; the structure may have been intended to serve as a strengthening buttress.

Sometime after 1130 a minor addition apparently was made to the main room block of Kin Kletso. A kiva about 15 feet (4.6 meters) in diameter and two surface rooms were placed along the east wall near the south corner, recalling similar late additions at Casa Chiquita. About the same time a rectangular room within

the room block was remodeled to receive another 15-foot- (3.6-meter-) diameter kiva.

No exterior doors penetrate the perimeter walls of Kin Kletso; roof hatches and ladders presumably were the primary means of access to the pueblo. Like Una Vida, Pueblo Bonito, Pueblo del Arroyo, and several other Chacoan pueblos, Kin Kletso had a turquoise workshop suggesting its relation to the Chacoan trade network. Today a part of the Chaco Culture National Historic Park, the well-preserved remains are readily accessible to visitors by way of a nearby road.

CASA CHIQUITA
Chaco Canyon Anasazi

The early-twelfth-century pueblo of Casa Chiquita is situated on an irregular, boulder-strewn site approximately one mile (1.6 kilometers) west of Pueblo Bonito on the floor of Chaco Canyon. Meaning "little house" in Spanish, Casa Chiquita lies on uneven terrain sloping up toward the northeast near the base of the north cliff. Many of the compact pueblo's architectural characteristics are similar to those of its nearby contemporaries, Kin Kletso and New Alto.

The reconstruction presented here is based primarily on information published by Stephen H. Lekson (1987:246–251). In plan Casa Chi-

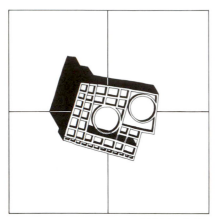

CASA CHIQUITA

quita measures at most 60 by 75 feet (18 by 23 meters) and contains possibly fifty-six rooms, two kivas, and a compartmented south wall very similar to Kin Kletso's. The three-story room block steps down to the central kiva, which the sloping ground elevates to the second-floor level.

Casa Chiquita is composed of eighteen three-story rooms lining the west wall, twenty-two two-story rooms west and south of the central kiva, and perhaps sixteen single-story rooms. A single-story wall is located 2 feet (60 centimeters) south of the two-story south wall and parallel with it. Perpendicular walls interconnect the parallel walls forming compartments about 4.5 feet (1.4 meters) long, perhaps for the purpose of strengthening the south wall.

The architectural massing of Casa Chiquita is oriented toward the northeast, not toward the south or southeast, which is the more traditional arrangement for Anasazi pueblos. The building seems to have been erected in a single phase of construction late in the development of Chaco

Canyon, probably between 1100 and 1130. Relatively uniform and small in size, the rooms of the unexcavated pueblo contain an average of roughly 45 square feet (4.2 square meters).

The walls of Casa Chiquita are built in the McElmo style, a type of masonry composed of dominantly large, somewhat coarsely fitted sandstone blocks in often uneven courses. Unlike Pueblo Bonito, Chetro Ketl, and other great houses of Chaco Canyon, Casa Chiquita is small in scale, lacks a plaza, represents a single construction phase, and uses masonry employing mostly large blocks. These architectural characteristics resemble those of structures found north of the San Juan River.

Although Casa Chiquita is much in ruins today, several original wall sections remain standing to the third-floor level along the south and east sides of the room block. The remains lie a short distance from the modern road through Chaco Canyon. A foot trail provides access to the ruins. The remnants of the ancient pueblo are part of the Chaco Culture National Historical Park and are open daily to the public.

NEW ALTO

NEW ALTO
Chaco Canyon Anasazi

The highly symmetrical pueblo of New Alto lies about 400 feet (120 meters) west of Pueblo Alto and approximately 3,500 feet (1.1 kilometers) north of Pueblo Bonito in Chaco Canyon. Much smaller and better preserved than its nearby neighbor, New Alto measures in plan perhaps 72 by 77 feet (22 by 23.5 meters). More heavily reduced Pueblo Alto is entirely one story in height while New Alto is predominantly two stories high.

The reconstruction proposed here is based on information published by Stephen H. Lekson (1987:251–256). Oriented slightly east of south like Wijiji, the almost square plan is composed of a grid of six rooms in both directions with four rooms near the center removed to accommodate a kiva. The circular chamber is built on the ground floor; its rooftop forms a small terrace facing south on the second-floor level.

All of New Alto's rooms are two

stories high except the single-story south row and the central kiva. The compact pueblo has twenty-six rooms two stories high and six ground-floor rooms, a total of fifty-eight rooms and one kiva. The round room has an estimated outer diameter of possibly 25.4 feet (7.75 meters); six pilasters on its interior perimeter imply influences from sources north of the San Juan River.

Remarkably uniform in size, the ground-floor rooms in New Alto have an average area of some 76.4 square feet (7.1 square meters). The typical areas of second-floor rooms seem to be roughly 11 to 27 square feet (1 to 2.5 square meters) larger due to diminished wall thicknesses. Doors within the unexcavated pueblo generally are located perpendicular to the kiva.

The masonry of New Alto characteristically is McElmo style consisting primarily of large sandstone blocks. Tree-ring dates are lacking, but architectural similarities to Kin Kletso suggest that New Alto probably was built in a single construction phase about the same time, between 1100 and 1130. By contrast Pueblo Alto was erected in probably five construction phases over a period of 120 years or so.

Pueblo Bonito, Chetro Ketl, and other Chacoan great houses characteristically are large in size, consist of multistory structures terracing down to plazas, utilize large and small stone masonry, and are built in several phases over extended periods of time. However New Alto, like its contemporaries Tsin Kletsin, Kin Kletso, and Casa Chiquita, exhibits McElmo characteristics, such as being smaller in size, usually lacking plazas, having compact masses, utilizing large stone masonry, and being built in single phases of construction.

The introduction of McElmo influences from areas north of the San Juan River illustrates the cultural elaboration present in Chaco Canyon during the early twelfth century. Variations in great house architecture apparently occurred concurrently with the continued occupation of traditional small-scale communities, mostly on the south bank of Chaco Wash. The people of Chaco Canyon seem to have accommodated simultaneously a rich variety of new and old ideas from both external and internal sources.

Recently stabilized by the National Park Service, the relatively well preserved walls of New Alto today continue standing in places to the second-story level. Largely free of fallen debris, the ruins are part of Chaco Culture National Historic Park and are accessible to visitors by way of a foot trail from Pueblo Alto.

BEE BURROW

BEE BURROW
San Juan Basin Anasazi

About 14 miles (23 kilometers) south of Pueblo Bonito lie the ruins of Bee Burrow on the south side of a low mesa. Situated on the San Juan Basin floor at an elevation of 6,410 feet (1,954 meters) above sea level, the pueblo probably was constructed and used between A.D. 1050 and 1200. Sandstone cliffs to the north, east, and west restrict visibility from the gently sloping site. Seven Lakes Wash, a stream sometimes known to flow in spring and summer, lies half a mile (0.8 kilometers) to the north in a valley suitable for farming (Marshall et al. 1979:27-29).

Bee Burrow is a well-ordered pueblo measuring at most 59 by 82 feet (18 by 25 meters). The building is oriented generally to the south-southeast and once contained at least eleven ground-floor rooms and two kivas. Exterior walls vary in thickness from 20 to 24 inches (50 to 60 centimeters) and consist of face veneers on both sides of rubble cores.

The closest source for the dark tabular sandstone of the walls is a quarry located roughly one thousand feet (300 meters) to the northeast. The wall heights of Bee Burrow probably ranged originally from about 6.6 feet (2 meters) in the south to some 13 feet (4 meters) in the north, suggesting the likelihood of perhaps five second-floor rooms. Room dimensions vary from 6 to 23 feet (1.9 to 7 meters) and areas from 106 to 392 square feet (9.9 to 36.4 square meters).

No windows or doors are apparent in Bee Burrow's standing walls. Both of the pueblo's kivas are constructed at ground level, and both originally were enclosed by rectangular masonry walls. The approximate interior diameters of the east and west kivas are 18 and 16.7 feet (5.5 and 5.1 meters), respectively.

An ancient road some 27 miles (43 kilometers) long once linked Chaco Canyon with Kin Ya'a to the south of Bee Burrow. The road traverses the site a short distance west of Bee Burrow. A second north-south road passes about 5 miles (8 kilometers) to the east (Frazier 1986:106).

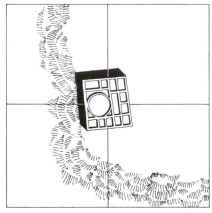

CASA CIELO

CASA CIELO
San Juan Basin Anasazi

Casa Cielo is one of Indian Creek Community's two main room blocks. Both blocks are single-story structures of intermediate size, and both lie on the floor of the San Juan Basin roughly 17 miles (27 kilometers) west-northwest of Pueblo Bonito. The greater community contains a total of twenty recorded house mounds.

Casa Cielo is situated near the south tip of the mesa about 1,600 feet (500 meters) east of Indian Creek and 100 feet (30 meters) above the valley floor. Located at an altitude of 6,100 feet (1,860 meters) above sea level, the site enjoys excellent visibility. The pueblo's walls rest only 7 to 16 feet (2 to 5 meters) from the mesa's steep edge to the west and some 40 feet (12 meters) from the edge to the south.

Neighboring Casa Abajo lies about 2,000 feet (600 meters) to the west on a site 80 feet (24 meters) lower in elevation. In plan the massive masonry walls of Casa Cielo measure at most 46 by 51 feet (13.5 by 15.5 meters).

The pueblo's area is less than half the size of Bee Burrow, its contemporary some 18 miles (29 kilometers) to the southeast. Within its rectangular walls the house contains a total of twelve rooms and a single kiva.

Casa Cielo is impressive because of its massive, well-preserved walls, some of which exceed 8 feet (2.4 meters) in height. Room dimensions range from an estimated 5.6 to 21 feet (1.7 to 6.4 meters), and room sizes vary from 48 to 124 square feet (4.4 to 11.5 square meters). A single entry into the pueblo is found in the south wall, and the remains of several portals appear in interior walls.

Casa Cielo's kiva has an interior diameter of approximately 21 feet (6.3 meters). Rubble and mortar fill the corners between the kiva's outer wall and the rectangular enclosure. Angular stones project from the core of the west enclosing wall, indicating that the kiva was planned in advance. Similar roughened walls are found at neighboring Kin Bineola, 7 miles (11 kilometers) east of Casa Cielo. Whether the projecting stones are intended to improve masonry bonding, to assist with scaffolding, or to serve other purposes is unclear (Lekson 1987).

The massive walls of Casa Cielo very likely rose originally to a height of 10 feet (3 meters). The walls consist of outer veneers having carefully fitted stones over rubble cores with generous quantities of mortar. No mortar at all is used in the exterior masonry joints. Averaging 24 to 28 inches (60 to 70 centimeters) in thickness, the walls are faced with thin brown tabular sandstones averaging from 4 to 8 inches (10 to 20 centimeters) in length, with occasional blocks up to 20 inches (50 centimeters) long.

Ceramic samples collected at Casa Cielo suggest that the site was constructed and used only briefly about A.D. 1050, toward the end of major activity at Indian Creek Community. By contrast, Casa Abajo, the settlement's other major room block, seems to have been built earlier and to have been used over a more extended period of time (Marshall et al. 1979:45–55).

CASA ABAJO
San Juan Basin Anasazi

Casa Abajo and Casa Cielo are the two main pueblos of Indian Creek Community. Located on the floor of the San Juan Basin, the site lies more or less 17 miles (27 kilometers) northwest of Pueblo Bonito. Casa Abajo is situated on a low mesa elevated slightly above the flood plain of Indian Creek some 330 feet (100 meters) to the southwest.

In plan the pueblo is L-shaped and consists of nine rooms with an irregularly shaped plaza oriented to the southeast. The room block and plaza measure overall 52.5 by 54 feet (16 by 16.5 meters) and encompass an area similar to that of Casa Cielo. The room dimensions of Casa Abajo range from 6.6 to 23 feet (2 to 7 meters), and room sizes vary between 54 and 226 square feet (5 and 21 square meters).

The masonry wall enclosing the plaza originally was 20 inches (50 centimeters) thick and probably rose to the height of 5 feet (1.5 meters). A single gate into the plaza appears in

CASA ABAJO

the south wall. The plaza measures at most 25 feet (7.5 meters) from north to south by 31 feet (9.5 meters) from east to west. No evidence of a kiva or other structure is found in the plaza.

The walls of both the pueblo and the plaza are of compound construction. The stones in the walls average from 8 to 16 inches (20 to 40 centimeters) in length and have occasional chinking. Due to Casa Abajo's advanced state of deterioration, the walls for the most part appear as linear piles of rubble.

Ceramic samples collected at Casa Abajo suggest a comparatively long period of occupation with major use between A.D. 900 and 1000. Human activity may have begun more than a century earlier and continued into the 1100s. An alternate interpretation is that Indian Creek Community was abandoned and subsequently reoccupied during the twelfth century (Marshall et al. 1979:45–49).

KIN KLIZHIN
San Juan Basin Anasazi

Kin Klizhin is one of the smaller main sites of the San Juan Basin. The pueblo has perhaps sixteen ground-floor rooms, at least four second-floor rooms, two surface kivas, a tower kiva three stories high, and a semicircular plaza to the southeast (Lister & Lister 1981:fig. 79). The ruin is located around 6.5 miles (10.4 kilometers) southwest of Pueblo Bonito on a small tributary of Chaco Wash. The terraced structure is situated on a sandy knoll elevated slightly above the nearby flood plain to the north and west.

Elevated 6,080 feet (2,160 meters) above sea level, the orderly ruins of Kin Klizhin can be seen from a considerable distance in all directions. The pueblo is composed of rooms of generous dimensions, massive and beautifully finished walls, and distinctive terraces descending from multiple stories on the southwest to single stories along the plaza. The unbroken west wall measures some 141 feet (43 meters) in length. From east to west the room block extends at most 57 feet (17.4 meters).

The surviving walls in the vicinity of the tower kiva generally are well preserved. However, the north group of rooms either never was completed or was enclosed only partially. In 1901 S. J. Holsinger examined the plaza wall, a compound structure about 16 inches thick (40 centimeters). The wall enclosed an elliptical area measuring overall possibly 92 by 184 feet (28 by 56 meters). The plaza wall may have been removed and reused for local building materials in recent years.

Kin Klizhin's rooms range in dimen-

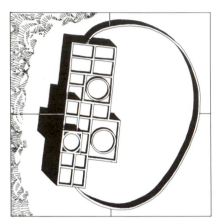

KIN KLIZHIN

sions from 11 to 20 feet (3.4 to 6.1 meters) except for the 7-foot-wide space immediately east of the tower kiva. Some of the rooms buttress the tower kiva. The north and south surface kivas had interior diameters of roughly 20 and 21 feet (6.0 and 6.4 meters), respectively. Solid masonry originally filled the spaces between the outer kiva walls and their rectangular enclosures.

The extraordinary tower kiva of Kin Klizhin may have consisted of three cylindrical chambers stacked one on top of the other. The ground-floor room measures 16.4 feet (5 meters) or so in diameter and is set in the center of a 20-by-22-foot (6-by-6.7-meter) masonry wall enclosure. The structure's four corners are filled with solid masonry. The ceiling beams rest on a 6-to-8-inch- (15-to-20-centimeter-) wide stone ledge in the perimeter wall some 8.2 feet (2.5 meters) above the ground floor.

The second-floor kiva's diameter increased to 18 feet or more due to diminishing wall thicknesses as the tower rose, and the ceiling height increased to almost 9 feet (2.7 meters). The third-floor kiva is estimated to have a diameter of 19.5 feet (5.9 meters) and walls up to 12 feet (3.7 meters) high. Reconstructed drawings of the structure (Marshall et al. 1981: 71) suggest an overall tower height of 30 feet (9 meters).

The massive walls of Kin Klizhin are 24 to 36 inches (60 to 90 centimeters) thick and consist of veneered cores with banded dark sandstone facings. Courses of small stones 4 to 8 inches (10 to 20 centimeters) long and 1 to 2 inches (2.5 to 5 centimeters) thick alternate with courses of large stones 12 to 20 inches (30 to 50 centimeters) long and 2 to 4 inches (5 to 10 centimeters) thick. The carefully laid and sensitively scaled stone walls traditionally were covered with a finish coat of stucco. The stones must have been carried a long way as no quarries are located nearby.

A prehistoric dam built of earth and masonry lies some 650 feet (200 meters) northeast of Kin Klizhin on the valley floor. Navajo farmers have renovated the 230-foot- (70-meter-) long structure and continue to use it today. In 1901 S. L. Holsinger observed that an irrigation ditch conveyed water from the dam "to a tract of about 200 acres of agricultural fields" (Lister & Lister 1981: 51).

An ancient highway once led straight from Chaco Canyon to Kin Klizhin. The road then continued west and passed a mile and a quarter (2 kilometers) north of Kin Bineola. Architectural features of Kin Klizhin suggest that the pueblo probably was a contemporary of the classic Chacoan monuments built between A.D. 1020 and 1120. Tree-ring dates and ceramics indicate major construction activity during the 1080s.

WHIRLWIND HOUSE
San Juan Basin Anasazi

Located at an altitude of 5,740 feet (1,750 meters) some 30 miles (48 kilometers) west of Pueblo Bonito, the Chaco outlier of Whirlwind House is one of the westernmost Anasazi communities in the San Juan Basin. The room block is built on a low mesa overlooking the confluence to two unnamed tributaries of the San Juan River. The pueblo is situated in the center of Whirlwind Lake Community, a medium-size settlement estimated to have a least two hundred rooms (Marshall et al. 1979: 89).

Whirlwind House has twelve ground-floor rooms, perhaps four second-floor rooms, a wall-enclosed surface kiva, and a small rectangular plaza. The room block consists of six pairs of rooms in a row measuring more or less 53 by 102 feet (16 by 31 meters). The heights of rubble mounds in the ruin suggest the likelihood of a number of second-floor rooms. Four such rooms appear in this reconstruction along the north wall; they terrace down to single-story masses to the southeast.

The kiva of Whirlwind House measures about 18 feet (5.5 meters) in diameter. Masonry walls at most 28 by 33 feet (8.5 by 10 meters) long enclose the kiva. Walls possibly 7.2 feet (2.2 meters) high surround the roughly 26-foot (8-meter) square plaza at the south corner of the room block. This unroofed space may have been intended to enclose a never completed kiva.

The walls of Whirlwind House are composed of sandstone face veneers with rubble cores. They range in thickness from 20 to 24 inches (50 to 60 centimeters) and have irregularly

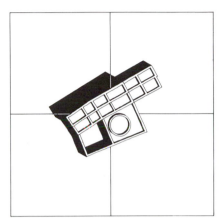

WHIRLWIND HOUSE

coursed facings with no visible chinking. The wall surfaces are composed of dark tabular sandstone slabs 2 to 20 inches (5 to 50 centimeters) long.

Greater Whirlwind Lake Community consists of at least twenty masonry-walled house ruins in an area of 2.3 square miles (6 square kilometers). Each house contains from two to twenty rooms, and many have kivas and small enclosed plazas. Agricultural plots and ponds in the nearby flood plain are valuable domestic resources for the community.

Like other settlements on the floor of the San Juan Basin, the limits of Whirlwind Lake Community were clearly defined. No other villages are located in the immediate vicinity. Ceramics associated with Whirlwind House suggest that the pueblo most likely was constructed and occupied between A.D. 1000 and 1100.

KIN BINEOLA
San Juan Basin Anasazi

Kin Bineola was one of the largest Anasazi communities in the San Juan Basin. Apparently occupied for more than two centuries, the pueblo's initial phase of construction seems to date from the A.D. 940s. At that time Kin Bineola probably was relatively self-sufficient in terms of basic subsistence and conducted trade with neighboring settlements and Chaco Canyon some 10 miles (16 kilometers) to the northeast. Located in a fertile valley at an altitude of 6,060 feet (1,847 meters) above sea level, Kin Bineola presumably was developed for the purpose of pooling resources and facilitating redistribution (Frazier 1986).

The site of the greater community is a flood plain bounded by low-lying mesas to the east. Within an area extending from the pueblo more than one mile (1.6 kilometers) to the west and two miles (3.2 kilometers) to the south lie the remains of numerous habitations, roadways, irrigation structures, great kivas, shrines, and other prehistoric features. Kin Bineola was once the focus of a substantial population.

Perhaps the most distinctive design characteristic of the pueblo is its E-shaped ground-floor plan. Measuring at most 153 by 350 feet (46.5 by 107 meters), the terraced structure steps up from one to three stories to the north. The pueblo consists of an estimated 105 ground-floor rooms, fifty-eight second-floor rooms, thirty-four third-floor rooms, ten kivas, and two large plazas oriented toward the south-southeast (Marshall et al. 1979:60). Still largely unexcavated, Kin Bineola appears to contain an overall area of 36,180 square feet (3,361 square meters).

All ten kivas were constructed in orthogonal rooms above grade, and all except two were a single story high. The highest kiva may have been a three-story structure resembling a tower. Stephen Lekson (1987) observed that the outer surfaces of the kivas' cylindrical walls and the inner surfaces of their rectangular enclosures were unusually rough. Whether the roughened masonry was intended to support scaffolding during erection, to increase bonding with rubble fill in the corners, or to serve some other purpose is unknown.

An unusual feature of Kin Bineola is its 158-foot- (48-meter-) long double wall along the full length of the pueblo's west end. Both walls are massive; they have veneered cores and are separated by a void ranging from 22 to 30 inches (55 to 75 centimeters) in width. Seven short walls divide the void into cells of varying lengths. The outer, or westernmost, wall is only one story high while the inner wall rises two stories. Long parallel walls most likely serving as buttresses also appear along the south walls of Kin Kletso and Casa Chiquita. The outer walls seem to act as buttressing supports for the inner walls.

Two quarries for Kin Bineola's stone walls are found on nearby mesa tops. The larger quarry is located about 1,230 feet (375 meters) to the northwest; the smaller one, 1,000 feet (300 meters) to the northeast.

Kin Bineola's rectangular plazas appear to be devoid of structural features. The smaller west plaza measures roughly 80 by 95 feet (24 by 29 meters) and opens to the south. A masonry wall possibly 20 inches (50

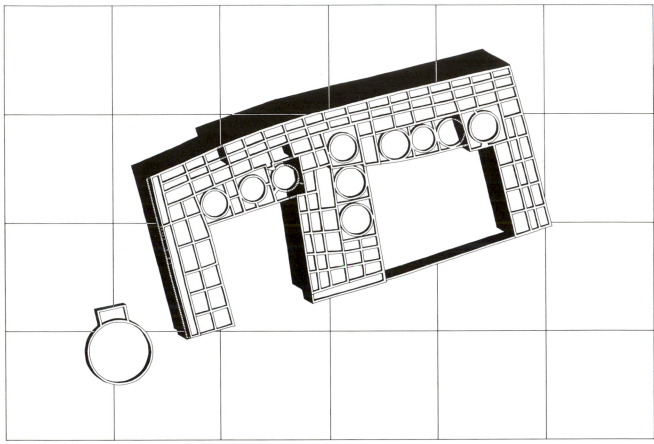

KIN BINEOLA

centimeters) thick encloses the approximately 95-by-122-foot (29-by-37-meter) east plaza. The wall lacks an obvious indication of an entry portal or gateway.

Around 33 feet (10 meters) from the pueblo's southwest corner lies a great kiva having an interior diameter of approximately 56 feet (17 meters). This dimension is only seven feet (2.3 meters) smaller than the diameter of Casa Rinconada, the largest kiva in Chaco Canyon. The great kiva may have been associated with the earlier

period of construction and occupancy at Kin Bineola.

Most of the pueblo's walls consist of carefully laid masonry facing veneers on both sides of rubble cores. The veneers are built with evenly coursed layers of sedimentary stone slabs, each an inch or so (2 to 3 centimeters) thick and 4 to 8 inches (10 to 20 centimeters) long. The resulting walls have exceptionally diminutive scales and very likely were coated originally with stucco. The thickness

of typical walls is more or less 20 inches (50 centimeters).

During the eleventh and twelfth centuries a major roadway linked Kin Bineola to Chaco Canyon. Tree-ring dating indicates that the site was constructed and expanded between A.D. 1111 and 1124. Obviously the focus of an extended community, Kin Bineola seems to have become fully integrated into the Chaco system by the early twelfth century.

PUEBLO PINTADO
San Juan Basin Anasazi

Situated on the edge of a broad flood plain east of Chaco Canyon, the impressive three-story ruins of Pueblo Pintado are visible for a considerable distance in all directions. Centuries ago a major roadway connected the site with Pueblo Bonito some 17 miles (27 kilometers) to the west. The easternmost of the major Chacoan communities, Pueblo Pintado once contained an estimated 135 rooms.

The site lies about 650 feet (200 meters) south of Chaco Wash at an altitude of 6,520 feet (1,987 meters) above sea level. Twenty-seven tree-ring dates from various parts of the ruins indicate major construction activity at the site around A.D. 1060. Ceramic samples suggest occupancy in the vicinity of Pueblo Pintado from 900 until 1250. Primarily a cultural affiliate of Chaco Canyon, the pueblo probably was abandoned and reoccupied during the thirteenth century (Marshall et al. 1979).

In plan the massive pueblo has two terraced wings forming a right angle with an enclosed plaza to the southeast. The main room block measures at most 175 by 217 feet (53 by 66 meters). Both wings are mostly two stories high and three rooms wide. The structure terraces down from three stories near the outer corner to a single story in the interior corner.

A formal building constructed according to a clear architectural plan, Pueblo Pintado once had most likely ninety ground-floor rooms, forty second-story rooms, five third-floor rooms, five kivas, and a subterranean great kiva. Rooftop hatches may have been the primary means of gaining

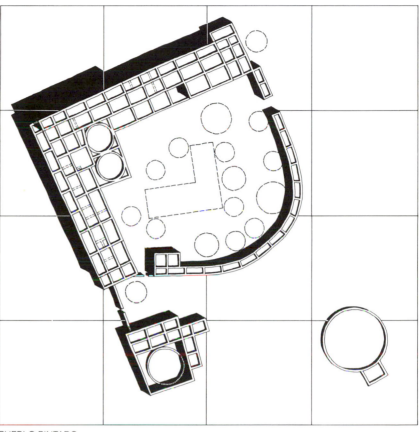

PUEBLO PINTADO

access to the ground-floor rooms; no evidence for doors is found in the exterior walls of the first floor.

A curving arc formed by perhaps nineteen long, narrow rooms encloses the plaza. Each of the rooms is one story high and has dimensions of possibly 5.6 by 16.4 feet (1.75 by 5 meters). Walls formed by single rows of rooms also enclose plazas at Chetro Ketl, Peñasco Blanco, Pueblo del Arroyo, Pueblo Bonito, Hungo Pavi, Tsin Kletzin, and Una Vida.

The plaza's maximum dimensions

are in the range of 160 by 180 feet (49 by 55 meters). A gateway 15 feet (4.5 meters) wide provides entry into the plaza roughly 26 feet (8 meters) south of the north wing. A second entry may be located in the southwest corner of the plaza.

Both of the kivas at the northwest corner of the plaza have diameters of 25 feet (7.6 meters) or so. Solid masonry originally filled the corners between the kivas and their rectangular enclosures. A third kiva approximately 21 feet (6.5 meters) in diameter is located near the south end of the west wing. Remains of a fourth subterranean room, possibly 20 feet (6 meters) in diameter, are found at the east end of the north wing.

Approximately 50 feet (15 meters) south of the main building, and connected to it by a straight wall, was a single-story structure consisting of ten rooms and a kiva. The kiva has two components. The lower chamber is a subterranean kiva perhaps 34 feet (10.4 meters) in diameter. The upper component seems to be a walled courtyard measuring more or less 40 by 45 feet (12.5 x 14 meters).

Roughly 85 feet (26 meters) southeast of the plaza wall are the unexcavated remains of a subterranean great kiva having an interior diameter of 57 feet (17.5 meters). The dimensions of the alcove on the kiva's southeast side are about 13 by 18 feet (4 by 5.5 meters).

In the plan presented here figures drawn with dashed lines represent fourteen subterranean kivas varying in diameter from 20 to 30 feet (6 to 9 meters), and an L-shaped house measuring at most 64 by 70 feet (19.5 by 21.3 meters). These structures are attributed to the reoccupation of almost all of Pueblo Pintado during the A.D. 1200s. The latecomers also built flimsy walls of soft limestone and overly abundant mortar to subdivide rooms in the pueblo. Similar evidence of later reoccupation is found at Salmon and Aztec.

The exceptionally well built walls of Pueblo Pintado contrast sharply to the inferior quality of later construction. These magnificent examples of Chacoan craftsmanship have stood exposed to the elements for more than nine centuries. More than half of the original walls remain in place today, including some three-story sections 26 feet (8 meters) high.

Reasons for the durability of Pueblo Pintado's walls include thicknesses of 20 to 40 inches (50 to 100 centimeters), the use of hard tabular sandstone material, and the very sparing use of mortar resulting in tightly fitted masonry joints. Typical exposed stones are relatively small in size with occasional blocks as large as 3 by 12 inches (8 by 30 centimeters). A quarry for the stones is located some 500 feet (150 meters) southeast of the pueblo.

The wood floors and roofs of Pueblo Pintado were built in much the same way traditional structures were built all over the Southwest until recently. Large, undressed logs called *vigas* span the shorter distances between parallel bearing walls. The *vigas* range in diameter from 6 to 12 inches (15 to 30 centimeters). Structurally, they act as main beams and are spaced as far apart as possible, presumably because of the relative difficulty of obtaining large timbers for construction.

Smaller wood joists called *latillas*, usually 2 or 3 inches (5 to 8 centimeters) in diameter, bear on the *vigas* and end walls. The *latillas* are placed close together and support ceiling mats. The ceiling heights at Pueblo Pintado typically are some 8 feet 2 inches (2.5 meters), unusually high for Chacoan rooms.

Numerous house mounds have been found in the immediate vicinity of Pueblo Pintado. Fourteen residential sites containing 116 surface rooms and nineteen pit houses or kivas are found near the pueblo. The kivas usually are located south or east of their associated houses. Further research at Pueblo Pintado is expected to expand our present knowledge of typical Chacoan communities.

ANDREWS
San Juan Basin Anasazi

The Andrews ruin is the largest of at least twenty-five masonry structures constituting the greater Andrews Community. The site lies on the north side of Red Mesa Valley approximately 43 miles (69 kilometers) south of Pueblo Bonito. The multistory pueblo is built on relatively open and level ground, although a deep arroyo cuts through the site immediately north of the structure. The greater community extends for about a mile and a quarter (2 kilometers) along a gently sloping hillside with an average elevation of 7,000 feet (2,133 meters) above sea level.

Andrews Community apparently was well established before A.D. 800. In all, the settlement probably had at least twenty-one residential structures containing some 106 rooms, but not all were in use at the same time. During the ninth century two great kivas were constructed and occupied, quite likely serving as social and religious centers of a large, dispersed population. One of the great kivas had the extraordinary diameter of 78 feet (24 meters), distinguishing it as one of the largest chambers of its type known in the Southwest. The presence of two great kivas suggests a relatively large population (Marshall et al. 1979:117–129).

During the period of 950 to 1000 the nuclear Andrews Community seems to have expanded, the multistory community center and third great kiva most likely were built, and earlier structures including the original great kivas presumably were abandoned. During the same period Casamero Community was established on a site 3 miles (4.8 kilometers) to the northwest.

The Andrews Ruin appears to have had originally fourteen rooms, five kivas, and possibly two plazas. Generally in good condition, the ruins extend roughly 130 feet (34 meters) from north to south. The estimated diameters of the kivas range from 14 to 16.4 feet (4 to 5 meters). The west kiva is elevated on fill above grade and has a 30-by-40-inch (75-by-100-centimeter) ventilator tunnel leading to the south.

Rectangular courtyards measuring 18 by 40 feet (5.5 by 12 meters) and 20 by 23 feet (6 by 7 meters) enclose the two east kivas. A crescent-shaped, perhaps 90-foot- (27-meter-) long wall defines a plaza area around the detached kiva. The 20-inch- (50-centimeter-) thick curving wall retains plaza fill 30 to 40 inches (75 to 100 centimeters) above the surrounding grade. At the east end of the pueblo a wall 5 feet (1.5 meters) high encloses a 16-by-39-foot (5-by-12-meter) plaza, which opens to the east.

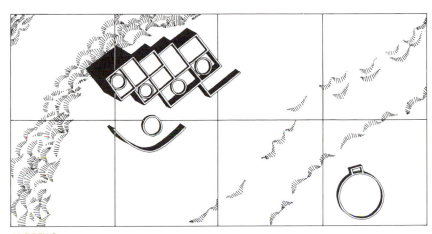

ANDREWS

About 150 feet (45 meters) southeast of the Andrews Ruin are the unexcavated remains of a great kiva with an estimated interior diameter of 41 feet (12.5 meters). This is well more than twice the diameter of any of the room block's kivas and more than six times their average floor areas. Probably contemporary with the pueblo, the great kiva seems to have been a semisubterranean chamber with walls originally projecting perhaps 40 inches (1 meter) above grade. A 10-by-15-foot (3-by-4.5-meter) alcove appears along the great kiva's north wall.

The masonry walls of the great kiva and the room block were of both compound and core-veneer types. Sandstone predominates, but some limestone also is found. For example, the pueblo's southwest wall consists of 16-inch- (40-centimeter-) thick, core-veneer masonry with 4-by-6-by-6-inch (10-by-15-by-15-centimeter) stones showing pecked and ground surfaces.

The great kiva's walls are of compound construction. Stones in the walls range from 4 to 8 inches (10 to 20 centimeters) in thickness and are up to 14 inches (36 centimeters) long. The massive upper walls of the great chamber measure from 24 to 32 inches (60 to 80 centimeters) in thickness.

CASAMERO
San Juan Basin Anasazi

Casamero Community is situated at the base of a mesa in Red Mesa Valley overlooking Casamero Draw. Located approximately 42 miles (67 kilometers) south of Pueblo Bonito, the set-

CASAMERO

tlement consists of a large multistory room block, an associated great kiva, and fourteen smaller ruins. The main building in the compact, half-mile- (800-meter-) long site lies at an elevation of 6,920 feet (2,110 meters) above sea level.

The L-shaped pueblo measures about 65 by 98 feet (20 by 30 meters). Oriented to the east, the structure contains twenty rooms and a wall-enclosed kiva on the ground floor, probably nine rooms on the second floor to the west, and a plaza to the southeast. Low masonry walls enclose the 36-by-58-foot (11-by-18-meter) plaza. Remains of what may have been a subterranean kiva some 18 feet (5.5 meters) in diameter are found in the north end of the plaza.

A number of doorways, all elevated above floor level, provide access for ground-floor rooms. Two of the portals are T shaped, but the others are rectangular. Many 20-to-28-inch- (50-to-70-centimeter-) square ventilation openings appear low in the walls. Typical floor features include storage bins, cists, fire boxes, and hearths,

some of which have fallen from upper rooms. Trash filled one room, and a burial was found in another.

In plan Casamero's walled kiva is shaped like a keyhole 14.3 feet (4.35 meters) in diameter. At some unknown time the kiva was reoriented from south to southeast. Traditional appointments of the kiva include a perimeter bench, a subfloor ventilation shaft, a hearth about 12 inches (30 centimeters) in diameter, a draft deflector, an alcove to the southeast, and a *sipapu*, or spirit hole, in the floor.

Casamero's exterior walls consist of stone veneers on rubble cores typically measuring 20 inches (50 centimeters) in thickness. Interior walls generally are compound structures more or less 14 inches (35 centimeters) thick. The main building materials are limestone blocks in the range of 8 to 20 inches (20 to 50 centimeters) long with frequent chinking. Alternating bands of sandstone blocks also appear.

Wall foundations roughly 18 inches (45 centimeters) deep and wide were built of limestone rubble with generous quantities of adobe. Masonry wall coursing begins possibly 3 inches (8 centimeters) above the present floor level. The walls show evidence of stucco finishes. Ceiling *vigas* of piñon and juniper originally spanned between the walls, supporting closely spaced *latillas* covered with fiber mats and adobe.

The great kiva associated with the Casamero room block lies perhaps 213 feet (65 meters) to the south. The unexcavated subterranean chamber has an interior diameter of at least 69 feet (21 meters) and may have four surface alcoves around the perimeter.

Casamero Community seems to

have been established around the year 900 as a colony of the Andrews complex 3 miles (4.5 kilometers) to the southwest. Once Casamero had attained a sufficient size, the first great kiva apparently was built, presumably to serve as a social and religious center. During the eleventh century, as was the case at most of the settlements in Red Mesa Valley, a large multistory pueblo was constructed near the great kiva.

In Andrews and other Red Mesa Valley communities, the original great kivas were abandoned when later and somewhat smaller great kivas were built. The opposite seems to have occurred at Casamero where the older chamber apparently continued to be maintained and used. Ceramic samples and dendrochronology suggest construction and occupation of the more recent structures between 1000 and 1125. During this period additional Anasazi sites are known to have existed in the vicinity of Casamero (Marshall et al. 1979:131–140).

FORT WINGATE

San Juan Basin Anasazi

Fort Wingate is located on a sand-stone-capped hill in Red Mesa Valley possibly 50 miles (80 kilometers) southwest of Pueblo Bonito and a short distance east of Casa Vibora. Situated at an altitude of 6,780 feet (2,067 meters), the site lies in open grassland with dense stands of piñon and juniper to the north and south. Ceramic remains collected at the site suggest an initial occupation perhaps around A.D. 850 to 950, abandonment for a century or so, and reoccupation from perhaps 1050 to the 1300s.

Probably constructed mainly during the latter period of occupation, Fort Wingate consists of two room blocks, seven kivas, and one great kiva. Built of stone, the pueblo is arranged along a northeast to southwest axis and generally is oriented toward the southeast. The main room block is roughly F shaped and measures at most 70 by 160 feet (21 by 49 meters).

The ground floor of the central structure contains forty-four rooms and a wall-enclosed kiva some 15 feet (4.5 meters) in diameter. The northwest wall of the room block most likely was two stories high; here about sixteen more rooms were situated on an upper floor. The northeast structure appears to have ten ground-floor rooms and a wall-enclosed kiva more or less 16.4 feet (5 meters) in diameter.

At the southwest end of Fort Wingate lies the great kiva with a maximum interior diameter of roughly 40 feet (12.2 meters). A masonry bench 40 inches (1 meter) wide encircles the chamber, whose floor is sunken an estimated 5.6 feet (1.7 meters) below the surrounding ground level. Evi-

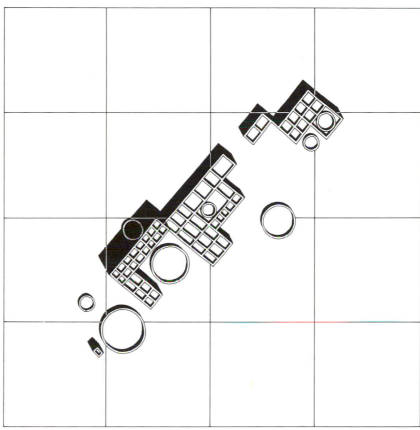

FORT WINGATE

dence of four pillars or roof supports was found during the excavation of the great kiva. The circular structure seemingly fell into disuse before the pueblo was abandoned; its stones may have been reused to build rooms elsewhere on the site.

Fort Wingate's walls are constructed of sandstones ranging in size from spalls to blocks measuring up to 4 by 14 by 14 inches (10 by 35 by 35 centimeters). The remains of an extensive residential community are found in the immediate vicinity of the site. One pueblo may have had forty rooms, and another probably was two stories high and measures around 100 feet (30 meters) square in plan (Marshall et al. 1979:155–158).

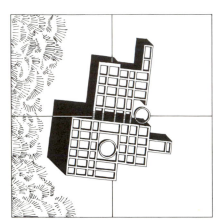

LAS VENTANAS

LAS VENTANAS
San Juan Basin Anasazi

In the midst of a substantial Anasazi community some 70 miles (113 kilometers) south of Pueblo Bonito lie the ruins of Las Ventanas. The site consists of a compact multistory pueblo with an estimated ninety rooms, a tower kiva, possibly a subterranean kiva, a great kiva to the southeast, and the remains of a prehistoric roadway. Unlike the neighboring communities of Haystack and San Mateo, Las Ventanas seems to be a frontier settlement lacking Chacoan characteristics in many respects (Marshall et al. 1979:187–193).

The site is located on a sandstone ridge overlooking a broad valley to the east and an extensive area covered with basaltic lava to the west. The pueblo is constructed in an open woodland of piñon and juniper at an elevation of 6,680 feet (2,036 meters) above sea level. Ceramic samples suggest that Las Ventanas was occupied between A.D. 1050 and 1200.

The north structure of Las Ventanas seems to have twenty-five single-story rooms and a subterranean kiva about 16.4 feet (5 meters) in diameter. The contiguous south room block apparently is a two-story structure with thirty-five or so chambers on its ground floor, perhaps thirty rooms on the second floor, and a two-story kiva near its center. The west wall probably approached 25 feet (7.5 meters) in height. Due to the ruinous condition of the largely unexcavated remains, the plan presented here is largely conjectural.

The tower kiva appears to consist of two chambers built one on top of the other. Each kiva has a diameter of approximately 15.4 feet (4.7 meters), and each lies within a rectangular enclosure measuring roughly 21 by 26 feet (6 by 8 meters). Rubble fills the corners between the enclosing walls and the kiva. The lower kiva lacks the usual perimeter bench and is built predominantly of basalt blocks with occasional sandstones.

A ledge 10 to 12 inches (25 to 30 centimeters) wide is recessed into the perimeter wall around 8.2 feet (2.5 meters) above the floor of the lower kiva. The purpose of the encircling ledge presumably is to support the structure of the second floor. The curving walls of the upper chamber are composed entirely of small sandstone blocks not exceeding 8 inches (20 centimeters) in length.

The masonry of the Las Ventanas pueblo consists primarily of sandstone slabs and blocks with an average size of 5 by 8 by 12 inches (13 by 20 by 35 centimeters). The walls west of the kiva are of core-veneer construction 24 inches (60 centimeters) thick. The only place in the pueblo where basalt appears is the lower kiva. Here blocks 8 to 16 inches (20 to 40 centimeters) long are laid in beds of abundant mortar to form walls 40 inches (1 meter) thick. Some chinking occurs with small sandstone spalls.

The great kiva of Las Ventanas lies more or less 820 feet (250 meters) south of the pueblo. The interior diameter of the subterranean chamber is estimated to be 54 feet (16.5 meters). Four alcoves are spaced around the perimeter at equal distances. The kiva's compound walls 16 inches (40 centimeters) thick are built with sandstone blocks ranging in length from 8 to 16 inches (20 to 40 centimeters).

A prehistoric road some 20 feet (6 meters) wide enters the site from the northeast and terminates more or less 330 feet (100 meters) southeast of the pueblo. The road is discernible for a distance of more than 400 feet (120 meters). Large stone slabs and blocks 16 to 60 inches (40 to 150 centimeters) in length form curbs along the edges of the road.

The relationship of Las Ventanas to its well-documented Anasazi neighbors is unclear. Multistory room blocks, tower kivas, and great kivas are characteristics of Chacoan architecture. The lack of a plaza, the absence of a dominant orientation to the southeast, the apparent mixture of construction systems and materials, and the disorganized massing of Las Ventanas are not characteristic of Chacoan architecture.

SAN MATEO

San Juan Basin Anasazi

The largest known Chacoan ruin in the Red Mesa Valley is San Mateo. The massive structure is located about 50 miles (80 kilometers) south of Pueblo Bonito and a short distance east of Haystack and the Andrews ruin. Situated at an altitude of 7,200 feet (2,195 meters), the site lies on a low rise above a flood plain with scattered piñons and low grasses in the immediate vicinity. The remains of two great kivas and an extensive prehistoric community of unknown extent are found nearby. Ceramics collected at San Mateo suggest major activity between A.D. 1000 and 1125.

The multistory room block measures at most 170 by 203 feet (52 by 62 meters). The building terraces down from three stories along the northwest wall to the fully enclosed plaza at grade to the southeast. The ruins of the largely unexcavated pueblo are estimated to contain fifty to sixty-seven ground-floor rooms, a number of second-floor and perhaps third-floor rooms, and at least five kivas. San Mateo most likely contains in all around one hundred rooms. Room dimensions range from 10 to 30 feet (3 to 9 meters), and areas vary from 97 to 388 square feet (9 to 36 square meters).

The plaza measures roughly 66 by 105 feet (20 by 32 meters). An unusual feature in the pueblo is a street or passageway entering the northwest room block from the plaza. The approximately 8.2-foot- (2.5-meter-) wide street extends some 52 feet (16 meters) into the pueblo. Its purpose may be to provide surface access to interior rooms or to the kivas. An-

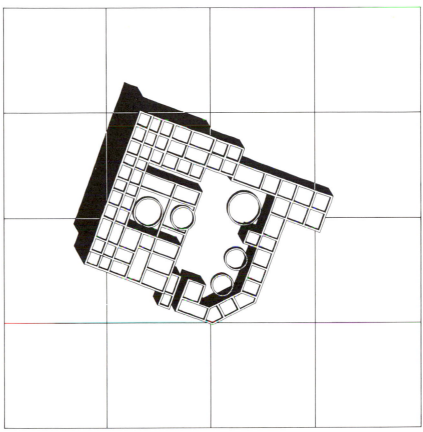

SAN MATEO

other narrow street enters the plaza from the south. Additional plaza entries from the east and north seem probable.

The wall-enclosed kiva fronting on the plaza has a diameter of 20 feet (6 meters). Not centered in its 23-by-26-foot (7-by-8-meter) enclosure, the chamber's southeast wall protrudes into the plaza. The larger of San Mateo's wall-enclosed kivas has a diameter of 26 feet (8 meters) or so. All of the kivas in the plaza appear to be subterranean. The larger chamber to the north measures conservatively 33

feet (12 meters) in diameter. The plaza's two smaller kivas have possibly 20-foot (6-meter) diameters.

None of San Mateo's walls extend above the present surface of the ruins at most 13 feet (4 meters) high. Soft sandstone slabs and blocks of poor quality contribute to inferior masonry at the site. Main walls may be of core-veneer construction about 20 inches (50 centimeters) thick. Buff-colored stones 1 to 4 inches (2 to 10 centimeters) thick and up to 10 inches (25 centimeters) long predominate.

The remains of numerous masonry unit houses, many with middens, have been found in the immediate vicinity of San Mateo. Quite likely a dense Anasazi community existed nearby, but its nature and extent remain to be determined (Marshall et al. 1979).

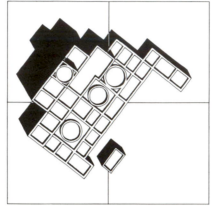

KIN YA'A

KIN YA'A
San Juan Basin Anasazi

Best known for its remarkable four-story kiva, Kin Ya'a is a medium-size Chacoan town located roughly 26 miles (42 kilometers) south of Pueblo Bonito. The site lies in open terrain on the western edge of a broad flood plain at an elevation of 6,780 feet (2,067 meters) above sea level. The sparse grasslands surrounding the site are suitable for agriculture. A cluster of tree-ring dates suggests major construction at Kin Ya'a around A.D. 1106. Well-defined roadways connected the pueblo with Chaco Canyon and other towns in the San Juan Basin and beyond (Marshall et al. 1979:201–206).

Oriented to the southeast to capture the winter sun, Kin Ya'a is estimated to have twenty-six rooms and three wall-enclosed kivas on the ground floor, nine rooms on the second floor, four third-floor rooms, and a tower kiva. The spire-like remains of the tower today rise more than 33

feet (10 meters) above the plain, although the original tower is thought to have been 7 feet (2.1 meters) or so higher. No evidence remains of the low wall enclosing a plaza to the southeast that was reported by Fewkes (1917:13).

The room block originally measured perhaps 116 by 149 feet (35.5 by 45.5 meters). Room dimensions range from 8.2 to 24.6 feet (2.5 to 7.5 meters) with areas from 125 to 270 square feet (11.5 to 25 square meters). The roofs of the ground-floor rooms and kivas form an elevated terrace about 40 by 130 feet (12 by 40 meters) in size. The terrace probably provided access to upper-floor rooms and the tower kiva. The surface kivas measure 16 to 20 feet (5 to 6 meters) in diameter.

The original height of Kin Ya'a's tower kiva is believed to be 40 feet (12 meters). The tower apparently once contained four cylindrical chambers set one on top of the other. Massive foundation walls 5 feet (1.5 meters) thick support the tower. The walls are

built of the largest stones in the pueblo, some measuring 8 by 48 inches (20 by 120 centimeters) in size.

The walls diminish in thickness to 2 feet (60 centimeters) at the top of the tower due to an arrangement of ledges in the walls at each floor level. The interior diameters of the tower kiva's chambers increase from 14.6 feet (4.45 meters) at the ground floor to possibly 16.4 feet (5 meters) at the fourth floor because the walls taper. A masonry tower some 20.7 feet (6.3 meters) square encases the cylindrical rooms.

Ledges 4 to 8 inches (10 to 20 centimeters) wide appear on the tower's northwest walls, most likely to assist in scaffolding during construction. Interior bearing ledges 6 to 10 inches (15 to 25 centimeters) wide occur at each floor level just above exterior wall pockets for beams. Possible scaffolding pockets are reported on the exterior face of the tower 9.2, 18.7, and 28.2 feet (2.8, 5.7, and 8.6 meters) above grade.

The masonry walls of Kin Ya'a typically are of core-veneer construction 20 to 24 inches (50 to 60 centimeters) thick. The veneers consist of dark brown sandstone slabs up to 8 inches (20 centimeters) thick and 4 feet (1.2 meters) long. However, the slabs average only 4 by 12 inches (10 by 30 centimeters) in size. Smaller stones measuring about 1 by 4 inches (3 by 10 centimeters) are used in the tower.

Kin Ya'a's tower kiva is sturdily built. The height of the tower is less than twice the width of its base, a conservative proportion. Adjacent rooms appear to buttress the tower on two sides at the third floor and on three sides at the second and first floors. Massive walls and solid-filled tower corners further enhance structural stability. Considering the absence of maintenance for almost nine centuries and the lack of reinforcing for tension and shear, Kin Ya'a's tower kiva demonstrates the enduring qualities of ancient architecture in the Southwest.

A great kiva approximately 44 feet (13.5 meters) in diameter is situated 650 feet (200 meters) northwest of the room block. Ceramic samples suggest that the subterranean chamber probably served as a religious center for the greater Kin Ya'a community prior to the construction of the major room block. Four alcoves are found around the perimeter of the great kiva. Three of the alcoves measure perhaps 8.2 by 11.5 feet (2.5 by 3.5 meters); the fourth alcove, to the east, is somewhat larger.

Within the four-square-mile (10.4-square-kilometer) area around Kin Ya'a, 104 residential sites have been identified. The largest masonry remain contains some fifty rooms and several kivas. One of the ruins yields evidence of occupation between 950 and 1100. The remnants of irrigation structures also are found nearby.

Two roadways enter Kin Ya'a from the northeast. One leads straight to the neighboring community of Bee Burrow and then continues to Chaco Canyon. The second road proceeds more easterly toward Pueblo Pintado. A third roadway departs Kin Ya'a toward the southwest; it leads to the mountains about a mile and a quarter (2 kilometers) distant. This may have been a quarry road for rock and wood similar to those known at Aztec and Pueblo Pintado.

MUDDY WATER
San Juan Basin Anasazi

The extensive Anasazi community of Muddy Water contains many dozens of unit houses, three Chacoan pueblos, and a great kiva distributed over an area of several square miles (square kilometers). An active site for more than five centuries, the huge community lies possibly 26 miles (42 kilometers) southwest of Pueblo Bonito and 6 miles (10 kilometers) west of Kin Ya'a. The pueblos and kiva are recognized examples of public architecture, but the precise number of residential sites remains to be determined.

The pueblo presented here is situated near the center of the nuclear community on a site elevated slightly above the surrounding grassland at an altitude of 6,750 feet (2,057 meters) above sea level. The largest of Muddy Water's three major pueblos, the structure and its associated great kiva may have been in use between A.D. 900 and 1100. Muddy Water's other two pueblos probably were occupied around 1125 to 1175.

Basically an L-shaped structure with a partially enclosed plaza to the east, the room block measures approximately 72 by 115 feet (22 by 35 meters). In all, the pueblo probably contained originally twenty ground-floor rooms, four to six second-floor rooms, and two kivas. Today the remains of the Muddy Water pueblo are much reduced; they lie in a rubble mound at most 11.5 feet (3.5 meters) high.

Room dimensions range from 7 to 25 feet (2.1 to 7.5 meters), and areas vary from 100 to 400 square feet (9.3 to 37.2 square meters). Both kivas are

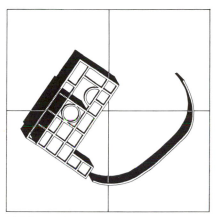

MUDDY WATER

wall enclosed on ground level, and both have interior diameters of perhaps 16 feet (5 meters). Like most kivas, the south kiva is circular, but the north chamber has an unusual semicircular plan.

A curving masonry wall, originally about 5 feet (1.5 meters) high, partially encloses the plaza. Open to the north, the plaza measures roughly 80 by 130 feet (25 by 40 meters). The primary building material for the walls of the plaza and pueblo is buff-colored tabular sandstone. Main walls appear to be of core-veneer construction some 20 inches (50 centimeters) thick.

The great kiva of Muddy Water is located about 440 feet (135 meters) southeast of the main pueblo. The chamber has an estimated interior diameter of 56 feet (17 meters). Four alcoves are spaced at equal intervals around the perimeter. The maximum dimensions of the alcoves are more or less 8 by 13 feet (2.5 by 4 meters).

One of Muddy Water's other two pueblos contains perhaps seven rooms and two kivas in a room block measuring up to 42 by 98 feet (12.7 by 30 meters). One of the kivas is built on ground level and is wall enclosed; its interior diameter is roughly 18 feet (4.5 meters). The other kiva, a subterranean room 26 feet (8 meters) in diameter, occupies a wall-enclosed plaza open to the sky.

The third major pueblo of the greater Muddy Water community apparently has fifteen ground-floor rooms, seven second-floor rooms, and a subterranean kiva some 20 feet (6 meters) in diameter. The circular chamber lies near the center of a rectangular, wall-enclosed plaza on the pueblo's east side. The room block measures overall 60 by 72 feet (18.5 by 22 meters).

The residential areas of Muddy Water are known to be extensive, but a comprehensive survey is lacking. For example, forty-six residential sites have been identified within a one-square-mile (2.6-square-kilometer) area west of the community's center. These ruins together contain an estimated 255 surface rooms and six kivas.

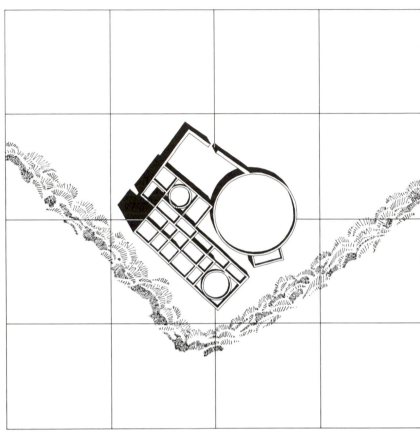

TOH LA KAI

TOH LA KAI
San Juan Basin Anasazi

The most exceptional feature of Toh La Kai is its orientation toward the northeast instead of the southeast, the usual arrangement for Anasazi pueblos. Located about 48 miles (77 kilometers) southwest of Pueblo Bonito, the site lies between Casa Vibora to the south and Tohatchi Village to the north. Situated on an alluvial slope immediately below a steep cliff, Toh La Kai commands an impressive view to the north (Marshall et al. 1979:235–238).

Open juniper grasslands with traces of piñon surround the site at an elevation of 6,450 feet (1,966 meters) above sea level. Several dry-land Navajo farms presently are under cultivation nearby. Ceramics collected from the ruins of the pueblo suggest probable construction and occupancy between A.D. 1000 and 1200. The remains of a pit house approximately 100 feet (30 meters) to the north suggest even earlier activity in the vicinity, perhaps around 750.

The architectural components of Toh La Kai are the multistory room block with a plaza and great kiva to the north and east. The overall dimensions of the complex are roughly 128 by 138 feet (39 by 42 meters). In all, the pueblo appears to contain eighteen ground-floor rooms, twelve second-floor rooms, possibly three third-floor rooms, and two kivas within rectangular enclosures.

The south kiva, some 25.6 feet (7.5 meters) in diameter, seems to be partially subterranean. The smaller north kiva has an interior diameter of only 19.7 feet (6 meters) and is flanked by three surface rooms. Their roofs form an estimated 1,840-square-foot (170-square-meter) platform on the pueblo's second floor.

Having a diameter of 75.5 feet (33 meters), Toh La Kai's great kiva is one of the largest such chambers recorded to date. The diameter exceeds by 12 feet (3.7 meters) the comparable dimension of Casa Rinconada, the largest kiva in Chaco Canyon. Probably only partly subterranean, the impressive structure appears to be contiguous with the northeast corner of the room block. A 10-by-26-foot (3-by-8-meter) surface alcove is found on the south side of the great kiva.

Slightly irregular in plan, the plaza's walls form the north corner of the complex. The open space measures more or less 40 by 53 feet (12 by 16 meters). A gate around 6.6 feet (2 meters) wide provides access through the northeast wall of the plaza.

Since Toh La Kai remains mostly unexcavated, the characteristics of its masonry walls are largely undetermined. One room in the ruins has core-veneer walls some 20 inches (50 centimeters) thick. Bonded but not chinked, the veneers consist of sandstone blocks 2 to 4 inches (5 to 10 centimeters) thick and 4 to 8 inches (10 to 20 centimeters) long.

HOGBACK
San Juan Basin Anasazi

The Chacoan community of Hogback lies approximately 54 miles (87 kilometers) northwest of Pueblo Bonito. The settlement occupies a sparsely vegetated gravel terrace some 50 feet (15 meters) above the nearby flood plain at an elevation of 5,100 feet (1,555 meters) above sea level. The town is situated on the west bank of the Chaco River about 10 miles (16 kilometers) southeast of its confluence with the San Juan River. Greater Hogback community's largest pueblo appears to have been occupied between A.D. 900 and 1050. Evidence of earlier human activity is found elsewhere in the 185-acre (75-hectare) settlement.

The community consists of north and south clusters of masonry residences containing an estimated three hundred rooms in thirty-five groups with numerous kivas. Located near the center of the north cluster, the main pueblo has Hogback's only enclosed plaza. The L-shaped room block has a semicircular plaza containing a kiva to the southeast.

Probably two stories high, the pueblo measures at most 52 by 72 feet (15 by 22 meters). The room block contains nine ground-floor rooms and perhaps six second-floor rooms to the northwest. A wall 20 to 30 inches (50 to 75 centimeters) thick encloses the roughly 30-by-43-foot (9-by-13-meter) plaza. Centered in the D-shaped plaza is a subterranean kiva possibly 23 feet (7 meters) in diameter.

Hogback's main walls are of core-veneer construction 16 to 20 inches (40 to 50 centimeters) thick. Facing veneers are built of sandstone blocks and slabs. The closest source of sand-

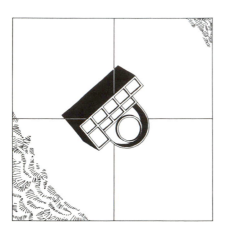

HOGBACK

stone is bedrock in the hills around 1,600 feet (500 meters) west of the pueblo.

The great kiva of Hogback lies in the south cluster 3,200 feet (1 kilometer) or so southwest of the main room block. The subterranean chamber may have an interior diameter of 52 feet (16 meters). A 26-by-43-foot (8-by-13-meter) structure on the north side of the great kiva suggests a large antechamber or possibly several surface rooms. An alcove measuring 8 by 13 feet (2.5 by 4 meters) appears on the chamber's south side. The great kiva most likely was built prior to the main room block and continued to be used while the latter was occupied (Marshall et al. 1979:241–245).

An exceptional feature of Hogback is the site's lack of productive soils nearby. Most Chacoan sites with public architecture, a great kiva, and numerous residences are closely associated with viable agricultural resources. An ancient road may connect Hogback with other communities to the south and with Chaco Canyon itself. One reason for Hogback's existence could be its strategic location for trade between the confluence of two major rivers to the north and an important roadway leading to the south.

WHITE HOUSE
San Juan Basin Anasazi

The unique Chacoan outlier known as White House consists of a cliff dwelling connected to a once-four-story-high room block at the base of a 500-foot (150-meter) cliff. The ruins are located in the dramatic natural setting of Canyon de Chelly about 2 miles (3.2 kilometers) east of its junction with Canyon del Muerto. According to Cosmos Mindeleff (1897), the site's name in Navajo is Kini-da-e-kai, a reference to the conspicuous white plastered walls of the cliff dwellings.

The earliest settlers probably arrived in Canyon de Chelly well before the beginning of the Christian era. By A.D. 300 to 400 the canyon's occupants were erecting small rooms with masonry walls in natural caves and elsewhere in the gorges. Agricultural plots most likely covered the fertile canyon bottoms, and between 700 and 1150, settlements and farms also appeared on the mesa-top plateaus around the canyon rims. Around 1150, Canyon de Chelly reached its maximum population of an estimated 600 to 800 people.

The need for agricultural lands may account for the location of room blocks on talus slopes and in natural caves overlooking the canyon floors. Compared with the Anasazi builders of Chaco Canyon and the Montezuma Valley, the residents of Canyon de Chelly constructed relatively few kivas and developed a less-sophisticated system of stone masonry. During the 1000s small numbers of people from the San Juan Valley appeared in Canyon de Chelly, bringing with them distinctive new ideas about architecture.

Lieutenant J. H. Simpson found White House during his 1848 expedition through Canyon de Chelly. The reconstruction presented here is based on a plan and description by Cosmos Mindeleff (1897:figs. 14, 15), comments by Ferguson and Rohn (1987), and my observations on the site in 1991. Several parts of Mindeleff's plan have been revised to incorporate more recent information. For example, the reconstruction shows a circular kiva at the west end of the lower ruin that was stabilized and partially plastered in 1967, a feature not recorded by Mindeleff.

At its peak of development White House seems to have had at most eighty rooms, a maximum of sixty in the earlier Chacoan room block and up to twenty in the later cave above. Tree-ring dates suggest that construction probably was underway on the lower structure by 1060 and continued in the cliff dwelling as late as 1275. The maximum population of the settlement may have been as many as one hundred people.

The reconstructed drawing shows the upper and lower ruins in a single plan, but the vertical elevation of the cave floor is approximately 35 feet

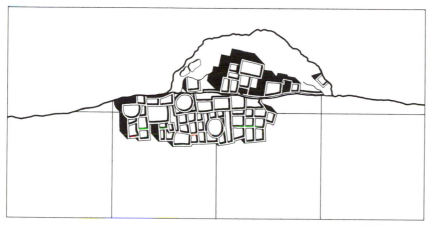

WHITE HOUSE

(10.7 meters) above the canyon floor. In plan the lower room block measures about 50 by 150 feet (15 by 45 meters). The walls in the east portion of the room block now rise 12 to 14 feet (3.7 to 4.3 meters) high, but marks in the cliff face indicate that a four-story tower near the room block's east end once rose to within 4 feet (1.2 meters) of the cave's floor.

Evidence of several circular kivas is found at White House. The roughly 18-foot- (5.5-meter-) diameter kiva near the center of the room block is built against the base of the cliff wall. Its floor is elevated some 10 feet (3 meters) above the floor levels of surrounding rooms and its wall cores are solid filled. Walls of rooms west of the central kiva typically are 12 to 15 inches (30 to 48 centimeters) thick. Several walls at the west end of the room block are of jacal construction consisting of vertical poles tied together horizontally and coated on both sides with mud plaster.

The upper ruin of White House presently has only ten rooms, perhaps half the original number. The cliff dwelling is entered by way of a well-defined portal in the wall along the south-facing cliff edge. The threshold of the portal is situated more or less 4 feet (1.2 meters) above the roof of the four-story tower rising from the canyon floor below.

Near the center of the natural cave is a large room measuring 12 by 20 feet (3.7 by 6 meters) or so, a landmark clearly visible from a considerable distance. The unusually large room has fine masonry walls 24 feet (7.7 meters) long to the south and possibly 7 feet (2.1 meters) to the east and west. Plastered with white stucco, the distinctive mass crowns the architectural composition of White House.

The rooms adjoining the principal structure also are constructed of stone, but the other chambers in the cliff alcove are of much more modest sizes and construction. Although the cliff overhang extends some 70 feet (21 meters) beyond the south edge of the cave, blowing rain and snow apparently required drains for the roofs of buildings in the cave. The distinctive masonry and large room size of the upper ruin imply the influence of builders familiar with architectural ideas from Chaco Canyon.

By 1300 White House and the other monuments of Canyon de Chelly apparently were abandoned. Over the centuries intermittent flood waters of the canyon stream have damaged or destroyed a number of rooms in the lower ruins; today only sixty rooms and four kivas remain. The remarkable cliff dwelling and room block are now part of Canyon de Chelly National Monument. The area is administered by the National Park Service and is owned by Navajo people, whose ancestors arrived in the enchanting valleys some three hundred years ago.

FAR VIEW

Northern San Juan Anasazi

Sometime around A.D. 900, Anasazi settlers in Mesa Verde began to build a remarkable reservoir called Mummy Lake on the north end of Chapin Mesa at an elevation of some 7,700 feet (2,347 meters) above sea level. Enlarged at least twice in the tenth century, the stone-lined reservoir measures about 90 feet (27 meters) in diameter and once could hold perhaps half a million gallons of water for the domestic needs of the surrounding settlements. During the eleventh century the Mummy Lake community grew to have possibly four hundred residents. They lived in at least eighteen settlements containing approximately 375 rooms with thirty-two kivas (Ferguson & Rohn 1987).

Mesa Verde is located in southwestern Colorado roughly 80 miles (128 kilometers) north of Chaco Canyon, a contemporary Anasazi center whose architectural ideas influenced several structures in the vicinity of Mummy Lake. Known as Far View Community, the settlement includes Far View House, Pipe Shrine House, Site 820, Far View Tower, and several other sites. Lushly covered with juniper, piñon, and other vegetation, Mesa Verde is less arid than other areas in the Southwest due to its higher altitude and more northerly latitude.

Far View House, the largest room block in the group, appears in the reconstruction presented here based on the plan published by J. Walter Fewkes (1917). The building derives its name from the commanding view available from its upper floors; in the distance to the southwest visitors can see the four corners of Utah, Arizona,

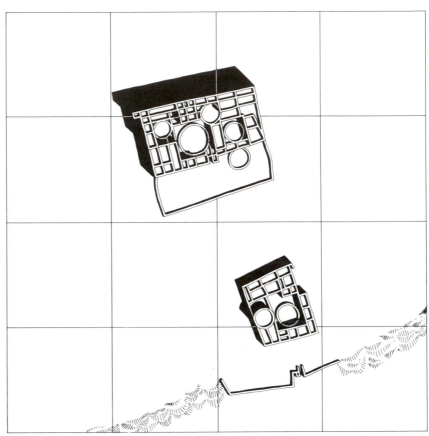

FAR VIEW

New Mexico, and Colorado. The reconstruction also shows Pipe Shrine House based on the plan published by Arthur H. Rohn (1977: fig. 13).

In plan Far View House measures at most 64.5 by 113 feet (19.7 by 34.4 meters). Oriented slightly east of south, the rectangular structure contains probably forty ground-floor rooms and five kivas in an orderly plan. The walls within the pueblo are arranged orthogonally and often continue in parallel alignments throughout the entire length of the structure. Room sizes appear to vary widely, averaging possibly 9.7 by 10.3 feet (3 by

3.2 meters), an area of about 100 square feet (9.3 square meters).

During his excavations in 1916, Fewkes found walls standing to a height of 10 to 20 feet (3 to 6 meters) above ground level, with clear indications of second and third stories. He conservatively estimated a total of fifty rooms for Far View House, but a larger number seems reasonable. The original massing of the room block apparently consisted of roof-top terraces stepping down to the south.

A low stone wall more or less 12 inches (30 centimeters) high retains an approximately 35-foot- (10.7-meter-) wide terrace or communal plaza along the south wall of the room block. A subterranean kiva 16 feet (5 meters) or so in diameter is recessed into the east side of the terrace next to the room block. Three doorways lead from the terrace into ground-floor rooms, and a fourth provides access into the structure from the north.

Views through the doorways reveal relatively large rectangular rooms of uniform sizes with high ceilings. The rooms are decidedly different from the small, irregular dwellings built in the cliffs around Chapin Mesa a century or so later. The ground-floor rooms of Far View House presumably were used primarily for storage. Upper-floor rooms most likely served as dwellings; some had doors opening onto rooftop terraces.

Ladders and roof hatches typically gave access to lower-floor rooms lacking doors. The three smaller kivas in Far View House are built on grade and are surrounded by masonry rooms. Accessible only through roof hatches, they range in diameter from 14.5 to 16 feet (4.4 to 4.9 meters).

The large central kiva, 33 feet (10 meters) in diameter, has eight pilasters and two floor vaults. It appears to be the oldest ceremonial chamber in the room block and closely resembles Chaco Canyon kivas in size. All five kivas have masonry deflectors, circular fire pits, *sipapus*, banquettes with pilasters, and above-floor ventilators replacing earlier subfloor ventilators of the Chacoan type.

Some 80 feet (24 meters) south of Far View House's communal plaza lies Pipe Shrine House, so called because of a cache of a dozen ceremonial clay pipes found in a pit in the kiva's floor. Probably one to two sto-

ries high, Pipe Shrine House has twenty-one ground-floor rooms arranged around a central kiva, and a round tower perhaps 16 feet (5 meters) in diameter with massive stone corners engaging the west wall. The nine rooms to the north were built first; their walls consist of single courses of stones with chipped edges.

Most of the remaining rooms in Pipe Shrine House have stone walls with double courses of stones. The kiva, around 21 feet (6.4 meters) in diameter, has six pilasters on a low, wide banquette, high walls, and a subfloor ventilator tunnel. Measuring more or less 57 by 69 feet (17.4 by 21 meters), the pueblo contains less than half the area of Far View House.

Roughly 26 feet (8 meters) south of Pipe Shrine House, a stone stair leads down to a lower level through an opening in a retaining wall. The wall provides a level, south-facing communal terrace for the room block. While excavating a midden southeast of Pipe Shrine House in 1922, Fewkes found a dozen undisturbed burials with pottery and other mortuary offerings surrounding them.

LOWRY

Northern San Juan Anasazi

The ruins of the large Anasazi town of Lowry are located at the end of an unpaved road approximately 9 miles (14 kilometers) west of Pleasant View

in southwest Colorado. The mostly unexcavated site lies in an oasis of piñon and juniper woodlands surrounded by irrigated fields of pinto beans. Fertile, well-watered farmlands were not typical of the prehistoric southwestern landscape.

The inhabitants of Lowry Pueblo, like their neighbors in Wallace, Escalante, Sand Canyon, and Hovenweep, were farmers who grew corn, squash, and beans in garden plots and supplemented their diets by hunting and gathering. The ancient towns lie in a 2,500-square-mile (6,475-square-kilometer) area of southwestern Colorado and southeastern Utah known as the Montezuma Valley. Teeming with perhaps thirty thousand inhabitants about eight hundred years ago, the Valley extends from Alkali Ridge in the west to Mesa Verde and the Dolores River Valley in the east.

The rich farmlands of the Montezuma Valley supported a much larger population than did the comparatively thin top soils of Mesa Verde. Between A.D. 1100 and 1300, Lowry may have been exceeded in size in the Montezuma Valley only by Yellow Jacket, which seems to have had a population in the range of 2,500 to 2,700 persons. Probably the Chacoan outlier farthest to the north, Lowry first was settled by Anasazi, who arrived most likely around 750.

Extending over an area of roughly one square mile (2.6 square kilometers), the town of Lowry consists of twenty-four recorded residential sites containing possibly twelve hundred rooms with an estimated population of fifteen hundred to eighteen hundred persons. Lowry's room blocks are organized in two distinct sections like those of Taos, Paquimé, Kinishba, Zuni, and other major towns of

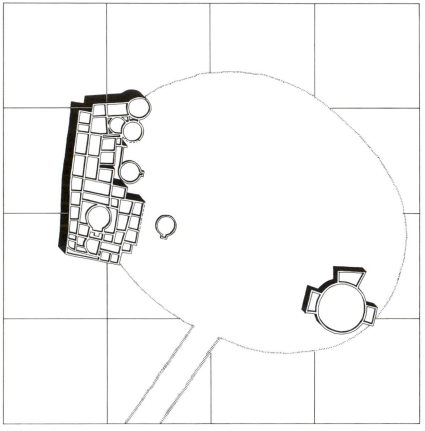

LOWRY

story rooms would increase the estimated total to between sixty and eighty-five.

Overall, the excavated room block of Lowry measures more or less 72 by 150 feet (22 by 46 meters) and contains eight kivas of which five at most were in use at the same time. Situated at an elevation of 6,915 feet (2,108 meters) above sea level, the ground-floor rooms range from a small storage room with an area of around 20 square feet (1.9 square meters) to a large dwelling room of some 240 square feet (22.4 square meters). The maximum roof span is 10 feet (3 meters) or so.

The kivas of Lowry Pueblo seem to range in diameter from 13 to 21 feet (4 to 6.4 meters). The largest round chamber is located near the center of the room block to the south. Here an earlier kiva was buried 8 feet (2.4 meters) below the present one, providing an impressive second-story base and elevating the more recent structure to a position of prominence in the room block. The impressive kiva has eight wall pilasters resting on a perimeter banquette.

The best known feature of the large kiva is a remarkably well preserved design painted on the plaster of its lower wall. Unfortunately, the painting presently is deteriorating; the view window in the kiva's roof has been boarded up and the room no longer is open to the public. The design recalls typical pottery decoration.

Tree-ring dates indicate that Lowry Pueblo's earliest rooms and kiva were built around 1089 or 1090. The large room sizes and masonry style resemble Chaco Canyon construction, but the kiva adheres to local tradi-

the ancient Southwest. Spring-fed East Cow Canyon divides Lowry into north and south sections and provides a constant source of water for the inhabitants and their farms.

Both sections of the town had a plaza, but only the north section had a great kiva. Lowry Pueblo, the site's only excavated room block, forms the west wall of the north section and faces the plaza and great kiva to the east. Three roadways radiate from the north plaza; they lead south to various parts of Lowry and to neighboring villages and hamlets. One

roadway appears today as a 30-foot- (9-meter-) wide shallow ditch leading southwest from the north plaza.

During the early 1930s Lowry Pueblo and the great kiva were excavated under the direction of Paul S. Martin of the Field Museum of Natural History in Chicago. The reconstructed plan presented here is based on the excavation report (Martin, Roys, & von Bonin 1936). Dr. Martin found the remains of thirty-seven ground-floor rooms and suggested that as many as fifty may have existed originally. Probable second- and third-

tions. Major expansion of the room block apparently occurred between 1103 and 1120, all in the local style of architecture. Three small, subsequent additions completed the structure.

Chaco-style rooms tended to be perhaps two or three times larger in size than Mesa Verdean rooms. Typical Chaco masonry walls in Lowry Pueblo consist of tabular sandstone slabs fitted very closely together and laid with sparing amounts of mortar. Local masonry utilized larger stones laid in less-regular courses with copious mud mortar joints and often chinked with small sandstone spalls.

The great kiva of Lowry demonstrates the town's former importance as a center of ceremonial rituals. The partially underground chamber appears to have an interior diameter of 46 feet (14 meters), an antechamber to the north, and foundations of somewhat similar rooms to the east and west. The great kiva seems to exhibit more Chacoan than Mesa Verdean characteristics, including an encircling bench lacking masonry pilasters, four massive column foundations, subfloor vaults, and a stair leading up to the north antechamber.

A single tree-ring date suggests that the great kiva was constructed around 1106. Lowry seemingly was abandoned about 1140 for unknown reasons, bringing to a close probably four hundred years of occupation. Now administered by the Bureau of Land Management, the site is open daily to visitors for self-guided tours.

AZTEC
Northern San Juan Anasazi

The largest Chacoan monument outside of Chaco Canyon, Aztec consists of more than a dozen mostly unexcavated ruins. The major structures presented in this reconstruction are the West Ruin, the East Ruin, the Earl Morris Ruin to the northeast, and a free-standing great kiva to the east. The large, well-preserved site is situated approximately 1,200 feet (366 meters) northeast of the Animas River at an altitude of more than 5,600 feet (1,707 meters).

Noted for both its Chacoan and Mesa Verdean characteristics, Aztec lies about 55 miles (88 kilometers) north of Pueblo Bonito and some 35 miles (56 kilometers) southwest of Cliff Palace. The plan of the West Ruin bears a distinct resemblance to Salmon, another Chacoan outlier located perhaps 10 miles (16 kilometers) to the south on the north bank of the San Juan River. A prehistoric roadway leads south from Aztec to Salmon and then continues to Chaco Canyon.

Tree-ring dates and ceramic samples suggest that construction began on the West Ruin early in the A.D. 1100s by people culturally affiliated with Chaco Canyon. A significant number of main roof beams were harvested between 1106 and 1115 (Lister & Lister 1990). Occupation seems to have continued until the late 1100s when the population apparently declined.

Some authorities believe that a brief period of abandonment may have occurred, but by the early 1200s the population began to increase once more. During the thirteenth century

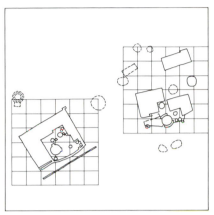

KEY PLAN OF AZTEC

decidedly Mesa Verdean influences appeared at Aztec, perhaps representing a shift in cultural affiliation rather than a migration of people (Cordell 1979). By 1300, after roughly a century of activity, the entire site was deserted.

A Chacoan pueblo surpassed in size only by Pueblo Bonito and Chetro Ketl, the West Ruin measures overall roughly 300 by 385 feet (91 by 117 meters). Based on the 1923 plan and a reconstructed model (Lister & Lister, 1990: 31, 238), the massive structure may contain 261 ground-floor rooms, 153 second-story rooms, seventy-five third-story rooms, thirty kivas, and a great kiva. The total of 489 rooms is somewhat greater than others have estimated; the increase seems to be attributable to the additional rooms and kivas shown at the east end of the plaza on the 1923 plan by Earl Morris.

Characteristics of Chacoan architecture in the West Ruin include the compact arrangement of rectangular rooms several tiers deep in a massive room block, multistory terracing of upper rooms stepping back from a

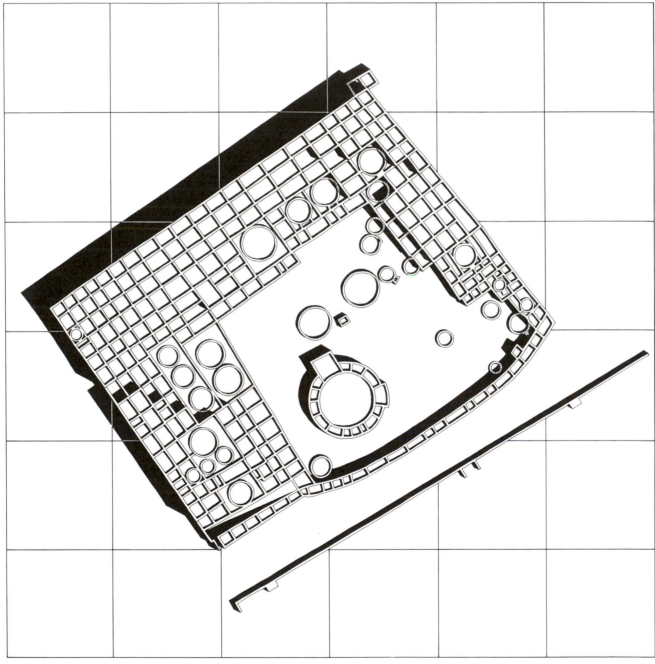

AZTEC, WEST RUIN

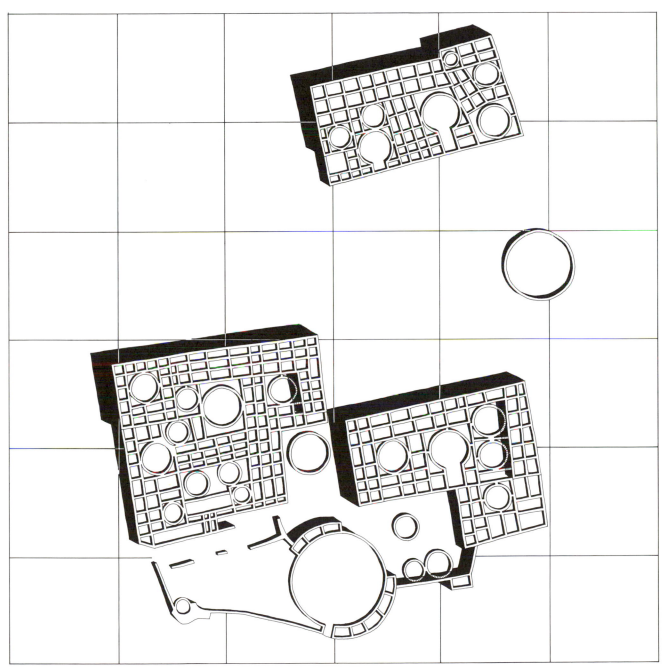

AZTEC, EAST RUIN AND EARL MORRIS RUIN

courtyard oriented to the southeast, and the introduction of numerous circular kivas both in the room block and in the plaza. The north wing of the West Ruin is seven rooms deep, the east wing contains at most five rows, and the west wing may be eight rooms deep but the area remains mostly unexcavated. A slightly bowing row of rooms encloses the plaza to the south, apparently the last major element built in the West Ruin.

Also reminiscent of the monuments of Chaco Canyon, the masonry walls of Aztec are dominantly sandstone block veneer laid on both sides of rubble cores. The masonry is laid in neat horizontal courses of thick block alternating with thinner slabs in a pattern called banded masonry. At several places in the west wing striking horizontal bands of green stones are laid four or five blocks high. The source of the green stone is unknown, but its color contrasts handsomely with the beige sandstone.

Aztec's masonry is not as fine as Chaco Canyon's because the local sandstone does not fracture in straight cleavage planes. Typically, mud plaster covers the masonry walls, giving them the appearance of being integral parts of the land from which they grow. Most of the interior walls are uncolored but some have red ocher wainscots below walls whitewashed with gypsum. The white surfaces occasionally have red painted or incised decorations. Inherent weaknesses in Aztec's masonry are the absence of bonding between veneers and cores, the lack of corner bonding, and the frequent alignment of vertical joints.

Fortunately, visitors today may enter a series of well-preserved rooms near the northwest corner of the West Ruin. Nineteen original ceilings remain in place; their heights range from 9 to 11 feet (2.7 to 3.6 meters). Of typical Chacoan construction, the main beams have large diameters and span the shorter dimensions of rectangular rooms. They support poles placed perpendicularly and overlaid with willow matting. Structural members are of pine, juniper, or cottonwood.

The kivas of Aztec are similar to those of Chaco Canyon except that they lack *sipapus*, or spirit holes. Doorways, hatchways, ladders, and small ventilation holes high in walls also are characteristically Chacoan. Other architectural details reflecting influences from the south are stone storage bins and *metates*, wall pegs and niches, and storage platforms of wood.

The West Ruin's plaza contains the only restored great kiva in the Southwest. Encircling the semisubterranean chamber are fourteen perimeter rooms at plaza level, each having a ladder down to the kiva floor. The exterior walls of the alcoves rise 10 to 12 feet (3 to 3.7 meters) above the plaza. Unfortunately, the height of the great kiva seems to have been increased during restoration, imparting a sense of formality to the interior space that most likely did not exist originally.

The interior diameter of the great kiva exceeds 48 feet (14.6 meters). Four masonry and wood columns nearly 3 feet (90 centimeters) square support the roof, a radially framed structure estimated to weigh more than 90 tons (81.6 metric tons). Surrounded by a low bench, the main floor contains traditional floor vaults, a central fire pit, and a number of small storage pits. The restored great kiva suggests the elaborate religious ceremonialism of the Anasazi people.

Roughly 150 yards (137 meters) to the east lies the East Ruin containing the largely unexcavated remains of two large room blocks, a plaza, and a great kiva. Overall, the group measures more or less 280 by 380 feet (85 by 116 meters). The reconstruction presented here indicates 199 ground-floor rooms, ninety-one second-floor rooms, nineteen kivas, and one great kiva having an interior diameter of probably 86 feet (26.2 meters). The ceilings of thirteen rooms remain in place in the East Ruin.

Tree-ring dates for the East Ruin, like those for the West Ruin, cluster in the early 1100s except for several in the 1230s. My guess would be that the two pueblos probably are contemporaries built in the 1100s and reoccupied in the 1200s. My guess is based on the facts that both pueblos utilize dominantly core-veneer masonry and their sizes are comparable. Both structures consist of multistory terraces stepping down to plazas oriented to the southeast. And, finally, structures similar to Aztec's are found in Chaco Canyon but not in Mesa Verde.

The Earl Morris Ruin is situated some 140 feet north (43 meters) of the East Ruin. The compact pueblo appears to measure overall 96 by 185 feet (29 by 56 meters) and to contain sixty-two ground-floor rooms, twenty-six second-story rooms, and eight kivas. The free-standing great kiva to the southeast has an interior diameter of around 61 feet (18.6 meters).

Not shown in this reconstruction is the Hubbard Tri-Wall, a circular ruin located about 200 feet northwest of the West Ruin. The unusual round structure consists of three concentric masonry walls with an outer diameter of 64 feet (19.5 meters) and a height of 12 feet (3.7 meters) or so. Around the central kiva are a total of twenty-two rooms, all presumably entered by means of roof-top hatches.

Nearby to the west, north, and northeast of Aztec are several closely associated communities with a number of pueblos, kivas, roadways, and irrigation systems. It seems likely that Aztec may have functioned as a subregional center interacting with its neighbors and conducting extensive trade with Chaco Canyon and beyond. The eventual abandonment of the Aztec complex seems to have been part of a more widespread migration of people away from the San Juan Basin in the thirteenth century.

SALMON
Northern San Juan Anasazi

The large multistory Chacoan outlier of Salmon is situated on the north bank of the San Juan River approximately 45 miles (72 kilometers) north of Pueblo Bonito in Chaco Canyon. The site lies on an alluvial terrace above flood level between Bloomfield and Farmington in northwestern New Mexico. One of seventy outliers identified within 50 miles (80 kilometers) of Chaco Canyon, the pueblo is named for Peter Milton Salmon, an early Mormon homesteader.

The ancient North Road connects the well-preserved outlier with Chaco Canyon. Like the West Ruin of Aztec, a contemporary room block located about 11 miles (18 kilometers) to the north, Salmon is a rectangular structure oriented slightly east of south with tiers of rooms terracing down to a large plaza containing a great kiva. Both Aztec and Salmon appear to be built according to a predetermined plan within a relatively brief span of time.

Excavated during the 1970s under the direction of Cynthia Irwin-Williams (1980), Salmon contains a total of perhaps 290 rooms, a great kiva, and a tower kiva recalling a similar structure at Chetro Ketl. The reconstruction presented here shows an E-shaped room block measuring more or less 190 by 386 feet (58 by 118 meters) and containing 140 ground-floor rooms. The walls are constructed of core-veneer masonry with distinctive bands of carefully fitted stones in the Chacoan style.

Most of the beams used to construct Salmon came from ponderosa pine, Douglas fir, white fir, and other large trees available in quantity only in areas some 50 miles (80 kilometers) from the site. Tree-ring dates indicate that most of the timbers were cut between A.D. 1088 and 1093, when all the ground-floor rooms and the second-floor chambers buttressing the tower kiva probably were built. Additional construction and refurbishing continued until perhaps 1116, when the building activities diminished in the pueblo.

The basic architectural module of the ground-floor plan is a suite of four rooms placed one behind the other and connected by doorways. The room closest to the plaza typically is a large, square living room measuring some 18 feet (5.5 meters) square. The dwelling space has a fire pit and a T-shaped doorway facing the plaza or a gallery leading into the plaza.

Behind the living room of each suite are three small, rectangular rooms all two stories high. Most likely used for storage, the interior rooms are connected to the dwelling space by doorways. The galleries along the south side of the north room block are covered passageways with doors to the plaza and living rooms.

The 50-foot- (15-meter-) diameter great kiva is entered by way of an alcove on the north side measuring possibly 12 by 20 feet (3.6 by 6 meters). As in the similar circular chamber at Aztec, four columns of stone and wood support the roof of Salmon's great kiva. Two stone-lined floor vaults are located near the center of the circular floor.

The tower kiva is located in the center of the room block on a platform of cobble stones. Special footings support the massive masonry walls of the 33-foot- (10-meter-) diameter tower and its contiguous rooms, which act as buttresses. The tower kiva very likely projected above the roof tops of adjoining rooms.

The foundations for the entire pueblo probably were laid out prior to the commencement of construction. Special-function rooms in Salmon include four milling rooms, each containing six to eight food processing stones, and a room apparently used exclusively for the manufacture and repair of *metates*. Evidence gathered on the site suggests close cultural connections with Chaco Canyon (Irwin-Williams 1980).

No indication of a socially or economically elite class is found at Sal-

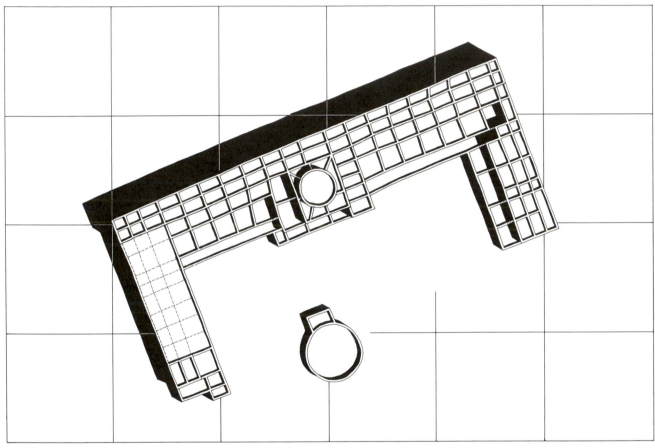

SALMON

mon. Not long after 1130 the original residents seem to have moved away from the pueblo. Around 1185 people with Mesa Verdean cultural characteristics may have reoccupied the entire pueblo; they undertook extensive renovations and built a large number of small kivas.

By 1263 or so, all the residents except a few stragglers seem to have abandoned Salmon for the last time, and the site began its centuries-long decline. As a result of a community-wide effort in the 1970s the site has been partially excavated and stabilized. Presently, Salmon and its modest museum are open daily to the public.

SQUAW SPRINGS
Northern San Juan Anasazi

Squaw Springs community is located some 24 miles (38 kilometers) south of Mesa Verde and 66 miles (106 kilometers) north of Pueblo Bonito. The 240-acre (98-hectare) site is situated near three springs in an area of desert grassland and open juniper. The average elevation of the nuclear community is 5,580 feet (1,700 meters) above sea level.

Perhaps as early as A.D. 500, early settlers began such activities as seasonal gathering and marginal farming in the vicinity of Squaw Springs. Around 900 the population started to increase, a community developed,

SQUAW SPRINGS

and a great kiva was built near its center. The great kiva has an estimated interior diameter of 56 feet (17 meters).

About A.D. 1000 the population concentrated in the vicinity of Squaw Springs, the multistory pueblo illustrated here was constructed, and a new great kiva was built roughly 66 feet (20 meters) north of the original one. Slightly smaller than its predecessor, the subterranean chamber has an interior diameter of approximately 50 feet (15 meters) with three alcoves, each measuring more or less 10 by 13 feet (3 by 4 meters), on its perimeter.

Possibly 215 feet (65 meters) north of the new great kiva lies a large, rectangular room block with two walled plazas to the south. The largest masonry building at Squaw Springs, the pueblo appears to have seventeen ground-floor rooms, six second-story rooms, and three kivas. The rectangular walls enclose an area of probably 75 by 82 feet (23 by 25 meters).

Today the remains of the pueblo lie beneath a mound of rubble up to 11.5 feet (3.5 meters) high. Wall thick-

nesses at the unexcavated site are difficult to ascertain; they may measure 20 inches (50 centimeters) or so. The principal building material is sandstone. Room sizes vary from roughly 67 to 258 square feet (6 to 24 square meters).

Originally, the plaza walls may have been at most 6.6 feet (2 meters) high and 20 to 24 inches (50 to 60 centimeters) thick. The east plaza measures about 31 by 39 feet (9.5 by 12 meters) and contains a subterranean kiva. The dimensions of the west plaza may be 28 by 30 feet (8.5 by 9 meters). A surface kiva some 15 feet (4.5 meters) in diameter lies almost enclosed within the room block in the plaza's north corner. The kiva outside the walls to the northwest is a subterranean chamber possibly 18 feet (5.5 meters) in diameter.

In the 500-acre (200-hectare) area surrounding the main pueblo, forty-three residential sites have been recorded. All of the sites have single-story masonry houses with one to thirty rooms, most have associated kivas, and many have plazas oriented to the south. In all, the greater community is estimated to have 354 rooms and thirty-six kivas.

In the 1,320-acre (534-hectare) area immediately southwest of Squaw Springs lie an additional fifty-five Anasazi sites. The sites are mostly one or several masonry rooms of modest size; they may have served as seasonal farmhouses or small storage facilities. These structures, and all the others in the Squaw Springs community, seem to have been abandoned completely by A.D. 1200.

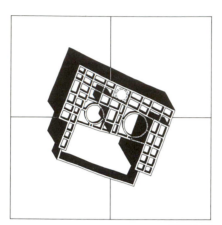

WALLACE

WALLACE
Northern San Juan Anasazi

The Wallace ruin contains the remains of a multistory pueblo several
miles east of the present-day city of
Cortez in southwestern Colorado. In
plan and architectural features the
pueblo bears a striking resemblance
to Wijiji in Chaco Canyon. One of
several sites in the prehistoric Lake
View Community, the Wallace ruin is
situated in the bottom of a valley.
Two earth mounds southwest of the
pueblo may be the remnants of an ancient road leading to the site.

The reconstructed plan presented
here is based on a report of investigations by Bruce A. Bradley
(1988:fig. 1). Originally, the room
block rose some three stories in
height and contained a total of perhaps one hundred rooms, three kivas,
and a walled plaza oriented to the
south. In plan the compact, nearly
symmetrical pueblo measures at most
93 by 105 feet (28 by 32 meters).

Construction of Wallace Pueblo
probably began early in the eleventh

century with the erection of four
multistory rooms in the western part
of the room block. The masonry walls
resemble those of Mesa Verde and
early Pueblo Bonito. Typically about
12 inches (30 centimeters) thick, the
walls consist of thin sandstone slabs
laid the full width of the wall in abundant mortar. A fifth room, also two
stories high, most likely was added to
the original structure sometime between 1075 and 1100.

Early in the 1100s the majority of
rooms were added and Wallace Pueblo
reached its final building form. The
main construction period somewhat
resembles Wijiji's single building
phase between 1115 and 1120. Wallace's well-executed, 20-inch- (50-
centimeter-) thick stone walls are examples of some of the finest masonry
produced in Chaco Canyon or its
outliers.

Foundations were excavated to a
depth and width of roughly 20 inches
(50 centimeters). Sandstone chunks
in liberal quantities of mud mortar
filled the footing trenches. The walls
consisted of carefully laid stone facings on both sides of a rubble stone
and mortar core. The facing stones
employed very little mortar and over-
lapped substantially to assure good
bonding. Limited chinking stones
were placed carefully to improve the
bearing capacity of the finished wall.

Wall penetrations included small
ventilation apertures just below ceiling lines, sockets for roof and floor
beams, rectangular doorways connecting interior rooms, and T-shaped
portals facing the plaza. At least one
row of three-story rooms appears to
extend the full length of the north
wall. Room sizes range in area from
possibly 43 to 129 square feet (4 to 12
square meters).

The average dimensions of the
slightly trapezoidal plaza are more or
less 40 by 70 feet (12 by 21 meters).
The pueblo's largest kiva measures
about 23 feet (7 meters) in diameter.
Access to the room block seems to
have been primarily by means of ladders to second-floor terraces from
which doors and roof hatches led to
interior chambers.

Built and occupied mainly between
1045 and 1125, Wallace Pueblo was
reoccupied briefly during the thirteenth century when minor alterations occurred in the room block.
Like nearby Escalante and Lowry,
Wallace is one of the most northerly
of the Chacoan outliers. Construction
of the pueblo quite likely was directed by experienced builders from
Chaco Canyon or Chacoan sites in
the San Juan Valley.

Presently under private ownership,
the partially excavated site is an appropriate subject for the ongoing
study of Chacoan influence in southwestern Colorado.

ESCALANTE
Northern San Juan Anasazi

The early-twelfth-century Chacoan
outlier of Escalante occupies a hill
crest about 9 miles (14 kilometers)
north of Cortez in southwestern
Colorado. Located on the south bank
of the Dolores River, the pueblo has a
commanding view of the McPhee

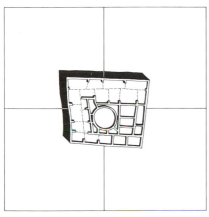

ESCALANTE

Reservoir to the north and a distant view of Mesa Verde to the southeast. Other nearby sites described in this study are Wallace, Sand Canyon, Hovenweep, Lowry, and McPhee Village.

The site derives its name from Fray Silvestre Vélez de Escalante, a Franciscan priest who happened upon the pueblo in 1776 while searching for a passage from New Mexico to California. Like Lowry Pueblo some 20 miles (32 kilometers) to the west, Escalante appears to be one of the northernmost outposts of the vast trading network established by the people of Chaco Canyon. The pueblo probably served as a center of exchange for the unfailing resources of the Dolores Valley and may have acted as a ceremonial or religious center as well.

The room block of Escalante measures at most 63 by 82 feet (19 by 25 meters) and contains an estimated twenty-five masonry-walled rooms of which seven have been excavated. Double rows of rooms to the north, east, and west and a single row to the south flank a central kiva. The ground-floor plan bears a striking re-

semblance in size and arrangement to the classic plan of New Alto in Chaco Canyon; however, the latter has one more row of rooms on the north side than does the former.

Some of Escalante's rooms were used for living and others served as storage. The largest excavated room measures about 10 by 16 feet (3 by 5 meters), much larger dimensions than those found in other settlements of the Montezuma Valley. The masonry walls are constructed in the Chacoan style of stone facings with cores of sandstone rubble.

The kiva's interior diameter is approximately 21 feet (6.4 meters). Typical of contemporary Chacoan ceremonial chambers, the structure has eight low pilasters on a wide banquette, a subfloor ventilator used to supply a fresh air draft, a centrally located fire pit, and a single masonry-lined floor vault. Tree-ring dates suggest that the main complex most likely was constructed around A.D. 1129 and continued to be occupied with two periods of abandonment, until the beginning of the thirteenth century.

Following the initial period of abandonment, Escalante was reoccupied perhaps about 1150 by people of the Montezuma Valley. Although the original architecture demonstrates Chacoan influences, pottery representing multiple periods of occupation is typical of the Northern San Juan area. A final occupancy, also by a small group of Montezuma Valley people, was of short duration around 1200.

Several small unit pueblos are found around the base of Escalante's hill. One is named Dominguez in honor of Francisco Atanacio Domínguez, a Franciscan priest who accom-

panied Escalante in 1776. The modest structure consists of four rooms with low stone walls constructed probably around 1123. The masonry walls are built with pecked stone blocks, which are characteristic of Montezuma Valley architecture.

A short distance south of the unpretentious room block lie the remains of a dirt-walled kiva 11 feet (3.4 meters) in diameter sunken 4 feet (1.2 meters) or so into the earth. Dominguez Pueblo may have been the home of eight to ten persons, who were members of an extended family. A contemporary of Escalante, Dominguez may have been associated with trading or ritual activities on the crest of the hill.

Excavations in the humble west room of Dominguez revealed one of the most remarkable burials discovered to date in the Southwest. Here were found the remains of a perhaps thirty-five-year-old woman of high status and influence. Interred with her were some 6,900 turquoise, jet, and shell beads, a unique shell-and-turquoise frog pendant, and other exotic grave offerings. The elaborate pendant suggests that she may have been a distinguished visitor from the Chaco area, perhaps related in some way to the trade network.

Escalante and Dominguez ruins are open daily to the public. Adjoining the site is the Anasazi Heritage Center, a museum operated by the Bureau of Land Management. The museum specializes in the study of prehistoric cultures in the Four Corners area, one of the richest concentrations of ancient architecture in the Southwest.

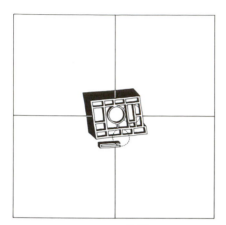

THREE KIVA PUEBLO

THREE KIVA PUEBLO
Northern San Juan Anasazi

Located in Montezuma Canyon of southeastern Utah, Three Kiva Pueblo lies approximately 50 miles (80 kilometers) northwest of Cliff Palace in Mesa Verde. The site contains a single-story Anasazi pueblo of medium size with fourteen rooms, a kiva, and a turkey pen. The surrounding terrain consists of rugged mesas and arroyos with occasional willows and cottonwoods (Noble 1981:43–45).

The first part of Three Kiva Pueblo probably was built during the A.D. 800s. The earliest occupants seem to have been affiliated culturally with the Kayenta branch of the Anasazi, who lived to the south and west. Following three successive occupations the pueblo apparently was abandoned about 1300. Later influences at the site appear to be more closely associated with the people of Mesa Verde and nearby Hovenweep.

The rooms of the pueblo form a rectangle measuring at most 37 by 50 feet (11.3 by 15.2 meters). A short distance to the south is an elongated stone enclosure some 20 feet (6.1 meters) long and 2 feet (61 centimeters) wide; it is believed to have been a turkey pen. An abundance of turkey bones at Three Kiva Pueblo suggests that the domesticated bird was an important source of meat and feathers.

The room sizes of the pueblo range from perhaps 42 to 165 square feet (3.9 to 15.3 square meters). In the center of the room block is a wall-enclosed kiva with an interior diameter of possibly 14 feet (4.3 meters). Dashed lines in the reconstructed plan presented here represent two additional kivas (Miller 1974).

During excavations two abalone shell pendants were found, indicating trade contact with the Pacific Coast. Stone artifacts also were found, including knives, scrapers, drills, projectile points, hammerstones, hoes, axes, mauls, dishes, *manos*, and *metates*.

Physically, Three Kiva Pueblo is about the same size as Casa Abajo, a roughly contemporary Chacoan community in the San Juan Basin. The latter, however, had fewer though larger rooms, no kiva, and a wall-enclosed courtyard. Today much of the land in southeastern Utah belongs to Ute and Navajo Indians, successors to the Anasazis who constructed and occupied Three Kiva Pueblo many centuries ago.

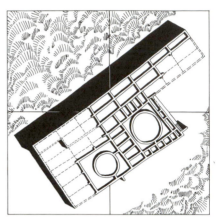

CHIMNEY ROCK

CHIMNEY ROCK
Northern San Juan Anasazi

Located on a spectacular ridge crest at an elevation of 7,600 feet (2,316 meters), Chimney Rock Pueblo occupies one of the highest sites in the prehistoric Southwest. To the west the dramatic ruin overlooks the winding green valley of the Piedra River, a tributary of the San Juan River in southwestern Colorado. To the north lies the continental divide, and to the northeast rise the towering twin peaks of Chimney Rock.

Here, in around 1075, colonists arrived from Chaco Canyon, approximately 93 miles (149 kilometers) to the south. The newcomers found a well-established community of perhaps as many as two thousand people living in high mesa sites situated between 600 and 1,000 feet (183 and 305 meters) above the valley floor. The Chacoans carried up the tons of stone, rubble, and earth fill required to build their pueblo on the narrow, waterless mesa top. A few hundred yards from Chimney Rock Pueblo down the rocky, sandstone ridge, the indigenous population lived in circular masonry structures.

The reconstruction presented here is based primarily on drawings and data recorded by Frank W. Eddy (1977:figs. 12, 19) during his investigations of the ruins in the early 1970s and the plan of Jean Allard Jeancon (1922:plate XII). The L-shaped pueblo is perched on a tiny rock platform with sheer drop-offs to the northwest and the southeast. The long axis of the room block lies along the crest of the ridge.

Measuring about 80 by 157 feet (24 by 48 meters), Chimney Rock Pueblo contains an estimated thirty-six ground-floor rooms, some thirteen second-floor rooms, and two kivas. Both kivas measure at most 28 feet (8.5 meters) in interior diameter and are enclosed by stone walls forming two 35-foot (10.7-meter) square courts. The walls rest directly on the bedrock of the mesa top. Earth fill about 10 inches (25 centimeters) thick is used to establish level floors.

Most likely, the first phase of construction at Chimney Rock Pueblo included the west kiva and the row of rooms to the northwest. Wall abutments suggest that the parallel walls running from northeast to southwest were constructed next. The short, perpendicular walls seem to have been filled in last. This sequence of building appears to support Jeancon's contention that the pueblo was laid out and constructed according to a predetermined plan (Eddy 1977:42).

Originally, the two northwest rows of rooms probably rose two stories, but their walls today rise only 6.6 feet (2 meters). Doorways interconnect the lower rooms, and hatchways with ladders presumably once gave access into upper rooms. The walls consist of alternating courses of tabular sandstone veneer with rubble core laid in the manner typical of Chacoan masonry.

By 1125, no more than fifty years after Chimney Rock Pueblo was constructed, the entire district was abandoned. Drought and possibly a breakdown in social organization may have contributed to the collapse of the Chaco system in the twelfth century. However, this would not explain the emigration of the indigenous inhabitants who had lived in their high mesa homes for perhaps two hundred years.

Today several of the ruins have been stabilized and are open to the public. The sites are part of San Juan National Forest. Persons desiring to visit Chimney Rock Pueblo are advised to make arrangements with the ranger station at Pagosa Springs, Colorado (Ferguson & Rohn 1987).

MAIN RIDGE
Virgin Anasazi

The large Virgin Anasazi community of Main Ridge is located on the shores of the modern Lake Mead near Overton, approximately 50 miles (80 kilometers) northeast of Las Vegas in southern Nevada. The agglomerated settlement originally lay on the east bank of the Muddy River, but the construction of Hoover Dam in the 1930s resulted in the partial flooding of the site. The name Virgin Anasazi refers to the nearby Virgin River and to the Virgin Mountains a few miles to the east.

The Muddy River villages were the westernmost settlements of the Virgin Anasazi, most of whom lived to the north and east along the banks of the Virgin and Colorado rivers in southwestern Utah and northwestern Arizona. In southern Nevada where rainfall averages only 4 inches (10 centimeters) per year, farmers cultivated plots in springs and swampy areas and possibly dug small diversionary canals for limited irrigation. Spring-fed Muddy River is a more reliable source of water than the Virgin River, which relies heavily on melting snow.

The heavily eroded site of Main Ridge lies at an altitude of roughly 1,160 feet (353 meters) above sea level. Due to a lack of stones suitable for masonry construction, adobe is the principal building material for the walls of the village. The closest sources for piñon, juniper, and limited quantities of ponderosa pine are the Virgin Mountains rising more than 8,000 feet (2,440 meters) above sea level and extending into southwestern Utah.

Sometime around the beginning of the Christian era, early settlers began to live part of the year in pit houses along rivers in southern Nevada. Between perhaps A.D. 500 and 800, storage cists appeared near the pit houses, sometimes in clusters. After A.D. 800, surface dwelling rooms gradually replaced pit houses, sites became more numerous, and storage shifted from cists below grade to curving rows of contiguous small rooms attached to dwellings.

The reconstructed plan presented here shows a 600-foot (183-meter) square area of Main Ridge as it may have appeared at its population peak between possibly 1050 and 1100. The reconstruction is based on the published work of Margaret M. Lyneis (1986). The site plan shows only sixteen of Main Ridge's estimated forty-four households. They extend over an area of possibly 1,800 by 2,200 feet (550 by 670 meters) encompassing more than 90 acres (36.8 hectares).

The households of Main Ridge are built along level contours in the irregular terrain. Each household consists of one to eighteen adobe rooms, usually contiguous and often forming gently curving, crescent-shaped arcs. Typical dwelling rooms have six small storage rooms together containing an average of some 70 square feet (6.45 square meters).

Notable characteristics of Main Ridge's community plan are the absence of such public features as a main plaza or meeting place, the lack of kivas of any size, and the scattered disposition of structures in the landscape. The settlement's forty-four households are estimated to have had a total of 193 rooms; of these, twenty-eight rooms probably were dwellings and the remaining 165 were used for storage.

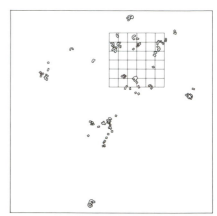

KEY PLAN OF MAIN RIDGE

Probably the most populous community along the Muddy River in 1100, Main Ridge and its neighbors probably were abandoned entirely by the 1160s for unknown reasons. During their last century in southern Nevada, the Virgin Anasazi produced distinctive pottery resembling designs of the Kayenta Anasazi to the east. Toward the end of occupation at Main Ridge, ceramics indicate contact with people along the lower Colorado River, perhaps in eastern California or western Arizona.

The large agglomeration of contiguous surface rooms at Main Ridge recalls somewhat similar plans of such Anasazi settlements as Coombs and Alkali Ridge in southern Utah, Badger House in Mesa Verde, and Grass Mesa and McPhee Village in the Dolores Valley of Colorado. Located approximately 280 miles (450 kilometers) northeast of Main Ridge, Alkali Ridge had an estimated 185 contiguous surface rooms of jacal construction, very nearly the same number as the Nevada site.

However, the storage rooms in Al-

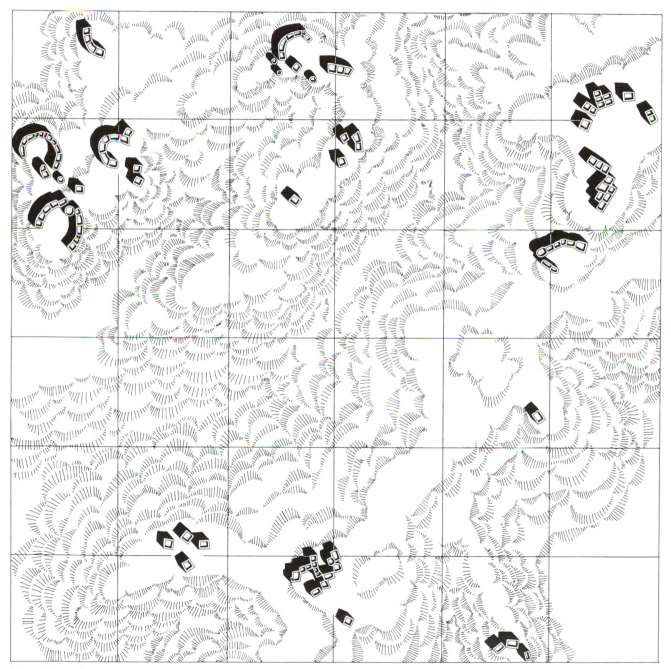

MAIN RIDGE, NORTHEAST HOUSEHOLDS

kali Ridge are located on the sides of dwellings while the rooms are placed end to end in Main Ridge. The Nevada site sprawls over thirty times the land area of the compact Utah site, and the former is arranged in four groups, each with up to sixty-seven rooms, while the latter has forty-four groups, each with at most eighteen rooms.

Main Ridge is one of a number of clustered settlements along the lower 16 miles (26 kilometers) of the Muddy River popularly referred to as Lost City or Pueblo Grande de Nevada. The area once had an estimated Virgin Anasazi population of possibly ten to twenty thousand people.

Beginning in 1924, Main Ridge and several other Lost City sites were excavated by Mark Raymond Harrington of the Museum of the American Indian for the Heye Foundation. Information on Lost City sites is on display in a small museum in Overton, including pottery, baskets, and ornaments. Some of the jewelry is made of turquoise mined by the Virgin Anasazi.

COOMBS
Kayenta Anasazi

Located in southern Utah at an altitude of 6,700 feet (2,042 meters) above sea level, Coombs Village shows simultaneously architectural influences of the Kayenta Anasazi to the south, the Virgin Anasazi to the west, the Fremont culture to the north, and Mesa Verdean ideas from the east. Probably built and occupied between A.D. 1050 and 1200, the community is situated on top of a 20-foot (6-meter) hill in Boulder, Utah. Sagebrush, greasewood, junipers, and grasses cover the landscape, and cliff-faced mesas rise beyond Boulder Creek about six-tenths of a mile (1 kilometer) west of the site.

The first settlers of Coombs Village most likely were Anasazi people from the San Juan area of northeast Arizona. They presumably were attracted by the availability of arable land, the permanent supply of water, the presence of building materials, an ample supply of firewood, and the abundance of game in the vicinity. The reconstruction presented here suggests the appearance of the community at the height of its development around 1100. The reconstruction is based on detailed drawings and descriptions published by Robert H. Lister and others (1959–1961).

Architectural and cultural diversity characterize the Coombs site. The architectural assemblage consists of a total of eighty-three recorded structures. These include thirty-seven dwellings, thirty-five store rooms, ten pit houses, and one *ramada*, or sunshade. Although Kayenta designs are associated with most of the pottery found in the village, the community plan and architecture recall such Mesa Verdean ideas as those found in nearby Alkali Ridge. The marked differences in design suggest multiple origins for the village founders.

Pit Houses Perhaps the most unusual aspects of Coombs Village are the simultaneous construction and use of jacal structures, masonry structures, pit houses, and at least one *ramada* and the apparent absence of kivas. All of Coombs' subterranean rooms are grouped together along the south slope of the hill in a sandy deposit where digging is relatively easy. True kivas in the San Juan area would be located near their associated dwellings regardless of the difficulty of excavation even in hard deposits, including bedrock.

The pit structures of Coombs Village lack perimeter benches, *sipapus*, and masonry-lined ventilator shafts, which are characteristic of Anasazi kivas. San Juan type kivas are not found in Fremont and Virgin communities, perhaps another indication of the multiple origins of the village settlers. The Coombs pit houses generally are square in plan and have rounded corners, and all ten dwellings contain approximately 120 square feet (11 square meters).

The walls and floors of the pit houses are plastered to prevent the soft sand from slumping. The floors are excavated to a depth of 3 to 5 feet (0.9 to 1.5 meters). Ceiling heights usually are about 6 feet (1.8 meters), and jacal or masonry walls enclose the portions of the pit houses above grade. Posts 4 to 8 inches (10 to 20 centimeters) in diameter are located in the corners of the typical pit houses. The poles support more or less square, horizontal wood roofs covered over with layers of earth or adobe and occasionally with thin sandstone slabs.

Hatches centered in the roofs and ladders usually ascending toward the north provide access into the pit houses. Ventilator shafts oriented toward the south are found in all but two of the structures. Stone-lined

COOMBS

hearths are recessed at least 12 inches (30 centimeters) into the floor near the center of each underground dwelling.

Jacal Structures The fifty-six jacal structures in Coombs Village are mostly dwellings that frequently adjoin one or more other rooms. The U-shaped cluster of rooms to the northwest consists of twenty-nine jacal and five masonry structures ranging in area from 43 to 165 square feet (4 to 15 square meters). Dwellings generally are larger than store rooms. Doors provide access into some rooms and roof hatches with ladders are used in others.

The walls of jacal structures are vertical; they consist of posts 2 to 8 inches (5 to 20 centimeters) in diameter with their bases recessed into the ground 6 to 12 inches (15 to 30 centimeters) apart. Stones often are placed between the posts to serve as the base of the wall. Interior and exterior wall surfaces frequently are plastered.

Roofs typically are composed of horizontal wood poles supporting matted twigs or reeds covered with earth or mud and sometimes with thin slabs of limestone. Occasionally, vertical poles prop up sagging roofs in random locations. Dwelling room floors are plastered with caliche or adobe, while store room floors often are paved with stones to discourage rodents.

Dwellings usually are equipped with open stone-lined bins, centrally located circular hearths, and ceramic storage jars recessed into floors with thin stone slabs for covers. Ten mealing bins and *metates* are found in Coombs Village; the grinding stones are located to serve several dwellings conveniently.

The jacal structures of Coombs resemble those of Alkali Ridge in construction and shape. Fremont jacal structures usually have thicker, sloping walls with more widely spaced posts and no stones between the posts. The Coombs walls may be described more accurately as being of wattle-and-daub construction.

Masonry Structures A total of sixteen rooms in Coombs Village are built of coursed sandstones and serve primarily as store rooms. Nine contiguous masonry rooms form the orderly row along the west side of the L-shaped cluster near the center of the community. Some of the interior partitions of the linear building are of jacal construction rather than of stone.

The dwellings attached to the north end of the linear row of stone rooms are constructed of both masonry and jacal. Varying from rectangular to almost round in plan, the rooms range in area from 26 to 76 square feet (2.4 to 7 square meters). Two large rectangular stone dwellings contain perhaps 240 square feet (22.3 square meters) each and have rows of posts along their centerlines to support their roofs.

The walls consist mostly of fine-grained sandstones dressed to form rectangular blocks 2 to 4 inches (5 to 10 centimeters) thick, 10 to 12 inches (25 to 30 centimeters) wide, and 10 to 24 inches (25 to 60 centimeters) long. Occasionally incorporating basalt boulders, the walls typically are a single stone wide and sometimes are plastered. Access into the masonry rooms is by means of roof hatches in flat roofs like those of the jacal structures.

The masonry structures erected in Coombs Village resemble those of the western San Juan area rather than the masonry associated with the Fremont and Virgin River areas, which characteristically employ unshaped stones in generous beds of mortar. Similarly, the grouping of structures around plazas or courts is customary in Anasazi villages but is rare in Fremont or Virgin River communities.

Coombs Village may have had a maximum population of two hundred or so people at a single time, assuming that a maximum of forty dwellings were occupied concurrently and a typical family consisted of five persons. Sometime around 1200, the entire village was burned, perhaps intentionally in view of the absence of foodstuffs and portable artifacts. Evidence of violence is lacking. The former residents quite likely returned to the Kayenta area to the south, never to reoccupy Coombs Village.

Following the excavation of the ruins in the late 1950s the site was reburied for protection. Anasazi State Park in Boulder today contains a replica of a six-room Anasazi dwelling and a museum displaying artifacts and exhibits about the ancient site. Some of the remains have been stabilized and are open to the public daily for self-guided tours.

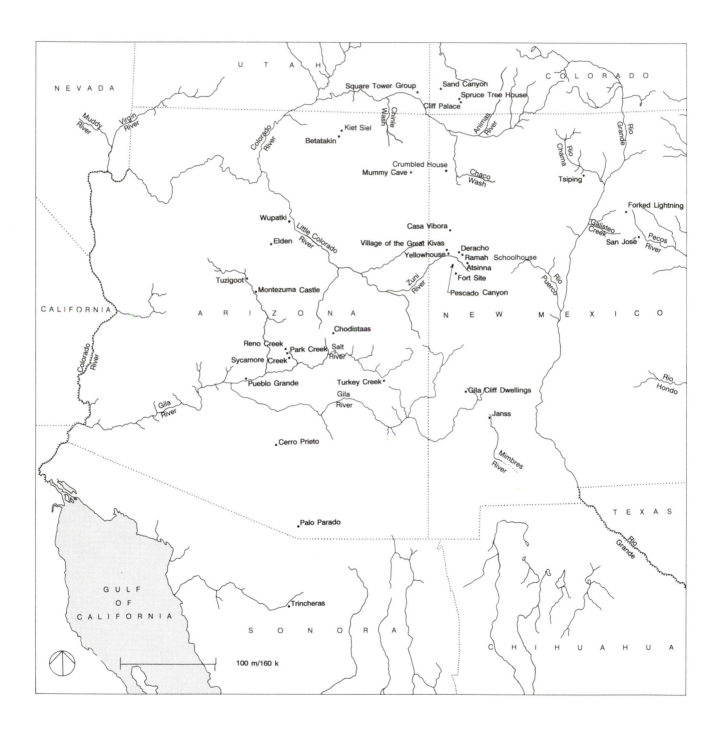

The time period from 1140 to 1300 spans the years from the cessation of architectural creativity in Chaco Canyon to the end of the region-wide Great Drought of 1276 to 1299. This seems to be a time of widespread unrest throughout the Southwest and of adjustment to varying local conditions. Mogollon pueblos continued to develop in the highlands of the Southwest. Platform mounds within rectangular enclosures gained increasing sophistication in Hohokam communities on the irrigated desert plains, while upland Hohokam settlements continued to develop in isolated sites to the south.

Salado towns in the upper Salt River and Tonto Basin areas appear to incorporate Hohokam ideas from the southwest, Anasazi influences from the north, and perhaps new ideas like wall-enclosed compounds and platform mounds from the southeast. During the restless period of the thirteenth century, Zuni people relocated to remote mesa-top sites at the east end of the Zuni Valley. The Sinagua community of Elden Pueblo was active near Flagstaff during the latter twelfth and early thirteenth centuries, and a short while later scattered settlements were concentrated in major pueblos of the Verde Valley.

Kayenta Anasazi constructed new communities in the relative safety of cliff dwellings overlooking fertile valleys in northern Arizona, such as Tsegi Canyon and Canyon de Chelly. Some of the northern San Juan inhabitants of Mesa Verde moved from mesa-top sites down into cliff dwellings, while many of those living elsewhere in the Montezuma Valley assembled in sizable towns or village clusters. Many Anasazi residents of the western Rio Grande Valley relocated to mesa tops above deep canyons, while those dwelling in more open areas to the east gathered into aggregated villages and hamlets.

Mogollon

Like the earlier Mogollon pueblo of Cameron Creek, Turkey Creek Pueblo in east-central Arizona is a single-story settlement divided into north and south sections, which may indicate social divisions called moieties. Larger and more orderly in plan than the Mimbres Valley sites, Turkey Creek has some 335 rooms, an unusually large rectangular kiva, and several streets and plazas predating those of later Hopi and Zuni pueblos.

Chodistaas, an eighteen-room farming hamlet with a wall-enclosed plaza oriented to the southeast, shows indications of lessening Hohokam influence and increasing contact with the Anasazi north of the Mogollon Rim. The Gila Cliff Dwellings in southwestern New Mexico illustrate an alternative type of Mogollon settlement during the latter thirteenth century.

Hohokam

The large complex of wall-enclosed compounds at Pueblo Grande is typical of a number of Hohokam settlements recorded on the valley floor of the Salt and

Gila River Basin. Closely related to an extensive canal system, Pueblo Grande was erected in at least four stages reflecting changes over time rather than a predetermined plan. The remarkable 20-foot- (6-meter-) high platform mound of Pueblo Grande appears to be a more sophisticated version of earlier Hohokam truncated mounds like the one in Snaketown.

Cerro Prieto, a Hohokam upland site north of Tucson, is possibly the largest terraced hill, or *trincheras*, site in the United States; *trincheras* often are found in northern Sonora. Cerro Prieto has more than 250 masonry rooms, an extraordinary covered way flanked by stone walls, and other unusual architectural features. Palo Parado, a Hohokam upland site south of Tucson, was an extensive pit house village during one of several occupations recorded on the terraced hillside site.

Salado

The term Salado sometimes is associated with a distinctive type of pottery known as Gila Polychrome. The ceramic is widely found in the southern Southwest after 1300 and is known to have been manufactured at different sites in various areas at the same time. The ancient people producing the pottery were not from one ethnic stock but represent diverse cultural groups. Not surprisingly, the architectural characteristics of the Mimbres Valley sites in New Mexico have little in common with those of Tonto Basin sites in Arizona although both areas are associated with the term Salado (Germick, personal communication 1992).

One of three Salado sites in the Mimbres Valley, Janss contains twenty-six or so relatively large rooms and is built with massive puddled adobe walls. The unusually large Salado compound of Sycamore Creek is located in the Mazatzal Mountains on the west side of the Tonto Basin. The rectangular compound contains no platform mound and is much less densely developed than such later Salado pueblos as Salome, Besh Ba Gowah, and Schoolhouse Point.

The impressive platform mound compound of Park Creek is a neighbor of the Sycamore Creek site, but is much smaller in size. The adobe-walled enclosure nevertheless contains twenty-seven rooms, a large platform mound, and nine spacious courtyards. Reno Creek, a smaller neighbor of Park Creek, contains only fourteen rooms and one small platform mound; the walled compound probably served primarily as a storage facility for its larger neighbor.

Zuni (Anasazi)

During the twelfth and perhaps the early thirteenth centuries, influences from Chaco Canyon to the north and the Mogollon region to the south began to appear in the intermediate area along the Pescado and Nutria rivers in western New Mexico, the headwaters of the Zuni River. Casa Vibora, a Chacoan outlier with more than 150 rooms, has unusually small rooms, thin walls, and several other non-Chacoan architectural characteristics, suggesting a transition to Zuni ideas. The contemporary Village of the Great Kivas also exhibits characteristics of early Zuni architecture.

Between perhaps 1225 and 1275 the large Zuni pueblos of Deracho and Pescado Canyon were built on highland sites near the Pescado River. Oval-shaped Deracho contained likely more than six hundred rooms up to three stories high. The sprawling room block of Pescado Canyon, a contemporary of Deracho, also is three stories high and probably has more than 720 rooms, most of them very small in size.

During the latter half of the thirteenth century, the Zuni pueblo called the Fort Site was built on a high mesa top near the sites of Pescado Canyon and Atsinna. The rectangular, two-story room block has more than two hundred rooms arranged around a central plaza. Between possibly 1275 and 1325, Yellowhouse, an impressive three-story pueblo with some 425 rooms, was erected on the Pescado River.

Constructed at the same time, neighboring Ramah Schoolhouse is an orderly, two-story pueblo containing an estimated 186 rooms. The last highland Zuni pueblo mentioned in this discussion is Atsinna, a three-story rectangular structure having possibly 875 rooms. During the early fourteenth century most of the Zuni people began to return to the lowlands of the fertile Zuni River Valley to the west.

Sinagua

The volcanic eruption of Sunset Crater caused widespread environmental changes after 1065 for people living in the vicinity of the San Francisco Peaks in north-central Arizona. An example of the ensuing developments is two-story Elden Pueblo, a Sinagua settlement with sixty to seventy rooms in possibly four room blocks and at least nine pit houses. The largest of a number of Sinagua settlements in the vicinity of Flagstaff, Elden Pueblo may have had two community rooms and possibly a ball court.

The thirteenth-century ridgetop pueblo of Tuzigoot contains an estimated 110 rooms overlooking the fertile valley of the Verde River where Sinagua farmers practiced irrigation, an indication of probable Hohokam influence. The spectacular cliff dwelling of Montezuma Castle, one of forty major Sinagua settlements in the Verde Valley, was erected by Sinagua builders who may have learned the art of pueblo building from the Kayenta Anasazi to the north.

Kayenta Anasazi

Three spectacular cliff dwellings and a large surface pueblo in northern Arizona illustrate Kayenta Anasazi architecture during the twelfth and thirteenth centuries. The 150-room pueblo of Kiet Siel occupies a dramatic cave overlooking Tsegi Canyon in the Navajo National Monument of northwestern Arizona. The somewhat smaller but equally impressive cliff dwelling of neighboring Betatakin probably was built according to a predetermined plan and occupied by a single group of people.

Mummy Cave in Canyon del Muerto occupies two caves containing some ninety rooms linked by a distinctive structure in the Mesa Verde style of architecture. Possibly the residence of as many as sixty people, the cliff dwelling contains three or four kivas, including an unusual roofless ceremonial area in the east cave.

The focus of several Kayenta settlements north of Sunset Crater, Wupatki is a multistory pueblo having more than one hundred rooms, a community plaza, and a rare ball court built of stone. The Kayenta Anasazi eventually abandoned their traditional residences, and many probably migrated to the vicinity of the Hopi mesas where their descendants live today.

San Juan Anasazi

Between 1200 and 1300, probably more than thirty thousand northern San Juan Anasazi lived in the settlements of the Montezuma Valley in southwestern Colorado and southeastern Utah. The largest and perhaps most famous cliff dwelling in Mesa Verde, Cliff Palace has some 220 rooms. The dramatic structure was built in the early thirteenth century by the former occupants of mesa-top settlements like Far View Community. Neighboring Spruce Tree House accommodates perhaps one hundred or more residents in a dramatic cave containing about 114 rooms, eight kivas, and several interior streets and plazas.

The large bipartite pueblo of Sand Canyon contains an estimated 420 rooms, ninety kivas, fourteen towers, and a number of other distinctive architectural features. One of several small clusters of masonry-walled ruins in southwestern Utah, the Square Tower Group is composed of an isolated tower in a narrow valley between two mesa-top pueblos. Located on the slopes of the Chuska Mountains west of Chaco Canyon, the dramatic Anasazi pueblo of Crumbled House consists of a wall-enclosed village with distinctive corner towers built on the point of a mesa top high above a terraced pueblo on the talus slope below.

Rio Grande Anasazi

Situated on a mesa top like many of its contemporaries, Tsiping is a linear arrangement of some 350 rooms in the Chama Valley area of north central New Mexico. One of the easternmost pueblos in this study, oval-shaped San José lies in the Galisteo Basin between the Great Plains and the Rio Grande Valley. The adobe village of Forked Lightning is a straggling aggregation of 143 ground-floor rooms along a tributary of the Pecos River northwest of the San José site.

Contemporary World Architecture

During the thirteenth century, architectural creativity reached new heights of achievement in the Eastern United States. Two large ceremonial centers with truncated earth platforms flanking large double plazas, Winterville and Lake George, were under construction in the Lower Mississippi Valley. On a peninsula formed by the Harpeth River south of Nashville, the geometrically disciplined site of Mound Bottom consisted of more than a dozen truncated platforms oriented with respect to a main plaza bounded by an embankment. Meanwhile, in the Ohio Valley construction began on the Angel and Kincaid sites, two exceptionally large, D-shaped ceremonial centers having extensive residential areas within perimeter palisades (Morgan 1980).

About the same time in Mesoamerica, the Toltec occupation of the Yucatán Peninsula introduced new ideas from the Central Plateau of Mexico to Maya architecture. Examples at Chichén Itzá include a circular astronomical observatory, the monumental Temple of Kulkulcán, and extensive colonnades with slender columns and relatively thin walls. One of the three principal Maya cities in the Yucatán, Mayapán gained increasing power and urbanity, while architectural and artistic creativity declined.

Early in the thirteenth century, Chichimec invaders from the north established their first capital at Tenayuca on the Central Plateau of Mexico. The newcomers introduced the distinctive new architectural idea of twin temples with twin stairways on the same platform, an idea subsequently widely adopted by the Aztecs and others (Heyden & Gendrop 1973).

On the Micronesian island of Phonpei, elaborate megalithic construction utilizing immense basalt columns began in Nan Madol under the leadership of the *saudeleur*, the paramount chief who unified the districts of the island for the first time in the 1200s. On the island of Kosrae the initial phase of expansion began at Leluh late in the thirteenth century with the erection of modest coral and basalt compounds in the shallow lagoon. Around the same time construction and occupation of villages reached its peak on the Rock Islands of the Palau archipelago, and the construction of special purpose houses elevated on stone foundations called *latte* continued in the Mariana Islands (Morgan 1988).

TURKEY CREEK
Mogollon

About 60 miles (96 kilometers) east of Globe in east-central Arizona lies Turkey Creek Pueblo, a thirteenth-century ruin containing possibly 335 rooms. The site is situated on a low, grassy ridge on the south bank of Turkey Creek at an elevation of about 6,000 feet (1,829 meters). Pine, juniper, and piñon dominate the surrounding area.

The single-story masonry pueblo is organized in north and south divisions, or moieties as dual social divisions are called in the present-day pueblos of the Rio Grande. Near the center of the pueblo is a rectangular great kiva measuring approximately 35 by 50 feet (11 by 16 meters). The great kiva adjoins both of Turkey Creek's room blocks, serving to separate as well as to join the two divisions.

The reconstructed plan presented here is based on thorough documentation by Julie C. Lowell (1991). Together the room blocks measure at most 245 by 270 feet (75 by 82 meters). Two small plazas are located in the north block, and a large plaza lies southeast of the great kiva between the two divisions. One street leads west from the great kiva, and another interconnects the two small plazas.

Turkey Creek also contains four early pit houses, several outlying room blocks, and a circle of eight midden and burial mounds containing at least twenty-seven cremations and a larger number of burials. Volcanic tuff and basalt found in the vicinity of the site were used to construct the pueblo's masonry walls. Bones recovered from the site are of

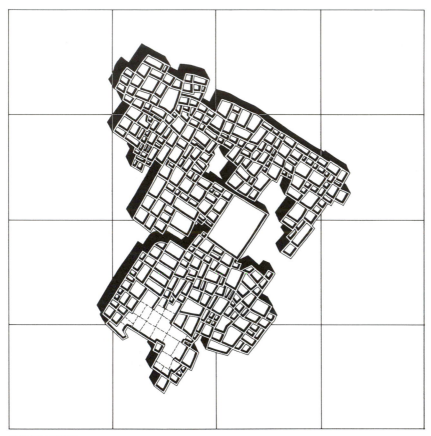

TURKEY CREEK

crements and was abandoned gradually, perhaps by one household at a time. The last residents may have moved to nearby Point of Pines pueblo, a contemporary community about 3 miles (5 kilometers) to the south. Why Turkey Creek was abandoned is unknown. Prehistoric people living in the vicinity quite likely thrived for another century and a half.

Archaeologists from the University of Arizona excavated all but twenty-one of the pueblo's estimated 335 rooms in 1958, 1959, and 1960. Material collected at Turkey Creek is stored in the Arizona State Museum. After the rooms were excavated and photographed, they were backfilled for preservation.

rabbit, deer, antelope, rodent, dog, bighorn sheep, turkey, and bear.

Tree-ring dates and ceramics collected on the site suggest construction and occupation of Turkey Creek between A.D. 1225 and 1286. Earlier pit house villages in the vicinity are designated Mogollon, but later surface structures generally are referred to as Western Pueblos.

A typical dwelling in Turkey Creek quite likely consisted of one large habitation room, one or two intermediate-size activity rooms, and two or three small store rooms. A full range of domestic and manufacturing ac-

tivities occurred in the dwelling. Roof hatches in living or working rooms appear to provide access into dwellings, and doors interconnected rooms within typical suites.

At its height Turkey Creek seems to have been organized on four social levels. The basic unit was the household. Households formed perhaps twenty groups. In turn eight groups comprised the south division, and an estimated twelve groups made up the north division. The fourth social level was the pueblo as a whole represented by the great kiva.

Turkey Creek probably grew by in-

CHODISTAAS
Mogollon

The small Mogollon farming settlement of Chodistaas is located in the forested mountains of east-central Arizona approximately 100 miles (160 kilometers) northeast of Phoenix. The site lies on a bluff overlooking a large, fertile valley about a mile (1.6 kilometers) north of Grasshopper Pueblo. Chodistaas contains eighteen one-story rooms built with dressed stone walls and a relatively large walled open space or community plaza, which may reflect the activities of the pueblo's inhabitants.

One of several farming settlements established in the vicinity of Grasshopper during the thirteenth century, Chodistaas measures overall roughly 157 feet (48 meters) square. The somewhat irregularly shaped plaza has maximum dimensions of possibly 79 by 92 feet (24 by 28 meters). Several of the rectangular rooms in the small pueblo seem to be U-shaped; apparently they have walls on only three sides and are open on the fourth. The basis of the reconstruction proposed here is a 1984 plan published by J. Jefferson Reid (1989 : fig. 10).

Tree-ring dating and careful excavations at the site have produced a relatively well defined sequence for the building of Chodistaas. Initial construction probably began around A.D. 1263 with the north group of nine rooms and perhaps the plaza. The four contiguous rooms near the southwest corner of the plaza very likely were added in 1280. All of the remaining rooms and features apparently were completed during the mid 1280s.

The period of the Great Drought from 1276 to 1299 appears to have

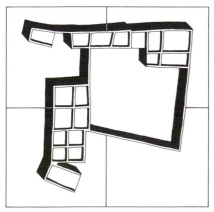

CHODISTAAS

been a time of unrest in the Grasshopper region and elsewhere in the Southwest. One reason for adding rooms to Chodistaas during the 1280s may have been to increase the storage capacity of the pueblo, thereby enhancing its ability to survive environmental adversities. Before 1300 Chodistaas and two nearby contemporary pueblos were burned and abandoned. Some of the former residents may have moved a short distance to the south where Grasshopper Pueblo was being established.

The room sizes at Chodistaas ranged most likely from 170 to 540 square feet (16 to 50 square meters). The average area was 312 square feet (29 square meters), almost twice that of Grasshopper, where the average room contained only 175 square feet (16.3 square meters). A typical Chodistaas household seems to have consisted of two rooms serving variously for manufacturing, storage, cooking, and sleeping. Compared with the residents of Grasshopper, those of Chodistaas may have made greater use of outdoor areas and shared domestic spaces and activities on a more informal basis.

Initially, occupancy at Chodistaas appears to have been part-time, but toward the end the residents may have lived in the pueblo throughout the year. The change in the pattern of occupancy may reflect a reduced emphasis on hunting and gathering subsistence and an increased reliance on dry farming to produce corn, beans, squash, and cotton. In the Grasshopper region the thirteenth century also seems to have been a period of decreasing contacts with Hohokam people to the south and increasing influences from the Anasazi to the north.

GILA CLIFF DWELLINGS
Mogollon

Located in southwestern New Mexico approximately 44 miles (70 kilometers) north of Silver City, the Gila Cliff Dwellings occupy six natural caves some 180 feet (55 meters) above the floor of a rugged canyon in the Mogollon Mountains. The creek flowing through the canyon joins the West Fork of the Gila River about 2 miles (3 kilometers) west of T J Ruin. The caverns extend roughly 500 feet (152 meters) along the south-facing cliff face and are at most 33 feet (10 meters) high.

Situated at an altitude of well more than a mile (1.6 kilometers) above sea level, only the easternmost cave is inaccessible. The other five cliff dwellings contain the relatively well preserved remains of rooms housing possibly forty to fifty residents. Passageways interconnect the three central caverns. The earliest settlers in the vicinity most likely were Mogollon people who lived in pit houses and raised limited crops on modest plots along the edges of creeks and on riverbanks; they also hunted game, gathered wild plants, and traded with neighboring communities.

Around the year 1000 strong Anasazi influences from the north appeared in the Mimbres region. Surface room blocks were built, sometimes with T-shaped doorways, coursed masonry walls, and two-story structures. Tree-ring dates provided by numerous surviving wood beams suggest that the Gila Cliff Dwellings were built during the 1270s and continued to be occupied for an estimated thirty to forty years.

The caverns contain a total of forty rooms, which accommodated perhaps

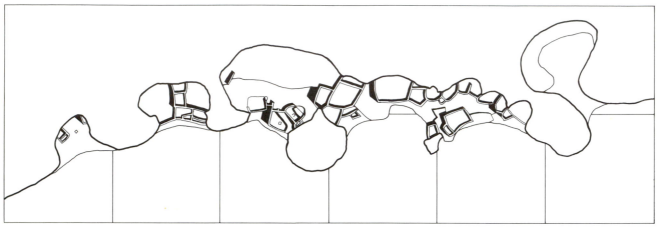

GILA CLIFF DWELLINGS

ten or fifteen families. The nearby creek afforded a dependable source of water throughout the year. Douglas fir, ponderosa and piñon pines, Arizona walnut, Gambel oak, canyon grape, and yucca supplied building materials and fuel for cooking and heating. Other wild plants provided food, clothing, and medicine, and the surrounding wilderness abounded with deer, rabbits, and other game.

Of volcanic origin, the site recalls somewhat the character of Walnut Creek near Flagstaff where Sinagua people briefly inhabited natural caves, although the population there was much greater and the scale was less intimate than I found the Gila Cliff Dwelling to be. The first recorded visit to the caverns was made in 1884 by Adolph Bandelier, the noted geologist, archaeologist, and historian who traveled extensively in the Southwest.

The rooms of the Gila Cliff Dwellings typically have uneven floors cut into the stone in some places and filled in others. The floors often occur on several levels and are plastered. Fire pits are located in the floors of living rooms, and the roofs of the caves are blackened with soot, indicating the repeated use of hearths. Stone-lined grain bins, *metates*, and *manos* denote spaces used to grind corn.

The stone walls of the cliff dwellings are laid with mortar and are plastered on their interior surfaces. Some rooms are entered by means of one or more doors, while others are entered through roof hatches. A few of the rooms are two stories high where the vertical clearance within the cave permits; other structures appear to be unfinished.

Narrow catwalks, ladders, and passageways interconnect the rooms of the three central caverns. During pleasant weather most activities presumably took place on roof tops or in plazas, recalling similar functional spaces at Cliff Palace and Spruce Tree House in Mesa Verde. The caves of the Gila Cliff Dwellings face south to capture the sunlight during long alpine winters when snow drifts several feet high accumulate in the shadows of mountain valleys and canyon walls.

One of the most beautiful and extensive wilderness regions of the Southwest, the area around the Gila Cliff Dwellings during the latter nineteenth century was the stronghold of Geronimo, the legendary Apache guerilla leader who for many years eluded capture by the American army. Now part of the Gila Cliff Dwellings National Monument, the caves are open to the public and may be entered and viewed at first hand.

PUEBLO GRANDE
Hohokam

The large earthen mound of Pueblo Grande contains the remains of one of the largest Hohokam platform mound compounds still in existence. Incorporated today into a City of Phoenix park, the prehistoric site is located on the north bank of the Salt River about 8 miles (13 kilometers) northwest of its ancient contemporary, Los Muertos. The Hohokam people were desert farmers who lived in southern Arizona from early in the Christian era until about a century before the Spanish arrived in the Southwest.

The prehistoric people constructed extensive canal systems to provide river water for their settlements and farm plots. They grew corn, cotton, and other crops, traded over a wide geographical area, and were accomplished stone and shell carvers. Hundreds of pit houses and adobe compounds, numerous cemeteries and middens, and other features probably remain buried at Pueblo Grande (Downum and Bostwick 1993).

Traces of more than a dozen prehistoric canals are situated less than 1,500 feet (457 meters) south of the platform mound. The extent of the greater settlement is estimated to have been perhaps 1,100 acres (450 hectares) in an overall area measuring possibly 1 by 2 miles (1.6 by 3.2 kilometers). Central Pueblo Grande is believed to encompass some 400 acres (162 hectares) of which only one-fourth lies within the municipal park.

The site's most impressive feature is the 20-foot- (6-meter-) high platform mound constructed of adobe, caliche, stone, river cobbles, and wood posts. According to the plan provided by Christian E. Downum and dated 21

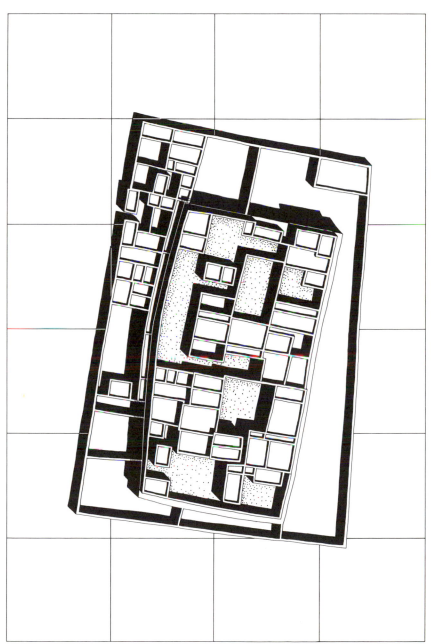

PUEBLO GRANDE

November 1991, the south and west walls of the compound measure 264 and 383 feet (80.5 and 116.8 meters), respectively. The dimensions of the platform mound inside the compound are at most 151 by 281 feet (46 by 85.5 meters).

The platform mound of Pueblo Grande is one of more than forty such structures recorded in south-central Arizona; of these, twenty-three are found in the Salt River valley (Gregory 1987). Platform mounds are known to have been constructed well before the Christian era at Poverty Point in the Eastern United States and San Lorenzo in Central Mexico (Morgan 1980: 3). Clear evidence exists, however, for the indigenous development of the idea of platform mounds at several well-documented Hohokam sites.

The low circular platform mound at Snaketown represents an earlier stage in the development of Hohokam platform mounds. The mound was approximately 40 feet (12 meters) in diameter and 4.25 feet (1.3 meters) high; its sides sloped and its summit was flat. In time the platform was capped by the first of eight layers of caliche, the last cap being encircled by a palisade of posts perhaps anticipating a later adobe wall enclosure (Gregory 1987: 186).

The platform mound of Pueblo Grande most likely was constructed in at least four phases between perhaps A.D. 1150 and 1350. It appears to have reached its ultimate size and shape through the merging of two smaller rectangular mounds, one to the north and one to the south. Retaining walls were built of coursed caliche adobe, and the platform area was filled with household trash, architectural debris, and sterile soil.

Internal walls are built in some mounds, perhaps to act as buttresses. Rectangular wall enclosures surround later platform mounds, such as those of Los Muertos and Casa Grande as well as Pueblo Grande. With a single known exception, rectangular Hohokam platform mounds are oriented with respect to a north-south axis.

Residential structures with adobe walls and courtyards with *ramadas* are found on top of the platform mound of Pueblo Grande. Many of the rooms have plastered floors. A 35-by-60-foot (11-by-18-meter) courtyard appears in the north-central area of the platform. Spectators could sit on the rooftops and walls surrounding the courtyard while watching ceremonies.

The main entry into the compound seems to be located toward the north end of the west wall. Here two rooms flank the 7-foot- (2.1-meter-) wide entry like guard houses. Only six other rooms engage the perimeter wall. Access to interior rooms apparently is by means of doorways and roof hatches with ladders.

Over two hundred ball courts are recorded in Arizona; of these eighty are in the Salt River Valley but many have been destroyed. The remains of three ball courts are found at Pueblo Grande, one each to the north, northwest, and south. Presumably built between 1050 and 1200, the small ball court to the north measures 35 by 82 feet (11.7 by 25 meters). The north court is oriented north to south and has stone markers at both ends and in the middle.

The maximum population for Pueblo Grande is estimated to be one thousand people, about twice the number estimated for Snaketown. The community appears to control the supply of canal water to several populous villages and may have been an administrative center for a larger area of the Salt River Valley. Carved marine shell, distinctive pottery, and other items suggest that Pueblo Grande also was an important trade center.

In 1964 the National Park Service designated Pueblo Grande a National Landmark. Today the City of Phoenix maintains a one-hundred-acre park containing the archaeological remains and the Pueblo Grande Museum. Located at 4619 East Washington Street, the site is open to the public daily.

CERRO PRIETO
Hohokam

The terraced hillside village of Cerro Prieto is located approximately 40 miles (64 kilometers) northwest of Tucson in south-central Arizona. The well-preserved, thirteenth-century Hohokam site overlooks Los Robles Wash and the Santa Cruz River to the northeast. Meaning "dark hill" in Spanish, Cerro Prieto is literally carved into the lower slopes of an 800-foot- (244-meter-) high volcanic mountain some 5 miles (8 kilometers) west of the town of Red Rock.

Cerro Prieto technically is referred to as a *trincheras* site. The word *trinchera* means "entrenchment" in Spanish; an early European observer

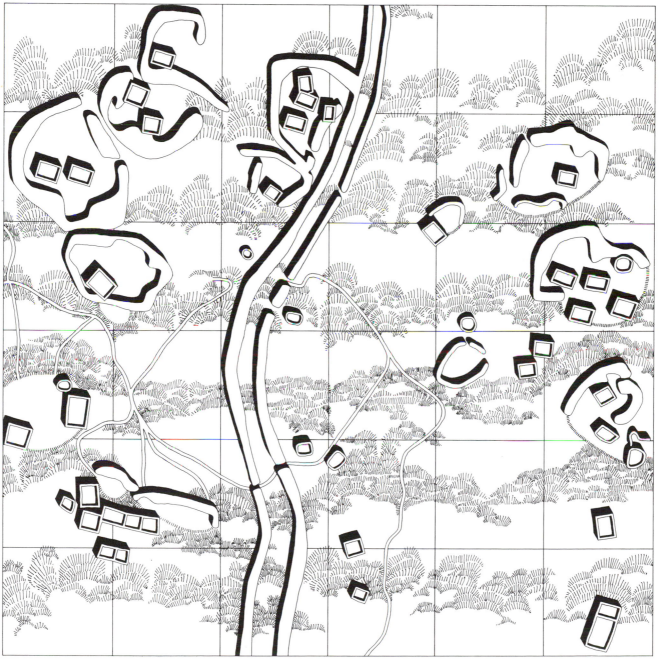

CERRO PRIETO, NORTHWEST AREA

referred to a series of stone walls on a hillside as a hillside fortress, or *cerro de trincheras* (Di Peso 1974: 365). Perhaps the largest *trincheras* site in the United States, Cerro Prieto appears to be an adaptation of hillside terracing systems developed in northern Mexico.

The largest and best preserved *trincheras* site on the continent, Cerro de las Trincheras, is located near the town of Trincheras, Sonora, about 135 miles (216 kilometers) south of Tucson. From a distance the entire mountain takes on the appearance of a stepped pyramid, an impression that some observers suggest is intentional (Downum 1990).

In all, Cerro Prieto contains more than 250 rectangular and circular stone rooms, dozens of artificial terraces and wall-enclosed plazas, an elaborate system of trails and passageways dug into the hillside, concentrations of fire-cracked rocks associated with roasting pits, and parallel stone walls dividing the community into east and west precincts. The partial reconstruction presented here is based on a map prepared by Christian E. Downum, Douglas B. Craig, and John E. Douglas between 1983 and 1986.

The stone walls, terraces, and other components of Cerro Prieto extend over an area measuring perhaps 1,600 by 2,300 feet (500 by 700 meters). The reconstruction presents a 600-foot (183-meter) square area in the northwest section of the site showing walled compounds, rooms, trails, and the central passage way. This is the densest concentration of structures on the hillside.

Most of Cerro Prieto's extensive structures are built on the lower third of the north-facing hillside. A large

prehistoric stone quarry occupies the summit at an elevation of 2,860 feet (842 meters) above sea level. At the base of the hill, prehistoric cornfields are found still intact; here many centuries ago farmers cleared fields and dammed slopes to divert water into small garden plots.

The architectural elements of Cerro Prieto are distributed along a roughly 2,300-foot- (700-meter-) long arc between the elevations of 1,800 and 2,100 feet (550 and 640 meters) above sea level. Here the site is covered by fallen stones, scattered pottery, shell jewelry, stone tools, broken grinding stones, and burned human and animal bones. Ceramics recovered from the site suggest occupancy between possibly A.D. 1150 and 1300 to 1325 or so (Downum 1990).

The massive stone walls dividing the site form a corridor or passageway ranging in width from more or less 10 to 30 feet (3 to 9 meters). The huge parallel walls are constructed of boulders stacked up to 6.6 feet (2 meters) above grade and varying in thickness from around 3 to 10 feet (1 to 3 meters). The massive structure ascends the hillside probably 460 feet (140 meters) vertically in a horizontal distance of an estimated 1,150 feet (350 meters), a slope ratio of 1 to 2.5.

A total of 232 rooms are recorded at Cerro Prieto. Of these, 169 seem to be arranged in forty-six clusters of two to nine rooms each. The remaining rooms are found in isolated locations; they may represent storage facilities or serve other special purposes. Whether rectangular or curvilinear, all the rooms appear to serve domestic functions.

The masonry walls of Cerro Prieto are constructed either of rough stacks of large stones laid horizontally one

on top of the other or of rubble cores consisting of pebbles and small cobbles filling the space between two parallel courses of larger stones. Both types of masonry present flat stone surfaces on the interior sides of walls. The site's largest recorded room measures most likely 15.4 by 24.3 feet (4.7 by 7.4 meters).

All twelve of Cerro Prieto's walled compounds are concentrated generally in an area of 300 by 1,000 feet (90 by 300 meters). Five compounds lie east of the walled passage and seven lie to the west. Large, often irregularly shaped boulder walls 3 to 6 feet (1 to 2 meters) high usually enclose the compounds on one or more sides. The compounds contain one to four rooms, except for one compound that has none.

The most extensive compound in Cerro Prieto appears to measure 92 by 105 feet (28 by 32 meters). The compounds usually are constructed by a combination of cutting into the hillside upslope and filling in downslope. The masonry walls of the compounds generally display a high quality of workmanship.

At least thirty terraces are found at Cerro Prieto, some retained by stone walls 13 feet (4 meters) high and up to 200 feet (60 meters) long. Five huge terraces are arranged like steps up the northeast face of the hillside. The function of the terraces is unknown; possible uses include garden plots, outside work areas for houses or house clusters, or such rituals as cremations.

The numerous trails of Cerro Prieto create an elaborate pedestrian network sometimes involving switchbacks. Generally 20 to 30 inches (50 to 75 centimeters) wide, the trails often have smooth surfaces consisting of bedrock cemented with caliche. Recessed into the rocky surface of the hill, two trails lead across the walled passage bisecting the site.

About half a mile (800 meters) east of Cerro Prieto lies Pan Quemado, one of Arizona's largest collections of rock art. Petroglyphs also are found in association with many of the house clusters in Cerro Prieto. In addition, Pan Quemado is the site of a prehistoric reservoir, probably an important source of water for inhabitants of the nearby *trincheras.*

Other *trincheras* sites in Arizona are Fortified Hill near Gila Bend and Linda Vista 15 miles (24 kilometers) northwest of Tucson. Unlike such Hohokam sites as Snaketown or Los Muertos, the structural remains of Cerro Prieto lie on the surface, not buried beneath the ground. Certainly one of the most remarkable Hohokam sites, Cerro Prieto now is a State Park and is listed on the National Register of Historic Places. However, site visits are not allowed at the present time.

PALO PARADO
Hohokam

The extensive Hohokam pit house village of Palo Parado lies on a 50-foot- (16-meter-) high bluff west of the Santa Cruz River in southern Arizona. Located approximately 50 miles (80 kilometers) south of Tucson, the site lies between the towns of Tumacacori and Nogales on the border with Mexico. The reconstruction presented here shows Palo Parado as it may have appeared during the second of three successive periods of occupation.

The site probably was occupied initially from A.D. 800 or earlier until 1050 or later. During this period the residents built perhaps forty pit houses in several long irregular rows along the elevated terraces overlooking the river. A unique architectural feature of the community was a roughly 10-foot- (3-meter-) wide, stone-paved street extending possibly 237 feet (72.3 meters) along the east side of the pit house village.

A large dance plaza was situated east of the paved street on a level promontory close to the river. Unlike contemporary Hohokam villages of the Tucson Basin, however, no ballcourt is found at Palo Parado (Wilcox 1987:235). Cremations and burial rituals in the village closely parallel Hohokam practices, and iron pyrite mirrors found in the ruins clearly indicate trade with Mesoamerica.

The earliest occupants of Palo Parado may have been an independent group of local people who were beginning to assume Hohokam characteristics. After abandonment and an occupational hiatus of perhaps a century, the terraced site was reoccupied. The reconstructed drawing presented here shows the site during the second and most extensive period of development.

The basis of the reconstruction are drawings and a description published by David R. Wilcox (1987:fig. 4) based largely on reanalysis of site information developed by the late Charles C. Di Peso (1956). Possibly sometime between 1150 and 1200 a large, new pit house village began to appear on the terraced bluff of Palo Parado. The new settlement grew to have perhaps a dozen or more clusters with courtyards, each consisting of three to eight pit houses.

The residents of each cluster most likely were members of the same extended family or clan. The pit houses faced common courtyards with defined areas for work, cooking pits, sunshades called *ramadas,* storage areas, and burial grounds. Low walls enclose the perimeter of the site and define the limits of several clusters. The westernmost cluster appears to be the only one surrounded entirely by a low wall.

Because the large site extends some 1,100 feet (335 meters) along the bluff, the reconstruction is presented in overlapping north and south sections. In all, the reconstruction shows more than seventy pit houses, two reservoirs, all or part of twelve distinct courtyards, and a number of low walls. The pit houses range in size from 100 to almost 600 square feet (9.3 to almost 55.7 square meters).

The south section of the reconstruction shows all or part of nine clusters on two terraces, one about 13 feet (4 meters) lower than the other. Several more pit houses lie beyond the east edge of the drawing. The north section presents both of Palo Parado's reservoirs, all of five clusters, and parts of three others.

The linear courtyard extending from the north to south in the north section recalls the rows of pit houses built during the first period of occupancy at Palo Parado. Sometime around 1350 or so, the terraced site was abandoned for the second time. Many dwellings may have been

PALO PARADO, SOUTH PORTION

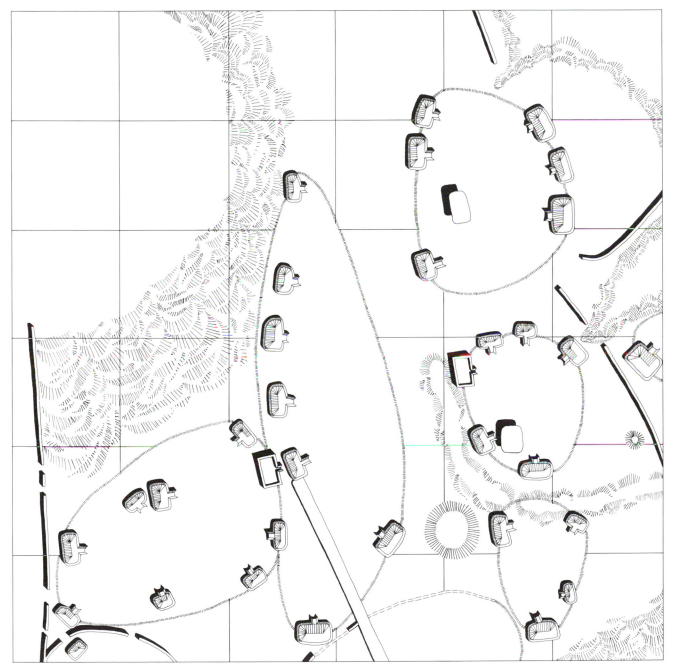

PALO PARADO, NORTH PORTION

burned simultaneously, suggesting the possibility of a ritual abandonment or possibly a catastrophe resulting from social unrest (Wilcox 1987:239).

Like other Hohokam pit houses, those of Palo Parado generally have short, relatively wide entries with several steps descending from exterior ground level to interior floor level. By contrast, entries into Mogollon pit houses often are comparatively long and narrow in order to accommodate entry ramps rather than stairs. The reconstructions for Harris, Mogollon Village, and early Cameron Creek illustrate the typical Mogollon pit houses.

After several centuries of abandonment, Palo Parado was reoccupied during the historic period for the third and final time. A small group of Tohono O'odham people constructed a sturdy compound and three adobe houses on one of the northeast terraces previously occupied by pit houses. The final occupation also concluded with a disaster of some kind, possibly during the eighteenth or nineteenth century (Wilcox 1987:247).

JANSS
Salado

One of three surviving Salado sites in the Mimbres Valley of New Mexico, Janss is located approximately 180 miles (290 kilometers) southwest of Albuquerque. The puddled adobe pueblo is situated on the first terrace above the Mimbres River at an elevation of 6,200 feet (1,890 meters) above sea level. Although Janss supposedly had thirty rooms, the reconstruction presented here shows only twenty-six in a single-story room block measuring overall roughly 70 by 115 feet (21 by 35 meters).

Janss is a relatively small Salado site. Each of the twenty-one known Salado sites in New Mexico has from thirty to one hundred rooms, and those in Arizona contain from twelve to 250 (LeBlanc 1976). Large rooms are characteristic of Salado architecture; those of Janss range in area from 60 to 390 square feet (5.6 to 36 square meters). The average size of Salado rooms recorded elsewhere is 226 square feet (21 square meters).

Another characteristic of Salado architecture is puddled adobe walls. Perhaps the best known example of this type of construction is Casa Grande, the multistory Hohokam great house located some 185 miles (300 kilometers) west of the Janss site. The geographical distribution of Salado sites is not entirely clear; they may be found from western Arizona across southern New Mexico and possibly into Texas.

The Salado phase of southwestern prehistory is imperfectly understood (Stuart & Gauthier 1988:208–210). Some authorities suggest the time frame of possibly A.D. 1150 to 1450 for Salado cultural developments, in-

JANSS

cluding particularly the distinctive type of pottery known as Gila Polychrome sometime after 1300. The pottery is not known to have been produced after 1450.

Whether the Salado phase represents a migration of people or the spread of ideas or both remains to be determined. The topographical settings for classic Salado communities usually are areas around riverine systems, particularly the Gila and Salt rivers. Salado means "salt" in Spanish.

The Salado culture seems to have developed in central Arizona from Anasazi and Mogollon ideas. In time the Hohokam people, participating in a larger sphere of interaction, took up such Salado ideas as building aboveground pueblos on their own. Similarly, the Salado apparently developed techniques for irrigation and stone and shell working.

SYCAMORE CREEK
Salado

The remains of a large Salado compound are located on the north bank of Sycamore Creek about 2 miles (3 kilometers) west of Tonto Creek of central Arizona. The site occupies a narrow ridgetop sloping down toward the east and defined by a deep ravine to the north. The cobble masonry walls of the compound extend approximately 555 feet (170 meters) along the ridge from east to west and at most 130 feet (40 meters) from north to south.

Situated in the uplands of the Mazatzal Mountains roughly 50 miles (80 kilometers) northeast of Phoenix, the Sycamore Creek site is one of the largest compounds in the Tonto Basin. The compound's walls extend to the outer edges of the ridgetop, but most of the spaces within the enclosure are open-air courtyards or plazas rather than roofed rooms. In all, the reconstructed plan presented here suggests fifty-seven rooms of modest size and thirty-six relatively large open spaces.

The reconstruction is based on a scaled map recorded by Joseph S. Crary and information provided by Stephen Germick of the Tonto National Forest in 1991. Although the perimeter walls of the Sycamore Creek compound enclose an area greater than that of Salome, the latter contains more than three times the number of ground-floor rooms but comparatively little open space. Sycamore Creek seems to represent a somewhat earlier stage of Salado architectural development involving lower site densities and single-story construction exclusively.

Like Hohokam compounds of the Salt and Gila Basin, early Salado com-

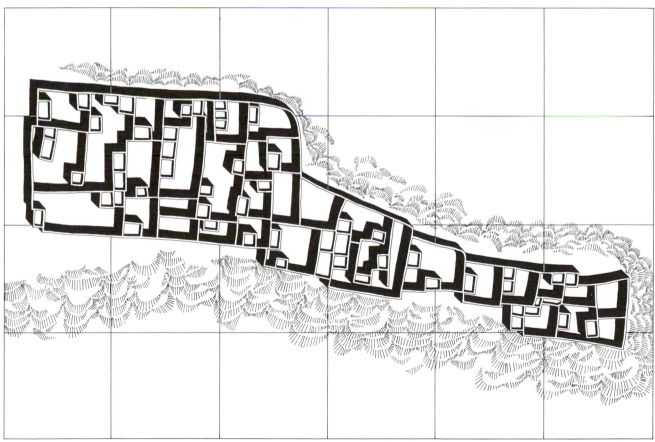

SYCAMORE CREEK

pounds are more or less rectangular in plan and have fewer enclosed rooms than courtyards or patios. The Salado community of Sycamore Creek appears to be an aggregation of compounds representing several stages of construction, rather than a structure built in a single phase according to a predetermined plan. In time rooms and courtyards were subdivided within each compound, resulting in more but smaller spaces as the community's population increased.

Large granite boulders frequently are incorporated into outer terrace edges and elsewhere in Sycamore Creek. An unusual architectural arrangement appears in the location of rooms near the middle of courtyard walls rather than in corners where only two walls would be required to enclose rooms. Apparently several rectangular rooms have only three walls; they are entirely open on the fourth side. Similar rooms are found at such Mogollon sites as Grasshopper, 50 miles (80 kilometers) or so northeast of Sycamore Creek.

Sycamore Creek is one of more than a thousand Salado sites recorded in the Tonto Basin. The walled site probably reached its maximum level of development sometime in the late 1200s and likely was abandoned around 1300. Contemporary Salado compounds in the Mazatzal piedmont described in this study are Reno Creek and Park Creek. Sycamore Creek was a much larger compound and had many more rooms than its neighbors, but it lacked a platform mound.

PARK CREEK
Hohokam

The impressive Salado platform mound site of Park Creek is located approximately 2 miles (3 kilometers) southwest of Punkin Center in the Tonto Basin of central Arizona. Situated at an altitude of roughly 2,600 feet (792 meters) above sea level, the ruins lie on the south bank of Park Creek in the Mazatzal piedmont about 50 miles (80 kilometers) northeast of Phoenix. The orderly rectangular compound measures at most 170 by 290 feet (52 by 88 meters).

The most distinctive architectural feature of Park Creek is the relatively large platform mound located in the northeast quadrant of the compound. The freestanding podium rises perhaps 6 feet (2 meters) above the plaza level and has seven small rooms on its level summit. Whether the rooms along the west side of the compound also were placed on an elevated base or were two-story structures is unclear.

In all, Park Creek appears to contain twenty-seven rooms and nine more or less rectangular plazas or courtyards. Possibly eighteen rooms are dwellings; the remaining nine may be used for storage or other purposes. The seven large rooms along the compound's west wall have average areas of some 266 square feet (25 square meters) each, while the seven small rooms on the central platform have estimated average areas of 121 square feet (11 square meters) each.

The central platform measures around 58 by 80 feet (17.7 by 24.4 meters) and is enclosed by a wall. A single room may occupy the small truncated mound located northeast of the main platform. Three large rooms on the west side of the east courtyard most likely served communal or ritual functions.

The unbroken wall surrounding Park Creek has no entries but presently is buried by sedimentation in several places. Along the north side the enclosure consists of adobe walls probably 6 feet (2 meters) high above stone foundation courses. A single portal 5 feet (1.5 meters) or so wide leads into the 50-by-60-foot (15-by-18-meter) courtyard west of the central mound.

Walls of rooms and courtyards in the southeast area of the compound consist of adobe reinforced with vertical poles set on base walls four stone courses high. The compound's seven west rooms are constructed of adobe courses reinforced with unshaped granite cobbles and slabs. A cluster of four rooms about 100 feet (30 meters) west of the compound indicated previous occupation of the site during the twelfth century.

Park Creek seems to be a ceremonial and administrative center built and used between 1250 and 1300. The lack of trash at the site suggests a comparatively brief period of occupancy. By comparison, major Hohokam platform mound sites in the Salt and Gila Basin like Pueblo Grande and Casa Grande may have reached their peaks around 1325 (Downum 1991).

First recorded by Adolph F. Bandelier in 1883, Park Creek is an anomaly because of its upland location; Salado platform mound compounds normally are found in river valleys. The 6-foot- (2-meter-) high platform mound presumably contained room-sized masonry cells filled with rubble to serve as the foundation for structures built on the level summit.

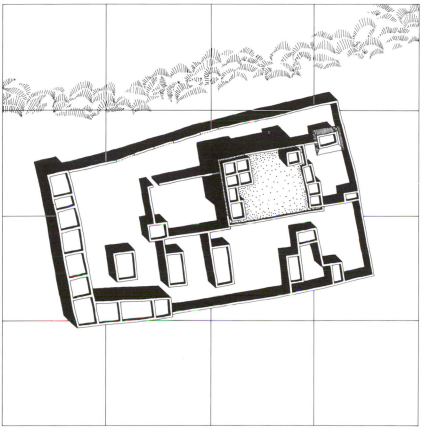

PARK CREEK

RENO CREEK
Hohokam

A Salado compound overlooking Reno Creek is located about 2 miles (3 kilometers) west of Punkin Center in central Arizona. Situated at an altitude of 2,650 feet (807 meters) above sea level, the rectangular enclosure occupies a north-south rise in the Mazatzal piedmont of the Tonto Basin. The ruins lie approximately 4,300 feet (1,300 meters) northwest of the Park Creek site.

The reconstructed plan presented here is based on information provided by Stephen Germick of the Tonto National Forest Office and Joseph S. Crary (Germick & Crary 1990: fig. 4). Overall, the Reno Creek compound measures roughly 150 by 336 feet (46 by 102 meters) and contains perhaps fourteen rooms and nine spacious plazas or courtyards. The site seems to be an aggregation of possibly four or five smaller units added over a period of time.

The most distinctive architectural feature of Reno Creek is the impressive platform mound centered in the south end of the compound. The story-high podium has overall dimensions of possibly 20 by 25 feet (6 by 7.6 meters). A room with stone walls occupies the summit, and another abuts the platform to the west.

The two rooms engaging the north side of the podium most likely are used for storage of some type. Nine of Reno Creek's masonry-walled rooms seem to be dwellings. Typically rectangular in shape, their plan sizes range from possibly 200 to 250 square feet (19 to 23 square meters).

The sizes and shapes of the remaining five rooms at Reno Creek suggest that they were used for storage. One

Within a one-mile (1.6-kilometers) radius of Park Creek, 174 prehistoric sites are found. The sites include residential compounds, house clusters, thermal enclosures, and fieldhouses associated with agricultural plots. Reno Creek, one of the neighboring compounds described in this study, lies less than a mile (1.3 kilometers) to the northwest. The two compounds are similar in size, but Reno Creek has a single small podium and relatively few rooms.

Park Creek may represent an attempt to integrate the resources of upland zones with riverine areas. For example, people living in the Mazatzal piedmont could have provided wood or stone materials in exchange for decorated ceramics, shell, or cotton available in the river valley. One of the reasons for abandoning the uplands around 1300 may be related to below-normal precipitation in central Arizona between 1280 and 1295 (Germick & Crary 1990).

such room lacks a wall on its fourth side, recalling similar spaces in the Sycamore Creek compound and in Mogollon sites like Chodistaas and Grasshopper 50 miles (80 kilometers) or so to the northeast. A formal entry at most 10 feet (3 meters) wide provides access from the east; a second portal around 16 feet (5 meters) wide gives access through the west wall.

Ceramics collected on the site indicate that Reno Creek probably was occupied sometime between 1250 and 1300. At this time Salado compounds were increasing in size and architectural complexity. At Reno Creek and other Salado sites, two dwelling rooms and one store room formed a discrete module, sometimes two stories high. This seems to be the basic module for the structures built on platform mounds.

In view of the site's proximity to Park Creek, Reno Creek more likely served as a local storage facility and administrative center rather than as an elite residence or major political center (Germick & Crary 1990). The development of platform mounds and compounds with spacious plazas may recall similar Hohokam ideas from the Salt and Gila Basin, but the introduction of open-sided rooms and compact room blocks introduces the possibility of Mogollon or Anasazi influences from the north and east.

CASA VIBORA
Zuni (Anasazi)

Casa Vibora illustrates the introduction of Chacoan architectural ideas into the developing Zuni culture. The site is located about 53 miles (85 kilometers) southwest of Pueblo Bonito and 26 miles (42 kilometers) north of present-day Zuni Pueblo. The large multistory pueblo of Casa Vibora is situated at the northeast end of a level ridge on the west side of Fenced-Up Horse Canyon.

Low sandstone cliffs form the southeast edge of the ridge. Open piñon and juniper woodlands cover the steep slope along the northwest edge. The ridge top rises 100 feet (30 meters) above the valley floor at an elevation of 6,900 feet (2,103 meters) above sea level. The remains of a large community extend from Casa Vibora along the ridge to the southwest for a distance of perhaps 1,700 feet (518 meters).

In all, the Fenced-Up Horse Canyon community appears to consist of sixteen masonry pueblos having more than 420 rooms, thirty-seven small kivas, a great kiva, and extensive middens. The community probably was once the focus of a number of widely dispersed settlements.

Architectural characteristics and ceramic samples suggest that Casa Vibora was constructed and occupied between A.D. 1100 and 1250. The massive pueblo seems to have 133 ground-floor rooms, possibly twenty second-floor rooms, at least eleven associated small kivas, an enclosed plaza, and a great kiva. The overall dimensions of the main room block are around 100 by 355 feet (30 by 108 meters).

The great kiva and twenty-six

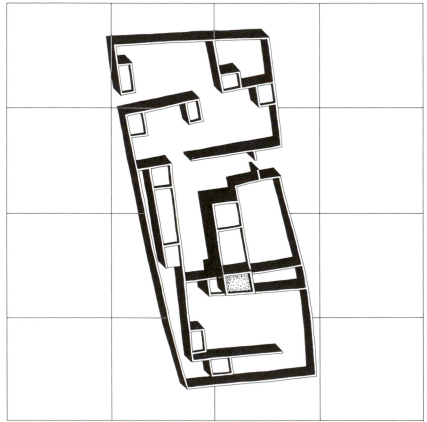

RENO CREEK

rooms in the relatively well preserved pueblo have been excavated. Typical room dimensions range from 6.5 to 13 feet (2 to 4 meters), and no long rooms are apparent. The average room size is more or less 81 square feet (7.5 square meters). Compared to rooms found in pueblos closer to Chaco Canyon, Casa Vibora's rooms generally are smaller in size and are less varied in proportion.

Interior walls average only 12 inches (30 centimeters) in thickness; they frequently are discontinuous, indicating random accretion rather than planned expansion. Within the roughly 57-by-105-foot (17.5-by-32-meter) plaza are the remains of five subterranean kivas, each 16.4 feet (5 meters) or so in diameter. A 26-foot (8-meter) diameter kiva lies southeast of the plaza.

Near the center of the room block's south wing are two subterranean kivas 14 to 16 feet (4.3 to 5 meters) in diameter. The chambers occupy small rectangular courtyards that may serve as antechambers. Subterranean kivas with a surface antechamber also are found at Pueblo Pintado, Muddy Water, Andrews Ruin, and other Chacoan sites in the San Juan Basin.

Immediately south of the pueblo is the community's great kiva, 56 feet (17 meters) in diameter, with an interior perimeter bench 2 feet (60 centimeters) wide. On the chamber's north side is an 8-by-13-foot (2.5-by-4-meter) semisubterranean antechamber or stair. To the west lies a surface structure containing six to eight rooms of varying sizes.

Casa Vibora's walls are built of reddish purple sandstone blocks measuring typically 6 by 12 by 16 inches (15 by 30 by 40 centimeters). Compound walls some 12 inches (30 centimeters)

thick predominate, and occasional core-veneer walls average 20 inches (50 centimeters) in thickness. Adobe most likely covered interior wall surfaces originally. Entryways are both rectangular and T-shaped.

Characteristics of Chacoan architecture found in Casa Vibora include an enclosed courtyard, a multistory room block, a closely associated great kiva, and terraced masses oriented toward the southeast. A number of architectural dissimilarities, however, indicate unique Zuni characteristics. These include small rooms of relatively uniform size, misaligned wings, arbitrary room placements, construction indicating growth by ac-

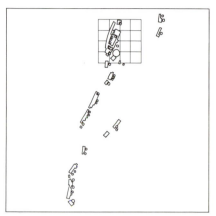

KEY PLAN OF FENCED-UP HORSE CANYON COMMUNITY

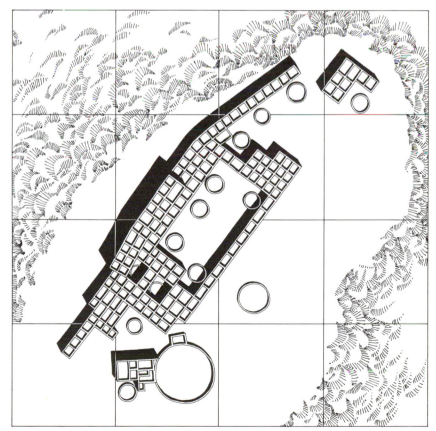

CASA VIBORA

cretion, compound walls of minimum thickness, and the absence of wall-enclosed surface kivas fronting on the plaza.

The relationship of Chacoan architectural ideas to those of the Zuni is not clearly understood. After major activity ceased in Chaco Canyon, the San Juan Basin largely was abandoned. Immigrants moving to the south and west may have contributed to the building traditions of the emerging Zuni culture (Marshall et al. 1979:149–153).

VILLAGE OF THE GREAT KIVAS
Zuni (Anasazi)

The Chacoan outlier called the Village of the Great Kivas is located about 67 miles (108 kilometers) southwest of Pueblo Bonito, some 17 miles (27 kilometers) northeast of Zuni. Despite its name, the community is relatively modest in size. The site is situated on a south-facing slope at the base of a mesa overlooking the broad Nutria Valley.

Ceramics collected on the site indicate human activity in the vicinity from the eleventh to the fourteenth centuries, with major construction during the A.D. 1100s. During this time Anasazi populations were increasing, and structures were added and modified rapidly in the Village of the Great Kivas (Woodbury 1979b). Overall, the site consists of three room blocks containing an estimated total of eighty rooms, three wall-enclosed surface kivas, four pit house kivas, and two great kivas.

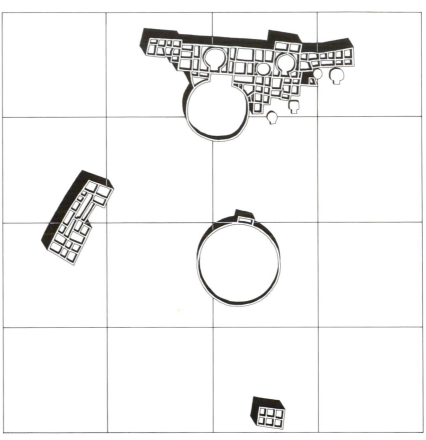

VILLAGE OF THE GREAT KIVAS

According to Frank H. H. Roberts (1932), construction of the one-story stone pueblo began with an orderly rectangular structure containing twelve rooms and two wall-enclosed kivas around 18 feet (5 meters) in diameter. Later additions were three rooms on the west end and the contiguous great kiva to the south. The semisubterranean chamber has an interior diameter of 54 feet (16.5 meters), a bench around its perimeter, and an alcove to the north adjacent to the room block. Four stone pillars 2 to 3 feet (60 to 90 centimeters) square supported the roof of the great kiva.

The initial structures seem to be carefully arranged, but subsequent additions are less orderly. Fifteen rooms grew to the south while the original structure was remodeled to accommodate a third walled kiva. To this were added misaligned room extensions to the east and west with four arbitrarily placed pit house kivas to the southeast. The additions brought the north room block to essentially its final form.

The Village of the Great Kivas also contains a small house with perhaps six rooms to the south, a twenty-room structure to the west, and a second great kiva near the center of the group. The wall enclosing the unexcavated chamber measures 78 feet (24 meters) in diameter. Few great kivas in the Southwest exceed this dimension.

The site presents evidence of people from the south with Mogollon traits living with others from the north having Anasazi traditions. Bonded masonry like Pueblo Bonito's and kiva features, such as floor vaults, illustrate Chacoan influences at the Village of the Great Kivas. During the 1200s Zuni village sizes increased, and many were built on the tops of mesas or hills with commanding views in all directions.

DERACHO
Zuni (Anasazi)

The thirteenth-century Zuni pueblo of Deracho is located on the north bank of the Pescado River possibly 10 miles (16 kilometers) west of the continental divide in west-central New Mexico. Neighboring sites described in this study are Ramah Schoolhouse and Lower Pescado. The site derives its name from the property's owners at the time of Leslie Spier's (1917) visit.

Deracho is situated on the floor of the Ramah Valley at the base of a mesa sloping steeply upward to the northwest. Intermittently flowing Cebola Creek, the closest source of water for the pueblo, lies some 650 feet (200 meters) to the southeast. The ruin occupies a grassy plain at an elevation of 6,850 feet (2,088 meters) above sea level.

The oval plan of Deracho is almost entirely filled with rooms. The pueblo's shape recalls those of the larger

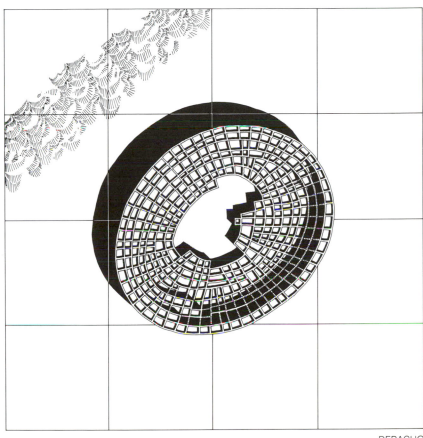

DERACHO

Cienega Site and other elliptical pueblos in the Zuni area. The maximum dimensions of the continuous outer wall are approximately 174 by 226 feet (53 by 69 meters).

Like its contemporary in Pescado Canyon, Deracho is constructed with tan, well-shaped sandstone. The rubble mounds now covering the ruins are more than 6 feet (2 meters) high. J. Walter Fewkes (1891) observed that building stones were being removed from the site to build the modern town of Ramah.

The reconstruction presented here is based on Keith W. Kintigh's plan (1985: fig. 4.10 after Spier 1917: fig. 4a). Assuming an average room size of 76 square feet (7.2 square meters), Deracho would contain almost 350 rooms on its ground floor. Further assuming that half of the rooms had second stories and one-quarter had third stories, the total estimated number of rooms would exceed six hundred.

The average room size and total number for the pueblo of Deracho are somewhat less than those for Pescado Canyon. Ceramic collections, however, suggest that both sites were constructed sometime before A.D. 1250 and that both were occupied until 1275 or so.

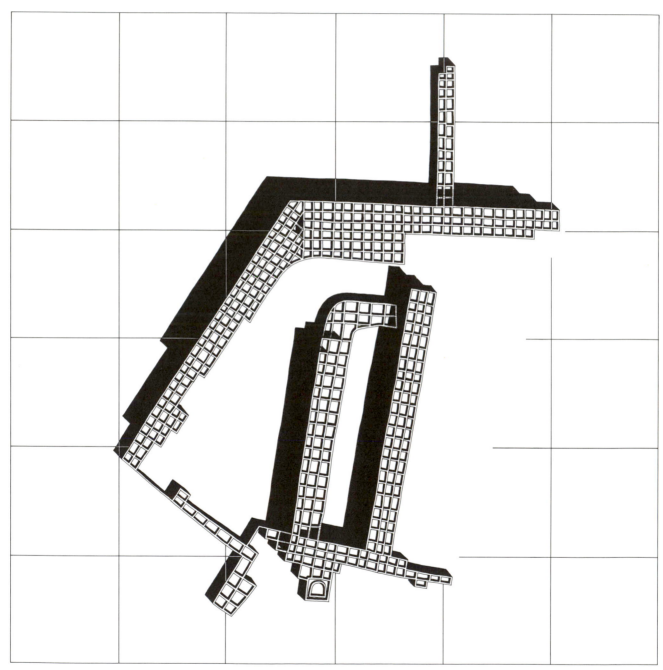

PESCADO CANYON

PESCADO CANYON
Zuni (Anasazi)

The large Zuni pueblo of Pescado Canyon is one of the most recently recorded major sites in Zuni prehistory (Kintigh 1985). Located more or less 4 miles (6.4 kilometers) south of the Pescado River, the pueblo lies roughly 110 miles (176 kilometers) west of Albuquerque in west-central New Mexico. Other prehistoric Zuni sites in the vicinity of Pescado Canyon are Lower Pescado, Deracho, and Yellowhouse.

The ruins are found in a ponderosa pine forest on a mesa top at an altitude of 7,390 feet (2,252 meters) above sea level. The site overlooks Pescado Canyon, a grass-covered plain with scattered juniper and piñon woodlands. At present a small spring in the arroyo wall about 2,300 feet (700 meters) north of the site is the closest source of fresh water.

The reconstruction presented here is based on the map prepared by Andrew Fowler and Barbara Mills (Kintigh 1985) on file with the Zuni Archaeological Program in Zuni, New Mexico. Overall, the Pescado Canyon ruin measures at most 400 by 510 feet (122 by 159 meters). Compared with the compact rectangular plans of Atsinna, Ramah Schoolhouse, or other contemporary Zuni pueblos, the plan of Pescado Canyon seems to be somewhat sprawling and unresolved. The irregular plan consists of linear rows of one to six rooms forming a large plaza oriented to the southeast.

The linear room block within the plaza contains a long, narrow courtyard. At the south end of the structure an approximately 20-foot (6-meter) square room appears to enclose a D-shaped kiva. A long row of some twenty-five rooms extends to the north. The kiva, the north row of rooms, and another row to the southwest seem to be appendages added to the pueblo rather than integral components of the plan like those at Atsinna and Ramah Schoolhouse.

The masonry walls of Pescado Canyon are constructed of well-fitted tan sandstones on both sides of rubble cores. Sandstone outcrops surround the mesa-top site. Some of the site's remaining walls presently rise more than 6 feet (2 meters) in height. Originally, some of the walls quite likely were three stories high.

The reconstruction presented here suggests more than four hundred ground-floor rooms for Pescado Canyon ruin. Assuming half again that number for second-floor rooms and one-quarter that number for a third story, the total estimated number of rooms would be 723. The average room size in one room block is around 86 square feet (8 square meters), somewhat smaller than such contemporary Zuni pueblos as Atsinna.

Ceramics collected at the site indicate that the pueblo probably was constructed sometime before A.D. 1250. About this time the Zuni population began to shift toward a relatively few, very large sites in the highlands toward the east end of the Zuni River Valley. Occupation seems to have continued at Pescado Canyon until 1275 or so.

FORT SITE
Zuni (Anasazi)

Also known as the Crockett Ruin, the Fort Site is perched on top of a mesa about 11 miles (18 kilometers) south of the Pescado River in west-central New Mexico. The site is located less than a mile (1.6 kilometers) from the southeast boundary of the Zuni Indian Reservation. The closest neighboring pueblos described in this study are Atsinna and Pescado Canyon.

Situated at an elevation of 7,510 feet (2,289 meters) above sea level, the Fort Site occupies the highest altitude of the Zuni pueblos in this study. The site is higher by 80 feet (24 meters) than Atsinna, the study's next-highest example. The mesa top is covered by a juniper and piñon woodland with scattered ponderosa pines. To the north is a commanding view of grass-covered Shoemaker Canyon.

This reconstruction is based primarily on a map by Ferguson and Gagner (Kintigh 1985:fig. 4:20) on file with the Zuni Archaeological Program file in Zuni, New Mexico. According to the map's published scale, the site measures very nearly 191 by 242 feet (59 by 74 meters), but Kintigh (1985:39) describes somewhat smaller dimensions. Like Atsinna, Ramah Schoolhouse, and other Zuni pueblos, the Fort Site is a rectangular, multistory room block with a central plaza.

Two-to-four-room-deep rows flank the plaza, forming a room block with a slightly rounded northwest corner. The sunken area in the plaza's southeast corner probably was once a kiva. A roughly 1,200-square-foot (110-square-meter) depression cut into the bedrock some 40 feet (12 meters) east

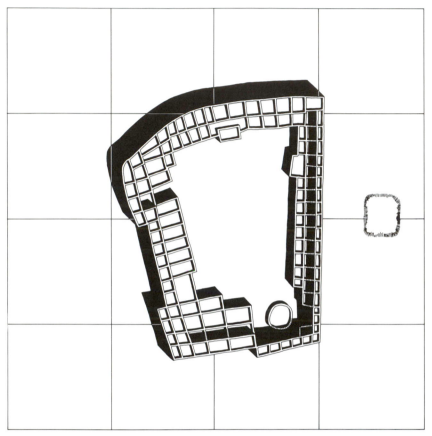

FORT SITE

of the pueblo may have served as a reservoir.

The room sizes shown in the reconstruction average perhaps 146 square feet (13.6 square meters), much larger than those of other thirteenth-century Zuni pueblos. The rooms depicted along the west and south sides of the plaza are particularly large. The reconstruction shows a total of 123 ground-floor rooms.

Leslie Spier's map (1917) of the Fort Site indicated 144 rooms of a somewhat smaller average size than the reconstruction shows. Using Spier's estimate and assuming that half of the ground-floor rooms had second stories, the total estimated number of rooms for the pueblo would be 216.

The masonry walls of the Fort Site are built of unevenly shaped, well-laid sandstone. Today the walls in some places continue to stand more than 6 feet (2 meters) high, and some have visible second-floor bearing holes. Ceramics collected at the site suggest that the room block was constructed and occupied between possibly A.D. 1250 and 1300, a little later than Deracho and Pescado Canyon.

YELLOWHOUSE
Zuni (Anasazi)

The ruins of Yellowhouse pueblo lie on the north bank of the Pescado River in the Zuni Indian Reservation of west-central New Mexico. Approximately one mile (1.6 kilometers) to the west the Nutria River flows into the Pescado, forming the Zuni River. The pueblo derives its name from Zuni words meaning roughly "yellow ruin."

The site is situated on a grass-covered plain at an elevation of 6,600 feet (2,012 meters) above sea level. A basalt outcrop is exposed in the riverbank some 65 feet (20 meters) to the south, and a sandstone outcrop appears possibly 165 feet (50 meters) to the west. Sparse juniper and piñon woodlands appear on the hillside 650 feet (200 meters) or so south of the site.

The dimensions of the L-shaped pueblo are at most 230 by 300 feet (70 by 90 meters). In plan Yellowhouse consists of two rectangular room blocks, each with its own plaza, one or two kivas, and several walled courtyards. Two unusual interior streets appear along the east and south sides of the east room block.

The pueblo's three circular kivas probably measure no more than 20 feet (6 meters) in diameter. The reconstruction presented here is based on a report by Rosalind L. Hunter-Anderson (1978) and a description by Keith W. Kintigh (1985). Originally recorded by Leslie Spier (1917), Yellowhouse has been mapped more recently, and presumably more accurately, by the Office of Contract Archaeology of the University of New Mexico.

Hunter-Anderson's report shows 234 ground-floor rooms for Yellowhouse, quite a few more than Spier's 145. The average room area is about 112 square feet (10.4 square meters), slightly larger than the room sizes of Atsinna, for example. Assuming that half of the ground-floor rooms of Yel-

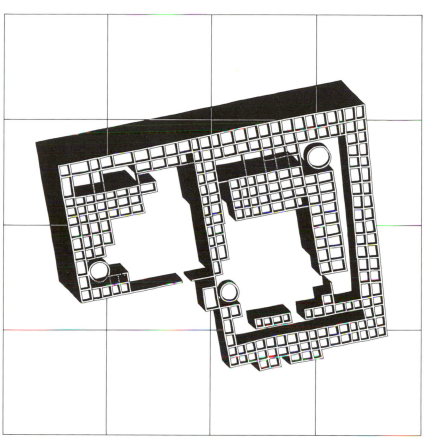

YELLOWHOUSE

lowhouse have two stories and one-quarter have three stories, the total would be an estimated 410. This is around half the number estimated for Atsinna.

The masonry walls of Yellowhouse are constructed of basalt and sandstone, both shaped and unshaped. Today some of the walls remain standing well more than 6 feet (2 meters) high. Ceramics collected at the site suggest construction and occupation between A.D. 1275 and 1325, somewhat later than the Fort Site.

RAMAH SCHOOLHOUSE
Zuni (Anasazi)

The ruins of the rectangular Zuni pueblo of Ramah Schoolhouse are covered almost entirely by buildings of the present-day town of Ramah in west-central New Mexico. The site is located on the floor of the Ramah Valley at an elevation of 6,885 feet (2,099 meters) above sea level. Situated roughly 10 miles (16 kilometers) west of the continental divide, the Ramah Schoolhouse ruins lie about a mile and a half (2.5 kilometers) east of the Deracho site.

Approximately 650 feet (200 meters) northwest of the pueblo is Cebola Creek, a tributary of the Pescado River. Deciduous vegetation covers the area near the watercourse, and grassy plains lie beyond. Some 1,300 feet (400 meters) to the east is a per-

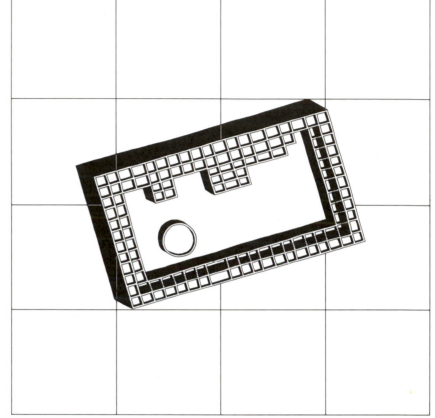

RAMAH SCHOOLHOUSE

haps 850-foot- (260-meter-) high mesa with juniper and piñon woodlands on its slopes.

The plan of Ramah Schoolhouse published by Keith W. Kintigh (1985) is the basis of the reconstruction presented here. According to Kintigh's graphic scale, the orderly pueblo's maximum dimensions are about 131 by 232 feet (40 by 70 meters). Rows two to five rooms wide form the perimeter of the room block and define the central plaza.

Presumably, the depression that Leslie Spier (1917) noted in the southwest corner of the plaza may have been a kiva, possibly similar in size to the circular chamber at Atsinna. The plaza is oriented toward the southeast, like the plazas of Atsinna, Yellowhouse, and other rectangular Zuni pueblos. Spier indicated that some of the rooms of Ramah Schoolhouse most likely were two stories high.

The reconstructed plan shows 124 ground-floor rooms, each with an average area of more or less 97 square feet (9 square meters). Assuming that half of the rooms had second floors, the total would be an estimated 186 rooms. The Fort Site was somewhat larger and Atsinna was around four times the size of Ramah Schoolhouse.

Ceramics collected at the ruins suggest that the pueblo probably was constructed and occupied sometime between A.D. 1275 and 1325. If so, Ramah Schoolhouse would have been contemporaneous with Yellowhouse, its neighbor 11 miles (17.5 kilometers) to the west.

ATSINNA
Zuni (Anasazi)

The thirteenth-century Zuni pueblo of Atsinna is perched dramatically on the edge of El Morro mesa overlooking the valley of the Zuni River to the north. From its altitude of 7,430 feet (2,265 meters) the mesa top drops off abruptly to the north, east, and west but slopes more gently down to the south. The ruins are located amid spectacular scenery some 120 miles (193 kilometers) west of Albuquerque in west-central New Mexico.

Below the grass-covered mesa top is Inscription Rock where early travelers recorded their names. Zuni workers excavating the ruins in the 1950s named the site Atsinna, meaning "where pictures are on the rock." El Morro derives its name from the Spanish word meaning "bluff" or "headland" (Noble 1981).

Early hunters and gatherers are known to have appeared in the Zuni River Valley area well before the beginning of the Christian era. Here between A.D. 400 and 900 a number of pit house villages probably were constructed and occupied. In time early pueblos came into use, but toward the middle of the thirteenth century the Zuni began to relocate from the lower river valley to sites in higher elevations 40 miles (64 kilometers) or so to the east.

The reasons for leaving the lower elevations are unclear, but one may have been to take advantage of increased precipitation at such higher altitude sites as El Morro. Here scattered individual farmsteads were established at first, but during the latter thirteenth century a new type of settlement seems to have developed. By then the Zuni were consolidating into

densely populated pueblos like Atsinna (Kintigh 1985).

Tree-ring dates indicate that the construction of Atsinna most likely began around 1275. Occupation presumably continued until at least 1350. Evidence gathered at the site suggests that the large pueblo was abandoned slowly when the Zuni began to move back downriver after living on the mesa top for perhaps two or three generations. By 1400 the large pueblo apparently was entirely abandoned.

The reconstructed plan of Atsinna presented here is based on a composite of information provided by Kintigh (1985), Amsden (1934), and the Museum of New Mexico's Laboratory of Anthropology in 1990. The maximum dimensions for the rectangular pueblo appear to be about 225 by 320 feet (68 by 97 meters). Rows of four to eight rooms flank the central plaza, which measures at most 115 by 185 feet (35 by 56 meters).

Atsinna's unbroken exterior wall is well made and once rose at least two stories in height, but evidence suggests that some rooms were added outside. Two kivas are found in the pueblo, one rectangular and the other round. The latter has an inner diameter of possibly 30 feet (9 meters) and protrudes into the north side of the plaza. Remains of walls found beneath the plaza may be those of an earlier structure.

At its peak Atsinna had an estimated 750 to one thousand rooms. This reconstruction proposes five hundred one-story, possibly 250 second-story, and perhaps 125 third-story rooms, a total of 875. The rooms of the massive pueblo were remarkably uniform in size; they seem to average 100 square feet (9.3 square meters) in

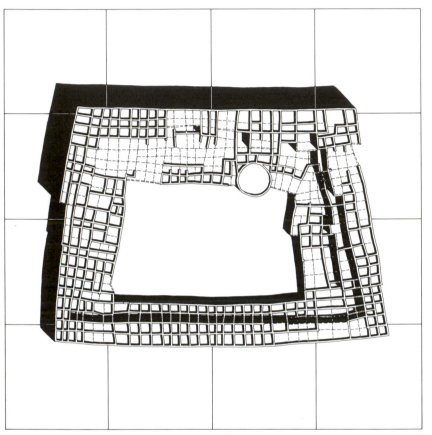

ATSINNA

area and to have typical dimensions of 10 by 10 feet (3 by 3 meters) or so.

Only the rooms closest to the plaza have hearths and benches, features implying spaces for daily living. Featureless rooms appear to represent storage. Five excavated rooms had stone-paved floors, and one had a wall painting on plaster.

Secure sources of water for Atsinna are found in several natural rock basins and pools in the mesa top. Three reservoirs lie south of the pueblo; one seems to measure 25 feet (7.5 meters) in diameter and 3 feet (1 meter) in depth. Similar features occur at Pueblo de los Muertos, a contemporary neighbor very similar to Atsinna in size and proportions.

The people of both Acoma and Zuni claim Atsinna as an ancestral pueblo. The ruins are part of El Morro National Monument some 30 miles (48 kilometers) east of Zuni, New Mexico. Visitors today may tour Atsinna's excavated wing consisting of a dozen or more masonry rooms and two kivas.

ELDEN PUEBLO
Sinagua

The remains of Elden Pueblo, also known as Sheep Hill Pueblo or Pasiwvi, lie in a ponderosa pine forest a short distance east of Mount Elden in the San Francisco Peaks. The site is located on the northwest side of Highway 89 near Flagstaff, Arizona. The ruins contain a perhaps sixty-one-room Sinagua pueblo, four smaller room blocks, at least nine pit houses, and more than 130 burials in three main cemeteries.

Ceramics and other data collected at Elden Pueblo suggest that the room block probably was built and used between A.D. 1100 and 1275. Sinagua settlers most likely selected the site because of its proximity to a permanently flowing spring and good farmland. Unshaped sandstone and basalt blocks found in the vicinity were used to construct the pueblo.

The reconstructed plan presented here is based primarily on information provided by the Coconino National Forest Office in Flagstaff (Pilles 1986: figs. 1, 2, 7). Overall, Elden's partially two-story room block measures approximately 125 by 140 feet (38 by 43 meters). The first structure built in the pueblo appears to be a nucleus of rooms near the center of the plan. Over time, blocks of four or more rooms were added to the nuclear core.

By far the largest of Elden's sixty-one ground-floor rooms is the 30-by-36-foot (9-by-11-meter) community room situated near the center of the southeast wall. A bench some 2.6 feet (80 centimeters) high engages the room's perimeter walls on all four sides. A ventilator tunnel, fire pit, and plastered floor with small holes to an-

ELDEN PUEBLO

chor looms indicate the specialized activities of the large room.

Other rooms in Elden Pueblo were used for such purposes as weaving, manufacturing stone tools, and producing pottery. Floors in various rooms yield evidence of fire pits, post holes, storage pits, multiple floor levels, and subfloor infant burials. The room block is known to be constructed over an earlier pit house village, a familiar pattern for many southwestern pueblos.

A very unusual feature of Elden Pueblo is the specially surfaced exterior activity area on the north, west, and south sides of the room block. Formalized surfaces of this type are unknown elsewhere in the Southwest. Future investigations may reveal remnants of special surfacing along the east side as well.

A social hierarchy may have existed at Elden Pueblo, judging by seemingly high status burials. One grave contained a carved bone hair pin, a sandstone nose plug, turquoise ear rings, an incised shell bracelet, and other rare artifacts. The burial of a stone

tool carver has obsidian cores, projectile points, hammers made of deer antlers and stones, and other tools.

During the early occupation of Elden Pueblo trade apparently was conducted primarily with Kayenta communities to the north. In time, trading shifted to other Western Pueblos and eventually to Hopi settlements. Other widely differing examples of Sinagua architecture discussed in this study are Montezuma Castle and Tuzigoot in the Verde Valley to the south and Nuvaqueotaka north of he Mogollon Rim.

The Hopi name for Elden Pueblo is Pasiwvi, meaning "the place of coming together" or "the meeting place." Several major Hopi societies are reported to have developed at or near Pasiwvi. Until the 1940s, Hopi travelers on their way to the nearby San Francisco Peaks stopped at the pueblo and offered prayers, a further indication of the Sinagua role in Hopi cultural development.

High-status burials, trade specialization, a large community room, and great quantities of nonlocal trade items indicate that Elden Pueblo once was a political and ceremonial center. Efforts presently are underway to excavate and stabilize the walls of the room block at a height of about 4 feet (1.2 meters) and to open the pueblo to the public. The site would add significantly to our understanding of Sinagua architecture.

TUZIGOOT
Sinagua

Probably built primarily during the thirteenth century, the Sinagua pueblo of Tuzigoot occupies a commanding limestone ridge some 120 feet (37 meters) above the winding Verde River in central Arizona. The site lies approximately 40 miles (64 kilometers) south of the somewhat earlier Sinagua settlements of Elden and Walnut Canyon near Flagstaff. Tuzigoot derives its name from the Apache word meaning "crooked water," a reference to an irregular crescent-shaped pond following the watercourse in the valley below. The characterful site recalls such historic Italian hilltowns as Pienza, which is perched on a Tuscan hilltop overlooking fertile farmlands south of Sienna.

Sometime, perhaps as early as the seventh century A.D., Hohokam farmers from the south began to settle in the valley near Tuzigoot. They established irrigation systems to water their fields and built one-room houses of jacal construction on the river terraces overlooking their farms. In time Sinagua people began to occupy pit houses in the nearby foothills and plateaus; they practiced dry farming and supplemented their diets by hunting and gathering.

Around 1125 Sinagua farmers moved from the uplands down into the valley where they adopted irrigation farming and above-grade construction. Kayenta Anasazi from the north most likely introduced the idea of building pueblos to the Sinagua people.

Early in the twelfth century Sinagua builders constructed several small clusters of rooms on the ridge-

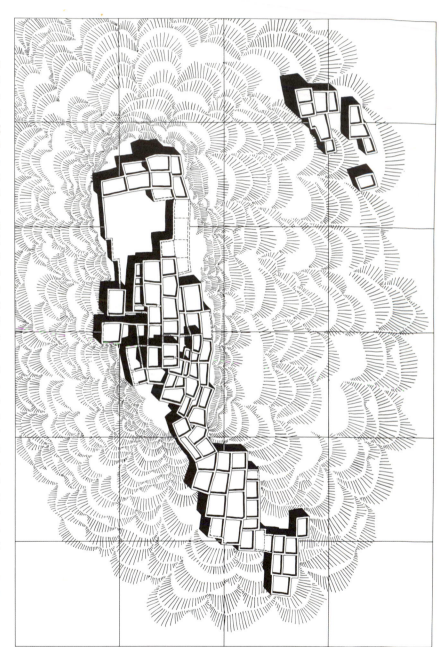

TUZIGOOT

top of Tuzigoot where possibly fifty people took up residency. During the early thirteenth century widespread droughts seem to have uprooted Sinagua people to the north, and newcomers migrated into the Verde Valley. The population of Tuzigoot doubled about 1225 and doubled again within decades, bringing the maximum population of the ridgetop pueblo to perhaps 225.

The reconstruction presented here shows Tuzigoot as it may have appeared at its peak of development when the pueblo measured overall about 275 by 485 feet (84 by 148 meters) in plan. At most two stories high in places, the pueblo is known to have at least seventy-six contiguous ground-floor rooms and more or less twenty-six second-floor rooms in the main room block. An annex of ten more chambers lies to the northeast. Dashed lines in the reconstruction suggest twelve additional rooms based on my impressions of the site in 1991.

The reconstruction presented here is based primarily on a map provided by the National Park Service in 1991. Most of the rooms presumably were entered by means of roof hatches and ladders; few doorways are found. Twenty-three tree-ring dates indicate major construction at Tuzigoot in the early 1100s, around 1200, and late in the 1300s (Lister & Lister 1989).

Excavations between 1933 and 1935 revealed several hundred burials within the pueblo and its middens. A large plaza found in the northwest corner of Tuzigoot may represent the pueblo's center of trading activity and community assembly. Although the Sinagua were daring and imaginative builders, their masonry compared poorly with that of the Anasazi, perhaps because of the inferior quality of stone available for construction.

The building stone of Tuzigoot is soft and breaks unpredictably; the walls are uncoursed and vary substantially in width. Mortar is used generously in compensation for the irregular shapes and sizes of stones. By contrast the Sinagua are exceptionally fine craftsmen and skillful traders whose mercantile network extended south to the Gila Basin and northeast to Nuvaqueotaka and the Hopi Mesa area.

Tuzigoot continued to be occupied from perhaps 1125 until the early 1400s when the Sinagua abandoned the Verde Valley for unknown reasons. Possibilities for their departure include too much pressure on natural resources by an increasing population and perhaps friction with such neighboring groups as the Yavapai, whom the Spanish found living in the valley when they arrived in 1583. Administered by the National Park Service, Tuzigoot and its associated museum are open daily to the public.

MONTEZUMA CASTLE
Sinagua

The spectacular Sinagua cliff dwelling of Montezuma Castle peers out from the face of a sheer limestone cliff on the north bank of Beaver Creek in

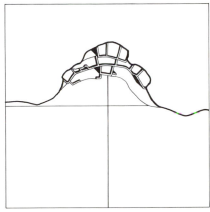

MONTEZUMA CASTLE

central Arizona. The exceptionally well preserved site is situated about 16 miles (26 kilometers) east of Tuzigoot and approximately 40 miles (64 kilometers) south of Elden Pueblo and Walnut Canyon near Flagstaff. The name of the site is a misnomer; early settlers gave Montezuma Castle its name in the mistaken belief that the Aztecs built the structure.

Containing perhaps twenty rooms, the five-story structure measures at most 40 feet (12 meters) vertically by 90 feet (27 meters) horizontally and is recessed into the cliff face to a depth of 40 feet (12 meters). The reconstruction presented here is based on information provided by the National Park Service, an article by Peter J. Pilles, Jr. (1981), and my observations on the site in 1991. Sinagua builders erected the walls of Montezuma Castle with small limestone blocks laid in mud mortar; sycamore beams support the roofs and upper floors.

Two paths provide access into the cliff dwelling, one from the valley floor 100 feet (30 meters) below and one along a ledge in the cliff face. Substantial effort undoubtedly was required to haul up into the cave the beams, stones, and fill needed to construct Montezuma Castle. Several small keyhole doors are visible today from the valley floor, but the principal means of communicating between the rooms and terraces seems to be by way of ladders and roof hatches.

Newcomers probably migrated into the Verde Valley during the twelfth century, bringing with them the knowledge of masonry construction possibly learned from Kayenta Anasazi builders to the north. In exchange the newcomers learned techniques of farming involving irrigation. The constantly flowing waters of Beaver Creek, the fertile river terraces, and nearby deposits of salt and minerals presumably were attractive resources to the builders of Montezuma Castle.

The latter thirteenth century appears to be a time of concentrating scattered settlements of the Verde Valley into possibly forty major pueblos, each surrounded by smaller room clusters, extensive farm plots, and field houses. Tuzigoot and Montezuma Castle are examples of this concentration. The large pueblos usually were multistory structures located close to flowing rivers or creeks; many had kivas and a community room, and at least one had a ball court that may date to the 1150 to 1225 period.

Montezuma Castle is strategically located between the Hohokam to the south, the Kayenta Anasazi to the north, Cohonina groups to the northwest, and the Mogollon to the east. Sinagua artisans carved fine tools of stone and bone, wove handsome cotton garments, created distinctive bas-

kets, and produced valuable ornaments of turquoise, shell, and stone. Never distinguished potters, the Sinagua imported decorated pots from their neighbors in the Hopi mesa area to the northeast.

During the early 1400s the Sinagua abandoned the Verde Valley for reasons that are unclear, perhaps depletion of natural resources, overpopulation, or friction with neighbors. Their descendants may have been absorbed into pueblos to the north. Hopi legends tell of a wandering tribe from the south that lacked ceremonies and priests; pottery and basketry traditions support the legends (Noble 1981).

The first Europeans to visit the Verde Valley appear to be members of Antonio de Espejo's expedition in 1583. The cliff dwelling of Montezuma Castle, the hilltop citadel of Tuzigoot, and Elden Pueblo in an alpine forest illustrate the adaptability and diversity of Sinagua architecture in broadly varying natural settings. Like Tuzigoot, Montezuma Castle is administered by the National Park Service and is open daily to the public.

KIET SIEL
Kayenta Anasazi

The largest cliff dwelling in Arizona, Kiet Siel also is one of the best preserved prehistoric structures in the Southwest. Also spelled Keet Seel, the name means "broken pottery" in the Navajo language. Betatakin, Inscription House, and Kiet Siel are the three major sites of Navajo National Monument located in northern Arizona approximately 120 miles (190 kilometers) northwest of Flagstaff. These three ruins, together with Mummy Cave in Canyon de Chelly and Wupatki near Sunset Crater, represent Kayenta Anasazi architecture in this discussion.

The spectacular pueblo extends some 340 feet (104 meters) along a cliff face oriented toward the southeast. Like the contemporary cliff dwellings of Mesa Verde, Kiet Siel derives warmth from the winter sun and shade from the summer sun by virtue of its favorable position in a natural cave. The site was discovered in 1895 by Richard Wetherill, the rancher from Mancos, Colorado, who also discovered Cliff Palace and other ancient monuments of the Southwest.

Kiet Siel is situated in an offshoot of Tsegi Canyon about 8 miles (13 kilometers) north of Betatakin. Tsegi is a Navajo word meaning "rock canyon." The earliest record of settlements in this vicinity dates to around 750 B.C. and the latest may be A.D. 1300, a period of more than two thousand years (Ferguson & Rohn 1987). Tree-ring dates suggest that construction of the cliff dwelling probably began shortly after 1250 and continued until 1286 or possibly a few years later.

The peak of building activity at

Kiet Siel seems to have occurred between 1272 and 1275 when the population of the settlement may have reached a maximum of 125 to 250 people. In all, the pueblo has an estimated 155 rooms, four kivas, and three ceremonial annexes.

Some of the rooms in the lower area of the cliff face have deteriorated due to their more exposed locations. Most of the large Kayentan structure is so remarkably well preserved that roof beams in many rooms are intact and original roofs and terraces survive. Even corncobs, woven baskets, and other perishable objects have been preserved.

The basis of the reconstruction presented here is an excellent plan with accurate section drawings provided by Jeffrey S. Dean (1969), a scholar who has studied the ruins carefully. He identified twenty-five room clusters, each consisting of a living room associated with one to four store rooms grouped around a courtyard. The same arrangement is found in the suites of Cliff Palace and other Mesa Verdean cliff dwellings. In several cases evidence indicates room abandonment and rebuilding and the reuse of beams in later structures.

The original method of gaining access to the cliff dwelling was by means of hand and toe holds carved into the cliff face. Shallow notches in the rock formed vertical trails for ascent from the natural cave to the mesa top or descent into the valley where the Anasazi cultivated corn, beans, and squash. Domesticated turkeys and wild game supplemented the diets of Kiet Siel's residents.

The Kayenta builders created level terraces on the sloping cave floor by constructing retaining walls and filling in behind them. A conspicuous ar-

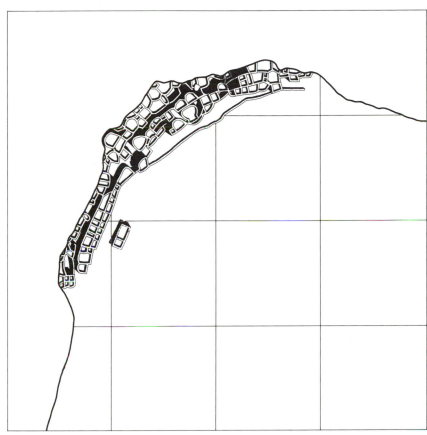

KIET SIEL

chitectural feature of Kiet Siel is an exceptionally large retaining wall roughly 180 feet (55 meters) long and 10 feet (3 meters) high near the east end of the cliff dwelling. The structure presumably represents a community effort. The fill behind the huge wall consists of tons of rubble and earth brought up from the valley below by means of baskets.

Another example of community cooperation for construction is the system of three streets parallel to the cliff edge. The streets interconnect room clusters, granaries where foodstuffs were stored in stone-lined bins, grinding rooms equipped with *metates*, and kivas. Near the center of the plan is a keyhole-shaped kiva perhaps 13 feet (4 meters) in diameter. The circular chamber has rubble core walls plastered and painted inside, an above-floor ventilation shaft and draft deflector like those of Mesa Verde, and holes in the floor to anchor looms.

The distinctive D-shaped room southwest of the kiva is believed to be an annex related to ceremonialism but lacking the features of a kiva. The annex is constructed of jacal, vertical poles tied together and coated with mud plaster containing limited quantities of stone. Jacal construction had ceased elsewhere in the four corners area by the latter thirteenth century but continued to be used in Kayenta architecture.

Typical room walls in Kiet Siel consist of single courses of unshaped stones laid in generous beds of mortar. Walls containing entry doors, however, usually are of jacal construction. As a rule rooms are entered either by means of T-shaped portals or by roof hatches and ladders. Unusual architectural features of Kiet Siel are

vertical poles projecting from the tops of jacal walls or placed along the edges of streets and terraces. The purpose of the poles is unknown.

Although four round kivas are found in Kiet Siel, only one kiva exists in Betatakin and its shape is decidedly rectangular. Ceremonial rooms with rectangular plans are customary in present-day Hopi, Zuni, and other Western Pueblos. Around the end of the thirteenth century the residents of Tsegi Canyon abandoned their cliff dwellings and relocated to the south, most likely becoming ancestors of the present-day Hopi.

BETATAKIN
Kayenta Anasazi

The large Kayenta Anasazi cliff dwelling of Betatakin is located about 8 miles (13 kilometers) south of Kiet Siel in the Navajo National Monument of northern Arizona. Meaning "ledge house" in Navajo, Betatakin originally may have had 135 rooms, about twenty fewer than Kiet Siel. Inscription House, the third-largest cliff dwelling in the area, has seventy-four rooms and one kiva; the site lies approximately 15 miles (24 kilometers) west of Betatakin.

The impressive cliff dwelling extends roughly 530 feet (162 meters) along a curving arc in a cliff face oriented a little east of south. From its rocky perch, the village overlooks

plentiful Tsegi Canyon filled with oaks, Douglas fir, aspen, and box elders. Discovered in 1909 by John Wetherill and Byron Cummings, Betatakin appears to be planned and built according to an overall plan and occupied by a single group of people (Ferguson & Rohn 1987).

Dwarfed by the cavernous overhang arching above it, the site probably was used first as a seasonal camp around A.D. 1260. Tree-ring dates indicate occupancy by possibly an advanced party of twenty people or so in 1267 and 1268. The small group apparently cleared the site and stockpiled beams for future use. Between 1275 and 1277 the main body of the community occupied the sheltered ledges and undertook major construction.

During the middle of the 1280s Betatakin most likely reached its maximum population of 125 residents. At this time some seven hundred Anasazis lived in Tsegi Canyon, tending food crops and raising cotton in farm plots on the fertile valley floor. After 1286 people began to drift away from Betatakin, and by 1300 the great cliff dwelling was abandoned after an occupancy of less than forty years.

Compared to the refined masonry structures of Chaco Canyon, Kayenta walls seem rudimentary. Uncoursed and only one row of stones thick, the walls contain more mud mortar than stone. Kayenta room clusters resemble those of Mesa Verde, but relatively few small kivas and no great kivas at all are found in Tsegi Canyon. Ceremonies involving the entire community may have been performed in open plazas under the overhanging cliff.

Betatakin's only kiva is a rectangular room with core-filled masonry walls situated near the center of the

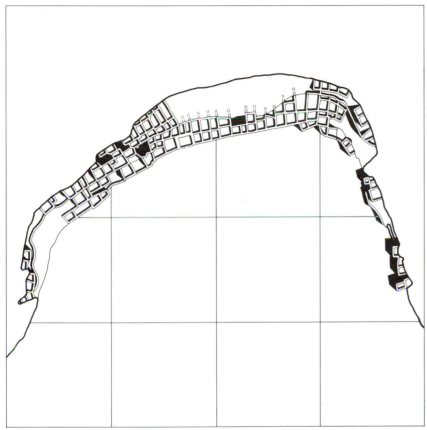

BETATAKIN

living room with one or more store rooms grouped around a small courtyard. Many of the rooms are of multistory construction, and courtyards occupy several rooftops. Interior floors are filled with rubble and dirt to establish level surfaces, walls typically are plastered, and fire pits are used to heat dwelling rooms. A main pathway or street leads along the centerline through most of the village.

The fact that no rooms in Betatakin are clearly larger or better finished than others suggests an egalitarian society with no privileged class. Storage free from rodents is placed on a ledge perhaps 30 feet (9 meters) above the closest roof; it is accessible only by ladder. After the village was abandoned a section of the cave's roof collapsed and destroyed a portion of the cliff dwelling, but today most of the rooms appear much as they did seven centuries ago.

One of the reasons for abandoning the cliff dwellings of Tsegi Canyon after relatively brief periods of occupancy may have been the result of arroyo cutting, a phenomenon brought on by a seasonal shift from gentle rains and snows during winters to torrential summer downpours. As a result arroyos cut deeply into the mesa tops, and watertables dropped too far to sustain agricultural systems. Droughts ensued, and residents relocated to more favorable environments.

The people of Tsegi Canyon appear to have migrated to the south where they eventually became the ancestors of the Hopi. Today the cliff dwellings are administered by the National Park Service and are open to the public. Betatakin is relatively accessible, but a visit to Kiet Siel requires preplanning and considerable time and exertion.

village. The room contains a bench along its north wall and has loom anchor holes in its floor. The south wall of the kiva is missing; it may have been of jacal construction.

Unusually high ceilings and the lack of associated structures identify the rectangular room as a kiva. Another kiva is found in a small cave upstream from Betatakin. Rectangular ceremonial rooms with floor holes for loom anchors are characteristic of Hopi, Zuni, and other Western Pueblos.

In common with other Kayenta and Mesa Verde cliff dwellings, the organizing element of Betatakin's plan is a

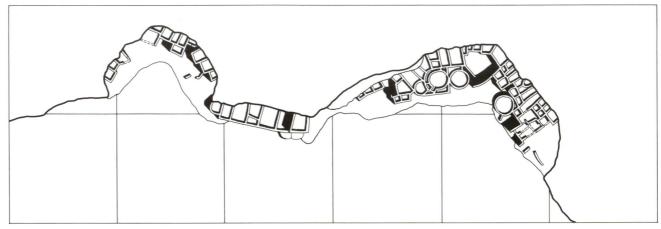

MUMMY CAVE

MUMMY CAVE
Kayenta Anasazi

The Kayenta Anasazi cliff dwelling of Mummy Cave occupies two caves connected by a narrow ledge some 300 feet (90 meters) above the stream bed of Canyon del Muerto in northeastern Arizona. Approximately 12 miles (19 kilometers) southwest of the ruins the valley joins Canyon de Chelly. The two spectacular gorges form Canyon de Chelly National Monument, the site of the best known examples of eastern Kayenta Anasazi architecture.

Canyon de Chelly lies a short distance east of Chinle, Arizona, about midway between the Kayenta ruins of Betatakin and Kiet Siel to the west and the monuments of Chaco Canyon to the east. The narrow, meandering canyons are formed by watercourses originating in the Chuska Mountains. At some points the gorges cut as deeply as 1,000 feet (300 meters) into the sandstone mesa, producing winding canyons with steep walls and flat, well-watered floors.

The predecessors of the Kayenta Anasazi may have arrived in Canyon de Chelly as early as 1000 B.C. In time they established farms, produced corn, beans, and squash, and grew cotton to be woven into textiles. The people raised turkeys and hunted rabbits and mule deer with bows and arrows. They located their settlements at the bases of cliffs and in natural caves in the canyon walls, perhaps to conserve the arable land on the canyon floors for agriculture.

The unique cliff dwelling of Mummy Cave extends possibly 400 feet (120 meters) along the east wall of Canyon del Muerto. The ruins lie in two large caves, a 100-foot- (30-meter-) wide alcove to the west and another twice as wide to the east. A narrow ledge interconnects the caves. The remains of twenty-two rooms with masonry walls, probably the first structures built in Mummy Cave, are found in the southeast corner of the larger alcove.

The early structures in the east cave seem to date from A.D. 300 to 400. Quite likely other remains from the same period lie buried beneath the floors of rooms built more recently. Major construction in Mummy Cave occurred during the thirteenth century; by 1300 the cliff dwelling most likely was abandoned.

At the height of its development Mummy Cave may have contained a total of ninety rooms and three or four kivas. The maximum population is estimated to have been perhaps sixty people. The largest component of the settlement, the east cave, may have been the first to be constructed. Here forty-five rooms are recorded, and ten more may have existed originally.

Rows of small storage rooms and large living rooms line the irregular wall of the east cave. The walls measure 6 to 15 inches (15 to 38 centimeters) in thickness and are built of small, uncoursed stones laid in generous beds of mortar. Two large retaining walls define the outer edge of the cliff terrace. Near the center of the east cave are three circular kivas, each about 16 feet (5 meters) in diameter. The wall of one kiva is decorated with abstract designs rendered in red and white.

Near the center of the east cave is found a large, roofless enclosure measuring perhaps 24 by 30 feet (7.3 by 9 meters) in plan. The lower 4 feet (1.2 meters) of the enclosing walls are painted burnt sienna in color and the upper surfaces are off-white. Niches, benches, and a paved platform within the enclosure suggest kiva-like ceremonial activities.

At present the west cave contains the ruins of fourteen rooms; it may have had six more originally. Accessible only by means of the narrow ledge to the east, the uneven floor of the smaller cave is covered almost entirely by the remnants of walls. The absence of a kiva in the west alcove suggests that ceremonial activities were held in the east cave.

The best preserved and most refined masonry structure in Mummy Cave is constructed on the 100-foot- (30-meter-) long ledge linking the east and west ruins. The building has seven exceptionally large, two- and three-story rooms with walls up to 2 feet (60 centimeters) thick. The room sizes and masonry style of the link clearly are characteristic of Mesa Verde architecture, not Kayenta.

A tree-ring date for the ledge building indicates construction in 1284, not long before the abandonment of Mummy Cave. The distinctive architectural style implies that some of the people who abandoned Mesa Verde relocated for a while in Canyon del Muerto before continuing their southward migration a few years later. The three-story tower at the east end of the ledge attests to the high degree of skill attained by the ancient masons.

Measuring up to 15 by 20 feet (4.5 by 6.1 meters) in plan, the ledge building's rooms are the largest in Canyon de Chelly. The floors and ceilings of the three-story tower consist of neatly placed mats of small poles laid perpendicular to beams 2.5 to 4.5 inches (6.4 to 11.5 centimeters) in diameter. The beams are placed parallel to each other and 18 to 24 inches (45 to 60 centimeters) apart; their ends project 2 feet (60 centimeters) or so beyond the wall face.

The ledge rooms of Mummy Cave appear to be interconnected by portals to facilitate movement between the adjoining caves. The reconstruction of the cliff dwelling presented here is based on a plan and description by Cosmos Mindeleff (1897: fig. 16), information by Ferguson and Rohn (1987), and my observations on the site in 1991.

Almost entirely abandoned by the Kayenta Anasazi by 1300, Canyon de Chelly continued to be visited occasionally by small numbers of Hopi. A short time after the Pueblo Revolt of 1680 to 1692, Navajo people occupied the scenic valleys; their decendents continue to live and tend farms on the fertile canyon bottoms today. Now open daily to the public and administered by the National Park Service, Canyon de Chelly is part of the Navajo Indian Reservation.

WUPATKI
Kayenta Anasazi

The southern Kayenta pueblo of Wupatki is located on a rugged sandstone outcropping approximately 100 miles (160 kilometers) south of Betatakin and Kiet Siel in northern Arizona. Meaning "tall house" in Hopi, Wupatki consists of a room block once having more than one hundred rooms, a walled circular plaza, and the northernmost ballcourt found in the ancient Southwest.

During the twelfth century, population of Wupatki is estimated to have been two hundred persons. Tree-ring dates indicate construction of the room block may have begun as early as 1106; the peak of building activity probably occurred during the 1150s. Although the structure appears in places to be four stories high, it consists mostly of single-story rooms elevated on natural rock outcroppings or on filled lower floors.

The reconstruction presented here is based on a site plan and information provided by the National Park Service and my observations on the site in 1991. Today Wupatki appears to have north and south components, but in plan the room block probably was once a single structure measuring overall possibly 140 by 345 feet (43 by 107 meters). In several places boulders too large to move are incorporated into walls; the natural rocks and stone masonry absorb heat from the sun during the day and release it at night, warming the rooms of the pueblo.

The coursed masonry walls of Wupatki are built of easily shaped sandstone blocks laid with minimum mortar. The coursed masonry, stone-lined fire pits, above-floor ventilators,

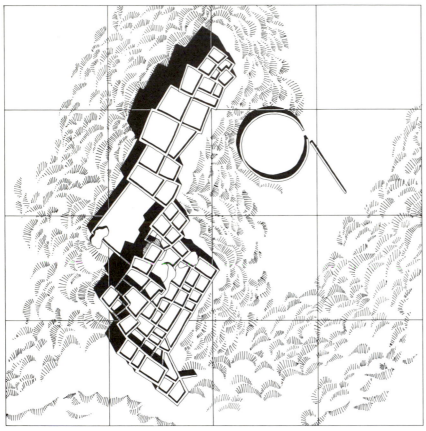

WUPATKI

The curving perimeter wall measures some 63 feet (19 meters) across. The absence of post molds or foundations suggests that the space may not have had a roof.

A continuous stone bench engages the interior base of the encircling wall. The enclosure is broken only by a portal facing downslope to the northeast, maybe to drain away rain water. Presumably a ceremonial gathering place, the roofless plaza lacks a *sipapu* and other features traditionally associated with a great kiva.

Another unusual architectural feature of Wupatki is the restored oval-shaped ballcourt placed on the valley floor a little more than 300 feet (90 meters) north of the room block. Generally oriented with respect to a north-south axis, the playing court measures overall 78 by 102 feet (24 by 31 meters) and has an opening at each end. Unlike the ball courts of Snaketown, Casa Grande, Pueblo Grande, and other Hohokam sites, the ball court of Wupatki is built of stone.

Ball courts traditionally are associated with religious rituals. Unlike the unique 6-foot- (1.8-meter-) high stone walls of Wupatki, the enclosures of Hohokam ballcourts usually are built of compacted earth or caliche. Ball courts imply trade and cultural exchange with such places as the Verde Valley or the Salt and Gila Basin.

Other small contemporary pueblos within 7 miles (11 kilometers) of Wupatki include Lomaki, the Citadel, and Wukoki. Like Wupatki, the neighboring settlements appear to be dominated culturally by the Kayenta Anasazi in the twelfth century. The stabilized remains of Wupatki and its neighbors presently are administered by the National Park Service and are open daily to the public.

and draft deflectors are characteristic of Anasazi architecture. The inner and lower rooms of the pueblo most likely were used for storage. Special-purpose rooms include several food-processing chambers, indicated by grinding stones, and a room containing seven infant burials in stone-lined pits.

A community courtyard or work area is situated on the west side of the room block near the center of the pueblo. The small plaza measures roughly 50 by 60 feet (15 by 18 meters). Roof hatches equipped with ladders and T-shaped doorways provide access into the rooms of the pueblo.

Four courses of dark basalt cobbles lend visual relief to the ubiquitous sandstone walls in one of Wupatki's upper-floor rooms.

Ponderosa pine beams supporting the floors and roofs of the room block were brought to the site from forests far away. Some of the beams still in place are more than eight hundred years old. The five southernmost rooms of Wupatki are partially subterranean storage rooms; they are accessible only by means of roof hatches.

An unusual circular enclosure is found at a lower elevation 30 feet (9 meters) or so east of the room block.

CLIFF PALACE

San Juan Anasazi

The largest cliff dwelling in Mesa Verde, Cliff Palace overlooks Cliff Canyon from the west wall of Chapin Mesa approximately 1.5 miles (2.4 kilometers) south of Spruce Tree House. The well-known Anasazi settlements in Mesa Verde are located in the high plateau country of southwestern Colorado 80 miles or so (130 kilometers) north of Chaco Canyon. Cliff Palace is part of the greater community of Cliff and Fewkes canyons consisting of thirty-three cliff dwellings where some six hundred to eight hundred people lived in the thirteenth century (Ferguson & Rohn 1987).

Cliff Palace was named by Richard Wetherill and Charlie Mason, two ranchers who discovered the ruins during a snowstorm in December 1888 while looking for stray cattle on Chapin Mesa. Like Spruce Tree House, Cliff Palace is oriented to the west-southwest for maximum exposure to the sun during the wintertime and maximum shade during the summer. The ruins lie in a natural cave measuring 324 feet (99 meters) in width, 89 feet (27 meters) in depth, and 59 feet (18 meters) in height.

The cave was formed as a result of water seeping into the highly porous sandstone cliff. In winter the water freezes and occasionally cracks loose layers of stone from the ceiling of the cave. In several locations fallen boulders were incorporated into the architectural masses of Cliff Palace when construction began around A.D. 1200.

Tree-ring dates suggest more or less continuous construction from 1209 into the early 1270s. In all, the ruin contains perhaps 220 rooms and

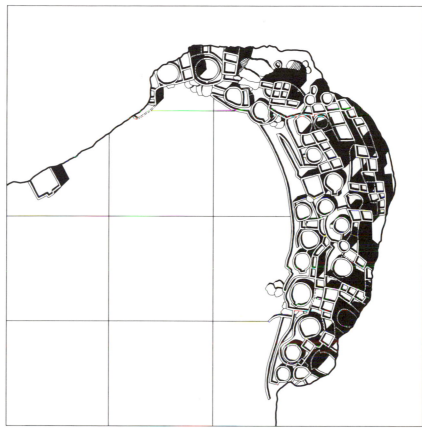

CLIFF PALACE

twenty-three kivas where possibly 250 persons lived in the thirteenth century. Water for Cliff Palace probably came from a spring at the base of the cliff on the opposite side of the canyon.

Two trails, one at each end of the cave, lead down into the canyon and up to the mesa top. The trails consist of finger and toe holds cut into the sheer cliff face. The steep paths are exposed to icing conditions during the wintertime. Presumably, considerable dexterity was required for the residents to ascend and descend the precarious trails while carrying cumbersome burdens on their backs or

water-filled vessels on their heads.

The reconstruction presented here is based on the report of Jesse Walter Fewkes (1917) of the Smithsonian Institution, who excavated the ruins in 1909. The rooms of Cliff Palace are mostly rectangular, but several have circular, trapezoidal, or irregular plans. Compared with the relatively orderly plan of nearby Far View House, the cliff dwelling's plan appears somewhat erratic due largely to the physical constraints of the cave and its highly uneven floor.

A round tower near the center of the ruin and two square towers to the south establish architectural reference points for Cliff Palace. An unusual aspect of the community plan is the relatively large area occupied by kivas. To create level terraces, the builders constructed a number of retaining walls and placed fill behind the walls.

A remarkable feature of Cliff Palace is the row of fourteen small storage rooms inserted between the cave roof and a narrow ledge. Accessible by short ladders, the rooms have ceiling heights of only 39 to 42 inches (1 to 1.1 meters). The store rooms are cool, dry, and out of reach of children and animals.

The kivas of the cliff dwelling ranged in diameter from roughly 16 to 24 feet (4.9 to 7.3 meters). The internal arrangements of the ceremonial chambers were similar to those of Spruce Tree House, but their sizes are somewhat larger and their numbers are substantially greater. The plaza-level room of the round tower provides additional ceremonial space for its two adjoining kivas.

Room sizes typically are about 6 by 8 feet (1.8 by 2.4 meters) in plan with 5.5-foot- (1.7-meter-) high ceilings. Small rectangular openings near the ceilings of some rooms apparently provided much-needed ventilation when fires were built inside for warmth in the winter. Some of the masonry walls exhibit exceptionally fine masonry with very straight surfaces and precisely square corners.

Rectangular and T-shaped doors typically provide access into rooms. The portals seem to be deliberately small perhaps in order to minimize heat loss and cold drafts during the wintertime. Sandstone slabs possibly 1 inch (2.5 centimeters) thick most likely served as doors in winter, while willow mats or animal hides over the

portals may have provided privacy in summer.

The four-story residence toward the south end of Cliff Palace contains an exceptionally well preserved wall painting. The lower walls of the third-floor room are painted burnt sienna and the upper walls are off-white. In the center of the upper walls are geometric designs featuring vertical zigzag lines side-by-side within rectangular borders.

The decorative designs of Cliff Palace are the most elaborate in Mesa Verde. The burnt sienna color is produced by powdered hematite mixed with water and fine clay. The off-white color results from the application of pure clay called kaolin. Earth tones are the most frequently used colors in Mesa Verde.

A tunnel interconnects the two southernmost kivas in Cliff Palace. A second tunnel leads from the end kiva to the room to the east. High benches between kiva pilasters typically were used to store pottery and other objects. Horizontal poles extending between pilasters in some kivas formed shelves for additional storage.

At its peak of population, Mesa Verde may have been the home of twenty-five hundred Anasazi. The reasons for its abandonment by A.D. 1300 after seven centuries of occupation are unknown. Possibilities include a prolonged drought between 1276 and 1299 and the depletion of soil, timber, and wildlife resources. The former residents may have moved southward, eventually joining pueblos in the Hopi, Zuni, Acoma, or Rio Grande areas.

SPRUCE TREE HOUSE
San Juan Anasazi

The large Anasazi cliff dwelling of Spruce Tree House overlooks Spruce Canyon from the southwest wall of Chapin Mesa in Mesa Verde National Park. Located about 4 miles (6.4 kilometers) south of Far View Community and some 1,000 feet (300 meters) lower in altitude, the dramatic structure is built in a natural cave measuring 216 feet (66 meters) at its greatest width and 89 feet (27 meters) at its greatest depth. The cave is oriented toward the southwest and receives a maximum amount of sunlight in the wintertime, but relatively little during the summer.

The first inhabitants of the cave most likely lived in pit houses centuries before the construction of Spruce Tree House began around 1200. After occupying settlements on the mesa top for hundreds of years, many of the inhabitants moved down into large dwellings in the faces of the mesa's sheer cliffs during the thirteenth century. The reasons for their relocation are unknown.

The cave is located near a large spring at the head of Spruce Tree Canyon in an area covered with piñon pines and juniper trees. Spruce Tree House was the focus of a community of fourteen sites near the springs where possibly 150 to two hundred people lived. Most of the residents more likely than not occupied the cliff dwelling.

Spruce Tree House was discovered in 1888 by Richard Wetherill and Charlie Mason, who misnamed the place for a large Douglas fir then growing in front of the cave. Exceptionally well preserved by the overhanging cliff, the site is one of sixteen

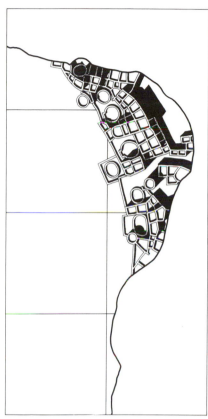

SPRUCE TREE HOUSE

in Mesa Verde excavated between 1908 and 1922 by Dr. Jesse Walter Fewkes of the Smithsonian Institution. The cliff dwelling appears to contain in all 114 rooms, eight kivas, an interior street, and several plazas or courtyards.

Two rock-cut trails in the sheer cliff face, one north of the cave and the other to the south, interconnect the cliff dwelling with the top of Chapin Mesa where the inhabitants cultivated corn, squash, and beans. The architectural components of Spruce Tree House are similar to those of the pueblos built earlier on the mesa top. The pueblos have rect-

angular masonry rooms two and three stories high, which flank plazas containing underground kivas. However, the shape of the natural cave precluded a rectangular room block, such as Far View House.

The average room size in the cliff dwelling is approximately 6 by 8 by 5.5 feet (1.8 by 2.4 by 1.7 meters) high. Seven kivas have interior diameters of roughly 15 feet (4.6 meters) each; the eighth kiva measures only 11 feet (3.4 meters) or so in diameter. The average room size is less than half the size of typical rooms in Far View House.

The reconstruction presented here is based primarily on information published by the Mesa Verde Museum Association in 1991 and Ferguson and Rohn (1987). A main street leads into the deepest part of the cave and divides the community plan into two major areas. Middens or refuse areas are found in the deepest recesses of the cave or along the cliff face downslope to the southwest.

Most of the rooms of Spruce Tree House are rectangular but several have curved walls. One room is D-shaped and two are cylindrical. Rooms with curved walls may be related to nearby kivas, recalling the arrangement of a circular tower adjoining a round kiva in the middle of nearby Pipe Shrine House. Rectangular and T-shaped doors typically provide access into rooms, sometimes by means of a balcony supported on the cantilevered ends of upper-floor beams.

Several exceptionally well preserved walls are plastered and still have their original finishes. In a number of rooms the lower walls bear traces of a burnt sienna coloration while the upper walls are painted white. An abstract, geometric design

rendered in sienna adorns the upper wall of one room.

Kivas are sunken below courtyards and plazas so that their roofs can serve as work areas or convenient places for community assembly. Hearths and stone-lined bins are found in courtyards where women once ground corn, made pottery, wove baskets, and prepared food. Men fashioned tools of stone and bone and blankets of turkey feathers or cotton. Small rooms deep in the cave and on upper levels generally were used for storing crops. Rooftops also served for drying foodstuffs and storing them.

During the coldest months of the year, fires may have burned twenty-four hours a day deep within the cave and room doorways likely were closed by animal hides or thin slabs of sandstone. In wintertime the easiest places to dig probably were in trash mounds, where burials are found. During inclement weather domestic activities moved from the courtyards into rooms equipped with hearths for heating, lighting, and cooking.

Kiva ladders project upward into one of the courtyards of Spruce Tree House where two underground chambers are restored. A typical kiva has a ventilation shaft leading from the surface to the kiva floor; a low wall deflects the fresh air draft to improve circulation within the room, and smoke escapes through the roof hatch above the fire pit. Six wall pilasters rest on high, narrow perimeter benches, and an alcove imparts a keyhole shape to the otherwise circular plan of the kiva.

The basic construction material for the tall, straight walls of Spruce Tree House is sandstone shaped into rectangular blocks about the size of a loaf of bread. The blocks are laid in mortar consisting of mud and water. Construction and occupation seem to have continued in the cliff dwelling until perhaps 1276. A drought between 1276 and 1299 may be one of the reasons Mesa Verde was abandoned toward the end of the thirteenth century.

The Mesa Verde people and their neighbors in the Montezuma Valley apparently migrated to the south, perhaps eventually joining the pueblos of the Hopi, Zuni, Acoma, or the Rio Grande area. Spruce Tree House is one of the foremost architectural achievements of the ancient Southwest. The ruins are open daily to the public during the summer months when Mesa Verde National Park receives visitors.

SAND CANYON
San Juan Anasazi

The late-thirteenth-century Anasazi community of Sand Canyon is located some 10 miles (16 kilometers) west of the present-day city of Cortez in southwestern Colorado. The monuments of Hovenweep lie several miles west of Sand Canyon, and Lowry is situated about 20 miles (32 kilometers) to the north. A deep canyon with a spring-fed stream divides the well-defined village into east and west zones.

The impressive pueblo contains an estimated 420 rooms, ninety kivas,

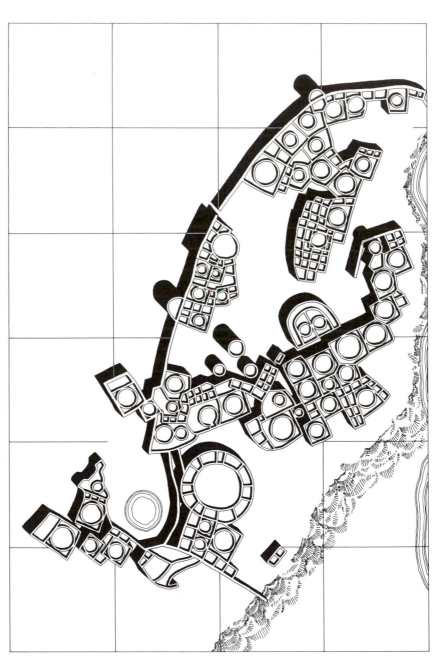

SAND CANYON, WEST AREA

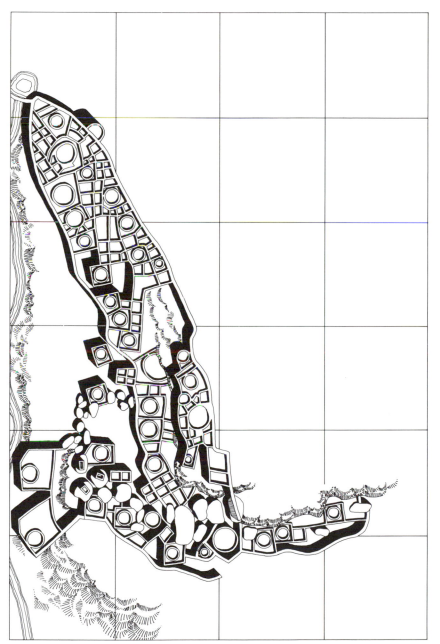

SAND CANYON, EAST AREA

fourteen towers, a great kiva, an unusual D-shaped public building, and a number of other distinctive features. The reconstruction presented here is based on a report prepared by the Crow Canyon Archaeological Center (Bradley 1990). Overall, the site measures approximately 490 by 690 feet (150 by 210 meters).

The first architectural element constructed at Sand Canyon pueblo was the massive, roughly 6.6-foot- (2-meter-) high stone wall surrounding the site. The impressive masonry enclosure appears to have been built in a single phase, perhaps representing a comparatively brief community-wide effort. The stones of the wall were quarried nearby and show signs of being erected rapidly.

Kivas with associated rooms in nine blocks dominate the western half of Sand Canyon pueblo. The blocks seem to conform to the site's topographical features. Near the center of the western section is a large plaza suggesting ceremonial activities or special functions. An unusual double-walled, D-shaped structure with two kivas occupies the southeast corner of the plaza.

Recently, a great kiva having an interior diameter of 44 feet (14.5 meters) was identified in the area south of the plaza not far from the cliff edge. The circular ceremonial chamber appears to be surrounded by perimeter rooms like those around the comparable structure in the courtyard of Aztec's West Ruin. A small reservoir is found in Sand Canyon Pueblo's southwest corner.

Tree-ring samples from room blocks in the pueblo's western area yield dates ranging from 1244 to 1274. Two-story rooms are associated with some of the kivas, but most of

Canyon's structures appear to be a single story high. The free-standing round tower in the south end of the Plaza once rose to a height of 16.4 feet (5 meters) or so, recalling similar structures in Hovenweep to the west.

A reservoir north of the perimeter wall along the upper stream bed served to assure the flow of water from the spring below. The eastern zone of Sand Canyon appears to contain a relatively high proportion of residential spaces and small court-yards suitable for domestic activities. The dwellings seem to have grown by accretion, but they are grouped in five distinct areas.

Tree-ring samples from Sand Canyon's residential zone yield dates of 1265 and 1267. Evidence gathered on the site indicates that the households were vacated at a relatively leisurely pace between possibly 1285 and 1300, when the site was abandoned completely. The ceremonial area to the west, however, appears to have been deserted very hastily for reasons that are unclear.

Today Sand Canyon Pueblo is the subject of ongoing research by the Crow Canyon Archaeological Center of Cortez, Colorado. Self-guided tours are available, and access is by way of a graveled-surfaced county road. The site lies in an area administered by the U.S. Bureau of Land Management.

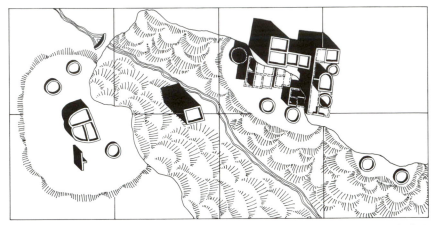

SQUARE TOWER GROUP

SQUARE TOWER GROUP
San Juan Anasazi

Square Tower Group is one of six clusters of masonry-walled Anasazi ruins found in Hovenweep National Monument. The group is located in southeastern Utah approximately 25 miles (40 kilometers) west of Cortez, Colorado. Meaning "deserted valley" in the Ute language, Hovenweep is part of the greater Montezuma Valley community in the Northern San Juan area.

Here about A.D. 1200, after living for generations on mesa tops and valleys in the vicinity, the people drew together for unknown reasons at the heads of shallow, box canyons fed by springs. Similar relocations occurred about the same time at Mesa Verde, in Canyon de Chelly, and in the Kayenta area of northern Arizona.

During the thirteenth century the population of Hovenweep, including two major settlements in Utah and four in Colorado, probably was at least twenty-five hundred persons. Situated at an altitude of 5,240 feet (1,597 meters), Square Tower Group lies roughly 16 miles (26 kilometers) southwest of Lowry and about the same distance west of Crow Canyon. The group consists of Square Tower House, Hovenweep House, Hovenweep Castle, and at least ten kivas.

The solitary monuments of Hovenweep are unique in the ancient architecture of the Southwest; here square, circular, oval, and D-shaped masonry towers stand like timeless sentinels. Their purposes are unknown, although ceremonialism, dwellings, watchtowers, signal platforms, celestial observatories, water reservoirs, and granaries have been suggested. Relatively few penetrations are found through the superbly constructed masonry walls; one tower has no portals at all, suggesting access by means of a roof hatch only.

The reconstruction presented here is based on information published by the National Park Service, a description by Ferguson and Rohn (1987), and my observation on the site in 1991. Among the best preserved and most impressive of the enigmatic Hovenweep ruins are those of the Square Tower Group. Square Tower House sits in the middle of the group on a huge sandstone boulder at the bottom of Square Tower Canyon.

On the canyon rim to the east is Hovenweep Castle, to the west is Hovenweep House, and at the north end of the canyon are the remnants of a check dam above a spring in the valley below. Most likely more than one hundred people lived in the farming village of the Square Tower Group. Originally three stories high, the isolated tower has a single T-shaped door facing south down the canyon and several small wall penetrations that may represent pockets for wood beams.

Square Tower is constructed of coursed, dressed stones recalling Mesa Verde masonry. Difficult to build and unsuitable for daily living, the structure is presumed to be a ceremonial building in view of its proximity to the spring and the absence of a nearby kiva. The tower's location in the bottom of the canyon suggests that it was not a stronghold, a lookout tower, or a signal platform.

So-called Hovenweep Castle once may have been the home of several families. Most of the walls of the pueblo's one- and two-story rooms have collapsed, leaving two citadel-like towers still standing on the mesa top. The better preserved of the two D-shaped structures is the tower closer to the spring; its massive outer walls are two and three stone courses thick, and its foundation is a solid rock.

The only ground-level doorway in Hovenweep Castle opens into the canyon several stories above the talus slope below. The multistory room block originally built on the soft talus

slope has fallen into ruins. Its highest rooftop may have provided access to Hovenweep Castle, recalling the relationship of the lower room block to the cliff dwelling of White House in Canyon de Chelly. A single kiva is found in the mesa top, but the remains of six additional kivas are located in the talus slope below.

Hovenweep House is a D-shaped ceremonial structure situated amid the ruins of a sizable pueblo now covered by sagebrush. The surviving structure is built on a rock foundation; walls lacking firm foundations have collapsed. Wall openings in Hovenweep House give rise to speculation that the structure may have been used for astronomical observations.

CRUMBLED HOUSE
San Juan Anasazi

The largest known Anasazi site in the Chuska Valley, Crumbled House is located in northwestern New Mexico roughly 65 miles (104 kilometers) south of Mesa Verde and about 45 miles (72 kilometers) west of Chaco Canyon. Culturally, the Chuskan Anasazis seem more closely related to the Mesa Verdean people than to the Chacoans. Situated at an average elevation of more or less 5,880 feet (1,792 meters) above sea level, the site consists of an upper room block on a mesa top above a lower room block on a talus slope.

Ceramics collected on the site suggest that Crumbled House was constructed and occupied between A.D. 1100 and 1250. The reconstruction presented here is based on a 1962 plan by Stewart L. Peckham (1969), the report of Michael P. Marshall and others (1979), and data provided by John R. Stein in 1991. Recent aerial imagery and ground examination indicate that the actual number of rooms in the unexcavated site may be about 20 percent fewer than those shown in Peckham's plan.

Sometimes called the "Castle of the Chuskas" the citadel-like upper room block is situated on the southwestern tip of a mesa 100 feet (30 meters) above the surrounding valley floor. Steep talus slopes descend from the mesa edges except to the northeast where it joins a large plateau. The panoramic view from the mesa top is unobstructed in all directions. The surrounding terrain is a sparsely vegetated, open grassland. Located 2 miles (3 kilometers) or so southwest of the site, the Chuska Mountains provided fir, oak, and pine for the construction of Crumbled House.

In plan the mesa-top site forms an isosceles triangle measuring perhaps 155 feet (47 meters) along the wall to the northeast and extending some 265 feet (81 meters) toward the southwest. Three circular towers, each possibly 13 feet (4 meters) in diameter and more than two stories high, define the corners of the triangular plan. The massive towers have 20-inch- (50-centimeter-) thick walls of large, coursed block recalling Mesa Verdean masonry.

The castle-like upper room block has high masonry walls lining the mesa edges, a deep moat, and a stout wall separating the site from the ad-

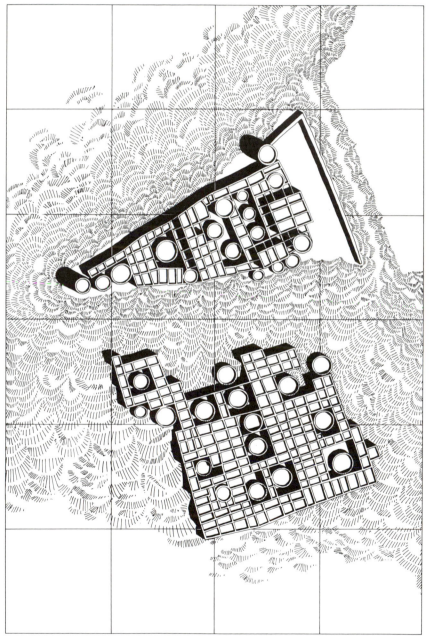

CRUMBLED HOUSE

joining plateau. Peckham's reconstruction of the unexcavated room block proposed more than one hundred ground-floor rooms and thirteen kivas for the site, but more-recent estimates suggest eighty rooms may be more likely. Probably twenty-five second-story rooms also seem reasonable.

Typical rooms in the upper section of Crumbled House measure approximately 10 by 13 feet (3 by 4 meters). The fourteen depressions in the ruins seem to represent keyhole-shaped, subterranean kivas ranging in diameter from 13 to 20 feet (4 to 6 meters). Masonry walls generally are constructed of unshaped sandstone cobbles with typical dimensions of 8 by 12 by 12 inches (20 by 30 by 30 centimeters). Stones of this size abound on the mesa's talus slope.

The bases of multistory walls are thicker than single-story walls; they vary from 20 to 40 inches (50 to 100 centimeters) in width. An unbroken wall located 30 feet (9 meters) or more northeast of the room block originally rose an estimated 12 feet (3.7 meters) above the bottom of the outer moat. Around 3 feet (1 meter) in thickness, the massive wall is constructed of stones larger than those used for house construction.

The moat isolating Crumbled House's upper room block from the plateau is a highly unusual structure. The excavation measures roughly 175 feet (54 meters) in length and 33 feet (10 meters) in width. Keyhole-shaped kivas and Mesa Verdean style masonry at Crumbled House imply influences from the Northern San Juan Valley area.

More or less 70 feet (21 meters) south of the citadel, a large room block descends the steep talus slope.

The gridded structure is organized on five or six terraces stepping down a vertical distance of possibly 65 feet (20 meters). The rectangular complex measures at most 180 by 200 feet (55 by 60 meters) and contains 150 or so rectangular rooms and sixteen circular kivas.

One or more stairways most likely interconnected the upper and lower room blocks of Crumbled House. Unlike the mesa-top structure, the lower house is constructed of dark, tabular sandstones taken from the base of the talus slope west of the site. The precise nature of the irrigation system in the vicinity of the site is unclear, but apparently some of the ancient ditches, channels, and reservoirs continue to be used today.

Like White House, the earlier Anasazi pueblo situated about 35 miles (56 kilometers) to the west, Crumbled House is organized vertically into two distinct components. The extraordinary Castle of the Chuskas is a unique example of ancient architecture in the Southwest. Part of the Navajo Indian Reservation and much in ruins, the remote site has no visitor facilities.

TSIPING

Rio Grande Anasazi

Tsiping is situated at the edge of a volcanic tuff mesa in the Chama River area approximately 45 miles (72 kilometers) northwest of Santa Fe. The pueblo ruins occupy a commanding site 800 feet (244 meters) above the surrounding valleys near the present-day community of Abiquiu. Tree-ring samples and ceramics indicate occupation from roughly A.D. 1200 to 1325 (Stuart & Gauthier 1988).

The period of 1250–1300 is believed to have been a time of stress for Anasazi people. By then the Chacoan population had left the San Juan Basin some 85 miles (140 kilometers) to the west, and a severe drought was in effect. At this time isolated sites like Tsiping were widespread in the Southwest.

Built of cut and shaped tuff blocks, the stone pueblo contains perhaps 335 rooms, sixteen kivas, a linear central plaza, and a walled enclosure to the north. Cavate dwellings are recorded in the southeast side of the mesa below Tsiping. A trail leads down the cliff face to the northeast, and stone walls are found to the southwest.

The remains of Tsiping extend about 675 feet (206 meters) along the mesa edge and at most 140 feet (43 meters) to the northwest. The roughly 140-by-240-foot (43-by-73-meter) walled enclosure at the north end of the pueblo contains three kivas and has an entry portal facing north. Ranging from possibly 10 to 90 feet (3 to 27 meters) in width, the street-like plaza extends for an estimated 450 feet (137 meters) through the pueblo.

Ten kivas are found in the linear plaza, three are situated in the north

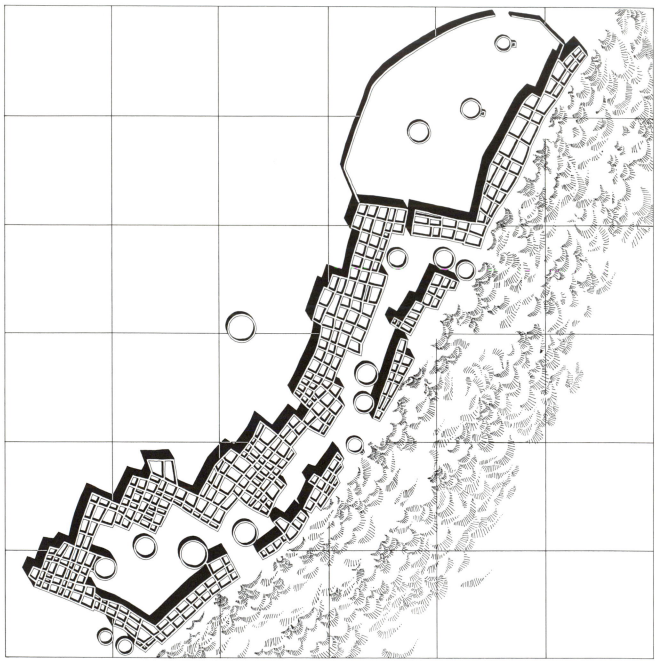

TSIPING

enclosure, and three lie outside the pueblo. Three kivas have entries or perimeter alcoves oriented to the southeast. The disposition of elements in the community plan seems random; no grouping or alignment is apparent.

The room proportions of Tsiping generally are orthogonal with respect to the mesa's edge. The overall plan suggests an aggregation of elements over time rather than a predetermined plan. Tsiping's linear character, size, orientation, and mesa-edge location recall somewhat Walpi, the Hopi pueblo built on First Mesa several centuries after the abandonment of Tsiping.

SAN JOSÉ
Rio Grande Anasazi

The oval pueblo of San José lies in the Galisteo Basin of north-central New Mexico, approximately 65 miles (104 kilometers) east of Albuquerque and perhaps 5 miles (8 kilometers) southwest of the Pecos River. The Anasazi community probably was built and occupied between A.D. 1200 and 1300, a short time before construction began in the neighboring villages of San Cristóbal and Pecos to the west and northwest, respectively. San José is situated on a grassy mesa at an altitude of some 6,900 feet (2,103 meters).

The reconstruction presented here

is based on a preliminary survey of the unexcavated pueblo by Harry P. Mera for the Laboratory of Anthropology in Santa Fe. Solid lines in the reconstruction follow the configuration recorded by Mera; dashed lines suggest possible wall locations pending more accurate information. The plan of San José resembles a roughly 100-by-170-foot (30-by-52-meter) oval with its long axis oriented from north to south and a northerly extension measuring more or less 28 by 40 feet (8.5 by 12.2 meters).

Two concentric rows of rooms may have lined the oval perimeter, forming a central open space some 50 feet (15.2 meters) or so across. Mera noted two kiva-like circular rooms at the north and south ends of San José's elliptical plaza. The reconstruction proposes sixty-one rooms with mostly trapezoidal shapes and typical dimensions of possibly 10 by 11 feet (3 by 3.4 meters).

A passageway about 4 feet (1.2 meters) wide gives access into the central court through the east side of the oval pueblo. San José presumably was a single story high. Pueblos with elliptical, circular, or other curvilinear plans began to be built in the Anasazi area of the Southwest around A.D. 1200; the trend apparently continued for the next two and one-half centuries.

In the Arizona area tiny Fire House appeared near the Hopi mesas and large Kin Tiel was constructed farther to the south. At least six curvilinear Zuni pueblos are known, including Nutria, Lower Pescado, and Deracho. In the Rio Grande area oval-shaped Tyuonyi was erected and the early, circular pueblo of Gran Quivira was built and occupied probably between 1300 and 1400. The impetus for build-

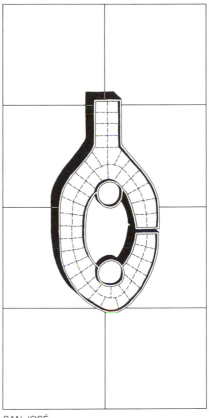

SAN JOSÉ

ing pueblos with curving walls seems to have subsided by the late 1400s, almost as suddenly as it began.

With the possible exception of Tyuonyi, no curved-wall pueblos continued to be occupied by the time the Spanish entered the Southwest in 1540. Anasazi town plans reverted to rectangular or linear room blocks, sometimes forming plazas or streets. By the time the historic period began in the Southwest, San José most likely had been abandoned for two centuries or more. Today, the unexcavated ruins lie on privately owned property and are not accessible to the public.

FORKED LIGHTNING

FORKED LIGHTNING
Rio Grande Anasazi

The adobe pueblo of Forked Lightning is located in a fertile valley of the upper Pecos River approximately 25 miles (40 kilometers) east of Santa Fe. The community lies on the east side of Arroyo del Pueblo about half a mile (800 kilometers) south of Pecos pueblo and some 5 miles (8 kilometers) east of Arrowhead. Forked Lightning is situated strategically between the agricultural communities of the upper Rio Grande to the west and the nomadic hunters of the buffalo plains to the east.

Minor arroyos cut into the terrain to the north and south, but the open hillside rises continuously to the west toward Glorieta Pass. Overgrown with piñon, juniper, and a scattering of pine, the site has been excavated only partially. The reconstructed plan of Forked Lightning is based on data recorded by Alfred Vincent Kidder (1958) in the late 1920s.

The coursed-adobe room block contains a limited number of stone walls. Forked Lightning seems to have 143 ground-floor rooms, four surface kivas, and a large but undetermined number of second-story rooms. The general absence of fire pits in lower-floor rooms other than kivas suggests that these chambers are predominantly store rooms. The plan shown here represents only a small part of the greater community; a short distance to the west are the badly eroded remains of another extensive room block.

The reconstructed pueblo measures overall perhaps 110 by 223 feet (34 by 68 meters). Additional rooms to the east may have been lost to erosion by Arroyo del Pueblo. Room sizes range from roughly 21 to 143 square feet (2 to 13 square meters). The central plaza's dimensions are at most 50 by 68 feet (15 by 21 meters). An entry passage less than 2 feet (60 centimeters) wide leads into the plaza from the west.

Forked Lightning consists of an aggregation of rooms grouped around a relatively small plaza facing toward the east. The room block seems to be a loose arrangement of single or multiple chambers. Many of the rooms are known to have been abandoned while others continued in use or were being constructed.

Presumably, not all of the rooms of the greater Forked Lightning community were occupied at the same time. A relatively large population probably was present at the site for less than a century. Ceramic samples indicate major activity between A.D. 1225 and 1300, with very limited use as early as 1115.

Red adobe with fragments of charcoal and a few pebbles produced the best construction at Forked Lightning. Typical adobe courses are 8 to 24 inches (20 to 60 centimeters) high, with an average of possibly 12 inches (30 centimeters). In many cases walls supported second floors, but such thicker walls or buttresses as those found at Pecos are absent at Forked Lightning.

Walls typically were built by depositing successive courses of puddled adobe into a movable wicker form. Horizontal adobe courses often extend the entire length of a room, but seldom do courses continue around corners. Walls are well laid with an almost uniform thickness of 11 inches (28 centimeters). A coat of plaster finishes interior walls and bases.

Foundations appear to be placed directly on the smoothed surface of the ground. Forked Lightning's few stone walls consist of laminated sandstones up to 20 inches (50 centimeters) long laid in beds of mortar. Flat stone faces are turned outward, imparting relatively smooth surfaces to the walls. Rubble fills voids between facing stones, and mortar is used sparingly.

Only ten doors are found in the room block; all are filled with adobe. Sills average 20 inches (50 centimeters) in height. Doors typically are around 17 inches (44 centimeters) wide and 20 inches (50 centimeters) high. Floors generally consist of 1- to 2-inch (2- to 5-centimeter) thick layers of clean adobe placed directly on the smoothed surface of the ground.

Two circular, subterranean kivas are found near Forked Lightning, but neither is shown on the reconstructed drawing. One is located an estimated 350 feet (107 meters) south of the pueblo; it has an interior diameter of 17 feet (5 meters) or so. The other kiva is situated in the ruins of the west pueblo. It measures possibly 11.6 feet (3.5 meters) in diameter and has an unusual interior finish of red adobe plaster.

Forked Lightning's four surface kivas range in size from 120 to 260 square feet (11 to 24 square meters). All the ceremonial kivas have doors facing east, and none are circular like their subterranean counterparts. White lime plaster walls are characteristic of most of the kivas.

Mounting pressure from neighboring groups may account for the aban-donment of the community around A.D. 1300. The more secure *mesilla* of Pecos, a short distance to the northeast, had relatively steep sides and good visibility in all directions. The new pueblo was close enough to be constructed by workers still living in Forked Lightning, and the distance for transporting household goods to new residences was relatively short.

Between 1300 and 1540, generally, the population in the Southwest consolidated into a limited number of large communities, often abandoning former areas and concentrating in the Hopi mesas, the valley of the Zuni River, and the upper Rio Grande area. The period spans from the end of the Great Drought of 1276–1299 to the arrival of Spanish explorers in the Southwest in 1540.

By the middle of the fifteenth century Grasshopper, Kinishba, Casa Malpais, and other Mogollon pueblos were abandoned and the people who built them likely had migrated toward the north and east where they may have joined Hopi, Zuni, or other Anasazi communities. The people who built Los Muertos, Casa Grande, and other great Hohokam towns may be the ancestors of the present-day Tohono O'odham (previously Pima) or Papago Indians of southern Arizona. The cultural identity of the Salado people seems to have disappeared gradually during the fifteenth century.

During the fourteenth century the Zuni people abandoned their isolated mesa-top sites at the east end of the Zuni River Valley and returned to the fertile lowlands where they established the six large pueblos the Spanish found in 1540. The population of the Hopi mesas seems to have been augmented by migrants, perhaps from the Northern San Juan region, the Kayenta and Virgin River areas, and the Little Colorado River basin. At the time of the *entrada* Oraibi and Awatovi were the only Hopi towns situated on mesa tops; the others were located by springs and farm plots on the canyon floors.

The population of the upper Rio Grande Valley area seems to have grown substantially during the fourteenth and fifteenth centuries. Exceptionally large communities appeared at Kuaua, Poshuouinge, Sapawe, Arroyo Hondo, Pecos, San Cristóbal, Paako, Gran Quivira, and many other Rio Grande sites. By the time Coronado's expedition arrived at Hawiku, a major shift toward the southeast seems to have been well underway in the ever-changing life of the Southwest.

Mogollon

The large Mogollon pueblo of Kinishba occupies a 12.5-acre (5-hectare) site in the mountains of east-central Arizona not far from Grasshopper. Composed of several multistory room blocks aranged in east and west groups, Kinishba contains well-ordered interior streets, plazas, and porticoes. The large pueblo's only excavated room block contains almost four hundred rectangular masonry rooms at most three stories high.

Around the time Kinishba was flourishing to the southeast, construction may have been well underway in neighboring Grasshopper, a Mogollon pueblo with some five hundred rooms arranged in thirteen room blocks one to three stories high. Spread over a 30-acre (12-hectare) site, Grasshopper's room blocks have interior streets and plazas recalling similar features in later Hopi and Zuni pueblos. The Mogollon community of Casa Malpais occupies a dramatic site in eastern Arizona consisting of several large terraces, a medium-size room block, a square great kiva, an extensive walled plaza, several cemeteries or catacomb areas, and other architectural components.

The magnificent city of Paquimé, also called Casas Grandes, is the grand Chichimecan trading center of the fourteenth century. Unsurpassed in architectural sophistication elsewhere in the Southwest, Paquimé, has a number of impressive room blocks up to seven stories high, an efficiently designed aqueduct, a large market, and an impressive assemblage of ball courts, plazas, ramps, colonnades, and ceremonial platform mounds. Although the vast city has an area of some 88 acres (36 hectares), Paquimé nonetheless is less than half the size of such contemporary Hohokam complexes as Casa Grande or Los Muertos in the Salt and Gila River Basin of southern Arizona.

The well-preserved eighteen-room cliff dwelling called the Cave of Las Ventanas overlooks the canyon of the Rio Garabato south of Paquimé. The small settlement is one of many agricultural communities related to the Chichimeca mercantile network. Located between Paquimé and the Cave of Las Ventanas, Olla Cave contains an enormous pot-shaped granary, which most likely was used to store corn.

Hohokam

Extending over an area of some 290 acres (117 hectares), Casa Grande occupies the largest site in this study. The vast Hohokam center includes thirteen adobe-walled compounds, a clan house, ball court, and central plaza. The massive adobe great house of Case Grande is the tallest and most impressive Hohokam structure surviving today. The roof top of the three-story citadel affords a clear view of all the surrounding community and the remains of its main canal extending northward toward its source of water, the Salt River in south-central Arizona.

Comprising thirty-five adobe-walled compounds, Los Muertos is one of the largest of forty Hohokam platform mound complexes recorded along the Salt and Gila River Basin. Typical Hohokam architectural characteristics found in Los Muertos are adobe-walled compounds and buildings, orthogonal town planning with respect to the cardinal points, disposition of compounds along a dominantly east-to-west axis, a distinctive platform mound in the large compound near the town's center, and a major canal connecting the community to the closest river. The absence of a ball court at Los Muertos suggests that the site may have been one of the last Hohokam settlements.

Salado

The ridge-top Salado pueblo of Salome appears to contain 150 ground-floor rooms and relatively few open spaces. The plan of Salome's compact room block is almost the opposite of the spacious compounds with few rooms that the Salado built a century earlier at such upland sites as Sycamore Creek, Park Creek, and Reno Creek. The fourteenth-century Salado cliff dwellings of Tonto contain possibly sixty-eight rooms in three caves overlooking the Tonto Basin to the east.

The two-story Salado pueblo of Besh Ba Gowah once may have contained more than 250 rooms. Built on the south bank of the upper Salt River, the room block has an unusual roofed corridor entrance leading to its central plaza, a remarkable sunken ceremonial room, unexplained variations in floor levels, and other distinctive characteristics. Like multistory Salome pueblo to the north, Besh Ba Gowah is very compactly planned, has masonry walls with stones laid in generous beds of mortar, and has relatively little open space on its ground floor compared to earlier Salado compounds.

The impressive platform mound compound of Cline Terrace is the best preserved and most elaborately organized of the surviving Salado communities in the Tonto Basin. Similar in size to the large Hohokam compound of Casa Grande, Cline Terrace contained an elite residence which was the focus of a complex hierarchical system. The neighboring Salado platform compound of Schoolhouse Point had more than twice as many rooms as Cline Terrace compactly arranged within its enclosing walls.

Zuni (Anasazi)

Constructed in eastern Arizona about halfway between the Hopi mesas and the Zuni pueblos, the multistory room blocks of Kin Tiel contain more than a thousand rooms up to three stories high. Completed around 1275 and abandoned sometime before 1540, Kin Tiel consists of an unbroken, curving perimeter wall enclosing room blocks that were added later in the construction sequence. A spring-fed drainage way divides the orderly pueblo into north and south halves recalling the architectural organization of Taos.

Reportedly the first pueblo to be seen by the Spanish in 1540, Hawiku is one of six Zuni pueblos established on the Zuni River in western Mexico late in prehistoric times. The large, accretional masonry village seems to comprise eight hundred multistory rooms in five densely clustered room blocks and several smaller structures. Hawiku's somewhat random grouping of compactly massed structures recalls to some extent the plan of Zuni Pueblo to which the inhabitants moved after the Pueblo Revolt.

Hopi (Anasazi)

Said by some to be the oldest continuously inhabited town in the present-day United States, Oraibi until recently was the most populous and influential of the Hopi pueblos. Established perhaps as early as the eleventh century, the famous Third Mesa village originally consisted of seven irregular, parallel rows of linear room blocks arranged in a street-type plan like Santo Domingo's. The enigmatic Second Mesa pueblo of Chukubi may have contained 250 ground-floor rooms and a single kiva; the settlement may have been abandoned around the beginning of the historic era in the Southwest.

The historic Hopi pueblo of Awatovi on Antelope Mesa had about 260 or so rooms in a multistory room block when the Spanish visited the site in 1540. Other Hopi people destroyed the pueblo in the winter of 1700–01, apparently because of their opposition to Christianity, which was embraced by the residents of Awatovi. Situated northwest of Awatovi, the fourteenth-century Hopi pueblo of Fire House comprised an estimated forty ground-floor rooms in a unique elliptical plan recalling the curvilinear perimeter walls of Kin Tiel to the southwest.

Sinagua

The large Sinagua pueblo of Nuvaqueotaka originally consisted of three large room blocks up to three stories high. The structures occupy a mountainous site north of the Mogollon Rim in central Arizona. Typical Sinagua architectural characteristics of Nuvaqueotaka include a probable ball court located between the three main room blocks and distinctive primary walls built parallel to each other throughout all three room blocks. Major construction probably occurred in the early fourteenth century, and Nuvaqueotaka seems to have been abandoned more than a century before the Spanish *entrada*.

Rio Grande Anasazi

Located on the west bank of the Rio Grande in central New Mexico, the large aggregated community of Kuaua includes more than twelve hundred rooms, three spacious plazas, six kivas, and other architectural components. Construction began on the puddled-adobe pueblo during the fourteenth century, and occupation seems to have continued until 1700 except for a brief period of abandonment after the Spanish siege in 1541. Otowi was one of the last active communities on the Pajarito Plateau north of Kuaua. The pueblo had more than eight hundred rooms in five orderly room blocks at most three stories high.

The largest of thirteen talus houses in Frijoles Canyon, Long House may contain 350 rooms in a combination of caves and adjoining multistory room blocks. Long House and Tyuonyi are nearby neighbors built and occupied during the fourteenth and fifteenth centuries on the floor of Frijoles Canyon in

Bandelier National Monument. Oval-shaped Tyuonyi is a masonry pueblo having almost six hundred rooms and at least three kivas.

The vast adobe pueblo of Poshuouinge may have comprised more than two thousand rooms in multistory room blocks defining immensely scaled plazas. Poshuouinge is one of at least ten large prehistoric pueblos erected between 1300 and 1500 in the Chama Valley. A contemporary of Poshuouinge in the upper Rio Grande Valley to the east, Arroyo Hondo most likely has more than one thousand rooms in twenty-four room blocks flanking ten plazas.

Considered to be the largest adobe pueblo in the Southwest, Sapawe appears to contain more than forty-four hundred rooms, at least nineteen kivas, and seven or more large plazas. The extensive remains occupy more than thirty acres (12 hectares) in the Chama Valley north of Poshuouinge. Abandoned in historic times, Sapawe may have had more than twice as many rooms as Poshuouinge and possibly four times the number of Arroyo Hondo and Kuaua.

One of the most extensive prehistoric pueblos in the Galisteo Basin, Paako is organized into north and south sections. Containing an estimated thirteen hundred rooms, Paako's north section has prehistoric room blocks built of puddled adobe to the east and later stone masonry structures to the west dating to the historic era. The large ruin of San Cristóbal in the Galisteo Basin consists of more than sixteen hundred masonry rooms in nineteen to twenty multistory room blocks.

A short distance north of San Cristóbal, construction began at Pecos about 1450 where four massive masonry room blocks are grouped closely together around a central plaza. The structures of Pecos grew into a compact and livable pueblo with more than twenty kivas surrounded by a low perimeter wall. Located west of Pecos in the Sangre de Cristo Mountains, Arrowhead is a small masonry pueblo with seventy-six single-story rooms arranged around a central plaza.

The study's final example of fourteenth- and fifteenth-century communities in the upper Rio Grande Valley is Gran Quivira, the largest pueblo in the Estancia Valley of central New Mexico. Displaying both Anasazi and Mogollon architectural characteristics, Gran Quivira is composed of seventeen room blocks, which housed an estimated three thousand people when Spaniards first visited the site in 1598. Occupied until 1672, Gran Quivira acted throughout its long existence as a trading center between the sedentary farming communities of the Rio Grande Valley and the roving hunters of the buffalo plains.

Contemporary World Architecture

In the Eastern United States architectural activity reached a climax during the late thirteenth and early fourteenth centuries; by the end of the fifteenth century a general decline had begun in most areas. Second in size only to Cahokia, the large and impressive ceremonial center of Moundville near Tuscaloosa had an extensive residential area and possibly twenty truncated platform mounds, including the main temple mound some 55 feet (16.8 meters) high. Another spectacular example of contemporary architecture was Etowah in the foothills of northwest Georgia, a D-shaped ceremonial center enclosed by a palisade and moat. The site contained an immense multiterraced platform mound exceeded in size only by Monks Mound at Cahokia (Morgan 1980).

On the Central Plateau of Mexico foundations were begun in 1325 for the Aztec capital of Tenochtitlán. The magnificient city had an impressive, wall-enclosed ceremonial compound dominated by twin temples on a single base recalling those of Tenayuca. In the Oaxaca region the new Zapotec capital of Mitla expressed new architectural ideas with its geometrically arranged quadrangles and with the extraordinary ornamentation of its façades. Along the rocky east coast of the Yucatán Peninsula, walls enclosed the city of Tulum on three sides. The buildings of Tulum were arranged to form perhaps the first recognizable streets in Mesoamerica (Heyden & Gendrop 1973).

During the fourteenth and fifteenth centuries in Micronesia, the royal tomb complex of Nandauwas and the royal residential compound of Pahnkadira, both magnificent examples of megalithic architecture, reached completion at Nan Madol on Pohnpei. About the year 1400 a paramount leader unified the island of Kosrae and began the great wall compounds of Kinyeir Fulat, Insru, Lurun, Posral, and others in central Leluh. The tradition of *latte* building continued with the erection of the House of Taga on Tinian, the highest stone foundation found in the Mariana Islands. A dozen megalithic columns originally elevated the house 16 feet (5 meters) above the ground level (Morgan 1988).

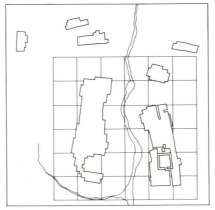

KEY PLAN OF KINISHBA COMMUNITY

KINISHBA
Mogollon

The large Mogollon community of Kinishba consists of seven room blocks in ruins on both sides of an arroyo in east-central Arizona. Three of the ruins appear in the reconstructed plan represented here based on the account of Byron Cummings (1940) recording his work at the site during the late 1930s. The remaining four ruins are modest in size; they lie close by to the north on both sides of the arroyo. The 30-foot- (9-meter-) deep arroyo drains south into the White River, a tributary of the upper Salt River.

Located approximately 115 miles (185 kilometers) east of Phoenix, the site is situated at an elevation of roughly 5,500 feet (1,676 meters) above sea level. In several respects Kinishba resembles Grasshopper, the contemporary Mogollon pueblo that lies some 40 miles (64 kilometers) to the northwest. Both sites are large in scale, and both consist of multiple room blocks arranged on both banks of a southward-flowing drainageway. However, Kinishba's site area is only some 12.4 acres (5 hectares), less than half the size of Grasshopper.

Centuries ago a spring-fed stream from the White Mountains north of Kinishba probably flowed through the arroyo. On the 3-by-6-mile- (5-by-10-kilometer-) wide hillslope south of the community, ancient agriculturalists cultivated corn, squash, and beans using dry land farming techniques. The fertile fields seem to be easily capable of sustaining Kinishba's estimated maximum population of fifteen hundred to two thousand people in the early 1300s (Noble 1981:74).

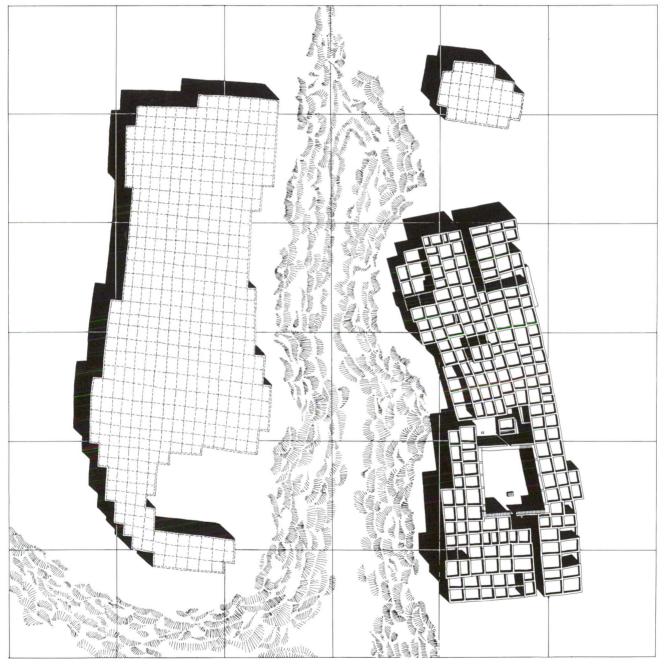

KINISHBA, MAJOR ROOM BLOCKS

The only room block excavated at Kinishba is shown to the east of the arroyo in the reconstruction presented here. The large ruin west of the arroyo and the small one to the north appear only in outline with shadows suggesting two-story heights. The following description applies primarily to the excavated room block; presumably, its construction was generally typical of the other structures at Kinishba.

The remains of numerous pit houses indicate an earlier Mogollon occupation and abandonment of the area. Sometime later new settlers most likely reoccupied the site and built a one-story structure, the remains of which underlie the pueblo presented here. Major construction and occupation of Kinishba most likely occurred after 1300, perhaps about the time Grasshopper flourished.

The large masonry pueblo measures at most 351 feet (107 meters) in length by an average width of 110 feet (33 meters). At its peak the structure may have contained 210 first-floor rooms, a large number on the second floor, and a few on the third floor for an estimated total of 389 rooms. Construction seemingly began at the north end of the room block and continued over time to the south in orderly increments. In the 1930s excavators found that some of Kinishba's west walls had collapsed and fallen into the arroyo.

The compact rectangular pueblo has two contiguous plazas and three entry passages. The first entry built is the 7-to-10-foot- (2.1-to-3-meters-) wide north passage some 62 feet (19 meters) long. The entry originally continued south to the plazas; later it was blocked by the nine rooms shown in the reconstructed plan. A short passage more or less 5.5 feet (1.7 meters) wide provides access from the west into the north plaza.

The main access into the larger south plaza seems to have been by way of the unique south passage with its remarkable offset entry. Visitors would proceed through the 7-foot- (2.1-meter-) wide passage to the north, a distance of about 75 feet (23 meters). Here a blank wall screens the plaza from view. Visitors then would turn left into a small, open-air forecourt measuring around 12 by 25 feet (3.7 by 7.6 meters). At the end of the outdoor room in the wall to the right is a 4.8-foot- (1.5-meter-) wide portal leading into the south plaza. The portal has neither a threshold nor a lintel.

The average dimensions of the south plaza are 54 by 62 feet (16 by 19 meters) or so. An unbroken bench some 20 inches (50 centimeters) high and 3 to 4 feet (0.9 to 1.2 meters) wide surrounds the plaza on all four sides. Two-story walls flank the plaza to the east, west, and southwest.

A distinctive roofed portico probably shaded the benches to the east and west, providing porches for second-floor rooms. Centered on the south entry portal and about 11 feet (3.6 meters) north of the benches is a rectangular altar. Perhaps a place for ritual offerings, the structure is built of adobe and stone to a height not exceeding 2 feet (60 centimeters).

The north wall of the large plaza rises 6 feet (1.8 meters) above bench level. Near the center of the wall is a slot-like portal around 21 inches (53 centimeters) wide. The opening provides access into the smaller north plaza. The floor elevation of the roughly 25-by-59-foot (7.6-by-18-meter) open space corresponds to the height of the south plaza's benches. Near the west end of the north plaza is a 2-foot (60-centimeter) square stone used for outdoor cooking.

Kinishba's only kiva is a rectangular structure sunken 8 feet (2.4 meters) below the level of the plaza. Access to the 10-by-11-foot (3-by-3.4-meter) subterranean chamber is by means of a ladder leading down through a roof hatch centered above the kiva's fire pit. Ritual paraphernalia presumably was stored in the 33-inch- (84-centimeter-) wide space along the south wall of the kiva. Very similar ceremonial chambers are found today in Hopi and Zuni pueblos.

The masonry walls of Kinishba consist of tabular sandstone with some basalt and limestone laid in clay mortar. Most walls are 12 inches (30 centimeters) or so thick, but some range up to 20 inches (50 centimeters) in thickness, perhaps to support third-floor rooms. Exterior walls and those facing plazas or passageways generally have ashlar facings backed up by rubble masonry.

Ashlar masonry consists of alternating courses of thick stone blocks with courses of thin flat stones. Other walls utilize large irregular stones and boulders chinked with spalls and backed up with rubble. Weaknesses in Kinishba's masonry were caused by failing to offset vertical joints and failing to interlock masonry facings with their backups. All of the walls were plastered by hand, the same way Hopi women apply adobe today.

The typical residential unit of Kinishba seems to have been two adjacent rooms, often a living room above a windowless storage space. Hearths for cooking and heating and often mealing bins or *metates* identify living rooms. Four large rectangular chambers ranging in area from 192 to 264 square feet (17.8 to 24.5 square meters) apparently are ceremonial rooms like those found in present-day Hopi pueblos.

Excavators found numerous ceremonial artifacts in the ruins of Kinishba. These include deer jawbones painted with symbols in red, black, and yellow and stone tablets with motifs representing the sun, water spirits, clouds, and lightning. The south plaza with its altar and perimeter benches seems to be a likely place for ceremonial dances and community activities (Cummings 1940).

The name Kinishba is derived from Apache and Navajo words meaning "brown house." Evidence gathered in the ruins indicates that the ancient people traded with Kayenta Anasazis to the northwest, the Tularosa to the east, the Hopi to the north, and the Hohokam of the Salt and Gila drainage to the south and west. Today the site is fenced off, deteriorating, and little visited. For access to the ruins, one may apply to the Fort Apache Tribe, administrators of the site, in Fort Apache, Arizona.

GRASSHOPPER
Mogollon

The large Mogollon pueblo of Grasshopper consists of some five hundred rooms on a large site bisected by an old channel of the Salt River Draw in east-central Arizona. The 30-acre (12-hectare) site lies in the midst of a broad, fertile valley approximately 100 miles northeast of Phoenix. The one- and two-story rooms of the large aggregated village are distributed in thirteen room blocks and fifteen outlying structures on both sides of the old channel.

Between A.D. 1275 and 1300 a small Mogollon farming settlement apparently occupied the Grasshopper site. Around 1300 the founders of the pueblo erected two small units of five to ten rooms and a larger block with twenty-one rooms. The latter structure may have been built by migrants from Chodistaas, a small nearby pueblo that burned and was abandoned just before 1300.

The three largest room blocks at Grasshopper appear to have been constructed between 1300 and 1330 by a rapidly growing population, perhaps augmented by successive immigrations. The main room block east of the old channel contains ninety-three contiguous ground-floor rooms. The two large room blocks to the west are grouped compactly around a large plaza measuring about 92 by 98 feet (28 by 30 meters).

The central structure has ninety-two ground-floor rooms and a 33-by-46-foot (10-by-15-meter) plaza. The open space seems to have been roofed over in the late 1320s and transformed into a great kiva. The west room block is L-shaped and consists of one hundred rooms. Northeast of

the main plaza is a small somewhat irregular courtyard measuring around 33 by 49 feet (10 by 15 meters). Room sizes at Grasshopper are relatively uniform, the average being possibly 175 square feet (16.3 square meters).

Two entries provide access to the main plaza, one by way of the north courtyard and the other through a passageway from the south. A cluster of tree-ring dates indicates that in 1320 a roof measuring roughly 10 by 33 feet (3 by 10 meters) was built over the south corridor, converting it into a covered way. At the same time the corridor leading east from the courtyard appears to have been roofed (Reid 1989).

By 1330 construction of the major room blocks at Grasshopper was complete. The large pueblo is an aggregation of small groups of rooms lacking a predetermined plan. Plazas and roofed corridors link some of the village structures, while other elements seem isolated or scattered. Covered ways recalling those at Grasshopper are found at such present-day Western Pueblos as Walpi, Shipaulovi, and Zuni.

After 1330 occupancy at the site shifted from continuous to intermittent. Modest low-walled structures were built and occupied in scattered locations around the periphery of the site. Many outliers were U-shaped structures with only three walls, like those of Chodistaas. After 1350 building activity declined markedly, and by 1400 Grasshopper Pueblo was abandoned completely.

Households at Grasshopper consist of one to three rooms serving the specialized functions of dwelling, storage, and manufacturing. The households may have been ritually linked in a hierarchy of kin-related social

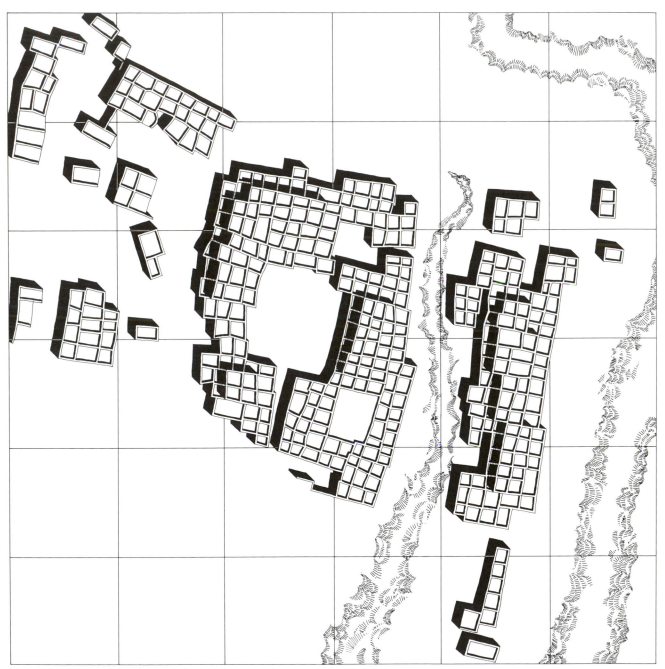

GRASSHOPPER

units. For example, three related households may have been associated with a ceremonial room, and six households with a kiva. The physical plan of Grasshopper may reflect directly its social organization.

Burials at the large pueblo consist of extended interments in simple rectangular pits, sometimes with associated burial offerings. Anasazi residents were of a minority group distinguished by greater wealth than most of the Mogollon, but they were not wealthier than the most prominent members of the Mogollon community. Anasazi, Mogollon, and perhaps members of other cultural groups apparently lived together peacefully at Grasshopper (Reid 1989).

Trade received major emphasis at the large community. Imported items include macaws and copper bells perhaps from Paquimé, white-fronted parrots perhaps from southern Sonora, shell ornaments from the Hohokam area, and pottery from the north. Possible exports from Grasshopper may have been turquoise, ceramics, salt, hematite, and chert.

Most of the items manufactured by the artisans of Grasshopper appear to be intended primarily for domestic consumption. The community may have been self-sufficient in food and raw materials until immediately prior to abandonment. It seems unlikely, however, that a political structure developed to the extent required for coping with the long-term problems of the large community.

The reasons for the decline and abandonment of Grasshopper are not clearly known. Overemphasis on trade and failure to intensify agriculture may have been contributing factors. The decades of below-normal rainfall between 1325 and 1355 also

could have proven to be a serious problem.

Where the former residents of Grasshopper eventually resettled also is unknown, but the Hopi, Zuni, or Rio Grande areas seem likely. The Mogollon always were known to be good hunters; they excelled at making arrow points and also were respected warriors. They probably were relatively free to move where they wanted.

CASA MALPAIS
Mogollon

The Mogollon community of Casa Malpais is located near the headwaters of the little Colorado River in east-central Arizona. The dramatic site is situated on five terraces ascending toward the southwest face of a sheer cliff that towers 155 feet (47 meters) above the valley floor. The ruins lie approximately 2 miles (3 kilometers) northwest of Springerville at an average elevation of roughly 7,000 feet (2,134 meters) above sea level.

Huge basalt boulders have fallen from the cliff face and rest in random piles on the broad, grassy terraces of the talus slope. Piñon, juniper, and oak woodlands cover nearby hillslopes, while pine, spruce, and fir forests are found at higher elevations. Fauna associated with the area include deer, antelope, elk, bear, lions, coyotes, rabbits, squirrels, raccoons,

and several species of birds, including American eagles.

The reconstruction presented here is based on a map and report prepared by John W. Hohman (1990: figs. 1–9). The sheer cliff face below the mesa rim appears in the northeast corner of the drawing. A narrow depression at the base of the cliff lies hidden from the view of the nearby terraces. Beyond the hidden depression the stepped terraces of the talus slope descended toward the river to the southwest. The settlement is situated near the fertile river valley but well above the level of the mosquito-breeding marshes. The community lies well below the path of cutting winter winds that sweep the mesa top.

Casa Malpais' highest terrace overlooks the valley to the southwest from an elevation some 100 feet (30 meters) above the flood plain. The large masonry room block on the terrace measures about 80 by 120 feet (24 by 36.5 meters). The structure contains forty-four formal rooms, a six-room annex associated with three patios or courtyard to the southeast, and an unusual room with a curvilinear wall on the northwest corner.

In all, the room block contains fifty-four recognizable spaces. Typical room sizes appear to measure perhaps 10 by 13 feet (3 by 4 meters), an average area of possibly 130 square feet (12 square meters). A single tree-ring date of A.D. 1268 was derived from a roof beam, but ceramics collected on the site suggest that Casa Malpais probably was founded and occupied between 1250 and 1400.

Around 50 feet (15 meters) northwest of the room block is an exceptionally well preserved great kiva measuring more or less 57 feet (17.5 meters) square. A bench probably 30

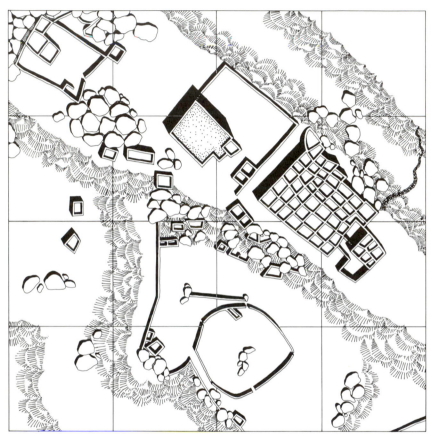

CASA MALPAIS, CENTRAL AREA

inches (75 centimeters) wide and 24 inches (60 centimeters) high may have engaged the base of all four walls. Casa Malpais' great kiva is remarkable for its large size and for the relatively late period of its construction and use.

Estimated to measure 50 by 90 feet (15 by 27 meters), a walled community plaza engages the great kiva's northeast wall. Three rooms of unknown function are found in the plaza southeast of the great kiva. The walls enclosing the plaza and its associated rooms are constructed of single rows of basalt boulders stacked two to four stones high.

Perhaps 90 feet (27 meters) northwest of the great kiva and on the same terrace is a walled compound enclosing three rooms. A square storage room engages the east corner of the compound, and four sacred chambers appear among the boulders north of the compound. Full-height walls of carefully fitted stones once sealed off the entrances into various burial vaults. Hohman refers to the cemetery as a catacomb.

Only one of Casa Malpais' four catacomb areas is shown on the reconstructed drawing. They seem to be among the first such burial chambers to be found in the Southwest. The large number of fallen basalt megaliths among the ruins provide numerous deep crevices and caves suitable for use as catacombs.

The extensive network of prehistoric trails on the site includes a walkway of fitted stones leading across the hidden depression at the base of the cliff. Here a spiral rock stair with hand holds ascends 55 feet (17 meters) to the mesa rim. The depression contains several special activity areas and numerous petroglyphs.

The next terrace to the southwest lies 26 feet (8 meters) below the level of the room block. The terrace contains seventeen or eighteen masonry rooms and a community plaza roughly 85 feet (26 meters) in diameter. A wall of basalt approximately 32 inches (80 centimeters) thick and possibly 50 inches (1.3 meters) high encloses the plaza.

Five narrow entries through the wall provide access into the large plaza. The function of the small masonry room on the north side of the plaza is unknown. A low masonry wall is built around the edges of the entire terrace, perhaps to control access during trading or ceremonial activities (Hohman 1990).

The next-lower terrace lies about 43 feet (13 meters) below the level of the room block. The terrace comprises several rooms with masonry walls and other features of unknown use. In all, more than two hundred interments with associated offerings, caches, and shrines have been identified at Casa Malpais.

Three distinct types of basalt masonry are used in the pueblo's structures, apparently according to their functions. The formal room block is constructed of small, tightly fitted stones with shaped outer surfaces. The great kiva, sacred chambers, and dance plazas are built of large, tightly fitted blocks most likely finished with a coat of plaster. Walls of compounds, patios, and the annex consist of medium-size cobbles with widely spaced joints using little or no mortar.

In Spanish the name Casa Malpais means "house of the bad lands," which seems to refer to the relatively

barren land at lower elevations to the north. The reasons for abandoning the community around 1400 are unknown, but drought and the collapse of more widespread economic or social systems are not ruled out. Casa Malpais presumably was one of the very last of the active Mogollon communities.

The final residents of Casa Malpais may have relocated to nearby Zuni pueblos or joined other Anasazi settlements to the north and east. During the past ninety years pothunters, looters, and vandals have caused extensive damage to the remains of Casa Malpais. Today a museum and field laboratory in the Casa Malpais Archaeological Park are open for visitation, and guided tours of the partially restored site are available by contacting the museum.

PAQUIMÉ
Mogollon

The splendid architecture of fifteenth-century Paquimé is unsurpassed elsewhere in the ancient Southwest. The remains of the once-magnificent city are located near the present-day town of Nuevo Casas Grandes approximately 190 miles (300 kilometers) southwest of El Paso and Ciudad Juárez in northern Chihuahua. Paquimé is situated at an altitude of 4,860 feet (1,481 meters) in a

KEY PLAN OF PAQUIMÉ

broad valley extending unbroken into southern New Mexico and Arizona. The tranquil valley and the surrounding Sierra Madres recall the valley surrounding Monte Albán in Oaxaca.

According to its excavator Charles C. Di Peso (1974), at its zenith the fallen trading center of the Gran Chichimeca spread its mercantile network over an area of perhaps 85,000 square miles (220,000 square kilometers). Trade items identified with Paquimé are found in ancient pueblos of the Southwest hundreds of miles to the north, in Mexico City some 940 miles (1,500 kilometers) to the south, on Webb Island off the Gulf Coast of Texas roughly 550 miles (880 kilometers) to the east, and along an estimated 900 miles (1,450 kilometers) of Mexico's Pacific Coast.

Casas Grandes is an alternate name for the city. The alternate is not used in this discussion because the name is easily confused with Casa Grande, the large Hohokam complex in southern Arizona. The name Paquimé first was recorded in the sixteenth century

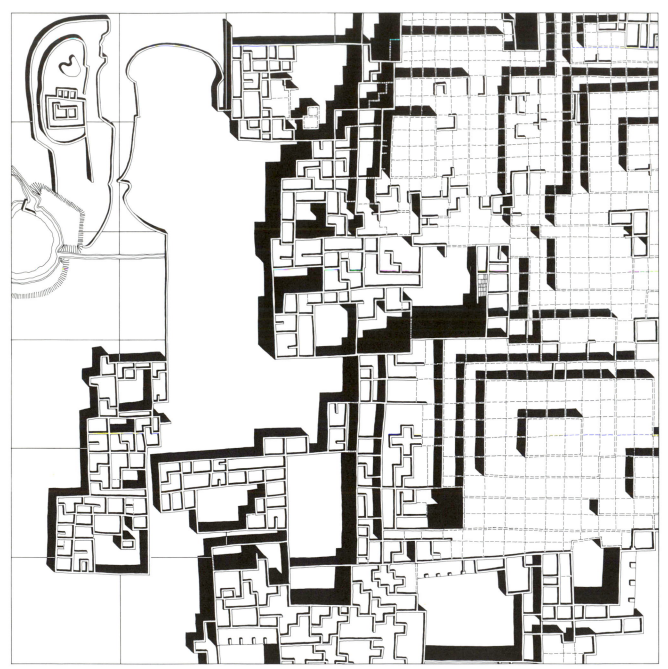

PAQUIMÉ, WEST-CENTRAL AREA

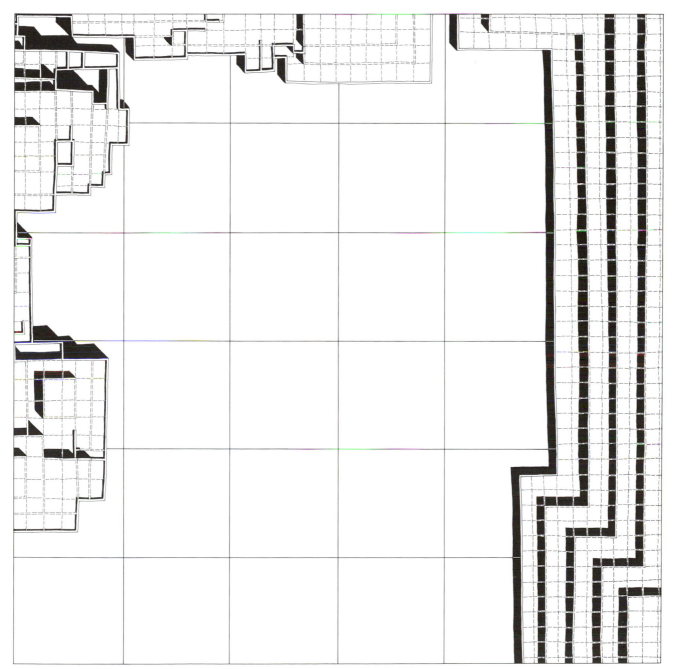

PAQUIMÉ, EAST-CENTRAL AREA

by General Francisco Ibarra, who quartered his troops in the ruins. The Spanish applied the name Paquimé to the city, the nearby river, and the valley (Di Peso 1974:295).

Paquimé's chronology initially was reported to fall between A.D. 1060 and 1340 based on wood samples recovered during excavations between 1958 and 1960. Subsequently, Jeffrey S. Dean of the University of Arizona's Laboratory of Tree-ring Research reexamined the specimens. He found that the wood lacks sapwood, which means that many rings are missing. The corrected chronology for Paquimé falls between A.D. 1275 and 1500.

Perhaps sometime around A.D. 900 barbarous people living on the northern frontier of Mesoamerica began to build mud-domed houses in pits forming hamlets in the vicinity of Paquimé. In time the modest settlements were modified and expanded. By the middle of the thirteenth century most villages counted a number of rudimentary surface structures facing central open spaces or plazas. About this time a small contingent of people, possibly Toltec-related traders called *puchteca* (Di Peso 1974), or *pochteca* (Cordell 1984), may have persuaded the indigenous Chichimeca to expand one of their settlements into a more substantial trading center.

During the next century and a half Paquimé grew into a sophisticated complex that by the fifteenth century probably resembled Los Muertos, the Hohokam complex in the Salt River Basin. At this time Paquimé most likely consisted of more than twenty self-sufficient, adobe-walled compounds, each with one- or two-story rooms, one or more open courtyards,

and storage facilities. The compounds of Paquimé, like those of Los Muertos, Casa Grande, and other major Hohokam settlements, were located at broadly dispersed intervals in the landscape.

A sophisticated aqueduct called the *acequia madre* was constructed to bring water into Paquimé from the mountains 2.3 miles (3.7 kilometers) to the northwest. The acequia was engineered carefully to convey water at a constant rate of fall although the vertical descent was only 64.6 feet (19.7 meters), a slope ratio of one unit in 181. Reservoirs, wells, cisterns, and a sewer system downstream augmented Paquimé's waterworks.

Other architectural features introduced in the twelfth-century city appear to be T-shaped doorways, raised fire hearths, heated sleeping platforms, square columns, and massive bearing walls built of caliche. The basic building material of Paquimé, caliche is a natural material underlying the surface of the desert floor. During this period Paquimé prospered, its trade networks flourished, and its population probably rose to at least seven hundred persons.

A major urban building program during the fourteenth century brought Paquimé to a high level of architectural development. The reconstruction proposed here shows the city as it may have appeared toward the middle of the fifteenth century. The reconstruction is based on information and drawings recording the well-documented excavation of Paquimé under the sponsorship of the Amerind Foundation between 1958 and 1961 (Di Peso 1974).

The reconstruction presents a 600-by-1,200-foot (183-by-366-meter) area in the center of Paquimé at the stan-

dard scale of this study. The area shown contains a major portion of the city's most sophisticated architectural elements, but even so the drawing represents less than one-fifth of the greater urban plan. During the fourteenth century Paquimé expanded to cover more or less 88 acres (36 hectares) of river terrace, twenty-seven times the area of Pueblo Bonito in Chaco Canyon but well less than half the size of Los Muertos or Casa Grande in the Salt River Basin.

Major components of the new city plan are ceremonial mounds, a large public marketplace, a ring of urban parks, an apartment building that may have been as high as seven stories, and a large plaza dividing Paquimé into two halves like Taos, Sand Canyon, Kinishba, Grasshopper, and other ancient sites in the Southwest. Visitors presumably were impressed by the vast city's grand ramps and stairways, colonnaded public halls, large public entries, multiple ball courts, spacious plazas, and monumental buildings.

The curvilinear retaining walls and broad ramps of the Mound of the Offerings appear in the northwest corner of the reconstruction. The solid-core structure contains three burials, perhaps the revered founder of Paquimé's mercantile system and a couple who may have succeeded him. The shrine's prominent location next to the central plaza and public market seems to anticipate large numbers of visitors.

Immediately south of the Mound of the Offerings is a large water reservoir retained by an earthen embankment. A stone-lined water channel leads east from the reservoir and passes under the public market on its way to the high-rise apartment complex. A row of sales booths lines the west side of the market. Nine or more portals provide convenient access from the apartment complex to the east. Four small subterranean houses along the perimeter of the market may have provided lodging for visiting merchants or served as small chapels.

The House of the Macaws appears in the southwest corner of the reconstruction. The handsome edifice consists of two single-story room blocks flanking the west entry into Paquimé. Rows of nesting boxes line the courtyards of the residence where people raising brightly colored parrots lived. Like the Mound of the Offerings, the House of the Macaws may have been a tourist attraction.

A short street separates the House of the Macaws from the House of the Dead at the south end of the market. Thirteen or so priests lived in the nineteen rooms of the House of the Dead; they seemingly specialized in raising turkeys used in connection with burial rituals. Unusually large numbers of human interments accompanied by the remains of headless turkeys and black ceremonial pottery were found in the compound's two plazas.

Southeast of the House of the Dead and apparently related to it both physically and ritually is Paquimé's most spacious compound, the commodious House of the Pillars. Only the north portion of the elegant building appears along the south edge of the reconstruction. About one-half of the ground-floor area is given over to ceremonial spaces, colonnaded galleries, a ritual ballcourt, and an unusual atrium flanked by two-story rooms.

Graced by rooms with the highest ceilings in Paquimé, the House of the Pillars contains several remarkable rooms characterized by multiple reentrant corners. These quarters may represent the dwellings of priests who were involved with the ceremonial reenactment of a sacred ball game. Other architectural components of the House of the Pillars are a special warehouse containing an exceptional number of seashells and the generously proportioned east entry colonnade with three massive pillars.

North of the House of the Pillars and extending from the East Plaza to the public market is the possibly seven-story House of the Skulls. The large room block contains almost two hundred rooms where more than five hundred residents may have dwelled in very modest circumstances. The building derives its name from several human trophy skulls found in the cruciform room in the building's west section. The least opulent of Paquimé's apartment blocks, the House of the Skulls lacks a special warehouse but has a large number of cooking hearths and culinary utensils.

North of the House of the Skulls and extending beyond the north edge of the reconstruction is the House of the Well where almost eight hundred persons may have resided in more than three hundred dwelling rooms. Sweat baths, a walk-in well descending 46 feet (14 meters) below plaza level, a generous water supply, and an efficiently functioning sewer indicate the residence of a privileged class of people. A warehouse in the House of the Wells contained millions of shells, turquoise, salt, selenite, more than fifty Gila Polychrome bowls, and copper ore, suggesting that copper workers lived here.

The basic planning module of Paquimé appears to be a rectangular room with a short wall projecting from one wall, creating two alcoves for beds raised around 3 feet (1 meter) above the floor. Caliche is the predominant material for walls, floors, and rooftops. The material was collected from hundreds of pits south and west of the city. Caliche also is used for scratch coats and final coats of plaster.

Timber used in the construction of Paquimé is mostly yellow and white pine felled in the forests of the northern Sierra Madre Occidental. Stout beams up to 33 feet (10 meters) long adequately resist bending stresses but often fail due to inadequate bearing seats. Timbers are shaped to serve as beams, lintels, stair nosings, and other components.

Locally quarried felsite provides 90 percent of the stones used for construction in Paquimé. Generally weak in compression, foundations of felsite often fracture under the weight of heavy walls. Stones usually are laid dry in retaining walls and are shaped into columns, capitals, lintels, nesting box entrances, trough *metates*, *manos*, and other implements. Stone cobbles and jacal construction frequently are used for nonbearing partitions.

Some six hundred doorways are found in excavated portions of Paquimé, an average of one and one-half doorways per room. The portals often are T-shaped, sometimes are rectangular, and very rarely are circular. Windows, niches, and shelves resemble those found elsewhere in the Southwest.

At its zenith the population of Paquimé may have been in the range of 2,240 people (Cordell 1984:275). Following its greatest period of architectural efflorescence, the prosperity of the trading center of the Gran Chichimeca apparently began to decline. The city eventually was set upon by an unknown enemy and destroyed, never to be rebuilt.

Mexican authorities have attempted to preserve carefully the areas excavated by the Amerind Foundation, and major portions of the extensive site remain to be examined. Since interpretive facilities are lacking, prospective visitors may be well advised to review in advance the three-volume study of Paquimé compiled by the late Charles C. Di Peso (1974). His comprehensive work sheds important light on the role of Paquimé in the development of ancient architecture in the Southwest.

CAVE OF LAS VENTANAS
Mogollon

The largest cliff dwelling in the canyon of Rio Garabato, the Cave of Las Ventanas is situated at an altitude of 6,824 feet (2,080 meters) in the Sierra Madre Occidental of northwestern Chihuahua. The Cave of Las Ventanas, meaning "the windows" in English, is located in a natural cliff alcove some 450 feet (137 meters) above the valley floor. The well-preserved remains lie about 45 miles (72 kilometers) southwest of Olla Cave and approximately 55 miles (88 kilometers) south of Paquimé, the noted fifteenth-century Chichimeca trading center.

East facing like Olla Cave, the Cave of Las Ventanas derives its name from the second-floor room of its southeastern structure. Eighteen small windows in the north and east walls of the room command views of all the approaches to the Cave of Las Ventanas. The cavern measures possibly 175 feet (53 meters) in width at its mouth and is perhaps 35 feet (11 meters) deep.

The cliff dwelling's eighteen ground-floor rooms occupy almost all of the cave floor. The building probably had twelve rooms on the second floor and several more on the third-floor level, suggesting a total of at least thirty rooms. The structure consists of two parallel rows of rooms. The rooftops of the unusually long one-story halls along the cliff edge may have been used as outside work areas.

The reconstruction presented here is based on a plan and description by Arturo Guevara Sánchez (1986: figs. 12, 14) and information published by Robert H. Lister (1958:59). The walls of the cliff dwelling are built of puddled adobe with occasional flat stones, recalling the type of

construction used at Paquimé. Interior posts provide additional support for the roofs of larger rooms.

The average room size in the Cave of Las Ventanas is around 230 square feet (21.4 square meters). Smaller rooms and interior chambers on lower floors presumably serve as store rooms. Window openings are diminutive in size and are rectangular or round in shape. Doorways generally are T-shaped, but a few are rectangular, and some have elevated sills. Most of the bearing walls extend down to the natural stone floor of the cave.

Tree-ring dates for the Cave of Las Ventanas indicate that timbers for construction most likely were harvested between A.D. 1060 and 1205. Assuming that the timber samples lack sapwood just as the samples recovered in Paquimé did, the adjusted chronology for the Cave of Las Ventanas may be in the range of 1275 to 1400. Pottery and other cultural remains collected in the cliff dwelling also suggest a close affiliation with the ancient trading center of the Chichimeca.

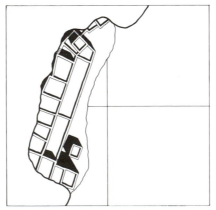

CAVE OF LAS VENTANAS

OLLA CAVE
Mogollon

The best-preserved and largest pot-shaped granary reported to date is found in Olla Cave, which overlooks the Río Piedras Verdes Valley in northwestern Chihuahua. The well-known cliff dwelling peers out from the west face of the canyon in the northern Sierra Madre Occidental approximately 25 miles (40 kilometers) southwest of Paquimé. The Spanish word *olla* means "round earthen pot," in this case a reference to the shape of large grass and adobe structures used for grain storage in Chihuahua, Sonora, and elsewhere in Mexico.

The granary constructed in the mouth of Olla Cave looks like an enormous ceramic pot some 12 feet (2.7 meters) in diameter and about the same dimension in height. The reconstruction presented here is based on a plan and description published by Robert H. Lister (1958:fig. 8). The cave opening measures perhaps 56 feet (17 meters) from north to south and 13 feet (4 meters) or so in height, barely high enough to clear the top of the granary.

Olla Cave's irregular plan consists of an open area to the east where at least fifteen rooms are situated and two deeper recesses in the cliff. The north recess extends roughly 170 feet (52 meters) into the cliff and contains two burials. Generally rectangular in shape, the rooms north of the granary are better preserved than those to the south. Room sizes range from possibly 42 to 165 square feet (3.9 to 15.3 square meters).

Olla Cave's larger rooms presumably served as dwellings while the smaller chambers were used for storage. Several rooms engage the walls of the cave, and some second-story rooms originally incorporated the roof of the cave into their ceilings. The walls of the rooms are built of puddled adobe with occasional stone slabs, recalling similar construction at Paquimé. The walls typically are plastered on both sides and have numerous doors but only a few small windows.

Undoubtedly used to store corn, the *olla*-shaped granary is constructed of large grass coils heavily plastered with adobe inside and out. Access to the granary's contents may be gained through the opening at the top of the vessel and through numerous circular apertures blocked with wood slabs when the container is full. As the level of corn decreases, lower portals may be unsealed to facilitate access.

The Chichimeca people who inhabited the fifteenth-century trading center of Paquimé are known to have used large, impressive adobe and basketry granaries like the one in Olla Cave. The granaries appear to be patterned along the lines of those still in use in Veracruz and Tlaxcala. The vessels resemble immense inverted jars sometimes 16 to 20 feet (5 to 6 meters) in height (Di Peso 1974:609).

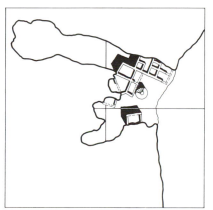

OLLA CAVE

CASA GRANDE
Hohokam

The tallest and most impressive surviving Hohokam structure, Casa Grande is situated in a large walled compound in south-central Arizona approximately 40 miles (64 kilometers) southeast of Phoenix. The greater Casa Grande community includes the remnants of thirteen measured compounds of various sizes, a clan house that is neither a room block nor a compound, an oval ball court, and a possible plaza where community activities may have occurred. The plaza is suggested around 300 feet (100 meters) northeast of the main compound.

The site measures overall some 3,150 by 3,870 feet (960 by 1,180 meters), an area of about 280 acres (113 hectares). This area is somewhat greater than that of Los Muertos, a contemporary Hohokam platform mound complex north of Casa Grande. Casa Grande's site is more than twice the size of Paquimé's in northwestern Chihuahua. All of Casa Grande's compounds are rectangular, and all but two enclosures are oriented slightly east of north.

The reconstruction presented here illustrates the plan of the largest compound based on information provided by John M. Andresen (1989) and David R. Wilcox (Wilcox & Shenk 1977). Situated at an altitude of roughly 1,420 feet (433 meters) above sea level, the largest compound contains more than sixty rooms enclosed within a 216-by-417-foot (66-by-127-meter) perimeter wall. A portal in the north wall is the only doorway opening into the compound. The residents probably used ladders to climb over the 7 foot (2.1 meter) or so high walls.

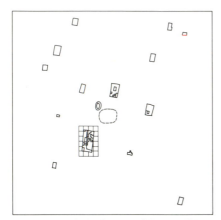

KEY PLAN OF CASA GRANDE COMMUNITY

In plan the great house is a compact rectangle with dimensions of 42 by 58 feet (12.8 by 17.7 meters). Lying west of the compound's center and slightly to the north, the main building of Casa Grande is composed of three parallel, rectangular rooms centered between two end halls. All of the interior spaces are more or less 9 feet (2.7 meters) wide, the inner rooms are perhaps 24 feet (7.3 meters) long, and the halls measure nearly 35 feet (10.7 meters) in length.

The main building dominates its orderly site with a citadel-like presence. The perimeter walls of the massive structure once rose three stories high, and a single fourth-story room was built in the middle of the rooftop. The ground floor, however, was filled for the first 5 feet (1.5 meters), thus reducing the interior height of the great house to two stories.

Small doors centered in all four sides of the structure provided access to interior rooms. The entry portals occurred at the second- and third-floor levels requiring ladders for access. The overall height of Casa

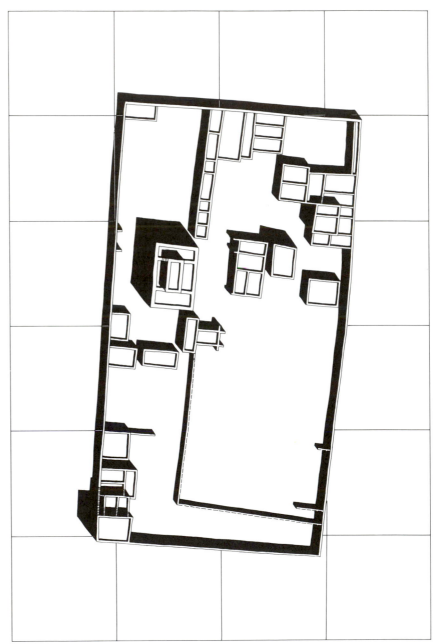

CASA GRANDE

Grande's great house is 35 feet (10.7 meters).

The massive walls of the great house diminish from a maximum thickness of 54 inches (137 centimeters) at the base to around 21 inches (53 centimeters) at the parapet. The walls are constructed of caliche, a subsoil with a high lime content occurring in natural deposits 2 to 5 feet (.6 to 1.5 meters) below the desert floor. Caliche was mixed with water and deposited by hand on the walls, forming successive layers.

Each of the layers of caliche is estimated to be an average of 26 inches (65 centimeters) thick. Caliche plaster provides a hard finish for the walls. Beam pockets in the stout walls received pine, fir, and juniper beams. Some of the timbers came from sources more than 50 miles (80 kilometers) distant. Saguaro ribs and reeds placed on the beams were capped with a layer of caliche, forming the level surfaces of upper floors and roofs.

Most of the other buildings in the compound were a single story high, but a three-story structure is incorporated into the southwest corner of the perimeter wall, perhaps for the purpose of minimizing labor. A two-story structure is located east of the great house, and other multistory rooms may have been built in the compound. Casa Grande and its associated enclosures represent a very high level of achievement in Hohokam architecture and town planning.

Hohokam people probably appeared in the vicinity of Casa Grande early in the Christian era. Meaning "those who came before" in the Tohono O'odham language, the Hohokam in time developed extensive agricultural systems irrigated by an extraordinary network of canals. The desert farmers built an estimated 600 miles (960 kilometers) of canals on the flat plains of the Salt and Gila valleys. The canals typically range from 2 to 6 feet (.6 to 1.8 meters) in width and roughly 3 feet (.9 meter) deep.

Still visible in places are segments of the ancient canal leading 16 miles (26 kilometers) north from Casa Grande to the Gila River. Canals, ball courts, and platform mounds near plazas seem to suggest influences from Mexico. The construction of compounds and room blocks began to appear in the twelfth century; the ideas may have been introduced through the Salado people in and around the Tonto Basin to the northeast.

The compound of Casa Grande probably was built and occupied between 1200 and 1450. The great house likely was constructed in the early 1300s. By the middle of the fifteenth century Hohokam cultural traits were no longer discernible, and Casa Grande apparently was abandoned. The descendants of the Hohokam may be the Tohono O'odham and Papago Indians whom the Spanish found living in the vicinity.

The first European known to visit Casa Grande was the Jesuit missionary Eusebio Francisco Kino, who recorded the Tohono O'odham name for the site in Spanish, meaning "great house." The function of the impressive structure remains as obscure today as it was to early observers. A number of small openings in the massive walls suggest the possibility of astronomical observations. Ceremonialism, public administration, and storage are alternative speculations.

The remarkable remains today are part of Casa Grande Ruins National Monument under the administration of the National Park Service. The site is open daily to the public. A museum near the ruins contains information on the Hohokam and their accomplishments, including beautiful shell and turquoise mosaics demonstrating a remarkably high degree of craftsmanship.

LOS MUERTOS
Hohokam

The vast Hohokam platform mound complex of Los Muertos is located about 6.5 miles (10.5 kilometers) south of Tempe Butte on the Salt River in south-central Arizona. The reconstruction presented here is based primarily on the survey of the ruins by the Hemenway Expedition in 1887 and 1888 (Haury 1945). The remains of the site underlie the present-day Phoenix suburbs of Chandler and Tempe.

Los Muertos is one of the largest of the forty Hohokam platform mound complexes recorded along the Salt and Gila rivers (Bostwick 1989). Meaning "the dead" in Spanish, Los Muertos derives its name from the large number of both buried and cremated remains reported by early observers. Cremation often was practiced by the Hohokam, the area's original settlers, but interment usually was the practice of the Salado people, newcomers who lived peaceably among the Hohokam.

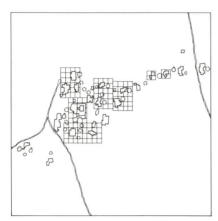

KEY PLAN OF LOS MUERTOS COMMUNITY

Like other major Hohokam settlements, Los Muertos depended on river water conveyed by an extensive network of canals to irrigate its fields and to provide for the daily needs of its sizable population. The main canal supplying the site appears along the east edge of the key plan shown here. From the canal three large ditches proceed westward to the immediate vicinities of the settlement's residential compounds.

In all, the Hemenway Expedition measured thirty-five compounds at Los Muertos and prepared detailed plans for twenty-five. Of these, the plans of only nineteen compounds were available for publication by Emil Haury in 1945. Presented on these pages are twelve detailed compound plans together with the outlines of two missing plans.

Los Muertos illustrates several characteristics of Hohokam community planning. For example, the dominant east-to-west axis of the village lies perpendicular to the main canal, which is oriented north to south, and most of the village compounds are

LOS MUERTOS, PLATFORM MOUND GROUP

LOS MUERTOS, NORTHWEST GROUP

rectangular with their longer axes oriented from north to south. The largest compound contains a distinctive platform mound and is located very near the geometric center of the community; ten compounds lie west of it and thirteen are to the east.

Los Muertos covers an area of approximately 1,800 by 4,700 feet (550 by 1,430 meters), the equivalent of 194 acres (78 hectares). The community occupies a somewhat smaller area than Casa Grande, the large contemporary Hohokam site to the south. Unlike most of its contemporaries, however, Los Muertos lacks a ball court. Twenty-five of the thirty-five known Hohokam platform mound sites had at least one ball court, and some had two. The absence of a ball court at Los Muertos may indicate a relatively late founding date for the community (Gregory 1987).

As is the case at other Hohokam sites sharing occupancy with Salado people, burials at Los Muertos often are found in the floors of rooms or plazas and near the exterior walls of compounds. Crematory urns usually are found in or near middens, or refuse heaps. Cremation pits, rarely exceeding 2 feet (50 centimeters) in depth, and trash mounds most frequently are located north or east of their associated residential compounds and very seldom are shared with other compounds (Haury 1945).

The basic building material of Hohokam architecture is adobe laid in successive layers to form walls up to four stories high. Adobe bricks were unknown in prehistoric times. The ancient builders mixed caliche, a calcareous formation found in such arid regions as the Salt River Valley, with local clays to form adobe walls of substantial durability. Stones suitable for construction are not available in the desert-like environment of Los Muertos.

Rainfall limited to 8 inches (20 centimeters) or so per annum minimizes maintenance on adobe walls but does not produce forests yielding construction timber. The elevations of nearby mountains rise only to 2,600 feet (792 meters), not high enough to support coniferous trees commonly used for construction in other areas of the Southwest. The broad, level river plain with fertile soils was the ideal environment for canals supplying water to communities and their agricultural fields.

Summer temperatures in the vicinity of Los Muertos sometimes reach 118 degrees Fahrenheit (48 degrees Celsius), and daily fluctuations may be as great as 60 degrees Fahrenheit (28 degrees Celsius). The relatively low humidity in the desert provides relief from the oppressive temperature to some extent. Massive adobe walls absorb solar heat during the day and release it at night, enhancing the livability of interior rooms in the arid Southwest.

For the purpose of this discussion, the term "compound" refers to a walled, rectangular enclosure containing usually single-story surface rooms, often contiguous and customarily orthogonal. Compounds serve such residential functions as living, cooking, sleeping, food processing, storage, and other domestic activities. One or more open courtyards admit light and ventilation into each compound. The twelve compounds of Los Muertos presented here range in size from eight to fifty-one rooms.

For the purpose of this study, the term "group" refers to a cluster of two or more neighboring compounds.

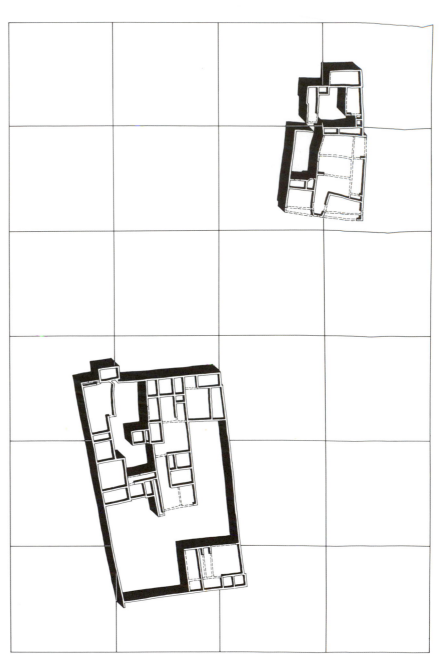

LOS MUERTOS, WEST PORTION OF CENTRAL GROUP

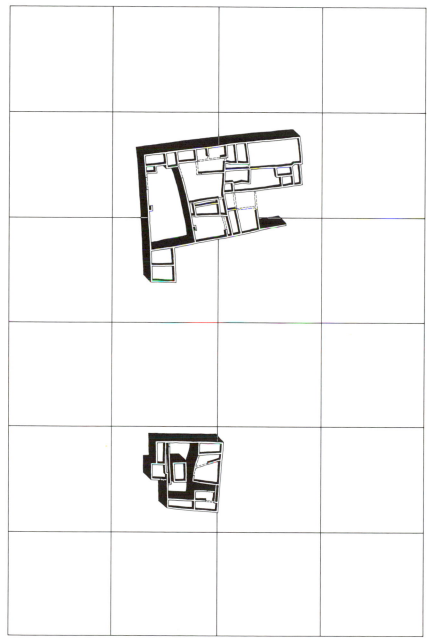

LOS MUERTOS. EAST PORTION OF CENTRAL GROUP

Compounds in Los Muertos are grouped to facilitate comparative analysis and to illustrate the spatial relationships of architectural elements as well as details within individual plans. The use of groups is strictly for the convenience of organizing the study.

Platform Mound Group When members of the Hemenway Expedition visited the largest ruin of Los Muertos in 1887, they observed a rounded mound some 15 feet (4.6 meters) high (Haury 1945:17). After partially excavating the remains, they found a massive perimeter wall measuring in plan roughly 210 by 315 feet (64 by 96 meters). The impressively large, unbroken wall enclosing the compound was constructed of adobe, in some places 7 feet (2.1 meters) thick. Its original height is unknown; the reconstruction proposes 10 feet (3 meters).

Within the walled enclosure, a large adobe structure rose perhaps as high as 40 feet (12 meters); in plan it measured approximately 80 by 135 feet (24 by 41 meters). Like other Hohokam buildings of this type, the freestanding edifice was rectangular, its long axis was oriented north to south, and it was situated on a platform mound near the center of the north wall. The survey records twelve rooms or compartments within the structure; these presumably represent a residence for special persons (Gregory 1987).

The remaining area within the platform mound compound seems to have been partitioned to form living and storage rooms or other functional spaces in support of the primary residence. The Hohokam often remodeled their adobe structures, and the ruin was not entirely excavated. Consequently, the reconstruction shows assumed wall locations with dashed lines.

About 95 feet (29 meters) west of the platform mound enclosure is an eight-room adobe block measuring no more than 45 by 100 feet (14 by 30 meters). Oriented with respect to a north-south axis, the house apparently expanded to the north by the addition of three rooms. A small midden associated with the ruin lies some 125 feet (38 meters) to the northeast.

Engaging the south wall toward the west end of the platform mound compound is a more or less 113-foot (34-meter) square enclosure for which the field map and data unfortunately are missing. This would seem to be a favorable location for an annex or facility supporting the platform mound enclosure, but information about the ruin is lacking.

Northwest Group The accompanying reconstruction of the northwest group in Los Muertos presents the plans of two compounds in detail. A third plan is shown in outline only due to the absence of the survey drawing and descriptive data. The latter measures overall roughly 170 by 205 feet (52 by 62 meters).

The well-ordered compound shown to the south in the group lies possibly 200 feet (60 meters) north of the platform mound compound. The 105-by-134-foot (32-by-44-meter) plan appears to be composed basically of a rectangular enclosure oriented from north to south with rooms disposed around an irregular courtyard. This arrangement is characteristic of Hohokam architecture in the Gila and Salt River Basin.

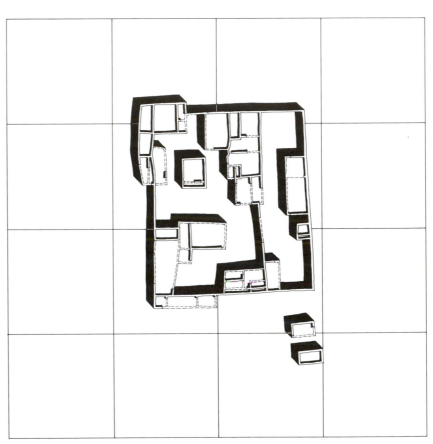

LOS MUERTOS, WEST PORTION OF SOUTH GROUP

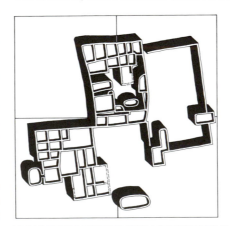

LOS MUERTOS, WEST PORTION OF EAST GROUP

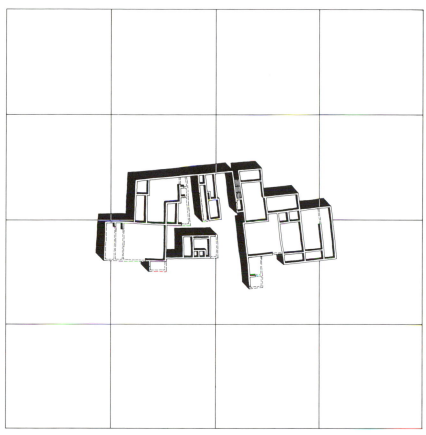

LOS MUERTOS, EAST PORTION OF SOUTH GROUP

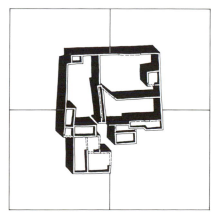

LOS MUERTOS, EAST PORTION OF EAST GROUP

The two northeast rooms and those along the west wall seem to be later additions, bringing the total number of rooms in the compound to twenty-two. Four unusual pits found in room floors seemingly served as granaries. The remains of a crematorium are centered about 40 feet (12 meters) east of the compound; well beyond to the east was the midden.

About 450 feet (137 meters) north of the platform mound compound lies a sprawling aggregation of fifty-one rooms in a structure measuring at most 155 by 240 feet (47 by 73 meters). Shown to the north in the northwest group, the somewhat rectangular plan appears to consist of five clusters of rooms with an equal number of irregular courtyards. The midden associated with the compound is situated some 70 feet (21 meters) to the east with a number of crematory urns on its south edge.

Central Group Some 300 feet (90 meters) northeast of the Los Muertos platform mound compound lies a large, well-organized walled enclosure with maximum dimensions estimated to be 135 by 230 feet (41 by 70 meters). The structure is the southwest compound in the plan presented here as the central group. All except one of the enclosure's thirty-one rooms lie within the quadrangle. As at most of the other compounds in Los Muertos, the major axis is oriented from north to south, and midden and crematory remains are found to the east.

The northwest enclosure in the central group consists of eighteen rooms and two small plazas measuring around 70 by 140 feet (21 by 42 meters). The rooms and plaza to the north appear to be added to the original structure. Middens lie both to the southeast, an unconventional location for Los Muertos, and to the east of the compound.

A nearly 65-foot (20-meter) square enclosure containing ten rooms is the southeast structure of the central group. Two rooms seem to have been added to the west, and an unusual freestanding room with no shared walls appears on the west side of the small courtyard. A midden and crematory remains are located to the east, the conventional arrangement in Los Muertos.

The central group's northeast compound consists of twenty-eight rooms and one courtyard organized on an east-west axis, an unconventional orientation for Los Muertos. The 125-by-150-foot (38-by-46-meter) structure lies some 800 feet (244 meters) northeast of the platform mound. Another unusual feature appears to be the sharing of the midden and crematorium to the east with another compound farther to the east.

South Group Two ruins comprising the south group lie more or less 300 feet (91 meters) south of the platform mound. The 160-by-195-foot (49-by-59-meter) west compound is a good example of the use of an enclosing perimeter wall to clarify architectural order; rooms outside the enclosure presumably are later additions. The structure's three freestanding rooms are exceptions to the architectural rule for Los Muertos, where chambers almost invariably are contiguous.

The approximately 115-by-225-foot (45-by-69-meter) east room block of the south group lacks a perimeter wall and is organized on a mainly east-west axis. These are exceptional features for Los Muertos. In several

rooms of the ruin investigators found square pedestals of adobe 16 inches (40 centimeters) high and a low bench of adobe (Haury 1945). Midden and crematory remains are situated to the north of the compound.

East Group The two ruins representing the east group lie more than 1,600 feet (490 meters) east-northeast of the platform mound in Los Muertos. The forty-two-room compound to the west is the larger of the two ruins. Measuring overall some 165 by 190 feet (50 by 58 meters), the structure is one of only two in Los Muertos organized with respect to an east-west axis. Two wings, each with a small plaza to the east, order the plan. The wings lie north and south of a commonly shared east-west wall.

The north wing has an unusual freestanding oval-shaped room in its interior court. A second oval room measuring possibly 12 by 28 feet (3.7 by 8.5 meters) stands free to the south of the room blocks. A third room with an oval shape is tenuously connected to the southwest corner of the ruin. Rooms with oval plans are not unusual features for Hohokam sites.

The smaller ruin in the east group measures about 100 by 120 feet (30 by 36 meters). Oriented generally from north to south, the modest compound contains eleven rooms and three relatively large courtyards. The structure is located near the eastern limits of Los Muertos.

Canals The map indicating the canal systems in the immediate vicinity of Los Muertos is based on the original survey by the Hemenway Expedition (Haury 1945: fig. 24). The survey omits additional Hohokam canals known to have existed north of the

Salt River. The aggregate length of canals serving Los Muertos exceeds 75 miles (120 kilometers).

The principal irrigation canal serving the Los Muertos system leaves the Salt River about 3 miles (5 kilometers) east of Tempe. The canal branches several times and turns south across the flat desert plain, bypassing the communities of Las Acequias, Los Hornos, and Los Guanacos, all contemporaries of Los Muertos. The communities are located well apart from each other and perpendicular to their main canals.

The ditches serving the compounds and farm plots of Los Muertos are interconnected and linked to secondary canals to assure the balanced distribution of water. At this point about 7 miles (11 kilometers) from the intake, the main canal measures approximately 30 feet (9 meters) in width and some 7 feet (2.1 meters) in depth. In the bottom of the canal is a small ditch, perhaps a method of conserving water when the flow of the river was low (Haury 1945:41).

Ditches leading from the canal supplied water to several reservoirs in Los Muertos. The storage basin near the center of the north group was roughly 100 feet (30 meters) wide, 200 feet (60 meters) long, and 15 feet (4.6 meters) deep. The ancient builders dug all of the canals, ditches, and reservoirs entirely by hand.

Los Muertos was a typical large Hohokam platform mound site of the Salt River Valley. The community's canal system and architectural structures probably were built and occupied sometime between A.D. 1300 and 1400 (Gregory 1987).

SALOME
Salado

The fourteenth-century Salado site on Salome Creek is the largest known multistoried masonry ruin in the upland areas of the Tonto Basin. The highly compact room block represents an important new direction in the evolution of Salado architecture. For example, thirteenth-century upland communities of the Tonto Basin, such as those on Reno Creek, Park Creek, and Sycamore Creek, consist of wall-enclosed compounds having relatively few rooms and proportionately large numbers of spacious plazas or courtyards.

The site is designated Tuzigoot-on-Salome, but in this study the ruin is referred to as Salome in order to avoid confusion with Tuzigoot, the important Sinagua pueblo in the Verde Valley (Germick & Crary 1989). Salome is located on the piedmont slope of the Sierra Ancha approximately 4 miles (6.4 kilometers) north of Lake Roosevelt.

The masonry-walled room block rests on a ridge overlooking Salome Creek to the northwest from an altitude of perhaps 2,530 feet (771 meters) above sea level. Salome Creek originates high up in the Sierra Ancha and normally flows from January into May or June as a result of winter snow melt. Overall, the structure measures possibly 125 by 445 feet (38 by 136 meters) and contains more or less 150 ground-floor rooms (Germick & Crary 1989:fig. 7).

The Salome room block may have been two or three stories high during the peak of its occupation around the middle of the fourteenth century. Assuming that one-half of the ground-floor rooms had second stories and

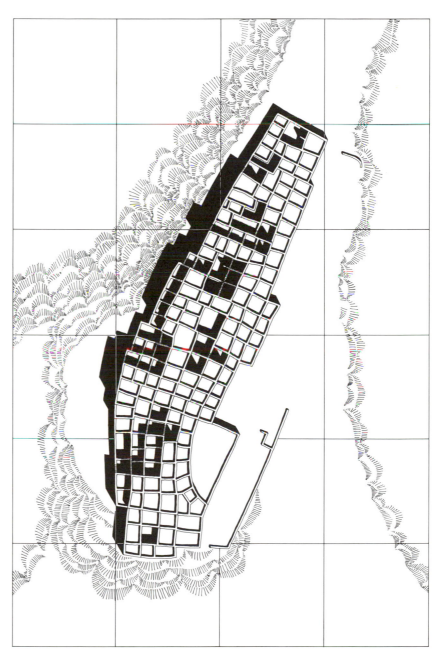

SALOME

one-quarter had third stories, the compact structure would have 260 or so rooms. The site apparently was constructed in two distinct phases: an earlier section to the south consisting of a compound converted to a room block, with a later addition to the north. The average room size appears to be about 164 square feet (15.2 square meters).

Sometime between A.D. 1000 and 1150 masonry house clusters and garden plots may have occupied the Salome site. During the thirteenth century walled compounds appeared. Early compounds usually consist of two or more structural components, each having one or two rooms and a large courtyard or plaza. Over time new components were added, thus increasing the number of rooms and open spaces in the compound.

Between 1300 and 1400 Salome was converted into a room block by compartmentalizing former open spaces with walls to form additional rooms and small courts and by adding second- and third-floor rooms. This process of architectural development differs conceptually from that of sites like Kin Tiel, where new room blocks were added in parts of a large central plaza surrounded by perimeter rows of rooms built during the initial phase of construction.

Surface ceramics at Salome confirm probable construction and occupancy between 1250 and 1400. Around 1350 displaced persons from other Tonto Basin sites and elsewhere apparently concentrated at the site, and the population likely reached its zenith. Some of the newcomers may have brought with them new architectural ideas, quite likely through contact with influences from the north or east.

The community pattern of Salome consists of a multitiered hierarchical pueblo comprising a single urban center surrounded by a number of smaller compounds, house clusters, and field structures. The large urban center occupied a favorable position for trade between the riverine communities of the Tonto Basin and the upland settlements of the Sierra Ancha. The prosperity of the densely populated site may have depended more heavily on regional economics than on agriculture.

Between 1356 and 1385 the economy and agricultural systems in central Arizona appear to have collapsed and Salome, like many other communities, was abandoned. Ceramics and architectural developments at Salome and elsewhere in the Tonto Basin suggest limited affiliation with indigenous people of the Sierra Ancha. Hohokam influence north of Theodore Roosevelt Lake may have been more in the form of trade rather than of settlement (Germick & Crary 1989).

TONTO
Salado

The fourteenth-century Salado cliff dwellings of Tonto overlook the Tonto Basin from high above the south bank of the Salt River in southeastern Arizona. Located approximately 55 miles (88 kilometers) east of Phoenix, Tonto is named for a group of Apache who ranged in the area during the nineteenth century. Although nomadic people probably moved through the Tonto Basin thousands of years earlier, the first settlers most likely were Hohokam. The colonists apparently moved from the lower elevation of the Salt and Gila River Basin up into the Tonto Creek vicinity around A.D. 750 or 800.

The Hohokam established pit house villages on the fertile flood plain along the Salt River where they practiced irrigation farming. By 1150 changes in settlement patterns, construction techniques, and pottery indicate the emergence of the Salado culture. Well known for surface dwellings of masonry, Gila Polychrome pottery, and distinctive cotton fabrics, the Salado continued to practice irrigation farming and to supplement their diets by hunting and gathering.

The Salado exchanged surplus food and goods with neighbors and joined trade networks that extended north to the Montezuma Valley, southeast to Paquimé in Chihuahua, and southwest to the shores of the Gulf of California. Between 1250 and 1300 some Salado moved from the river valleys into the uplands, where they founded such settlements as Sycamore Creek, Reno Creek, and Park Creek some 15 to 20 miles (24 to 32 kilometers) to the north. About the same time construction may have begun on Tonto's cliff dwellings.

Tonto consists of Upper Ruin and Lower Ruin, which has an annex. The accompanying reconstruction illustrates only Upper Ruin. The remains of both sites lie in shallow, east-facing caves formed by natural erosion. Lower Ruin has sixteen ground-floor

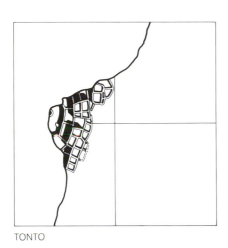

TONTO

rooms of which three have second stories. Next to the structure is an annex containing twelve rooms.

More inaccessible than Lower Ruin, Upper Ruin is situated at an altitude of roughly 3,400 feet (1,036 meters) above sea level. The apartment-like cliff dwellings are built of large, irregularly broken stones, laid in mortar containing small stones which are typical of Salado construction. The reconstruction presented here is based primarily on maps and information provided by the National Park Service.

Upper Ruin comprises thirty-two cave-floor rooms of which eight have second floors. The cave measures at most some 98 feet (30 meters) in width, with a maximum depth exceeding 50 feet (15 meters). The overhanging roof of the alcove together with the semiarid climate have preserved a number of fragile Salado cultural remains, including cotton fabrics and macaw feathers.

The largest room in Upper Ruin measures perhaps 10 by 16 feet (3 by 5 meters). Tonto's larger rooms

presumably were dwellings. Smaller rooms, some only 15 square feet (1.4 square meters) in area, appear to be used for storage. Like the large Salado room block of Salome west of Tonto Creek, the cliff dwellings of Tonto probably were built and occupied between 1250 and 1400.

Following the widespread collapse of agricultural systems and trade networks in the Southwest during the latter fourteenth century, the Salado culture disappeared from the Tonto Basin. Ceramic evidence suggests that some Salado people may have been absorbed into the Mogollon area to the east. Now designated a National Monument, the cliff dwellings of Tonto are administered by the National Park Service and are open daily to the public.

CLINE TERRACE
Salado

The spectacular Salado platform mound of Cline Terrace is located a short distance north of Theodore Roosevelt Lake near Punkin Center, some 50 miles (80 kilometers) northeast of Phoenix. The salient architectural features of the large site are massive enclosing walls, an extensive platform almost 10 feet (3 meters) high, and a group of two-story rooms and towers. The reconstruction presented here is based on a description (Rice & Redman 1992) and an accu-

rate map recording excavations of the ruins in the early 1990s by Glen E. Rice and others.

Situated at an altitude of 2,190 feet (667 meters) above sea level, the outer dimensions of Cline Terrace's perimeter walls are at most 250 by 440 feet (76 by 134 meters). The dimensions are somewhat greater than those of the contemporary Hohokam compound of Casa Grande and are 46 feet (14 meters) longer than the walls enclosing Pueblo Grande.

The impressive walls enclosing Cline Terrace are at least 8 feet (2.4 meters) high and equally wide. By comparison, Casa Grande's perimeter walls probably were almost as high as Cline Terrace's but were only 1.75 to 4.5 feet (.5 to 1.4 meters) thick. Cline Terrace's highest structures tower about 15.4 feet (4.7 meters) above the perimeter courtyards, less than half the height estimated for Casa Grande's great house.

The great Salado enclosure generally is oriented from northeast to southwest. The terrain rises gently toward the northeast but descends at a roughly 8 percent grade toward Tonto Creek, now Theodore Roosevelt Lake, to the southwest. Like other Salado and Hohokam walled platform mounds, Cline Terrace has a large, elaborate platform built of earth, stone, and debris enclosed within a cellular structure of masonry walls.

Although the compound is the largest Salado site presented in this study, Cline Terrace has only twenty-three or so ground-floor rooms and perhaps nineteen second-floor rooms, fewer than fifty in all. This is less than one-half the number for Schoolhouse Point. The stippled areas shown in the reconstruction indicate the platform

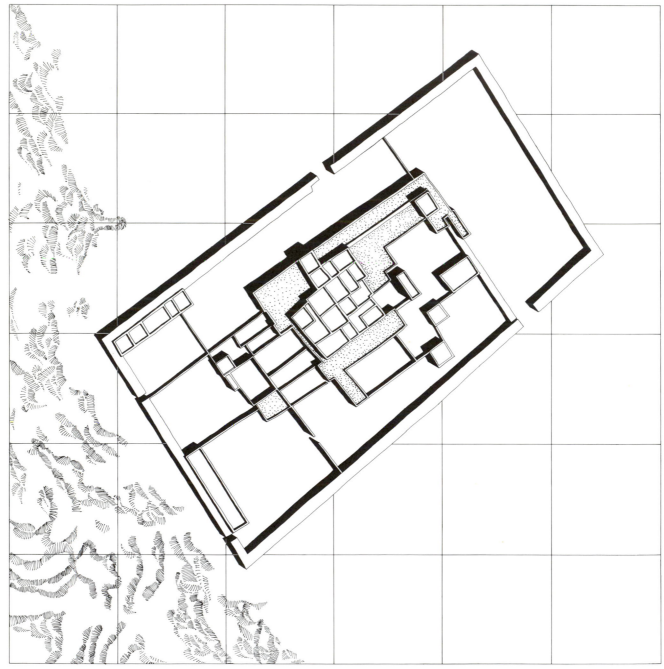

CLINE TERRACE

consisting of the rooftops of fourteen ground-floor rooms and the surfaces of solidly filled masonry cells.

Four entries provide access through Cline Terrace's enclosing wall into the perimeter courtyards of the compound. The largest of the entries is an 18-foot- (5.5-meter-) wide portal through the southeast wall providing access into the northeast courtyard. A massive wall measuring 5 feet (1.5 meters) in height and thickness separates the northeast courtyard from the rest of the compound. Several walls less than 3 feet (1 meter) high divide the perimeter area into six courtyards and a number of smaller patios. A solid-filled stage-like platform possibly 3.3 feet (1 meter) high occupies the north corner of the south courtyard.

The walls of Cline Terrace are constructed of stone cobbles laid in generous beds of mortar, sometimes faced with shaped rectangular slabs of soft white gypsum. Ceilings consist of closely spaced branches or dried saguaro ribs supported by stout pine or mesquite beams. Wood posts and beams near midspan support the roof beams of larger rooms.

One of the large rooms surrounded by other rooms on top of the platform is a workshop entered by means of an opening in the roof. Here deer bones were ground into sharp-tipped awls used for sewing and weaving, and shells obtained from the Gulf of California were fashioned into beads and ornaments. Also found in the room were spear points, large ceramic storage jars, brightly decorated serving vessels, and special minerals, such as azurite, copper, and iron sulfide used as pigments for ceremonial decorations.

A spectacular rectangular tower once stood at the foot of the mound on the southwest side of the inner plaza. The tower's foundation was made of successive layers of adobe and cobbles forming a solid block some 6 feet (1.8 meters) high. A room measuring about 8 by 24 feet (2.4 by 7.3 meters) in plan was placed on top of the foundation.

The tower rose approximately 15.4 feet (4.7 meters) above the level of the perimeter courtyards and was visible for a considerable distance except from the west where the rooms on top of the platform blocked the view. A veneer of shaped gypsum slabs faced the northeast façade of the tower, and an unusual doorway on the second-floor level overlooked the plaza.

The large room in the east corner of the inner plaza probably represents a meeting room where visitors were received and entertained. An unusual L-shaped room opens onto the northwest side of the plaza and leads some 24 feet (7.3 meters) into the mound itself. Partially lined with a gypsum veneer, the cave-like space was a repository for tidy groups of large storage jars, pieces of azurite and other minerals used for paint, small axes, special projectile points, turquoise jewelry, and decorative serving vessels.

Cline Terrace most likely was built and occupied between A.D. 1200 and shortly after 1450, a few decades before the voyages of Columbus. By 1320 the platform mound compound probably commanded the surrounding area of 10 to 15 square miles (26 to 39 square kilometers) where four villages were built for the lower-ranking members of the greater community. The remainder of the area contained small field houses,

communal food-roasting pits, and gardens.

Evidence gathered at the site indicates that the people living on the platform mound may have been members of important families, local rulers, and priests. The residents dined on venison while the commoners relied on rabbit for their source of meat, clearly indicating a hierarchical social organization. The occupants of Cline Terrace apparently commanded the large labor force required to construct the massive walls and platforms and to build and maintain extensive irrigation systems for the surrounding agricultural community.

During the fourteenth century the irrigable flood plain of the Tonto Basin encompassed an estimated 7,000 acres (2,800 hectares) of potential farmland capable of supporting perhaps ten thousand people. Of the eight platform mounds known to have existed in the Tonto Basin in 1300, five were covered by the waters of Roosevelt Lake in the early twentieth century. Cline Terrace is the best preserved and most elaborately organized of the three surviving Salado platform mound villages.

The focus of a larger community like Schoolhouse Point to the south, Cline Terrace represents an administrative center and elite residence in a complex hierarchical settlement system. The compound is noteworthy for the relatively lavish amount of courtyard and platform space it contains compared to its few dwellings and store rooms, an architectural idea recalling such Hohokam compounds as Los Muertos. The spacious walled compounds contrast sharply with Salome, Besh Ba Gowah, and other compact Salado sites that contain aggregations of rooms with relatively limited courtyard areas; these communities more closely resemble such neighboring Mogollon villages as Grasshopper and Kinishba.

One of eighty Salado sites known to have been active during the fourteenth century, Cline Terrace was burned and abandoned for unknown reasons almost a century before the Spanish *entrada.* Suggestions offered for the general collapse of the Salado culture during the early fifteenth century include internal friction, drought, failure of political and social systems, such environmental depredation as deforestation and pollution, epidemics, overpopulation, and combinations of these factors.

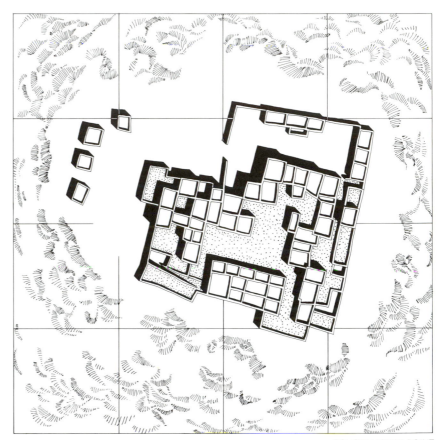

SCHOOLHOUSE POINT

SCHOOLHOUSE POINT
Salado

The large Salado platform mound and walled courtyard site of Schoolhouse Point is located in the lower Tonto Valley approximately 60 miles (96 kilometers) east of Phoenix. Originally situated on the south bank of the Salt River, the ruins presently overlook Theodore Roosevelt Lake on three sides from a low hill some 2,175 feet (663 meters) above sea level. A planned increase in the height of nearby Theodore Roosevelt Dam will cause the water level of the reservoir, Roosevelt Lake, to rise and inundate the ancient site.

The platform mound of Schoolhouse Point is a large, L-shaped structure containing a total of perhaps 115 rooms on two main levels. The compound measures overall perhaps 207 feet (63 meters) square, including the courtyard to the north but excluding the four freestanding rooms that lie a short distance to the west. The bases of the reconstruction presented here are accurate survey drawings provided by Glen E. Rice of Arizona State University and publications by J. Scott Wood (1986, 1989) of the Tonto National Forest.

Forty-five of Schoolhouse Point's rooms are located on the second-floor level. Many of the original ground-floor rooms were filled in with earth, stones, and debris to form the platform at an average height of 7 feet (2 meters) or so above the ground level. Room sizes range from perhaps 80 to 460 square feet (7.4 to 43 square meters), and roof heights vary greatly with some rising up to 19 feet (5.8 meters) above the level of the courtyard.

The plan of Schoolhouse Point resembles the contemporary Salado community of Besh Ba Gowah in several respects. The rooms of both sites were added incrementally rather than according to a predetermined plan, resulting in a jumble of often non-aligning walls enclosing rooms with widely varying floor elevations. Room rows and walls enclose the main courtyard and several smaller patios, and a narrow interior street leads south from the courtyard into the east side of the room block, recalling the covered entry in Besh Ba Gowah.

The stippled area shown on the reconstructed plan of Schoolhouse Point indicates the extent of the platform and the rooftops of ground-floor rooms. In the southeast corner of the room block a ramp ascends to the platform level where the largest of the elevated rooms is located. The circuitous, controlled access leading around the compound and up to the summit suggests some type of ceremonialism.

In the lower-floor rooms of Schoolhouse Point, excavators discovered large numbers of baskets, large ceramic jars, and granaries constructed of woven branches covered over with mud plaster. Each jar had a capacity in the range of 55 to 60 gallons (208 to 227 liters). The store rooms would be capable of holding quantities of surplus corn, beans, and other food sufficient to sustain the community through a number of successive crop failures. The estimated maximum population for Schoolhouse Point was around two hundred people.

One of the largest of the eighty or so known fourteenth-century Salado communities in the Tonto Basin, Schoolhouse Point was the center of a larger agricultural community controlling an estimated 2,000 acres (810 hectares) of irrigable corn and bean fields capable of producing three crops annually. Like the contemporary Hohokam compounds of the Salt and Gila Basin, Salado platform and courtyard compounds are located at 3-to-5-mile (5-to-8-kilometer) intervals along the 44-mile- (70-kilometer-) long flood plain of the Tonto Basin.

The construction of extensive irrigation canals and massive platform mounds clearly suggests coordination and control by a central authority, which also was responsible for the redistribution of food from the store rooms when crops failed. Schoolhouse Point appears to represent an elite administrative, residential, and ceremonial center in a complex hierarchical settlement pattern of the imperfectly understood Salado culture (Wood 1986).

Like their Hohokam neighbors, the Salado people participated in an extensive trading network that stretched from California to New Mexico and from Colorado to Mesoamerica. An example of their trade specialization is the production of the distinctly beautiful pottery known as Gila Polychrome, which was widely traded in the Southwest after 1300. Also like the Hohokam, the Salado developed a characterful and unique architecture appropriate to their unyielding desert environment.

BESH BA GOWAH
Salado

The fourteenth-century Salado pueblo of Besh Ba Gowah occupies a broad ridge overlooking Pinal Creek, a tributary of the Salt River in southeastern Arizona. The ruins are located on the outskirts of Globe approximately 75 miles (120 kilometers) east of Phoenix. Besh Ba Gowah means "place of metal" in Apache, a reference to the vast mining operations in the vicinity of the site.

Pinal Creek flows through a fertile valley interconnecting the upland canyons of the Salt and the Gila Rivers. Pinal Peak rises to an altitude of 7,848 feet (2,392 meters) some 10 miles (16 kilometers) south of Besh Ba Gowah. The combination of a year-round water supply, productive soils, a temperate climate, plentiful game, edible plants, and the availability of construction materials attracted settlers into the valley probably as early as A.D. 550.

In time hundreds of villages and hamlets sprang up along Pinal Creek. Around 1150 people having Salado cultural characteristics emerged in southeastern Arizona. The Salado suc-

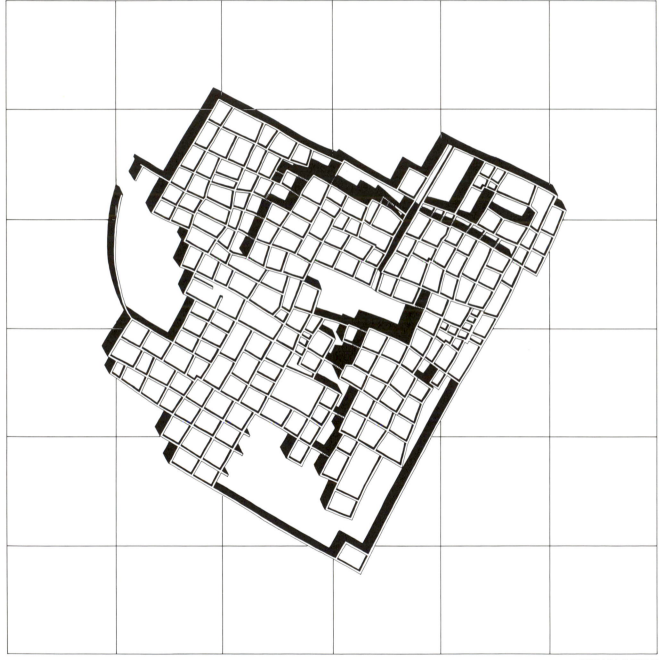

BESH BA GOWAH

cessfully incorporated attributes of the Hohokam and Mogollon cultures into their own distinctive lifestyles. Between perhaps 1225 and 1400, Salado workers built Besh Ba Gowah using cobble stones hauled up from the river valley and adobe mortar taken from the site.

The reconstruction presented here is based on a water color map prepared by Adolf F. Bandelier in 1883 combined with Irene Vickery's plan documenting her excavations between 1935 and 1940. Overall, the site measures possibly 335 by 390 feet (102 by 119 meters) and contains an estimated 208 ground-floor rooms and seven plazas. Assuming an additional forty-eight second-story rooms, Besh Ba Gowah would contain a total of 256 rooms.

Visitors to the reconstructed pueblo today will see neither the southeast perimeter row nor the thirty-five ground-floor rooms to the southwest noted by Bandelier. These structures were demolished in the late 1940s. Vickery recovered more than 350 burials from the ruins. She also recorded two distinctive interior corridors recalling similar features at the contemporary pueblos of Grasshopper and Kinishba about 50 miles (80 kilometers) to the north.

The principal entry into Besh Ba Gowah is by way of an unusual roofed corridor roughly 150 feet (46 meters) long. The corridor leads from the north side of the pueblo into the main plaza. Most likely the social and ceremonial center of the village, the plaza measures more or less 44 by 110 feet (13.4 by 33.5 meters). The central open space contained 150 burials, including community leaders whose elaborate tombs denoted their status.

The largest room in Besh Ba Gowah appears to be a 270-square-foot (25-square-meter) ceremonial room found in the room block about 20 feet (6 meters) east of the central plaza. The unusual chamber's floor level lies an average of 5.7 feet (1.75 meters) below the floors of surrounding rooms. High benches on the north and west walls presumably served for storage, while the lower bench along the south wall appears to be suitable for seating.

The large ceremonial room's floor has a surface of white clay plaster. The floor comprises a central hearth flanked by two circular quartzite stones resembling post bases for roof supports and a small rectangular box that may be analogous to a *sipapu.* Six small storage rooms, each having an area of nearly 43 square feet (4 square meters), line the south and east walls of the ceremonial room.

A second, smaller ceremonial room is situated at the west end of Besh Ba Gowah's central plaza. A variety of worked stone, bone, and antler tools, shells, ornaments, and other ceremonial paraphernalia was found in the rectangular chamber. A portal in the room's northeast corner leads to a small annex connected to the plaza. None of the other rooms around the plaza have access to the central open space.

The plazas and outdoor patios of Besh Ba Gowah appear to have been used for such daily activities as cooking, food preparation, tool making, ceremonies, and burials. Small windowless rooms may have been used to store food and supplies. Access to interior spaces usually is gained by means of ladders and roof hatchways. Where found, doorways are both rectangular and T-shaped.

Floor levels vary for unexplained reasons at Besh Ba Gowah. Foundation systems include horizontal stones laid end to end, rows of vertical slabs placed at regular intervals, and combinations of horizontal and vertical stones. The walls usually consist of two parallel rows of uncoursed river cobbles laid in generous beds of mortar. Walls for the most part are plastered. Wood posts support ceiling beams along the centerlines of larger rooms.

The architectural characteristics of the contemporary Salado pueblo of Salome about 40 miles (64 kilometers) to the north resemble those of Besh Ba Gowah in several ways. Both are multistory masonry pueblos, they have similar numbers of rooms, and both occupy more than an acre (0.4 hectare) of land. Besh Ba Gowah, however, has more plazas and a typical room area in the range of 228 square feet (21.2 square meters), compared to an average of only 164 square feet (15.2 square meters) for Salome.

The fourteenth century was an unstable time for both the Salado people and their Hohokam neighbors. For unknown reasons, perhaps drought, overpopulation, or environmental stress, Besh Ba Gowah apparently was abandoned around 1400. Today the partially restored site and the adjoining museum are part of a park operated by the City of Globe; the facilities are open daily to the public.

KIN TIEL
Zuni (Anasazi)

The large masonry pueblo of Kin Tiel is located approximately 22 miles (35 kilometers) south of Ganado in north-eastern Arizona, roughly halfway between Zuni Pueblo and the Hopi villages on First Mesa. The site is bisected by a drainage arm of Pueblo Colorado Wash, a tributary of the Little Colorado River. The architectural plan of Kin Tiel clearly differs from those of many Anasazi settlements, but its curvilinear outer walls recall to some extent those of Lower Pescado, Nutria, and even tiny Fire House.

The huge site appears to measure overall 310 by 560 feet (94 by 171 meters) and to contain within its walls an area of some 3 acres (1.2 hectares). The dimensions are almost identical with those of Lower Pescado. Kin Tiel's maximum length exceeds Pueblo Bonito's by 50 feet (15 meters) or so. However, the quality of the stone masonry compares poorly with that of the monuments in Chaco Canyon, and the kivas found at Kin Tiel are rectangular rather than round like those in the San Juan Basin.

When Victor Mindeleff (1989) visited the site in the 1880s, he observed major portions of the perimeter wall still standing two stories high. Apparently, the perimeter walls were completed first, perhaps to visually define the community. Generally regular in plan, the pueblo is divided into north and south wings by a spring. This recalls the division of Taos into halves by a flowing watercourse.

Very likely, the drainageway accounts for the location of Kin Tiel. Presumably, when the pueblo was inhabited some centuries ago the creek

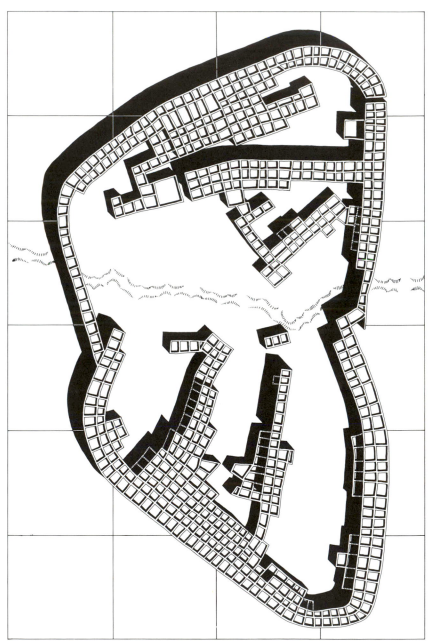

KIN TIEL

provided a usually reliable source of water for a sizable community. Within 6 miles (10 kilometers) of the site to the north and west, Mindeleff recorded two large drainage areas where water stood after rainstorms; these would have been favorable locations for prehistoric agriculture.

The openings recorded in the perimeter wall are very few and quite small, another distinctive characteristic of the pueblo. The reconstructed plan presented here shows more or less 611 rooms on the ground floor. Assuming that perhaps 427 may have second stories, it seems that Kin Tiel once may have contained possibly 1,038 rooms, although not all of them were occupied at the same time.

Only three entries are found in the perimeter wall. One portal lies on the east side south of the arroyo where the wall forms an offset. A second entry is situated on the rounded northeast corner of the pueblo, and a third is recorded in the north wall. One or more portals may exist in the south wall, but corroborating evidence is missing.

The terrain north and south of Kin Tiel slopes down about 7 feet (2 meters) to the level of the sandy wash. The room blocks added in the courtyard typically conform to the natural terrain; they are parallel with the arroyo to the north and perpendicular to it in the south. Access to all of the rooms is from the plaza, probably by way of roof hatches and second-story doorways. In the interest of maintaining an unbroken perimeter wall, the Zuni builders may have devised some method of bridging the watercourse, but evidence for such a feature is lacking.

In one room Mindeleff found a "stone-close," a doughnut-shaped slab with a hole around 18 inches (46 centimeters) in diameter carved through the center. The flat stone ring is roughly 7 inches (3 centimeters) wide; it forms a continuous head, jamb, and sill around the circular portal. The bottom of the stone-close is located in a masonry wall a few inches above the adjacent floor levels. One or more rectangular stone slabs leaned against the stone-close and propped in place would close the portal securely.

Kin Tiel appears to have been built, perhaps hastily, around 1275 when large numbers of people were abandoning the San Juan area and resettling elsewhere. The settlers often formed large aggregated communities like Kin Tiel. By the time the Spanish appeared in the Southwest, the large pueblo most likely had been abandoned. Such architectural features as the stone-close and square kivas support Zuni oral traditions that the people of Kin Tiel came to live in the Zuni heartland centuries ago.

HAWIKUH
Zuni (Anasazi)

Striking by virtue of its size and commanding position in the landscape, Hawikuh may have been the first pueblo in the Southwest to be seen by Spanish explorers. In 1539 Esteban, a Moorish scout for the expedition of Fray Marcos de Niza, reportedly entered the impressive hillside village where he was killed by the Zunis. Several days later Fray Marcos observed Hawikuh from a distance but did not attempt to enter the pueblo.

Fray Marcos seems to have mistaken Hawikuh's two- and three-story room blocks stepping up the hillside for six- and seven-story buildings. On the basis of the friar's report, Francisco Vásquez de Coronado visited and briefly occupied Hawikuh in 1540. Finding no gold or other precious metals, the conquistador continued on to the Rio Grande Valley in search of the fabled and perpetually elusive Seven Golden Cities of Cibola.

Hawikuh lies on the south bank of the Zuni River, a tributary of the Little Colorado River, approximately 15 miles (24 kilometers) south of Zuni Pueblo in west-central New Mexico. The historic village occupies the summit of a low rounded hill at an average altitude of 6,230 feet (1,899 meters). Open juniper and piñon woodlands originally covered the ridgetop, giving way to open grassland on the hillside (Kintigh 1985).

Hawikuh is one of six Zuni pueblos established before 1540, all concentrated in a 25-mile (40-kilometer) stretch of the Zuni River Valley in western New Mexico. Here the perennial flow of the river provides irrigation water for fertile farmlands.

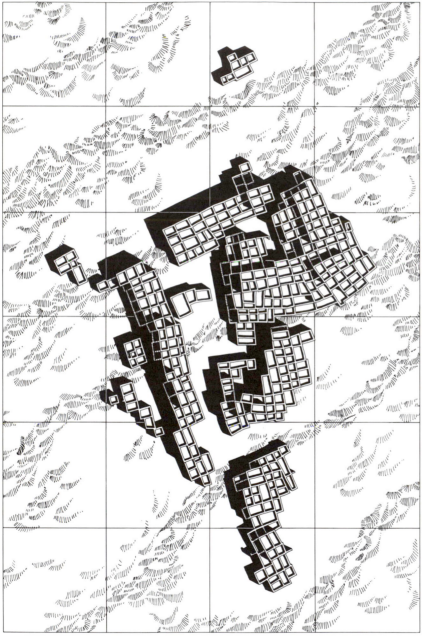

HAWIKUH

People probably first established pit house settlements in the valley between A.D. 700 and 800, or perhaps even earlier (Woodbury 1979b).

The large accretionary masonry villages of late prehistoric times probably date from the 1300s. Occupation of Hawikuh and the other five major Zuni pueblos continued until the Pueblo Revolt in 1680, when all were abandoned. The former residents of Hawikuh most likely joined their neighbors in establishing present-day Zuni Pueblo on the site of ancient Halona.

The reconstructed plan of Hawikuh presented here is based primarily on the room block plans published by Smith, Woodbury, and Woodbury (1966:figs. 6, 7, 10, 12, 13, 17). Victor Mindeleff's site plan (1989:plate XLVI) generally agrees with the scale of the reconstruction. Not shown are the lesser ruins to the east noted by Mindeleff; these include the remains of an adobe church and monastery founded at the base of the hill in 1629.

The aggregated architectural masses of Hawikuh recall to some extent the conceptual organization of Zuni Pueblo. Hawikuh consists of five major clusters of cells and several smaller room blocks. A highly irregular principal plaza, two smaller plazas, and a number of streets or alleys separate the dense, compact room blocks. Overall, the plan of Hawikuh measures roughly 319 by 514 feet (97 by 157 meters) and contains an estimated 457 ground-floor, 229 second-story, and 114 third-floor rooms, a total of possibly eight hundred rooms.

The average room size in the pueblo is about 93 square feet (8.6 square meters). The reconstructed plan of Hawikuh locates recorded wall foundations, while the reconstructed plan of Zuni shows roof parapets without reference to walls within suites. This accounts for the differences in scale of architectural elements in the two sites.

Hawikuh's once two- and three-story walls were built of red and tan sandstone quarried on and near the site. Today the ancient pueblo lies entirely in ruins; refuse up to 16 feet (5 meters) deep covers some areas of the once thriving pueblo. Only a few remnants of the abandoned church's adobe walls remain standing at the foot of the hill.

ORAIBI
Hopi (Anasazi)

The Third Mesa village of Oraibi once was the most populous and influential of the Hopi villages in northeastern Arizona. Located on an isolated mesa top approximately 7 miles (11 kilometers) northwest of Shongopavi, Oraibi may have been occupied continuously since around A.D. 1150. The only other populated settlement in the ancient Southwest that claims to be as old as Oraibi is Acoma, but the antiquity of both pueblos remains to be determined conclusively.

The reconstruction proposed here is based on information recorded by Victor Mindeleff (1989:plate XXXVI) in the early 1800s and by Stanley A. Stubbs (1950:fig. 21) in the late 1940s. At the time of Mindeleff's visit, Oraibi was one of the largest pueblos in the Southwest, containing as many residents as the combined populations of all six Hopi villages on First Mesa and Second Mesa. The parallel-street plan of the large pueblo recalls those of Shongopavi, Acoma, and Santo Domingo.

Although Oraibi is large in size, its architectural character is one of a small settlement on a large scale. The pueblo lacks the sophistication that characterizes the architecture of Paquimé, Pueblo Bonito, and Casa Grande. Oraibi consists of perhaps seven irregular rows of stone masonry room blocks, each oriented to the southeast and ranging in length from one or two rooms to more than 330 feet (100 meters). The rooms in five of the clusters attain heights of four stories, like several of the structures in Walpi.

Indications of orderly growth in a sequence of phases such as those in Mishongnovi are not found in Oraibi. The irregular streets between parallel room blocks are open at both ends, providing convenient access for residents and visitors alike. Unlike Oraibi, Zuni Pueblo originally was enclosed by unbroken blocks of perimeter rooms penetrated occasionally by relatively narrow passageways. Roof hatchways with ladders above the first floor are found frequently at Zuni but are rare in Oraibi.

The population of Oraibi in 1900 was six hundred persons, but by 1940 the number had declined to 112 (Connelly 1979). A longstanding factional dispute arose at Oraibi in 1906 resulting in the departure of a large segment of the village population. The departing group established Hotevilla, a present-day village on Third Mesa about 4 miles (6.4 kilometers) northwest of Oraibi.

In 1991, I observed a limited number of inhabited dwellings on the site and extensive remnants of former structures. The descendants of Oraibi today live in Old and New Oraibi, Upper and Lower Moenkopi, Hotevilla, and Bacabi. At the present time the Hopi people continue to follow a traditional way of life closely resembling that of their ancestors.

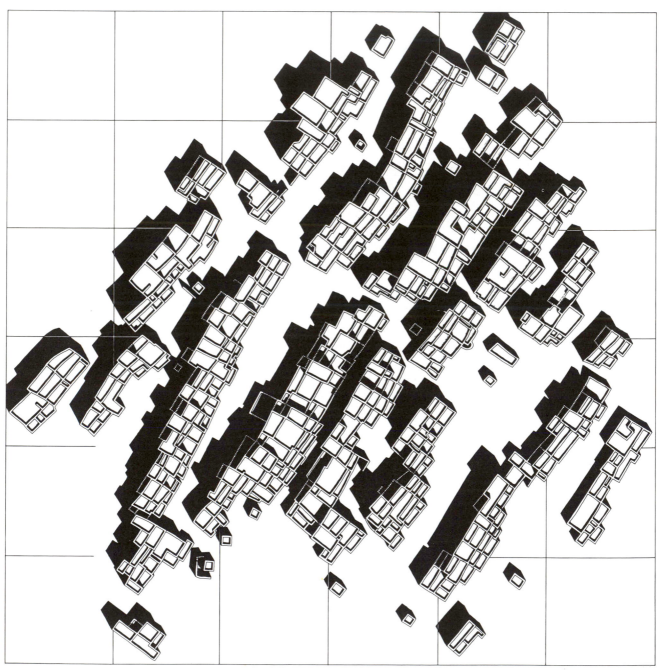

OR AIBI

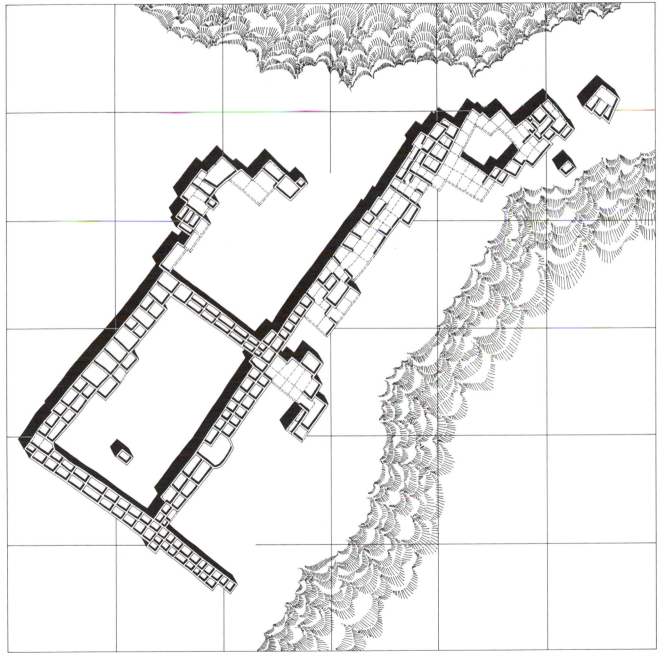

CHUKUBI

CHUKUBI
Hopi (Anasazi)

The abandoned Hopi pueblo of Chukubi lies on Second Mesa approximately 3 miles (5 kilometers) northeast of Mishongnovi. Now much in ruins, the village occupies a broad sandstone ledge similar to the site of Shipaulovi. The reconstruction presented here is based on the account of Victor Mindeleff (1989:plate XIII), who visited the site in the early 1880s.

More accessible than the nearby village of Payupki, Chukubi extends for more than 600 feet (183 meters) along the mesa. The remains consist of a large quadrangle to the southwest and a linear room block, which forms a connecting link with a small cluster of rooms grouped around an irregular courtyard to the northeast. Additional structures extend southeast and north from the quadrangle, but the purpose of these features is unclear.

Buildings two rooms wide enclose the plaza on all four sides. The rectangular plaza measures about 100 by 180 feet (30 by 55 meters) and contains the remains of a freestanding structure, possibly a kiva, toward the southwest. Chukubi's plaza is roughly the same length as Payupki's but is not as wide.

The reconstruction shows 250 ground-floor rooms and one kiva, but probably not all of the rooms were occupied at the same time. The rooms of Chukubi range in size from perhaps 60 to 280 square feet (5.6 to 26 square meters). Smaller rooms presumably were used for storage and larger rooms appear to be dwellings.

The orderly arrangement of Chukubi's west quadrangle recalls the village plans of Payupki and the east cluster of Mishongnovi, but the northeast cluster lacks clarity and resolution. Chukubi is composed of enclosed courts like Shipaulovi, not open-ended streets like those of Oraibi and Walpi. Chukubi is not recorded as an inhabited Hopi village at the time of the Pueblo Revolt in 1680.

AWATOVI
Hopi (Anasazi)

The large historic pueblo of Awatovi is one of the Hopi villages that was occupied at the time of the *entrada* but is in ruins today. The historic site is located on the southeast edge of Antelope Mesa overlooking Jeddito Wash approximately 90 miles (144 kilometers) northeast of Flagstaff. Called Awatubi by Victor Mindeleff (1989) and Talla Hogan by the Navajo, Awatovi is situated about 10 miles (16 kilometers) southeast of Walpi on First Mesa.

The four Hopi mesas, in order from east to west, are Antelope Mesa, First or East Mesa, Second or Middle Mesa, and Third or West Mesa. The geological structure of Black Mesa north of the Hopi mesas causes aquifers to feed springs along its south edge where the Hopi villages are concentrated. Here during the 1200s people from the Kayenta, Virgin River, and Little Colorado River areas joined local inhabitants in building such villages as Awatovi and Oraibi on the mesa tops and other settlements in the valleys below.

Although Awatovi appears unified in plan, the pueblo consists of distinctively separate historic and prehistoric components. The reconstruction presented here shows Awatovi as it may have appeared about 1692 based on the plans of Victor Mindeleff (1989:plate IX) and Harvard University's Peabody Museum (Montgomery, Smith, & Brew 1949:fig. 34). The original structures of Awatovi are the four hundred or so ground-floor rooms located generally northwest of the irregular central plaza.

In 1540 Coronado dispatched Pedro de Tovar with seventeen horsemen and three or four footmen to the Hopi area of northeastern Arizona in search of a practical route to the Gulf of California (Brew 1979). The first Hopi mesa the party visited was Awatovi, then one of the most prosperous of the Hopi settlements. The pueblo that Tovar observed probably measured some 240 feet by 440 feet (73 by 134 meters) and contained a large plaza enclosed by a low wall to the southeast along the mesa's edge.

The early Spanish explorers quite likely found second- and third-story rooms at Awatovi. The reconstruction suggests a conjectural total of perhaps four hundred or so original ground-floor rooms. Unlike the other Hopi villages, Awatovi appears to have a relatively orderly and symmetrical plan. Mindeleff recorded several rough stone walls standing up to 8 feet (2.54 meters) high to the south and low ridges of fallen masonry indicating original walls to the north.

A gateway possibly 15 feet (4.6 meters) wide provides access through the northeast side of the original pueblo.

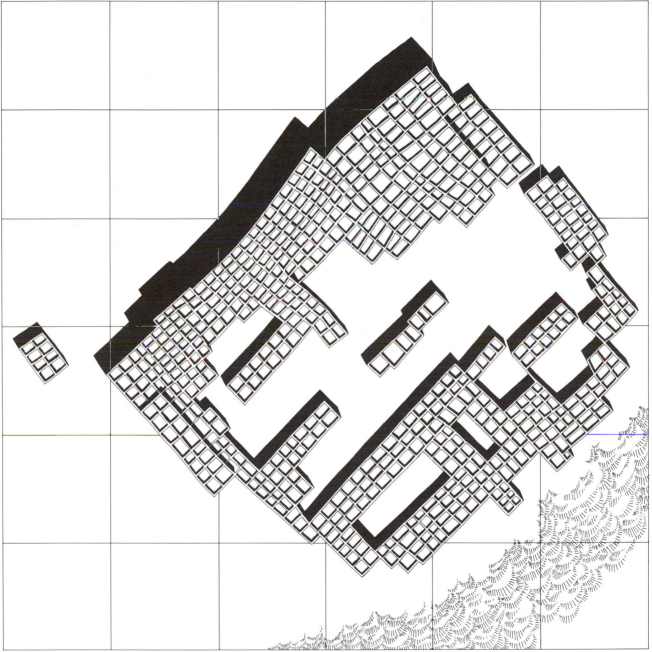

AWATOVI

The detached rooms roughly 35 feet (11 meters) from Awatovi's west corner also are believed to be the original features. Several subterranean rectangular kivas are said to be located in the plaza area, and excavators unearthed another kiva below the main altar of the mission church. The walls of the church's kiva contained extraordinary mural paintings, which can be seen today in the Museum of Northern Arizona and Harvard's Peabody Museum.

In 1629 two Catholic priests arrived in Awatovi where they founded a church, San Bernardo de Aguatubi, as a part of a larger effort to convert all the Hopi to Christianity. The effort failed everywhere except at Awatovi, and there it succeeded for only seventy-one years. One of the priests is said to have restored sight to a blind boy; this may be a reason Christianity was embraced in Awatovi and in no other Hopi villages.

During the Pueblo Revolt in 1680 the priests were killed, the church was destroyed, and the friary was transformed into a Hopi pueblo. Existing spaces were subdivided and new rooms were added, some probably several stories high. The reconstructed plan proposes 194 ground-floor rooms on the site of the former friary, increasing the estimated total of ground-floor rooms in Awatovi to almost six hundred. Assuming that half of the rooms had second stories and one-quarter had third stories, the total number of rooms in Awatovi would exceed one thousand.

The plan prepared during the Peabody Museum excavations of 1935 to 1939 locates the walls of the historic church and friary and those of adjacent Hopi structures. The Hopi rooms range in size from 45 to 110

square feet (4.2 to 10.2 square meters). The excavators recorded walls both of stone masonry and of straw-reinforced adobe, which is characteristic of Spanish construction.

Between 1680 and 1692 Hopi villages on First Mesa and Second Mesa moved from the valley floors up to the mesa tops for improved security during the tumultuous times. Refugees from the Rio Grande Valley and elsewhere helped to swell the populations of the relatively inaccessible Hopi mesas. During the Spanish reconquest of the Southwest in 1692, only Awatovi returned to Christianity; all of the other Hopi pueblos successfully resisted conversion.

Apparently, most of the Hopi people considered the presence of Christianity at Awatovi a threat to their traditional ways of life. Sometime during the winter of 1700–01 neighboring Hopi attacked and destroyed Awatovi, never to be rebuilt. A legend says the men were put to death and the women and children were captured. Archaeological evidence supports a rare occurrence in the ancient Southwest involving mass executions and cannibalism in connection with the destruction of Awatovi (Cordell 1984).

Tree-ring dating, architectural remains, and ceramic samples suggest that occupation in the vicinity of Awatovi may have begun as early as the A.D. 600s (Montgomery, Smith, & Brew 1949). Excavations of the prehistoric component of the ruined pueblo remain to be conducted. The remains may be visited, but a four-wheel-drive vehicle is advisable.

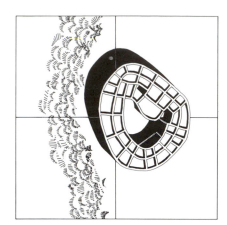

FIRE HOUSE

FIRE HOUSE
Hopi (Anasazi)

The elliptically shaped pueblo of Fire House is situated in northeastern Arizona around 20 miles (36 kilometers) northeast of Awatovi and a slightly greater distance from Walpi. Called by the Hopi Tebugkihu, Fire House derives its name from its legendary builders, the now extinct Fire Clan. The pueblo is remote from the Hopi heartland both geographically and architecturally.

The reconstruction presented here is based on a published account by Victor Mindeleff (1989: fig. 7) and his field notes in the files of the National Anthropological Archives in Washington, D.C. Compared to typical Hopi villages, the plan of Fire House is more unified and the workmanship is more skillful. The perimeter wall of the compact pueblo is remarkably well preserved, except along the edge of the cliff to the west.

The carefully fitted ashlar walls of Fire House resemble the masonry of

Chaco Canyon more than the stone-work of the Hopi mesas. The exterior walls contain the largest stones found in the ancient architecture of the Southwest. One of Mindeleff's engravings (1989:plate XI) shows a stone about 5 feet (1.5 meters) long by 1 foot (30 centimeters) high. Assuming that its width was not less than its height, the sandstone megalith would weigh at least 700 pounds (318 kilograms).

Lifting huge stones into place presumably would be a formidable task for the Hopi masons, who lacked modern construction equipment. Mindeleff's engraving shows several other shaped and fitted megaliths in the curving perimeter wall of Fire House. The largest stones are laid in the wall at least 3 feet (1 meter) above ground level. The masonry is all the more remarkable because pueblo masonry traditionally is distinguished by the use of very small stones.

In plan Fire House measures perhaps 90 by 108 feet (27 by 32.3 meters) and contains some forty ground-floor rooms. A single entry appears in the perimeter wall on the east side of the pueblo. Like the curvilinear perimeter wall of Kin Tiel, the Zuni pueblo possibly 40 miles (64 kilometers) to the southeast, the outer enclosure of Fire House seems to have been constructed first.

Interior partitions conform with the circumferential wall or follow radial alignments. A steep trail leads down the cliff face west of Fire House to a spring in the small canyon below. Bowl-like depressions in some of the rocks around the canyon rim may have been used to shape and finish stone implements.

Fire House and Kin Tiel may be two of the earliest examples of settle-ments with curvilinear walls in the ancient Southwest (Hayes, Young, & Warren 1981). Both probably were laid out between 1250 and 1300. Villages with curving walls, such as Deracho, began to appear in the Zuni area about the same time, and within a century at least half a dozen were built (Kintigh 1985).

The circular pueblo of Gran Quivira seems to have been built and occupied sometime between 1300 and 1400, and a similar structure at Tyuonyi most likely continued in use into the mid 1400s or so. Thereafter, as far as we know, ancient structures with curving walls like Fire House ceased to be built in the Southwest.

NUVAQUEOTAKA
Sinagua

The fourteenth-century Sinagua center of Nuvaqueotaka, formerly known as Chavez Pass, contains more than a thousand rooms distributed in three major room blocks, numerous smaller buildings, and related features. The large aggregated complex occupies low ridges and hillsides on Anderson Mesa at an average altitude of 6,600 feet (2,120 meters). The ruin lies north of Mogollon Rim approximately 45 miles (70 kilometers) southeast of Flagstaff in north-central Arizona.

One of Nuvaqueotaka's investigators, Fred Plog (1989), believes that construction may have begun at the large site sometime after A.D. 1270. The largest of numerous Sinagua communities in that vicinity, Nuvaqueotaka apparently represents the center of a complex hierarchy of settlements. Rather than combining all three room blocks into a single large structure on the south ridge, the Sinagua constructed three separate buildings and quite possibly located a ball court somewhere in the middle of them.

A unique architectural system appears in Nuvaqueotaka's massive masonry walls, which are oriented more or less in the east to west direction. Most of the thick, roughly shaped primary walls run continuously through their room blocks consistently forming long, parallel rooms. Later partitions of assorted architectural styles were added between the original walls, dividing the linear spaces into smaller rooms of various dimensions (Plog 1989).

All three room blocks may have been erected during a single phase of

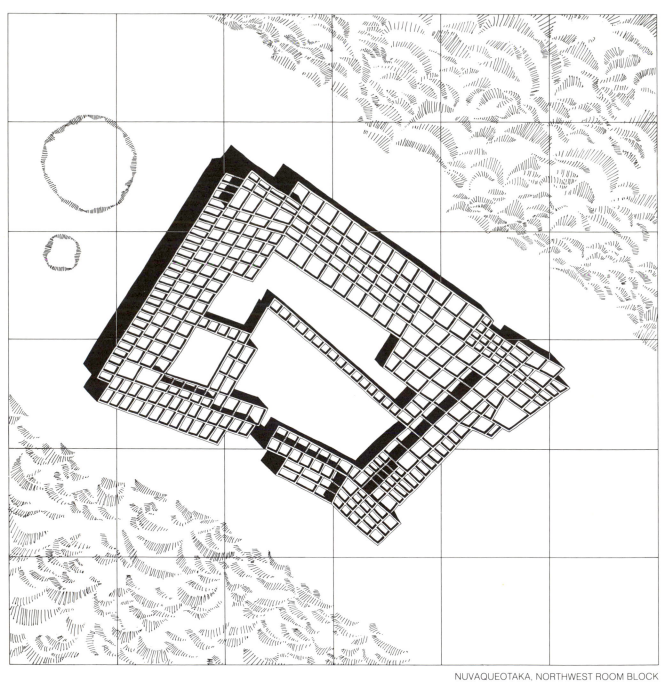

NUVAQUEOTAKA, NORTHWEST ROOM BLOCK

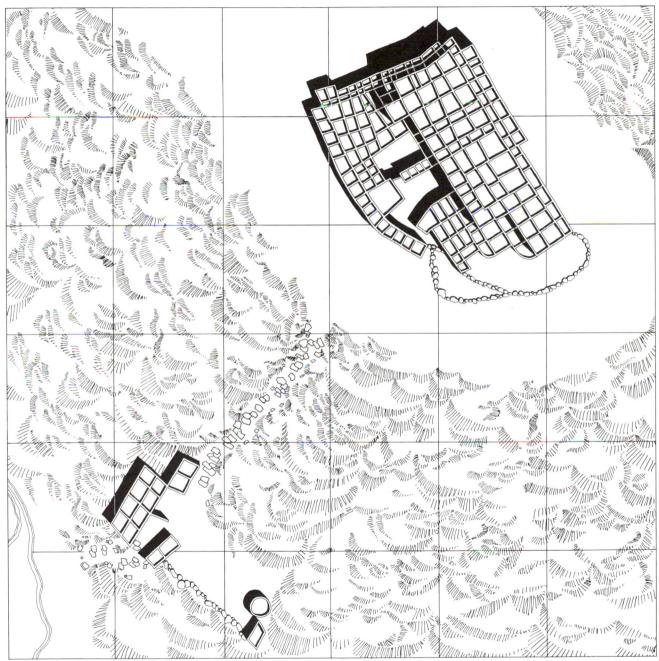

NUVAQUEOTAKA, SOUTHEAST ROOM BLOCK

construction. The reconstruction presented here omits the north room block. The larger of the two room blocks shown on the south ridge is the west (northwest) pueblo, which is located about 500 feet (150 meters) from the southeast pueblo. Other elements in the vicinity include a controversial stairway that may have descended to a spring complex, numerous agricultural terraces, check dams related to irrigation, reservoirs for rain water, and isolated field houses.

The reconstructed drawings of Nuvaqueotaka presented here are based primarily on the site plan of Upham and Bockley (1989:fig. 15.1) and the room block plans published by Upham (1982:figs. 46, 47, 48). The general place name for the ruin is Nuvaqueotaka, a Hopi word meaning "snow belt." An alternate spelling for the name is Nuvakwewtaqa (Upham 1982).

The northwest room block contains an estimated 434 rooms on the ground floor, half as many on the second story, perhaps thirty on the third floor, two large plazas, a rectangular great kiva, and a two-story perimeter wall that may have risen even higher at the pueblo's south and east corners. The great kiva measures some 46 by 56 feet (14 by 17 meters) and is surrounded by rooms perhaps used for storage.

Overall, the large pueblo measures possibly 260 by 380 feet (80 by 115 meters). A 16-foot- (5-meter-) wide entry portal in the southwest wall gives access into the main plaza. Reentrant corners flank the impressive portal. The dimensions of the quadrilateral open space average roughly 82 by 164 feet (25 by 50 meters).

Two noncontiguous rooms built later in the north plaza are omitted from the reconstructed plan. Two reservoirs for rain water, one almost 100 feet (30 meters) in diameter, are located about 80 feet (24 meters) northwest of the larger pueblo near the ridge of the hill. Middens and cemeteries lie on the hillside to the northeast and on the 500-foot- (150-meter-) long ridge to the southeast.

The southeast room block of Nuvaqueotaka steps up in terraces from single-story perimeter rooms to the northwest and southwest to at least three stories near the central core. The room block contains a kiva about 33 feet (10 meters) square, a rectangular plaza bisected by a row of smaller rooms, and plaza-like terraces to the southeast.

The southeast room block houses an estimated 180 single-story, ninety two-story, and forty-five three-story rooms, a total of 314 rooms compared to 680 rooms for the northwest room block. Anchoring the pueblo to the hillside is an exceptionally large retaining wall integrated with the architectural masses to the southeast and southwest. The southeast room block's overall dimensions are about 165 by 280 feet (50 by 85 meters).

Roughly 130 feet (40 meters) southwest of the smaller room block is an arrangement of stones that some observers believe may represent a stairway leading down the steeply sloping hillside to a spring, the area's only permanent source of water.

Other authorities believe that the stones are natural features, not manmade stairs. The elevation of the spring is nearly 120 feet (36.5 meters) below the top of the hill. The stair stones terminate on a 50-by-165-foot

(15-by-50-meter) plaza flanked by a small room block and related features. In some modern Hopi villages rituals are performed in areas below pueblos and close to water sources (Upham 1982).

The materials used to construct lower story walls at Nuvaqueotaka were basically basalt stones laid in abundant mortar. Ranging in size from footballs to small cobbles, the stones were laid in courses two stones wide. A limited number of walls three stones wide may have supported three-story structures.

Upper walls consistently were built of tabular sandstone or limestone, probably because they were lighter in weight and more easily shaped than basalt. Mortar also was used generously in the higher walls. Traces of white calcareous plaster were found on some of the interior walls and floors of rooms in the ruins of Nuvaqueotaka.

Presumably, larger rooms with hearths represent dwellings, while smaller spaces lacking hearths were used for storage. Dwelling rooms usually exceeded 10 by 10 feet (3 by 3 meters) in plan dimensions while store rooms seldom were more than 6 feet (1.8 meters) wide. Wood posts, often juniper but sometimes pine, typically supported roof spans in larger rooms.

A striking difference between the two room blocks appears in the ratio of living rooms to storage spaces. Only 43 percent of the spaces in the southeast room block seem to have been used for storage, while more than 70 percent of the spaces in the larger room block represent storage. The arable land available near Nuvaqueotaka may not have been sufficient to support the pueblo's large population during the fourteenth century (Upham 1982:184). The increased volume of storage suggests the possibility of stockpiling food.

The area in the vicinity of Nuvaqueotaka appears to have been densely inhabited by people living in smaller sites. Burial offerings indicate social ranking and perhaps a hierarchical social organization. Exotic imported items, such as turquoise, obsidian, marine shell, and copper bells, demonstrate evidence of an emphasis on trade, possibly at the expense of agricultural production.

KUAUA
Rio Grande Anasazi

The large adobe pueblo of Kuaua lies on the west bank of the Rio Grande at an elevation of 5,100 feet (1,554 meters) above sea level. Across the river to the east the Sandía Mountains rise to a height of almost 11,000 feet (3,353 meters). Located some 17 miles (27 kilometers) north of Albuquerque, the excavated remains contain more than twelve hundred rooms, three commodious plazas, six subterranean kivas, and a number of rectangular ceremonial rooms in several room blocks (Stuart & Gauthier 1988).

Like Paako, Pecos, Sapawe, Tyuonyi, Arroyo Hondo, and Otowi, Kuaua was built at a time of population aggregation into large communities in the Rio Grande area. Some of the settlements were occupied only briefly or were abandoned and reoccupied. During this time the population reached its prehistoric maximum. Characteristics associated with the large communities are decorated pipes, elaborate axes, carved bone tools, stone effigies, mural painting, and distinctive pottery (Cordell 1984).

Construction of the coursed adobe walls of Kuaua probably began in the early 1300s. The founders were Tiwa-speaking ancestors of the present-day residents of Sandia and Isleta pueblos. The Kuauans raised corn, beans, and squash in irrigated fields on the alluvial plain along the Rio Grande. Except for occasional Apache raids the residents of Sandía and Isleta pueblos. The Kuauans raised corn, beans, and squash in irrigated fields on the allu-

The extensive ruins lie 120 feet (37 meters) or more west of the riverbank. Kuaua occupies an overall area of about 450 by 490 feet (137 by 149 meters), the equivalent of roughly 5 acres (2 hectares). The northwest and south plazas measure more or less 150 feet (46 meters) square, while the 75-by-130-foot (23-by-40-meter) northeast plaza is less than half as large.

The plaza kivas of Kuaua have circular, square, or rectangular plans. One of the kivas contains one of the most spectacular finds in New Mexico: a polychromatic wall decoration with a geometric design (Lambert 1954:18). Colorful paintings also were found on the walls of kivas in Awatovi, Lowry, and Otowi, and fragments of wall coloring were recovered in a ceremonial room of the adobe pueblo at Paako and elsewhere in the ancient Southwest.

Some of the ceremonial rooms and plaza kivas of Kuaua, unlike those of Paako, have loom holes in their floors. Vents or small openings are found in many of the walls of Kuaua. Peckham (1969) observed small antechambers, or ancillary structures, on the east and south sides of two kivas and on the east side only of two other ceremonial chambers.

One of the square, subterranean kivas has a passageway through its side wall. This feature may represent an entry portal for participants during ceremonies, while the audience enters through the roof hatch of the kiva. Portals through or under walls recall the arrangement of entries into the large kiva of Casa Rinconada built during the latter eleventh century in Chaco Canyon.

Kuaua today is part of Coronado State Monument, named in recognition of the historic expedition led by Francisco Vásquez de Coronado. Dis-

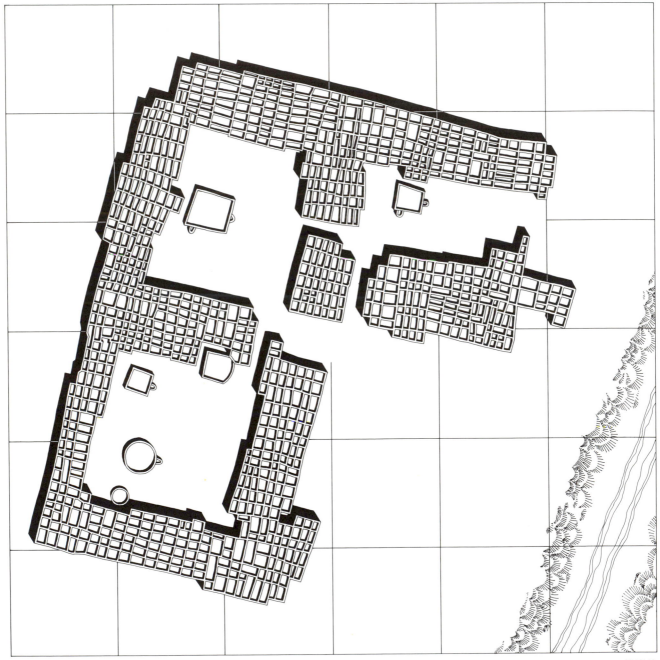

KUAUA

appointed by their failure to find gold in the Southwest, weary, cold, and hungry, the Spanish arrived at Kuaua in the winter of 1540–41. When the visitors began to appropriate food and clothing from the residents, hostilities broke out.

The enmity led to a siege, massacre of indigenous people, and a temporary abandonment by the residents of all the villages in the vicinity. Around 1700 the surviving residents of Kuaua and eleven other Tiwa-speaking communities consolidated into the pueblos of Sandia and Isleta. Visitors to the ancient site today will find informative cultural exhibits in a small museum and may take self-guided interpretive tours through the ruins.

A restored kiva may be entered by means of a ladder descending into a subterranean chamber, which is decorated with full-scale reproductions of the original frescoes. The much-eroded adobe brick construction visible in the walls today is not original. The masonry results from excavation and reconstruction at Kuaua during the 1930s by the University of New Mexico, the Museum of New Mexico, and the School of American Research.

OTOWI
Rio Grande Anasazi

The exceptionally large pueblo of Otowi is found on the Pajarito Plateau about 7.5 miles (12 kilometers) north of Long House and Tyuonyi in Bandelier National Monument. The striking site lies on a broad, grassy hillside between Pueblo Canyon and Bayo Canyon. The streams of the canyons converge a short distance to the east and flow into the nearby Rio Grande. Also called Potsuwii, Otowi contains five large room blocks, at least four plazas, ten circular kivas, two middens, and an artificial reservoir to the south.

The reconstruction presented here is based on the plan published by Edgar Lee Hewett (1938). Since Otowi never has been excavated systematically, the plan should be regarded as an approximation at best. While excavating a burial ground at Otowi in 1906, Hewett found beautiful polychrome bowls, distinctive glaze-ware, loosely woven cloaks of turkey feathers and rabbit fur, and other spectacular grave offerings (Stuart 1989).

Overall, the large site measures approximately 315 by 520 feet (96 by 158 meters). As at other pueblos of the Pajarito Plateau, the walls of Otowi are built of hand-cut volcanic tuff laid in adobe mortar. A talus house some 1.5 miles (2.4 kilometers) west of Otowi contains numerous cavates and colorful petroglyphs (Rohn 1989A). The relationship of Otowi to its neighboring talus house recalls the relationship of Tyuonyi to Long House in nearby Frijoles Canyon.

Quite likely all five of Otowi's room blocks were at least in part three stories high. The reconstruction presented here suggests 460 ground-floor rooms, possibly half as many second-floor rooms, and one-quarter the number of third-floor rooms, a total of 805 rooms in all. By comparison, the contemporary pueblo of Tyuonyi had an estimated 570 rooms, and Long House contained perhaps 353.

A wall along the north side of Otowi interconnects the three central, parallel room blocks. A second wall extends westward to engage the southwest structure. Of the community's ten kivas, two are contained in room blocks, and none exceeds a diameter of 25 feet (7.6 meters) or so. A reservoir about 33 feet (10 meters) in diameter lies near the south corner of the southwest structure.

The southwest structure is generally typical of Otowi's five rectangular room blocks. Measuring around 50 by 170 feet (15 by 52 meters) overall, it contains possibly 135 rooms and a kiva. Typical rooms are more or less square in proportion and measure along wall centerlines roughly 8.3 by 8.5 feet (2.5 by 2.6 meters). Otowi's room sizes are similar to those of the masonry rooms recorded at Long House, although the proportions of the latter are more rectangular.

The four tree-ring dates available for Otowi range from A.D. 1409 to 1491 (Rohn 1989a). Ceramics collected at the site indicate that the pueblo probably continued to be occupied well into the 1500s. If so, Otowi would have been one of the last active communities on the Pajarito Plateau. The Tewa-speaking residents of present-day San Ildefonso Pueblo in the Rio Grande Valley are believed to be descendants of people who once lived in Otowi and its

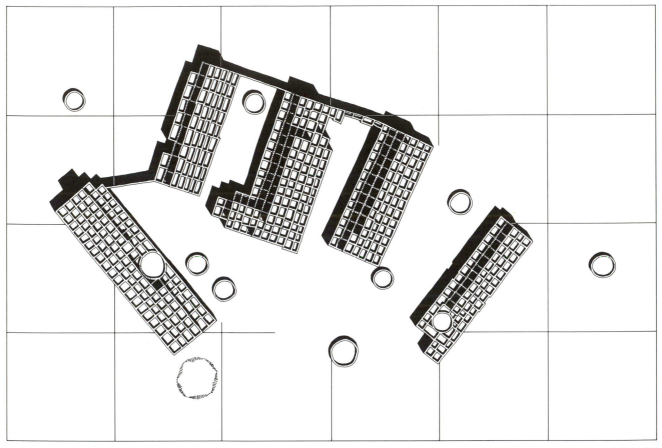

OTOWI

neighboring communities between Frijoles Canyon and Puye (Hewett 1938).

The Pajarito Plateau traditionally serves as an upland resource for the riverine pueblos of the Rio Grande. The higher elevations provide obsidian, game, edible natural plants, berries, acorns, and piñon nuts. Visitors to the remains of Otowi today will see little more than five low hillocks filled with wind-blown sand and a number of shallow depressions marking original kivas and the reservoir.

LONG HOUSE
Rio Grande Anasazi

Situated at the base of a sheer cliff in Bandelier National Monument, Long House combines masonry rooms with cave dwellings in a single structure. The site lies on the north side of a secluded gorge approximately 20 miles (32 kilometers) west of Santa Fe. The name of the gorge and the stream flowing through it is El Rito de Los Frijoles, meaning in Spanish "the ritual of the beans." The linear structure rests on a talus slope, an accumulation of debris that has fallen from the vertical rock cliff some 150 feet (46 meters) high. The surface of the talus slope is elevated 40 to 50 feet (12 to 15 meters) above the canyon floor.

The largest of thirteen talus houses in Frijoles Canyon, Long House stretches roughly 700 feet (213 meters) along the base of the south-facing cliff. Here the altitude of the canyon floor is more than 6,000 feet (1,830 meters) above sea level, and winter snows often cover the bases of north-facing cliffs for months on end. The rooms of the talus house generally are oriented for maximum exposure to the warming rays of the winter sun.

The reconstructed plan presented here shows 217 ground-floor rooms ranging from one to four chambers deep along the cliff face (Hewett 1938). Above these are traces of 136 additional rooms and caves, some up to four stories high. The squares shown in the cliff face of the reconstruction represent cavates, rooms artificially carved into the rock or under large boulders.

The north walls of rooms abutting the cliff sometimes are cut into the soft tuff for increased space. Sockets for roof beams and, occasionally, storage niches also are carved into the natural stone. Probably not all 353 rooms of Long House were occupied at the same time. Typical cave rooms in Long House measure perhaps 6 by 9 feet (1.8 by 2.7 meters) in plan and have ceiling heights of about 5 feet 8 inches (1.7 meters).

The height of the doorway to a typical chamber does not exceed 3 feet (90 centimeters) and is only half as wide. Often a small opening near the floor admits draft air for the fireplace, and one or more apertures near the ceiling emit smoke from the fire. A storage niche usually is carved into the stone wall, the walls and floors are plastered with mud, and a layer of soot invariably covers the ceiling.

A cave room of this type might serve as sleeping quarters for a family of five or six persons since no furniture occupied floor space (Wing 1961). Sometimes one cave room was connected to another by means of an interior portal. A typical masonry room in Long House measures about 7 by 10 feet (2.1 by 3 meters), not much larger than an average cave chamber.

The dwellings in the talus house are organized into five clusters, each containing from twenty-nine to almost one hundred rooms. Each cluster housed a group of families related by a common ancestry forming a clan. Each clan apparently had its own ceremonial structure, such as a kiva or plaza, and each was associated with distinctive patterns of rock art and decoration (Rohn 1989a).

The Anasazi builders of Long House customarily finished the interior walls of their living rooms by plastering the walls with one or two colors. Lower walls often are a red ocher color, while upper walls usually are white. Geometric designs sometimes embellish the interiors, often rendered by red lines on white backgrounds. Zigzags, triangles, and stepped pyramids appear frequently.

Along the cliff base to the west of Long House is Macaw House, another talus house. Snake House and Sun House, also talus houses, lie to the east, and Tyuonyi Pueblo is located a short distance to the southeast on the canyon floor near Frijoles Creek. The talus houses and the pueblo very likely were built and occupied at the same time.

Around A.D. 1300 relatively large numbers of people began arriving in the Pajarito Plateau area. In Spanish *pajarito* means "little bird," most likely a reference to the numerous wrens, swifts, swallows, bluebirds, woodpeckers, and other birds inhabiting the canyons. The settlers established communities housing sometimes one to two thousand people.

Daily life in Frijoles Canyon centered on cultivating plots of corn, beans, and squash in bottom lands where water was plentiful. The people also raised turkeys, hunted deer and rabbits in the nearby mountains, and gathered a wealth of edible natural plants and nuts. For two centuries or more life flourished in the canyons of the Pajarito Plateau. However, conditions changed in the early 1500s, and the canyon dwellers moved down to settlements closer to the Rio Grande, where their descendants live today.

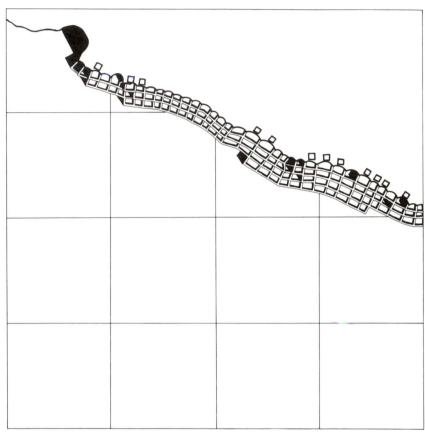

LONG HOUSE, WEST AREA

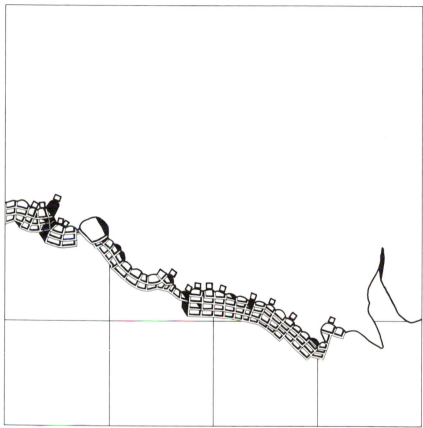

LONG HOUSE, EAST AREA

TYUONYI
Rio Grande Anasazi

The large masonry pueblo of Tyuonyi lies on the floor of Frijoles Canyon in north-central New Mexico. The canyon is one of many valleys formed by deep erosion into the soft and porous tuff of the Pajarito Plateau. A crystal clear brook called El Rito de Los Frijoles flows through the densely wooded canyon floor, providing a perennial source of water for nearby settlements and agricultural plots.

The bases of the reconstructed plan presented here are an acrial photograph published by David E. Stuart (1989), a plan drawing attributed to J. R. Terken (Hewett 1938), and my observations during a visit to the site in 1990. Originally, the massive, oval-shaped pueblo probably had a two- or three-story perimeter, but now the structure is much in ruins and has no walls standing more than 5 feet (1.5 meters) high. Fortress-like in appearance, the huge structure surrounds a central plaza containing three subterranean kivas.

The overall dimensions of Tyuonyi appear to be more or less 230 by 263 feet (70 by 80 meters). The approximately 134-by-149-foot (41-by-45.4-meter) plaza contains three circular kivas ranging in diameter from 20 to 27 feet (6 to 8.2 meters). Only the eastern kiva presently is excavated. A 6-to-10-foot- (1.8-to-3-meter-) wide entry corridor leads into the plaza through the east side of the room block.

The reconstructed plan proposes 325 rooms on the ground floor, half as many on the second floor, and a fourth as many on the third floor, for a total of possibly 570 rooms. Some authorities believe that one or more

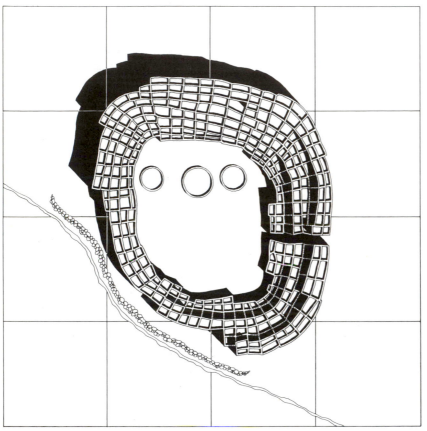

rows of rooms may have been built originally along Tyuonyi's southwest perimeter where the stream flows closest to the pueblo. Six hundred years ago Frijoles Creek flowed much closer to the walls than it does today, suggesting the possibility of flooding, which may have undermined foundation walls.

Future investigation of unexcavated areas in Tyuonyi may shed light on the construction systems and architectural details of the site. The pueblo seems to have been founded in the late 1200s and to have flourished between perhaps 1350 and 1450. Tree-ring dates for the site range from 1383 to 1466.

As many as eight rows of rooms appear in the north and east sides of the room block, possibly the result of successive construction phases. The southwest tiers, only three or four rooms wide, most likely were the last to be added. Access to the ground-floor rooms presumably was by means of roof hatches and ladders to the plaza level. Small doors interconnected interior rooms.

Tyuonyi was only one of a number of ancient settlements in the Frijoles Canyon. A short distance to the northwest is Long House, a structure comprising more than three hundred rooms strung along the base of the canyon's north wall. In preceding centuries pit houses and small masonry structures were built on the mesa tops. Human activity seems to have been intensive in the upland areas near Frijoles Canyon between 1160 and 1290 (Stuart 1989).

Tyuonyi apparently was abandoned in the late 1400s. By the time Coronado arrived in northern New Mexico some fifty years later, the former residents of Frijoles Canyon had resettled in Cochiti and other pueblos of the Rio Grande Valley a few miles to the east. An imaginary account of living on the banks of El Rito de los Frijoles during prehistoric times may be found in *The Delight Makers*, a colorful narrative written in the 1880s by Adolf F. Bandelier (1971).

POSHUOUINGE
Rio Grande Anasazi

The immense adobe pueblo of Poshuouinge is typical of the ten or more prehistoric settlements built along the Chama River between the Rio Grande and Abiquiu in north-central New Mexico. The Tewa name for the site has several translations, all more or less along the lines of "squash ridge village." A more popular name for Poshuouinge is Turquoise Ruin, although no turquoise is in evidence on this site. The ruins were excavated under the direction of Jean A. Jeancon (1923) in the summer of 1919.

Situated on a high bluff possibly 150 feet (48 meters) above the flood plain, the site lies on the south bank of the Chama River about 3 miles (5 kilometers) east of Abiquiu. The river valley in the vicinity of Poshuouinge is well suited to agriculture. Two springs some 500 feet (150 meters) south of the ruins most likely were sources of water for the prehistoric pueblo.

The mountain directly across the river from the site is known to the Tewa-speaking people as Tumayo, meaning "chief piñon mountain." Piñons and small cedar trees abound in the vicinity of Poshuouinge, particularly on the higher mesas to the south. The reconstruction presented here is based on the map and report published by Jeancon.

Like other late prehistoric sites in the Chama Valley, Poshuouinge's most striking features are the immense size and comparatively vast scale of the room blocks and plazas. Overall, the large pueblo measures about 630 by 656 feet (192 by 200 meters). These dimensions are so large that the north row of rooms enclosing the west plaza lie beyond the north edge of the reconstructed drawing.

For the most part, the north row of rooms is eroded to its foundations. Probably three rooms wide and two stories high, the north row contained a portal 29 feet (8.8 meters) wide leading into the east plaza and a circular room around 20 feet (6 meters) in diameter. Excavators speculated that the latter feature is a kiva or a watchtower on the edge of the bluff overlooking the river valley.

A distinctive architectural feature of Poshuouinge is its almost entirely multistory construction. Apparently only a dozen or so rooms are one story high. All the other rooms are two stories high except for two rows oriented from north to south; these reportedly had three floors.

The reconstruction presented here suggests 881 rooms on the ground floor, 869 on the second, and 250 on the third, an estimated total of two thousand rooms. Most of the room blocks are three rooms wide, but one row is four rooms wide. Average room sizes in Poshuouinge range from 65 to 94 square feet (6 to 8.75 square meters).

The west plaza measures possibly 260 by 285 feet (79 by 87 meters) and has no gateways, kivas, or other distinguishing architectural features. Poshuouinge's only single-story rooms flank the 18-foot- (5.5-meter-) wide gateway leading into the east plaza near the south end of the west row of rooms. Wood-framed *ramadas* line the west-central side of the larger plaza.

The walls of Poshuouinge are built predominantly of clay or adobe with very limited quantities of sandstones. Foundations consist of large stones laid in orthogonal rows oriented within 3 to 17 degrees of magnetic compass north. Typically 12 inches (30 centimeters) thick, the walls have exceedingly hard surfaces, especially after they are plastered.

Small openings 6 to 10 inches (15 to 25 centimeters) in diameter are located in walls near ceilings; the holes appear to serve as ventilators for rooms. Doors interconnect interior rooms, but no portals occur in exterior walls on the ground-floor level. Roof hatches and ladders provide access to lower floors, and doorways originally may have opened through exterior walls onto second- or third-floor roof terraces.

Floors are composed typically of a mixture of ash, grease, fine charcoal, adobe, and water. Great numbers of bottle-shaped storage pits 10 to 18 inches (25 to 46 centimeters) deep are found in floors throughout Poshuouinge, but wall niches are absent. More often than not, fireplaces are centered on interior walls. Roof construction is similar to the wood framing of other prehistoric Anasazi pueblos.

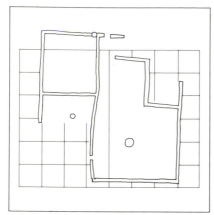

KEY PLAN OF POSHUOUINGE

A semisubterranean great kiva around 40 feet (12 meters) in diameter is located near the center of the east plaza. Four rectangular ceremonial rooms are found in the room blocks flanking the large plaza. Two are second-floor chambers centered in the plaza's north and west sides, and two are ground-floor chambers centered in the south and east sides. The locations of the ceremonial rooms in the plan of the pueblo correspond to the cardinal points.

A room in the southwest corner of the east plaza is a special kitchen for the preparation of "tissue paper" bread, called *buwa yave* in the Tewa language. The delicacy consists of many tissue-thin layers of bread rolled into a cylinder perhaps 1.5 inches (3.8 centimeters) in diameter and 6 inches (15 centimeters) in length. The *buwa yave* prepared by Hopi cooks on Second Mesa is made from purple corn and has an exceptionally delicate flavor.

Special grinding rooms at Poshuouinge contain as many as three *metates* each. In 1919 a man in his six-

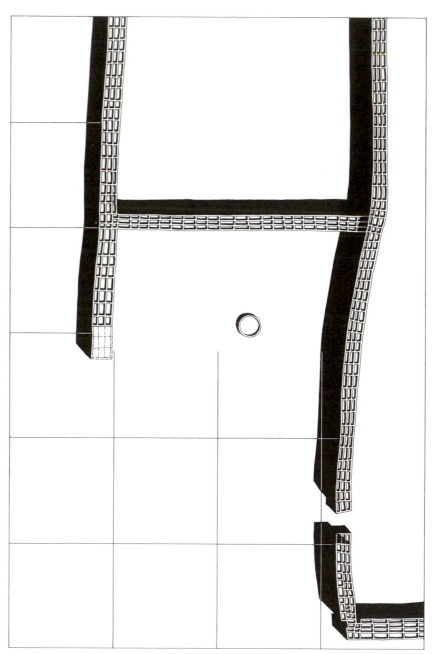

POSHUOUINGE, WEST PORTION

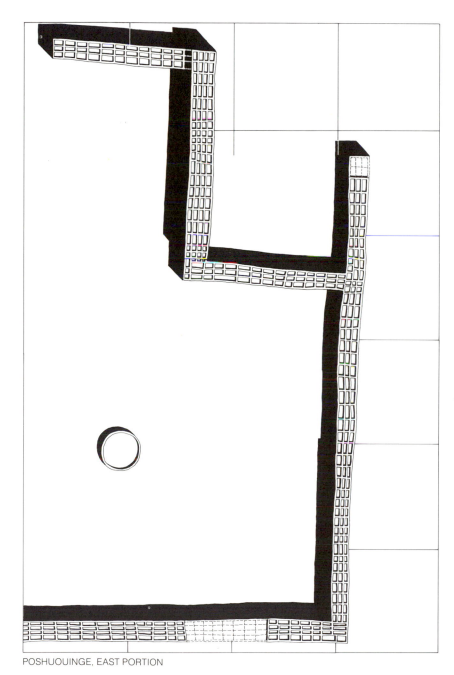

POSHUOUINGE, EAST PORTION

ties from Santa Clara Pueblo told Jeancon that in his youth it was customary for women to gather in special rooms to grind meal while men sang the mealing song. The activities took on the character of social gatherings. Many of the traditional practices of the present-day people in the Rio Grande Valley originated in pre-Hispanic times.

Poshuouinge and contemporary villages in the Chama Valley quite likely were founded during the fourteenth century. The communities seem to result from an amalgamation of migrants from the Northern San Juan and Mesa Verde area with indigenous people of the Rio Grande. Tewa-speaking people continued to live in the Chama Valley area until they joined their kin in the nearby Rio Grande Valley sometime between 1598 and 1620 (Schroeder 1979c:16). The inhabitants of both San Juan Pueblo and Santa Clara Pueblo claim ancestral ties with Poshuouinge.

SAPAWE
Rio Grande Anasazi

The immense adobe pueblo of Sapawe is considered to be the largest structure of its type in the Southwest. Also spelled Sapawi, the vast site occupies more than 30 acres (12 hectares) on the west bank of El Rito Wash approximately 8 miles (13 kilometers) north of its confluence with the

Chama River in north-central New Mexico. Extensively excavated in the 1960s by a team from the University of New Mexico, the ruins appear to contain the remains of several thousand rooms, at least nineteen kivas, and seven or more large plazas.

The basis of the reconstruction presented here is a map prepared in the 1930s by Harry P. Mera for the Laboratory of Anthropology of the Museum of New Mexico. The huge pueblo measures overall about 1,000 by 1,350 feet (305 by 412 meters) and would fill six pages if it were presented in its entirety at the study's standard scale. Because an accurate plan does not exist for Sapawe, only the room blocks defining two rectangular plazas in the west-central portion of the site are reconstructed here. Dashed lines in the plan represent assumed centerlines of walls.

The average room size suggested for Sapawe is in the range of 8.5 by 11 feet (2.6 by 3.4 meters), an area of roughly 94 square feet (9 square meters). Typical room sizes for the contemporary adobe pueblo of Poshuouinge range from 65 to 94 square feet (6 to 8.75 square meters), while the average room size in Arroyo Hondo generally is about 65 square feet (6 square meters). The reconstruction of the west-central portion of Sapawe proposes an estimated 1,063 ground-floor rooms.

Combining the dimensions shown for all the room blocks on Mera's map with the assumed room size, the estimated total number of ground-floor rooms in Sapawe would be 2,524. Further assuming that half of the pueblo's rooms have second floors and one-quarter have third floors, the estimated total number of rooms on all floors would be 4,417.

Although Frank C. Hibben (1937) reported at least nineteen kivas in Sapawe, Mera's map records only ten; these are shown on the small-scale key plan. The kivas range in diameter from 20 to 65 feet (6 to 20 meters). The great kivas of the Chama Valley are not known to have the sophisticated features associated with comparable structures in Chaco Canyon, Aztec, and other Anasazi sites.

An entry lane narrowing to perhaps 13 feet (4 meters) gives access into the west plaza, which measures possibly 200 by 400 feet (60 by 120 meters). Two kivas, each around 37.5 feet (11.4 meters) in diameter, are located toward the north end of the somewhat irregular west plaza. A single portal 10 feet (3 meters) or so in width interconnects the east and west plazas.

Like the west plaza, the slightly smaller east plaza has a more or less rectangular plan with its long axis oriented from north to south; its dimensions appear to be at most 170 by 330 feet (52 by 100 meters). House blocks consisting of five to eight parallel rows of rooms flank the open space on all four sides. The east plaza's four kivas range in diameter from 20 to 43 feet (6 to 13 meters).

Sapawe is one of several very large villages in the Chama Valley built between 1300 and 1500. During this period the population of the upper Rio Grande was consolidating into a few large communities for the first time. The Chama Valley sites apparently began to decline in population after 1500, but several pueblos, including Sapawe, continued to be occupied into the historic era. Sapawe quite likely is one of the four Tewa-speaking communities in the vicinity visited by Castaño de Sosa between 1540 and 1542 (Schroeder 1979c).

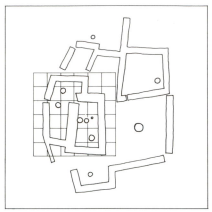

KEY PLAN OF SAPAWE PUEBLO

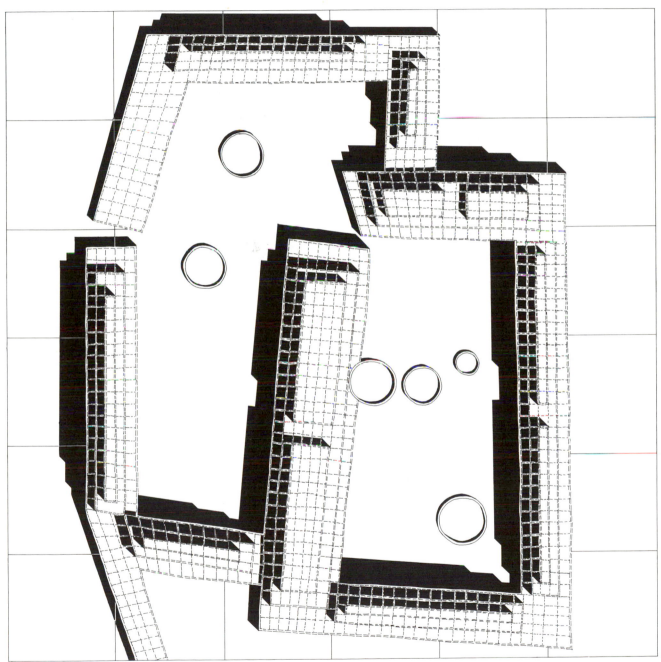

SAPAWE, WEST-CENTRAL ROOM BLOCKS

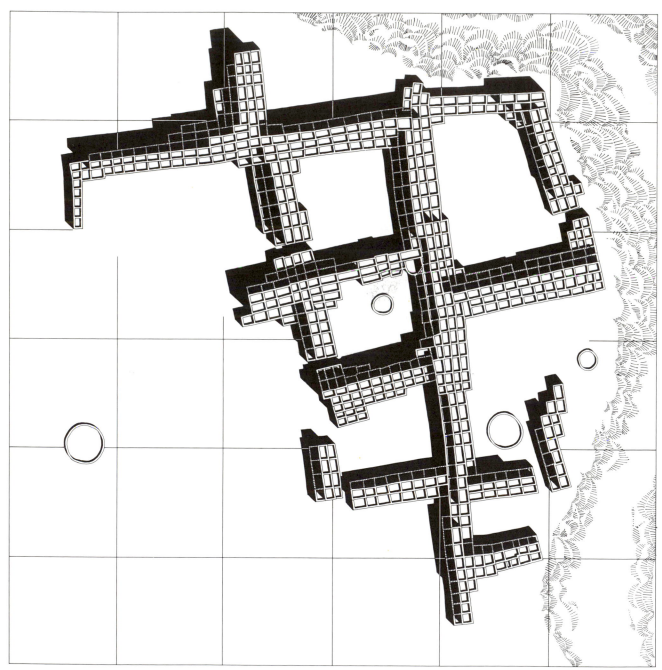

ARROYO HONDO

ARROYO HONDO

Rio Grande Anasazi

The large adobe pueblo of Arroyo Hondo lies on the southeast bank of a drainageway 6 miles (10 kilometers) or so south of Santa Fe in north-central New Mexico. Located in an open woodland zone of juniper and piñons, the site is situated at an altitude of 7,120 feet (2,170 meters) above sea level. The ruins were partially excavated and mapped during the 1970s by a research team from the School of American Research under the direction of Douglas O. Schwartz (Schwartz & Lang 1973).

Construction and occupation of the large structure probably began during the late thirteenth century, perhaps around A.D. 1295. This was a period in southwestern prehistory when the inhabitants of the upper Rio Grande were developing into fewer, larger communities. Between 1300 and 1330 Arroyo Hondo appears to have grown to the size shown in the reconstruction presented here. The plan is based on maps published by Ann M. Palkovich (1980: app. B).

Altogether, Arroyo Hondo occupies an area measuring roughly 510 by 530 feet (155 by 162 meters). At its peak of development the pueblo most likely contained more than a thousand rooms in some twenty-four house blocks defining ten plazas. By 1335, however, the site was in decline and much of it was being systematically dismantled.

The reconstructed plan for Arroyo Hondo shows house blocks two to six rooms wide. The structures are arranged orthogonally and are oriented generally toward the cardinal points. In Spanish the site's name means "deep gully," presumably a reference to the arroyo along the north and east sides of the pueblo.

The reconstruction tentatively proposes 636 ground-floor rooms. Some of the rooms have been excavated but many are estimated on the basis of surface observations only or are interpolated on the basis of the site's known room sizes. Assuming that half of the ground-floor rooms had second floors and one-quarter had third stories, the estimated total number for Arroyo Hondo would be 1,113.

A typical room in Sapawe measures perhaps 6.5 by 10 feet (2 by 3 meters) and has an area of 65 square feet (6 square meters). The large pueblo seems to contain at least five kivas. Four circular chambers are located in the plazas and are sunken below grade; their interior diameters range from 17 to 34 feet (5.2 to 10.4 meters). A fifth kiva is a D-shaped surface room found in the room block at the northeast corner of the central plaza.

Other large adobe pueblos in the upper Rio Grande area described in this study are Kuaua, Poshuouinge, Sapawe, and the early component of Paako. Compared with the contemporary adobe room blocks of Kuaua, Arroyo Hondo appears to be less regular in plan, to have similar overall dimensions but only about half the number of ground-floor rooms, and to have more but smaller courtyards or plazas. Both sites have several kivas with entries generally oriented to the south and east.

Around 1335, after only a few decades of occupation, Arroyo Hondo apparently was abandoned for a while. One of the reasons for the pueblo's decline may have been insufficient food resources. Skeletal remains of children and young adults demonstrate the ravages of malnutrition around the time of initial abandonment (Palkovich 198?).

In the early 1370s a second period of prosperity began at Arroyo Hondo. By 1400 the reoccupied village consisted of perhaps two hundred rooms in nine house blocks defining three plazas. Arroyo Hondo's second period of prosperity corresponds with a period of above-average rainfall in the upper Rio Grande Valley.

Around 1410 the adobe village once more began to encounter difficulties. A decade-long drought commenced in 1415, and a fire destroyed the pueblo in 1420. About 1425 Arroyo Hondo was abandoned for the second and final time.

Many other sites in the northern Rio Grande area also were abandoned about a century before the Spaniards entered the Southwest in 1540. The former residents of Arroyo Hondo quite likely relocated to one or more of the large Rio Grande pueblos known to be occupied in early historic times.

PAAKO

Rio Grande Anasazi

Located on the east side of the Sandía Mountains some 40 miles (64 kilometers) southwest of Santa Fe, Paako is one of the major pueblos in the Galisteo Basin. The community was a contemporary of Kuaua, Arroyo

Hondo, Poshuouinge, Sapawe, Pecos, and other well-known sites in the upper Rio Grande area. Here in time the people consolidated into a few large communities where the population reached its prehistoric maximum.

Paako is one of a number of pueblos associated with decorated pipes, elaborate axes, carved bone tools, stone effigies, mural painting, and distinctive pottery. The pueblo was occupied at the time of the Spanish *entrada*, as were Kuaua, Sapawe, Poshuouinge, and Pecos. Data gathered from the site suggest that construction probably began about A.D. 1275 and occupation continued until abandonment around 1425. Apparently reoccupied in the 1500s, Paako again was abandoned sometime during the seventeenth century (Lambert 1954).

The extensive site consists of north and south divisions, both located 100 yards (91 meters) or so west of San Pedro Arroyo. The two divisions grew west toward the Sandia Mountains and to the north and south until they almost joined. Ample land for agricultural production was reserved between the pueblo and the arroyo to the east.

The south division contains a group of buildings with several plazas. The much more extensive remains of the north division are presented here (Lambert 1954: figs. 2a, 2b, 2c). The north ruins of Paako extend over an area of roughly 500 by 670 feet (152 by 204 meters) encompassing approximately 7.7 acres (3.1 hectares). The reconstructed plan of Paako proposes an estimated total of approximately thirteen hundred rooms shown in dashed or solid lines.

Excavations in the north division include a prehistoric structure of coursed adobe to the east and a his-

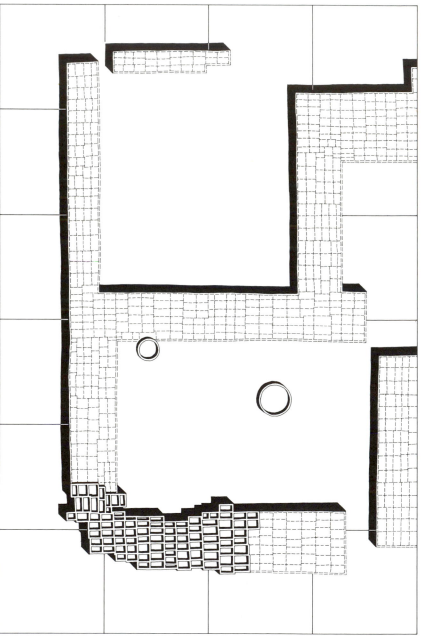

PAAKO, WEST AREA

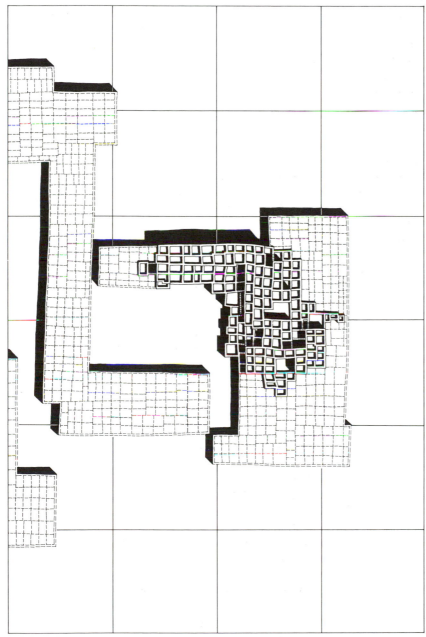

PAAKO, EAST AREA

toric building having stone walls to the west. The reason for changing in time from coursed adobe to stone construction is not known. Materials for both systems are readily available at Paako. A few buildings using both adobe and stone are found; they seem to represent a gradual transition in building systems. Immigrants from the Rio Grande area may have introduced new agricultural ideas to the builders in the Galisteo Basin.

Built closest to the arroyo, the prehistoric pueblo reconstructed here is L-shaped and measures perhaps 140 by 210 feet (43 by 64 meters). The structure contains 138 ground-floor rooms, possibly seventy-two second-floor chambers, and four ceremonial rooms inside the room block, recalling those of Forked Lightning and the quadrangle at Pecos. Typical room sizes range in area from 50 to 100 square feet (4.6 to 9.3 square meters). In shape the rooms generally are nearly square. Store rooms outnumber living and working spaces almost four to one.

Paako's ceremonial rooms quite likely served functions similar to kivas. Circular kivas appear only during the historic period at the site. The ceremonial chambers appear to range in area from 170 to 300 square feet (16 to 28 square meters) and generally are similar to those recorded at Kuaua except that no loom holes are found. Fragments of several colors of wall plaster were found in two ceremonial rooms at Paako. A similar chamber at Otowi has on one wall a fresco depicting a mountain lion.

Southwest of the two-story adobe pueblo lies a rectangular plaza measuring at most 80 by 130 feet (24 by 40 meters). Parallel dashed lines in the reconstructed plan indicate the walls of unexcavated room blocks enclosing the plaza. Entryways appear in the plaza's southeast and northwest corners.

The reconstructed structure at the southwest corner of Paako's north division represents the historic period. To the northeast are two circular kivas in a plaza almost four times the size of the earlier east plaza. The west house contains eighty-six rooms in an area 85 by 184 feet (26 by 56 meters).

Typical rooms in the stone pueblo are more rectangular in plan, more uniform in size, and somewhat larger in area than those of the earlier adobe room block. Like Pecos, the west house has a great kiva and seems to be composed of many six-room suites having narrow store rooms closest to the plaza. The floors of both the coursed-adobe and stone pueblos generally are adobe or mud and ash; stone paving is rare.

Paako's great kiva has an average diameter of 33.6 feet (10.2 meters) and an area of more or less 880 square feet (82 square meters). This area is almost three times the size of the largest ceremonial room in the adobe pueblo. The 21-foot- (6.4-meter-) diameter kiva in the plaza's northwest corner encompasses perhaps 350 square feet (32.5 square meters). The unexcavated remains of a third kiva are found in the west courtyard.

In 1581 and 1582 Spanish chroniclers recorded a number of large, active pueblos in the Galisteo Basin. Although today many Native American communities continue to be active in the Rio Grande Valley and elsewhere, none survive in the Galisteo area. All of the Galisteo settlements, like Paako, were abandoned earlier in historic times.

SAN CRISTÓBAL
Rio Grande Anasazi

The exceptionally large pueblo of San Cristóbal is one of the seven major communities in the Galisteo Basin excavated by Nels C. Nelson (1914) during the summer of 1912. Other extensive Rio Grande settlements occupied at the time of the Spanish *entrada* are Gran Quivira, Kuaua, Paako, Sapawe, and Poshuouinge. Abandoned early in the historic period, San Cristóbal probably was founded around A.D. 1300 (Stuart & Gauthier 1988).

The Galisteo Basin is a well-watered plain between the Manzano and Sandía mountains on the west and the less elevated buttes and mesas south of Pecos to the east. Situated at an altitude of between 6,000 and 6,500 feet (1,830 and 1,980 meters) above sea level, the valley's principal watercourse is westward-flowing Galisteo Creek. San Cristóbal is located approximately 50 miles (80 kilometers) northeast of Albuquerque along an arroyo in the east end of the Galisteo Basin.

The ruins of the large pueblo extend over an area of some 1,300 by 2,000 feet (400 by 600 meters) on both sides of San Cristóbal creek. At this point the creek emerges from a deep, rocky gorge and flows onto the open Galisteo plain to the west. The well-chosen site has the advantages of a constantly flowing source of water, tillable soils, ample stones for building, piñons and cedars on nearby foothills and mesas, and scattered pines with occasional cottonwoods in more remote canyons.

The historic component of San Cristóbal lies on the north bank of the creek near the center of the reconstruction presented here. The site plan is based on Nelson's (1914: vol. XV, plan 1) survey. More or less steep arroyo banks contain the site on three sides. About 500 feet (150 meters) north of the pueblo's northeast corner traces of a stone wall extend from canyon to canyon on the site's only exposed side.

Also found in the vicinity of the pueblo are rock shelters, petroglyphs, two artificial reservoirs, and several outlying structures. On a hilltop southwest of the site, Nelson recorded an unusual circular stone ruin roughly 33 to 36 feet (10 to 11 meters) in diameter. He speculated that the structure may have been a watch tower, kiva, or shrine.

Altogether, San Cristóbal consists of nineteen or twenty separate buildings. Some room blocks are simple rectangles in plan, but the majority are composed of several wings generally oriented with respect to the cardinal points. If they were placed end to end, the structures would extend for possibly 5,000 feet (1,524 meters), assuming a width of roughly 40 feet (12 meters).

The total number of ground-floor rooms at San Cristóbal is conservatively estimated to be 1,645, not all of which were occupied at the same time. Some of the room blocks are known to have second floors, and some may have had third floors. Assuming that half of the ground-floor rooms have upper floors, the large pueblo would contain a total of 2,467 rooms.

The southwest room block shown in the reconstruction is a prehistoric structure built on top of an earlier ruin. Probably originally rectangular in plan, the partially excavated building likely includes forty-five ground-floor rooms; additional rooms to the west may have been eroded by San Cristóbal Creek. Today the remaining walls of the room block rise only about 2 feet (60 centimeters) above the surrounding terrain.

The south-central room block appears to have 253 ground-floor rooms, more than any other building at San Cristóbal. The F-shaped building forms the boundary of courts to the north and west. The structure's soundly built walls are constructed primarily of stone slabs laid in mud mortar, though adobe sections are found in limited areas. The masonry walls typically are 11.5 inches (29 centimeters) thick.

The quadrangle shown in the middle of the reconstruction occupies the center of the historic pueblo. Early in the historic period around 650 ground-floor rooms probably were in use at San Cristóbal. Assuming that 325 upper-floor rooms also were occupied, the pueblo would have contained perhaps 975 rooms when Spaniards first visited the site.

A 200-foot- (60-meter-) square courtyard occupies the center of the quadrangle. A kiva possibly 36 feet (11 meters) in diameter is located in the northwest corner of the courtyard. An older building underlies the west wing of the quadrangle, where excavators found a comparatively large room with two fireplaces and walls covered with several coats of whitewash.

The building forming the east side of the quadrangle incorporates a kiva with an inner diameter of 20 feet (6 meters) at the floor level. Rectangular room walls apparently were removed to accommodate the circular chamber. On the kiva's tamped adobe floor excavators recovered several artifacts,

pottery shards, and bones of cattle and sheep, confirming the building's occupation in historic times.

The most unusual object found in the kiva is the fragment of a cast metal bell's rim. Bandelier (Nelson 1914:59) reported that raiders from the Galisteo Basin removed the Pecos mission bell to a high mesa in the direction of San Cristóbal. The incident occurred during the Pueblo Rebellion in 1680, presumably because of Pecos Pueblo's friendly relations with the Spaniards.

In retaliation, the people of Pecos reportedly joined the Apaches and others in driving the Tano-speaking people of San Cristóbal and San Lázaro out of the Galisteo Basin. Bandelier noted seeing the broken bell where it had been dropped near the head of a canyon leading down to San Cristóbal. Whether or not the bell fragment found in the historic kiva belongs to the Pecos mission rim is unknown.

Some of the well-preserved walls in the vicinity of the kiva rise as high as 8 feet (2.4 meters) above the floor. Lower-floor chambers with reduced ceiling heights recall similar spaces used for storage at Pecos. Some ground-floor rooms are paved with stones. Upper-floor chambers have fireplaces and plastered walls coated with several layers of fire-blackened whitewash.

The room block extending east from the quadrangle has the best preserved rooms in San Cristóbal. One chamber still has its ceiling beams in place and second story walls extending upward several feet (1 meter). Doors are conspicuously absent, suggesting access by means of roof hatches and ladders.

Typical ceiling construction con-

KEY PLAN OF SAN CRISTÓBAL PUEBLO

sists of beams 4 to 8 inches (10 to 20 centimeters) in diameter spaced fully 18 inches (45 centimeters) apart. The beams span the shorter dimensions of rooms and usually are of cedar, but some piñon and even cottonwood are used. Beam ends are cut to length by means of a dull instrument, such as a stone axe, or by burning.

Poles 1 to 3 inches (2.5 to 7.5 centimeters) in diameter are laid across the ceiling beams. Reeds or matted twigs are placed on the poles. Over these a layer of adobe is applied to serve as the roof, or the floor of an upper room. Blackened ceilings and walls are found in rooms with fireplaces. The average room size for San Cristóbal is approximately 82 square feet (7.6 square meters).

The room blocks shown to the east and west of the central group are prehistoric but closely resemble the historic buildings of San Cristóbal. Many human burials are found in refuse mounds, a traditional method of interment. Some of the middens are 4 to 12 feet (1.2 to 3.6 meters) deep, confirming occupation over an extended period of time.

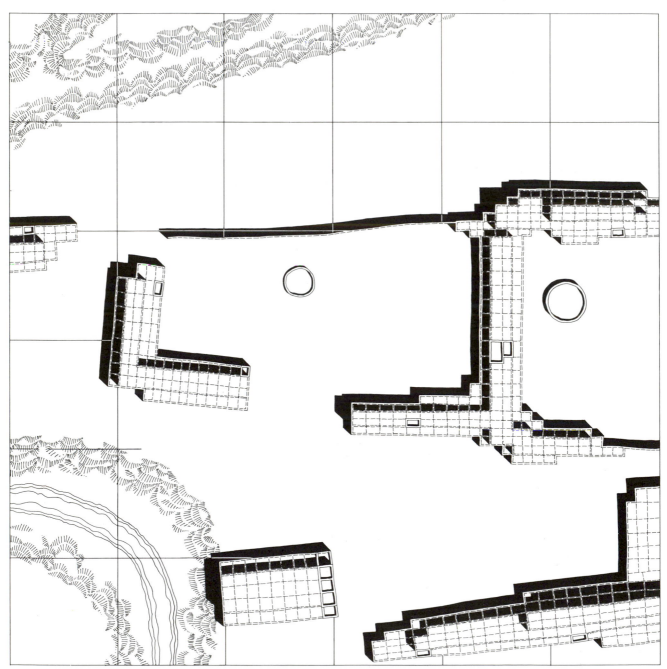

SAN CRISTÓBAL, WEST AREA

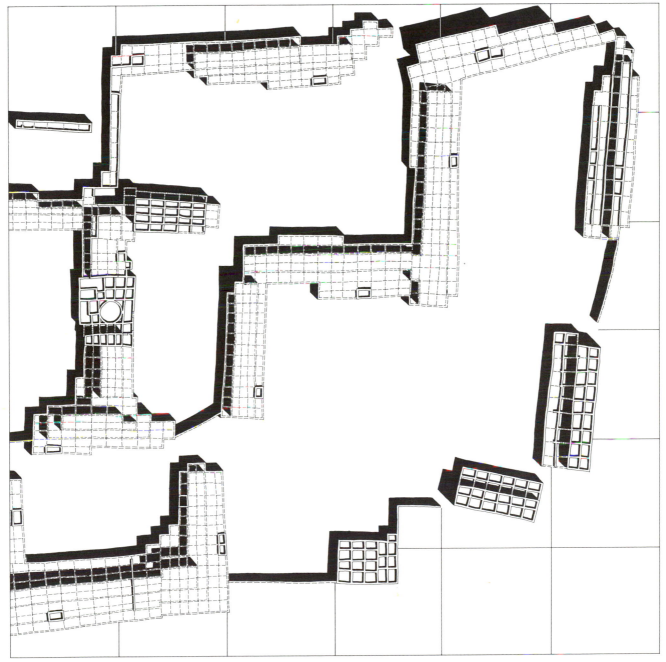

SAN CRISTÓBAL, EAST AREA

The earliest authenticated visit to the pueblo was made in 1590 by Castaño de Sosa who named it San Cristóbal. Bandelier determined that the native American name for the site is Yam-p-hamba (Nelson 1914:41). Most likely sometime before 1630, Spanish missionaries built a chapel a short distance south of the historic pueblo near San Cristóbal Creek.

The population estimated for San Cristóbal in 1680 was eight hundred, but that figure seems to be too large. During the Pueblo Revolt of 1680 to 1692, the pueblo appears to have been abandoned. According to Diego de Vargas, the Spanish general whose army reconquered New Mexico in 1692, the inhabitants resettled along the Santa Cruz drainage north of Santa Fe before finally dispersing in 1696 (Vargas Zapata 1914).

PECOS
Rio Grande Anasazi

Called Cicuye by early Spanish explorers, Pecos is situated on a small mesa in a fertile valley at an elevation of 6,950 feet (2,118 meters) above sea level. The site lies across the Arroyo del Pueblo from Forked Lightning, about 25 miles (40 kilometers) east of Santa Fe. Nearby, the Pecos River flows out of the mountains to the north and continues its long journey southward across the plains to join the Rio Grande in Texas. Toward the west the land rises to Glorieta Pass in the foothills of the Sangre de Cristo Mountains.

The settlement is located strategically between agricultural communities in the Rio Grande to the west and roving buffalo hunters of the Great Plains to the east. As a consequence, the people of Pecos were skilled at farming and trade. A highly distinctive and very livable architecture seems to have evolved at Pecos in response to the community's unique geographical position.

Between A.D. 800 and 1100 the increasing population of the Rio Grande Valley expanded into the upper Pecos River area, establishing a number of small, scattered settlements. In time the farming groups consolidated into larger communities. During the 1200s people concentrated into coursed-adobe pueblos with rare exterior doors and rectangular surface kivas next to rooms. Forked Lightning, for example, had rooms generally accessible only by means of roof hatches and four surface kivas adjoining the room block.

Around 1300 construction began on a rocky ridge at Pecos. Circular kivas detached from buildings and houses with stone walls appeared in various parts of the hilltop site. As at Forked Lightning, the initial construction at Pecos seems to lack a predetermined plan. Most of the randomly placed structures were only one story high. Also as at Forked Lightning, a number of the early rooms were burned and large quantities of corn were destroyed for unknown reasons.

About 1450 a new architectural plan was implemented at Pecos. The plan emphasized community definition and accessibility. A compact rectangular pueblo eventually four to

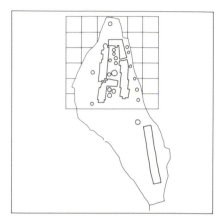

KEY PLAN OF PECOS PUEBLO

five stories high was laid out around a central plaza. No exterior doors appeared in the unbroken exterior walls. The north end of the mesa provided an abundance of easily broken sandstone slabs for walls of the four massive new room blocks.

People from other towns in the valley continued to relocate to Pecos and the expanding pueblo grew to incorporate 660 rooms with numerous kivas. The plan presented here measures overall some 200 by 400 feet (61 by 122 meters), including the two wings added later to the southeast and southwest. Rooms forming the basic quadrangle apparently were built first. Upper floors and ground-floor rooms fronting the plaza were added last. The latter reduced the plaza's dimensions to roughly 90 by 230 feet (27 by 70 meters).

Four staggered entrances provide access into the central courtyard. Kivas at three of the entryways recall somewhat similar features found at Forked Lightning. Two such kivas flank the east portal of Taos like reception rooms. Curved walls enclose the kiva to the northwest corner of

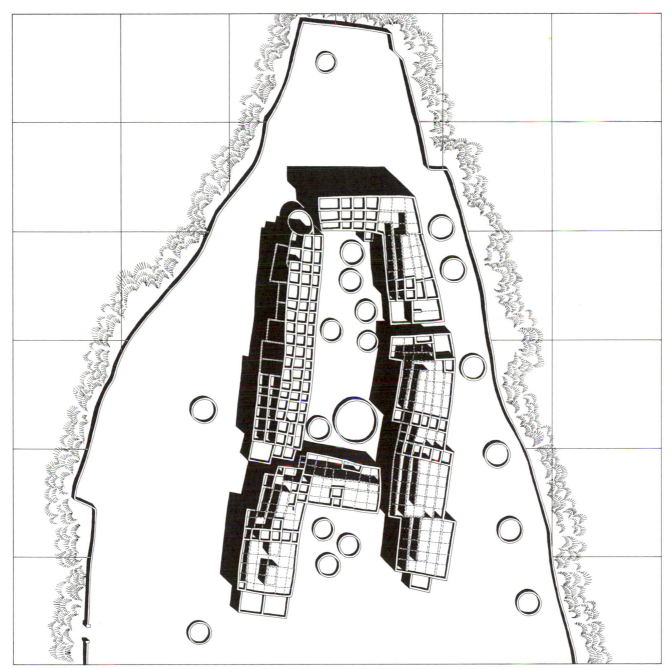

PECOS, NORTH PUEBLO

the plaza, and a rectangular kiva seems to guard the southwest portal.

The architectural module of Pecos appears to be a ground-floor unit three rooms deep and often two rooms wide, forming a six-room suite. Second- and third-floor rooms step back from the exterior, providing rooftop terraces with hatches and ladders descending to each floor. Interior doors or additional hatches lead to the rooms within the suite, but no openings occur in the ground-floor exterior or party walls.

Within each apartment several rooms typically were used for storage, one usually served for grinding or food processing, and the remaining spaces seem to have been used for sleeping or for the indoor activities of the residents. When the weather permitted, many domestic chores were done on outdoor terraces sometimes shaded by *ramadas*. Typical occupants were an extended family with perhaps eight or nine members. The household often consisted of the nuclear family, younger married kin, and, occasionally, elderly or infirm relatives.

Unlike the roughly contemporary pueblo of Tyuonyi, Pecos was built on very uneven terrain. Fill frequently was employed to provide a level base for foundations. Many walls were built on earlier ones or on uncompacted middens, which resulted often in settlement and sometimes in collapse.

Late in the construction sequence of the quadrangle, porch-like galleries were added on upper floors. Gallery roofs provided sheltered walkways interconnecting the various parts of the pueblo. Adobe walls serving as windbreaks appeared in the highest galleries. The galleries contributed a new degree of convenience and livability to Pecos.

A tunnel in the plaza interconnects one of the subterranean kivas with the west room block. Kidder (1958) estimated that each kiva at Pecos served four or more households, or about thirty-four adults. Perhaps the last structures built in the pueblo are the large rooms or walled enclosures added on the west side of the west room block. Possibly never roofed over, the walls are erected on top of earlier foundations. The enclosures last served as corrals during historic times.

A low stone wall about 3.5 feet (1 meter) high surrounded the entire mesa top. Perhaps more accurately described as a perimeter fence, the structure probably served to define clearly the geographical boundaries of the pueblo proper. A single entry appears in the west wall near the center of the mesa.

Typical rooms in the Pecos quadrangle measure approximately 9 by 10.5 feet (2.7 by 3.2 meters). Roof beams of yellow pine averaging 6 inches (15 centimeters) in diameter span the shorter dimensions of the rooms. Placed on roughly 24-inch (60-centimeter) centers, the beams support cedar or pine shakes and poles. These in turn bear matted twigs of cedar, willow, or wild cherry. Roof and floor surfaces consist of adobe some 2 to 8 inches (5 to 20 centimeters) thick placed over the wood substructure.

Ceiling heights shown in one of Kidder's (1958:96) carefully drawn sections range from around 4.4 feet (1.3 meters) for cellar rooms to 6.4 feet (2 meters) or so for upper-story rooms. Dimensions given are taken from the tops of adobe floors to the underside of ceiling beams. Lacking adequate ventilation and natural light as well as headroom, cellar rooms presumably served mainly for storage or as trash repositories.

The sandstone walls of Pecos range in thickness from more or less 14 inches (35 centimeters) to several feet. Buttressing is accomplished by adding a new wall next to an existing one and combining both into a single massive structure. Doorways are invariably rectangular and have sills 6 to 18 inches (15 to 45 centimeters) high. The portals usually are about 19 inches (48 centimeters) wide and 30 inches (75 centimeters) high. Roof hatches measure typically 18 inches (45 centimeters) clear between ceiling beams by possibly 30 inches (75 centimeters).

Sometime after the quadrangle was built, most likely between 1540 and 1590, a second large room block was constructed to the south near the middle of the mesa. The south pueblo measures 460 feet (140 meters) from north to south and is six rooms deep from east to west. Its rooms typically were some four feet (1.2 meters) longer than their counterparts in the quadrangle, suggesting an almost 40 percent increase in floor areas, assuming that the room widths remain constant.

In 1540 the members of the Coronado expedition approached Pecos by way of Glorieta Pass, a natural gateway to the plains. Eventually, the Spanish built a church and convent near the south end of the mesa where the newcomers introduced the technique of producing adobe bricks of uniform sizes in molds. Native Americans continued to live in Pecos until 1838 when the last residents journeyed 80 miles (130 kilometers) to the northwest to join relatives at Jemez Pueblo (Noble 1981).

The unrestored ruins of the quadrangular North Pueblo, the linear South Pueblo, and the partially restored ruins of the historic church and convent presently are part of Pecos National Monument. Administered by the National Park Service, the preserve contains 365 acres (148 hectares) and is open daily to the public.

ARROWHEAD
Rio Grande Anasazi

Arrowhead is situated in the southern foothills of the Sangre de Cristo Mountains around 18 miles (29 kilometers) east of Santa Fe. The pueblo lies at the east end of a hill crest some 200 feet (60 meters) above the adjacent terrain at an altitude of 7,726 feet (2,218 meters) above sea level. To the west Glorieta Pass provides convenient access to the riverine pueblos of the upper Rio Grande Valley and the Galisteo Basin. To the east 5 miles (8 kilometers) or so lie Pecos and Forked Lightning near the western edge of the Great Plains.

Technically on the ridge of a cuesta, the site commands an unobstructed view to the north, east, and south but slopes gently down to the west.

Like Forked Lightning, Arrowhead was relatively inaccessible on three sides but open on the fourth. About 450 feet (137 meters) to the north flows the creek in Arroyo del Pueblo, usually dry only during summer droughts.

Fertile agricultural plots are found in the alluvial plain of the nearby valley. Well-developed stands of ponderosa pine, aspen, spruce, and fir grow on the mountainous slopes above the hillside, and juniper and piñon up to 30 feet (9 meters) high surround the site. In the distance to the east the Pecos River leaves the mountains and flows more slowly across the southwestern plains toward Texas.

The plan of Arrowhead presented here shows seventy-six excavated rooms arranged generally around a central plaza containing a kiva in its southwest corner (Pearce 1937: fig. 1).

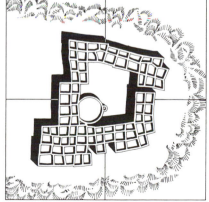

ARROWHEAD

The overall plan suggests an accretion of rooms rather than a predetermined architectural composition. The excavated room block measures at most 127 by 131 feet (38.7 by 40 meters), but the greater community originally extended considerably farther to the west.

An entry lane about 5 feet (1.5 meters) wide provides access from the east into the roughly 53-by-64-foot (16-by-19.5-meter) plaza. The semi-subterranean kiva has an estimated interior diameter of 25 feet (7.6 meters) and is circular in plan except on its west side, where it abuts the room block. Room sizes range from 36 to 130 square feet (3.3 to 12 square meters), substantially smaller than areas of Forked Lightning's chambers.

Tree-ring samples taken from wood beams at Arrowhead indicate that the trees were harvested between A.D. 1370 and 1392, a period corresponding with the earlier stages of construction at Pecos. Ceramics collected on the site suggest occupation into the 1400s and abandonment by 1450. The nearby adobe pueblo of Forked Lightning was abandoned possibly seventy-five years before work began at Arrowhead. Like Pecos, Arrowhead from the beginning was built of stone.

GRAN QUIVIRA
Rio Grande Anasazi

The largest pueblo in the Estancia Valley, Gran Quivira is located in central New Mexico about 65 miles (104 kilometers) southeast of Albuquerque. Formerly known as the Salinas Valley, the terrain forms an arid basin where precipitation collects in ephemeral lakes. Lacking an outlet, the water evaporates, resulting in the deposition of minerals, primarily salt.

The site lies on a limestone bluff between the Rio Grande 30 miles (48 kilometers) or so to the west and the Pecos River 90 miles (144 kilometers) or more to the east. The Estancia Valley served as an important trading center between the sedentary villagers of the Rio Grande and the roving hunters of the buffalo plains. Gran Quivira is situated on the southeast rim of the Anasazi world and the northeastern corner of the Jornada Mogollon region; both cultures influenced architectural development in the Estancia area.

By the A.D. 900s substantial Mogollon villages appear to have been flourishing in the vicinity of Gran Quivira. The inhabitants lived in pit houses, practiced rudimentary farming, hunted and gathered, and later began to build rooms above ground. The walls of the surface structures were constructed of jacal, which consists of vertical poles interwoven with twigs or branches plastered on both sides with adobe usually containing pebbles or small stones.

In the late 1100s Anasazi architectural ideas were introduced to Gran Quivira, probably by way of the Zuni area and the Acoma or Rio Grande pueblos. The innovations included

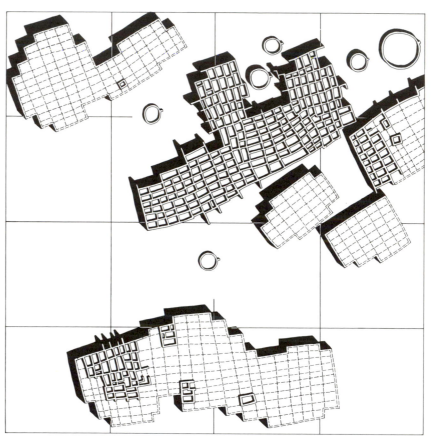

GRAN QUIVIRA, CENTRAL ROOM BLOCKS

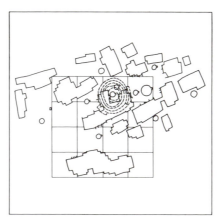

KEY PLAN OF GRAN QUIVIRA

room blocks with contiguous surface rooms of stone and adobe construction. By 1300 the Anasazi culture dominated developments in the Estancia Valley.

At Abó, Quarai, and Gran Quivira large stone complexes were built, each having hundreds of rooms and multiple plazas with numerous kivas. The area became one of the most populous centers in the Anasazi world, having reportedly more than ten thousand inhabitants early in the historic period.

Mesa Jumanes lies at the south end of the Estancia Valley. The inhabitants in the vicinity were called the Jumanos, from which the name Las Humanas may have derived. Las Humanas is an alternative name for Gran Quivira. The word Quivira refers to the fabled city of gold unsuccessfully sought by the Spanish all the way to Kansas.

Missed by Coronado in 1540, Gran Quivira was visited in 1598 by Don Juan de Oñate and four hundred Spaniards who sought to colonize New Mexico and to convert its inhabitants to Catholicism. At this time the population of Gran Quivira was estimated to be three thousand people. However, the environment proved too fragile for the Spanish colony, the situation deteriorated steadily, and the mission was abandoned completely in less than seventy-five years.

Agriculture failed, European diseases caused epidemics, famines and drought recurred, and Apaches raided with increasing frequency. Reduced to a population of perhaps 450 people, the survivors abandoned Gran Quivira in 1672. Some of the people initially joined other pueblos, but all left in the Spanish exodus to El Paso del Norte, present-day Cuidad Juárez, when the Pueblo Revolt broke out in 1680.

Gran Quivira contains the remains of seventeen room blocks, numerous kivas, and a colonial church and mission. The reconstruction presented here concentrates on an area 400 feet (122 meters) square near the center of the pueblo showing Mound 7, the best-documented prehistoric ruin in the roughly 500-by-800-foot (152-by-244-meter) site. The basis of the reconstruction is the thorough excavation report by Alden C. Hayes, Jon Nathan Young, and A. H. Warren (1981: figs. 3, 4, 5, 6) and my observations on the site in 1991.

Solid lines in the reconstruction represent walls believed to exist at the time of historic contact. Dashed lines are assumptions only based on the projections of known walls and average room sizes and proportions documented for the site. The south room block is presented 20 feet (6 meters) north of its actual location in order to include the structure in its entirety within this study's standard grid.

The room block of Mound 7 measures overall around 120 by 220 feet (37 by 67 meters) and may contain as many as 226 rooms and perimeter porches. All of the rooms consist of one-story stone walls built on top of earlier structures. The earliest structure was a circular pueblo probably built on original grade sometime between 1300 and 1400.

The round structure may have measured some 143 feet (43.6 meters) in outside diameter and may have contained 209 rooms; of these, eighty-eight rooms were excavated and recorded. The early pueblo most likely was planned as a complete structure and was completed in a single building phase. The rooms appear to be arranged in three to five concentric circles, one within the other, surrounding a central open space.

The average size of a typical trapezoidal room in the round pueblo is possibly 7 by 8.3 feet (2.1 by 2.5 meters), an area of approximately 58 square feet (5.4 square meters). The sturdily built walls average 13 to 18 inches (33 to 46 centimeters) in thickness. Many of the walls are intact up to a height of 6 feet (1.8 meters), and many have rectangular doorways. Typical walls are built of uncoursed stone blocks laid in beds of yellow mortar.

The interior courtyard of the circular structure measures more or less 60 feet (18 meters) across. In the middle of the open space is a subterranean kiva about 22 feet (6.7 meters) in diameter, a ceremonial chamber that continued in use well into historic times. The remains of five cisterns for storing rain water also are associated with the round pueblo. Further information on the remarkable circular and elliptical pueblos of the Southwest may be found in the text describing the Hopi pueblo of Fire House in this discussion.

Between 1400 and 1525 or so, the original round structure evolved into a more rectangular shape while occupancy continued in the pueblo. Some walls were razed and others were abandoned or rebuilt. The central kiva continued in use. Construction proceeded in seemingly unrelated stages with no apparent overall plan.

Walls continued to be built of uncoursed stone blocks laid in yellow mortar, but they were thinner, measuring no more than 12 inches (30 centimeters) in width. Early in the 1500s a building hiatus of maybe twenty years occurred while occupancy continued elsewhere in Gran Quivira.

Construction on Mound 7 resumed in 1550 and continued until the pueblo was abandoned. Building progressed in several increments, beginning at the west end, continuing from the east toward the center, and finally moving to the north. The reconstruction shows the room block in 1630 before the Spanish added eight rooms at the west end of the room block, interconnecting them with several existing chambers.

Walls projecting from the perimeter of Mound 7 are associated with porches or exterior work areas, perhaps with *ramada*-like sun shades but lacking permanent roofs. Seventeen porches are documented; one had walls on three sides. Sixty-one hearths indicate dwelling rooms where forty-five to fifty families may have lived.

A total of five small kivas are associated with Mound 7. Ranging from 17 to 22 feet (5.2 to 6.7 meters) in diameter, all of the chambers are round and have ventilation shafts oriented toward the east. Three are completely underground and two are semisubterranean. As at other Eastern Pueblos, the small kivas had short ventilator tunnels, lacked benches, and seldom had *sipapus,* or spirit holes.

A great kiva is found about 50 feet (15 meters) east of Mound 7. Measuring some 36.8 feet (11.2 meters) across and excavated about 5.5 feet (1.7 meters) into the bedrock, the circular chamber has a 6-foot- (1.8-meter-) wide perimeter bench. Simi-

lar large, free-standing great kivas are found at Pecos, Paako, Kuaua, San Cristóbal, and other ancient pueblos of the Southwest.

The Spanish burned and filled the kivas in an unsuccessful attempt to discourage native religious practices. In Mound 7 a number of rectangular surface rooms within the pueblo have most of the appointments associated with the destroyed kivas. The quadrilateral spaces may represent ceremonial rooms like those found in the room blocks of Acoma, Zuni, and other Western Pueblos.

Compared to the plans of the contemporary room blocks of Kuaua, Paako, or San Cristóbal, the arrangement of Gran Quivira seems somewhat random and incoherent. Considering the unevenness of the site's terrain and the four-hundred-year building sequence, however, Gran Quivira appears less irregular. Today the large pueblo is part of Salinas Pueblo Missions National Monument administered by the National Park Service and is open daily to the public.

First Mesa
Walpi
Sichomovi
Hano

Second Mesa
Shongopavi
Shipaulovi
Mishongnovi
Payupki

100 m/160 k

The final section of this discussion considers the effects of foreign impact on the ancient architecture of the Southwest between the time the Spanish arrived in 1540 and the present day. European ideas had little influence on southwestern architecture until Spanish colonists began to erect such structures as the mission buildings of Gran Quivira after 1598, of Pecos in the 1620s, and of San Bernardo de Aguatubi at Awatovi beginning in 1629. An important Spanish contribution to the region's construction technology was the introduction of adobe bricks made in molds with standard sizes.

For the purposes of this study the name "Anasazi" applies to the prehistoric people who inhabited various areas of northwestern New Mexico, northern Arizona, southern Nevada and Utah, and southwestern Colorado during the roughly 1,000-year period preceding the Spanish *entrada*. The modern Pueblo peoples who live in the Hopi, Zuni, and Rio Grande areas are descended from the ancient Anasazi. The Spanish word *pueblo* refers not only to a village or small town but also to its inhabitants.

Perhaps the most momentous event during this period was the Pueblo Revolt of 1680 to 1692, when the people of the Hopi mesas, Zuni Valley, and most of the upper Rio Grande and Athapaskan-speaking immigrants formed an alliance with the view of expelling the Spaniards from the Southwest and of restoring traditional authority to the Native American communities. Within little more than a decade the alliance disintegrated due to internal differences, the Spanish returned, and traditional pueblo architecture responded to the new realities according to a variety of strategies.

Immediately after the revolt the Zuni abandoned their six historic villages and, fearing Spanish reprisals, consolidated into a single very large, citadel-like pueblo with compact room blocks reportedly up to seven stories high. Following the Spanish reoccupation in 1692, religious and secular domination by the foreigners largely failed to materialize.

Over the years Zuni Pueblo began to modify its fortress-like architectural character. By the nineteenth century parallel rows of low-rise, easily accessible room blocks with open-ended streets extended eastward from the pueblo, and Nutria, Lower Pescado, and other new farming settlements were established to accommodate the needs of the increasing Zuni population.

In anticipation of Spanish retaliation after the Pueblo Revolt, the Hopi people relocated most of their pueblos from canyon bottoms to less accessible mesa-top sites where many remain today. Following the reoccupation, Spanish attempts to dominate the traditionally conservative Hopi pueblos largely failed. Consequently, such more recent mesa-top pueblos as Sichomovi were built less compactly and more openly than their immediate predecessors.

Refugees from Sandía and other Rio Grande pueblos hastily built sanctuaries in the Hopi mesas during the latter seventeenth century. When more peaceful times returned to the Southwest a few generations later, many of the refugees returned to their ancestral villages in the Rio Grande Valley.

Spanish efforts to gain religious converts proved more successful in the Rio Grande Valley than among the Western Pueblos. Even so, adobe churches and walled cemeteries remained well outside of traditional town plans in Acoma, Santo Domingo, Taos, and other Rio Grande pueblos. Although Christianity was accepted, traditional kivas and related ceremonial structures continued to be used in accordance with ancient practices.

In time many of the historic Rio Grande pueblos were abandoned. For example, Gran Quivira was deserted in 1672, Awatovi was destroyed during the winter of 1700–01, Kuaua was abandoned around 1700, and Pecos was vacated in 1836. The surviving Native American architecture of the Southwest today continues to accommodate change while preserving traditional architectural and spiritual values rooted in the distant past.

Zuni

Following the Pueblo Revolt of 1680 the Zuni abandoned their six former settlements and established the single large pueblo of Zuni. A compact, seemingly random concentration of rectangular rooms up to seven stories high developed around several small plazas, which were linked by narrow, winding streets sometimes covered over by adjoining room blocks. In succeeding years the Spanish built a church and wall-enclosed cemetery east of the pueblo, a large plaza developed around the religious precinct, and several mostly two-story, linear room blocks extended eastward from the pueblo, forming open-ended streets.

The architecture of Zuni Pueblo clearly responded to the arrival of the Spanish in the Southwest. First, six villages were transformed into a compact, seven-story citadel in anticipation of Spanish reprisals following the Pueblo Revolt. And second, when the European religious and secular authority generally failed to threaten the conservative Zuni traditions, the community became more open to growth and less compact.

In response to the increasing Zuni population during the nineteenth century, several seasonal farming settlements were established in the vicinity of the main pueblo. Erected on the remains of a prehistoric town built some six centuries earlier, Nutria has fifty-six ground-floor rooms in seven small blocks. Lower Pescado, also built on a prehistoric site, contains possibly 110 rooms arranged in a curving perimeter row similar in scale and configuration to the fourteenth-century Zuni pueblo of Kin Tiel.

Hopi

All of the First Mesa and Second Mesa towns date from shortly after the Pueblo Revolt in 1680 when the Hopi left their valley-floor sites near farm plots and springs and moved up to more inaccessible mesa-top locations. Only Awatovi on Antelope Mesa and Oraibi, the venerable mother village of Third Mesa, were situated on mesa tops when Spanish explorers visited the Hopi in 1540. Payupki, a Second Mesa pueblo built probably by refugees from Sandía Pueblo in the Rio Grande Valley, was abandoned around 1740 when the inhabitants returned to their ancestral home.

Walpi, the mother village of First Mesa, has a dense, linear grouping of rooms crowding the narrow southwest tip of the promontory. The last pueblo built on First Mesa, Sichomovi has no rooms higher than two stories; the community is a colonial dependency of Walpi in the village hierarchy. The guardian village of First Mesa, Hano was founded around 1700 by Tewa-speaking refugees from the Rio Grande seeking relative safety in the remote Hopi mesas of northeastern Arizona.

The mother village of Second Mesa, Shongopavi was established around 1680 and consists of three parallel, orderly rows of two-story room blocks flanking two streets. Dating to possibly 1700, Shipaulovi appears to be an upward extension of its rugged mesa-top site; the small pueblo has two-story room blocks grouped around a central square. The guardian village of Second Mesa, Mishongnovi was built in three successive phases of construction covering almost its entire plateau.

Rio Grande

Situated on a remote mesa top some 50 miles (80 kilometers) west of the Rio Grande and a roughly equal distance east of the Zuni Valley, the masonry-walled pueblo of Acoma serves in many ways as a symbolic transition between the Eastern Anasazi communities of the Rio Grande Valley and the Western Anasazi towns of the Zuni and Hopi. Acoma's town plan consists of three parallel rows of compact, multistory room blocks flanking two streets oriented from east to west, with a short perpendicular street near the town center serving as a plaza. Like Old Oraibi, Acoma apparently has been occupied continuously since perhaps as early as the eleventh century.

The very large Rio Grande Valley pueblo of Santo Domingo has a street-type plan formed by eight multistory adobe room blocks oriented from east to west and terminated by perpendicular room blocks running the length of the town. By contrast, the street-type plans of Acoma, Oraibi, and other Anasazi pueblos are open-ended; their plans lack the clarity and definition of Santo Domingo's. The two distinctive round, free-standing kivas of Santo Domingo symbolize the concept of duality that underlies many of the Rio Grande Valley's conservative traditions in architecture.

An example of plaza-type planning in the Rio Grande Valley, the adobe pueblo of Taos is divided into north and south sections on both sides of a large, irregular plaza bisected by a flowing creek. The multistory room blocks of present-day Taos retain to a major extent the impressive architectural character noted by the Spanish in 1540. With the possible exception of Pecos, Taos is the only pueblo known to be surrounded by a wall, and its kivas are the only subterranean ceremonial chambers that continue to be used in the Rio Grande Valley today.

Contemporary World Architecture

Although Native American architectural activity was in decline in the Eastern United States by the time European colonists began to arrive, many settlements continued to produce distinguished architecture. For example, the Fatherland site near Natchez continued to be occupied until 1730. The village is an excellent example of late linear site arrangements in the Lower Mississippi Valley. Big Mound City near West Palm Beach, a site containing a semicircular embankment with eight radiating causeways, continued in use until Spanish contact around 1650. During the late eighteenth century John and William Bartram visited the impressive remains of Mount Royal on the east bank of the St. Johns River. Here they found an extraordinary sunken processional way, or avenue, half a mile (800 meters) long interconnecting a truncated platform mound and an artificial lake (Morgan 1980).

Although the magnificent Aztec capital of Tenochtitlán and other Mesoamerican centers were destroyed partly or wholly in the wake of the Spanish Conquest, other monuments survived largely intact, and many may be visited today. With the loss of their traditional religious, political, economic, and social institutions, the Mesoamericans for the most part also lost their ancient architectural traditions. While modest residences with wattle-and-daub walls and thatched roofs continue to be built and used today in the Yucatán and elsewhere, traditional stone architecture with richly embellished public buildings largely has been relegated to the past (Heyden & Gendrop 1973).

In Micronesia, European contact came to different islands at different times over the period of three centuries. Magellan's ships visited the Marianas in 1521, but not until 1843 was contact established on a regular basis with the people of the Yap Islands. European visitors during the nineteenth century found ornately decorated meeting houses called *bai* elevated on stone platforms and piers in the Palau archipelago.

The spectacular island city of Leluh was newly completed when Europeans first visited Kosrae in 1824. By that time Nan Madol on Pohnpei, "the Venice of the Pacific," had been abandoned for two centuries or so and was overgrown by jungles. During his visit to the Mariana Islands in the early 1740s Lord Anson found all twelve of the original 16-foot- (5-meter-) high stone columns and capstones still standing in the House of Taga on Tinian. The colossal megaliths bear silent witness to the ancient architectural monuments of Micronesia and to the extraordinary spirit of the people who created them (Morgan 1988).

ZUNI
Zuni

The most populous present-day pueblo in the Southwest, Zuni is located in west-central New Mexico around 125 miles (200 kilometers) west of Albuquerque. The historic pueblo is situated on a small knoll on the north bank of the Zuni River, a permanently flowing tributary of the Little Colorado River. Beneath the northwest room blocks of the present village lie the ruins of Halona, one of the Seven Cities of Cibola that Coronado was seeking when his expedition appeared in 1540.

In order to understand more fully Zuni architecture in the context of the Southwest, it may be helpful to review architectural developments in the Cibola area during the millennium preceding the arrival of Europeans. Geographically, Cibola lies in an area of east-central Arizona and west-central New Mexico on the Pacific side of the continental divide. Traditionally, the area appears to have been influenced by Mogollon ideas from the south and Anasazi ideas from the north.

Zuni lies on the periphery to two cultural spheres of influence but maintains its own unique language. Not closely related to other Pueblo languages, Zuni has been linked tentatively to Penutian, a language of some prehistoric California peoples (Cordell 1984:11). Architecturally, Zuni also maintains a distinct identity while sharing many characteristics with the people of Acoma, the Hopi mesas, and other neighbors.

Between perhaps A.D. 500 and 1000 pit house villages similar to those of the Mogollon gradually were replaced by unit houses in the valleys of the

Little Colorado and Zuni rivers. A typical unit house consisted of a storage facility, pit house, service yard, and trash deposit arranged along an axis often oriented from northwest to southeast. Frequently, a small group of nearby unit houses forms a hamlet or farmstead.

Eventually, storage structures moved from below to above grade, sometimes having two or more rooms side by side. Pit houses had air shafts or vestibules like the Anasazis, not rampways like the Mogollon. An eastern Anasazi trait appeared in the form of circular rather than rectangular great kivas.

Between 1000 and 1130 or so, ideas from Chaco Canyon became dominant influences in Cibola. The pueblos of Fort Wingate, Casa Vibora, and the Village of the Great Kivas brought Anasazi ideas to the periphery of Cibola. At about this time or perhaps within a century thereafter, the population of Zuni is estimated to have reached possibly forty thousand, likely its prehistoric maximum (LeBlanc 1989).

The collapse of the Chaco system sometime after 1130 ushered in a period of reorganization and uncertainty in Cibola and elsewhere in the Southwest. During the 1200s Zuni people began to move up to remote mesa tops and ridges, possibly in anticipation of civil unrest. An example is the pueblo of Atsinna, built on a high elevation near the east end of the Zuni River Valley.

During the 1300s the Zuni abandoned their mesa tops and returned to the fertile valley of the Zuni River, where they easily could irrigate their farm plots. Here in a 25-mile (40-kilometer) stretch along the valley floor the Zuni established Halona, Hawi-

kuh, and the other four towns the Spanish found in 1540. The six Zuni pueblos were the heirs of the entire Cibola area.

The name Halona, meaning "red ant place" in Zuni, refers to ruins of an ancient village on both the north and south banks of the Zuni River in the vicinity of present-day Zuni pueblo. South Halona is situated on a terrace with an altitude of 6,725 feet (2,050 meters) above sea level, well above the flood plain on which the modern pueblo lies. The unexcavated ruins probably contain a large, roughly rectangular group of structures having some 250 ground-floor rooms and half as many second-floor rooms, an estimated total of 375 rooms (Kintigh 1985:47).

Ceramics collections suggest that Halona was occupied between 1275 and 1325. The fourteenth and fifteenth centuries were times of dwindling Zuni populations for reasons that are unclear. During this period major population concentrations centered in the Rio Grande Valley and the Hohokam area of the Sonoran Desert. Once more the Zuni found themselves on the periphery of two influential neighboring spheres.

By the time of historic contact the Zuni population had declined to five thousand or so people. Unrest and population reduction continued until the Pueblo Revolt of 1680, after which Halona fell into decay. Following the revolt the residents of the six former communities consolidated into the single pueblo of Zuni.

The earliest room blocks built at Zuni are found northwest of the central plaza. Here the room massing is exceptionally compact and crowded, recalling somewhat the configuration of such concentrated Zuni pueblos

as Atsinna. The plan reconstructed in this discussion is based largely on the plans and information recorded by Victor Mindeleff (1989) during his visit to the site in the early 1880s.

The massive pueblo lies along the north bank of the Zuni River on a highly irregular site, which is directly accessible to the surrounding farmlands. The closest quarry for stones is some 3 miles (5 kilometers) distant. The crumbled ruins of ancient Halona further contribute to the irregularity of the terrain, giving Zuni the appearance of height in addition to its building masses.

The variations in ground elevations of Zuni range up to 10 feet (3 meters) between adjacent terraces. Mindeleff recorded several rooms as high as five stories and noted that a traveler in 1850 had observed as many as seven stories. Six rectangular surface kivas, which are typical of Western Pueblos, are found within the eastern room blocks of Zuni. The kivas are said to represent the six Zuni cardinal directions: the four compass points, the zenith referring to Father Sky, and the nadir referring to Mother Earth (Swentzell 1990).

Within the northwest room blocks are two small plazas, both approximately 50 feet (15 meters) square. The west square is named Rat Plaza; the east, Torn Plaza. Not shown in the reconstruction are several pedestrian streets or covered ways interconnecting plazas and streets on ground level. The connecting ways lie below multistory masses whose rooftops are shown.

Architecturally, Zuni is an immense, highly irregular aggregation of rectangular cells generally conforming to an orthogonal geometry. The genesis of the town plan appears to

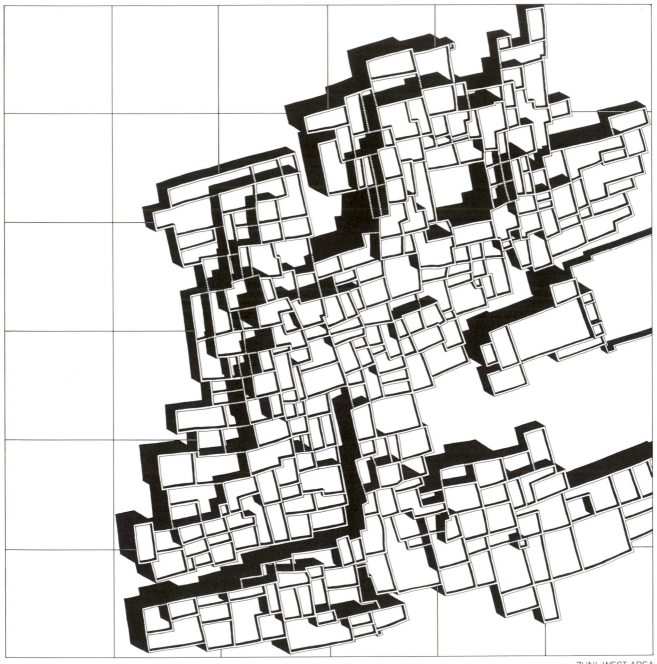

ZUNI, WEST AREA

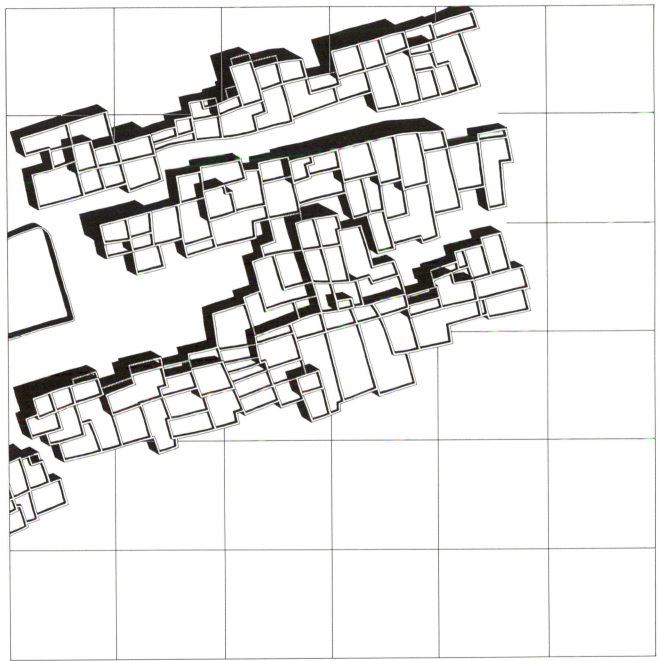

ZUNI, EAST AREA

have been the northwest room blocks. Masses seem to have been added to the earlier structures through time without the benefit of an overall plan. This contrasts sharply with the development of Kin Tiel, the relatively symmetrical Zuni pueblo that grew by filling in its large central plaza while preserving the original order of its enclosing walls.

Zuni's exceptionally large central plaza is very unusual. Here between 1629 and 1632 a church, friary, and cemetery were built. Burned in 1680, the church was reconstructed in 1699, abandoned in 1820, and restored in 1968. Unlike the people of the Eastern Pueblos, most of the Zuni and Hopi traditionally have been reluctant to embrace Christianity.

The eastern room blocks apparently were the last to be added to Zuni. Mostly one and two stories high, the new residences are arranged basically in three linear rows at most 500 feet (152 meters) in length. The rows form elongated streets more or less parallel with the river to the southeast.

The more recent room blocks generally have more commodious rooms in less crowded clusters than those in the earlier sections of Zuni. By 1750 the population had declined to thirteen hundred persons, but the pueblo began to establish outlying farm settlements in order to enhance its agricultural resources. In succeeding decades the villages of Lower Pescado, Ojo Caliente, Nutria, and Tekapo were founded.

By 1848 the population of Zuni and its agricultural communities had risen to 2,671, twice the pueblo's population a century earlier. By 1950 most of the houses were reduced to a single story, and very few of the original rooms survived (Stubbs 1950). The Bureau of Indian Affair's 1972 census listed 5,760 Zuni, quite likely the area's largest population since prehistoric times. The Zuni people today continue to carry forward their rich ancestral traditions in a greatly modified architectural environment.

LOWER PESCADO
Zuni

The Zuni farming community of Lower Pescado was constructed during the nineteenth century on top of a prehistoric ruin built perhaps five centuries earlier. One of the Zuni names for the village is Heshotatzina, meaning "marked house," probably a reference to pictographs found in a nearby ruin (Kintigh 1985:53). The remains of the ancient settlement form a rubble mound 7 to 10 feet (2 to 3 meters) deep along the eroding riverbank on the southwest side of the site.

Situated at an altitude of 6,700 feet (2,048 meters) above sea level, the site lies on a rise near the middle of the Pescado River Valley. Juniper and piñon woodlands cover the sides of the mesas several hundred yards to the north and south. The reconstruction presented here is based on the plan of the historic village recorded by Victor Mindeleff (1989:plate LXIX) during his visit in the early 1880s.

The walls of the modern pueblo seem to follow the outline of the prehistoric ruin. Although Mindeleff's plan shows about 120 ground-floor rooms, the ancient pueblo most likely had twice that number, judging by the room configurations of its fourteenth-century Zuni contemporaries. The depth of the remaining rubble base suggests that the previous structure was more likely than not several stories high (Kintigh 1985).

Assuming that half of the ground-floor rooms had second floors and one-quarter had third floors, the estimated total for prehistoric Lower Pescado would be 420 rooms. This is about the size of the late-thirteenth-century pueblo of Yellowhouse. Ceramics gathered from the eroding riverbank indicate occupation of the site from sometime after A.D. 1300 until possibly 1375.

During the nineteenth century the population of the Zuni people began to increase for the first time since the Spanish arrived in the Southwest. Accordingly, three seasonal farming communities were established to provide food for expanding Zuni Pueblo. A fourth outlying village, Tekapo, was established around 1912 to 1914. The agricultural settlements adjoin farmlands that cannot be reached conveniently on a daily basis.

One of the last farming communities to be established, Lower Pescado derives its name from the Spanish Ojo (del) Pescado meaning "fish spring" (Woodbury 1979b:481). The other three agricultural settlements of Zuni Pueblo are Ojo Caliente, located 15 miles (24 kilometers) or so south of the pueblo; Nutria, situated some 10 miles (16 kilometers) to the east; and Tekapo, about 7 miles (11 kilometers) to the southwest. Originally, when the harvest was com-

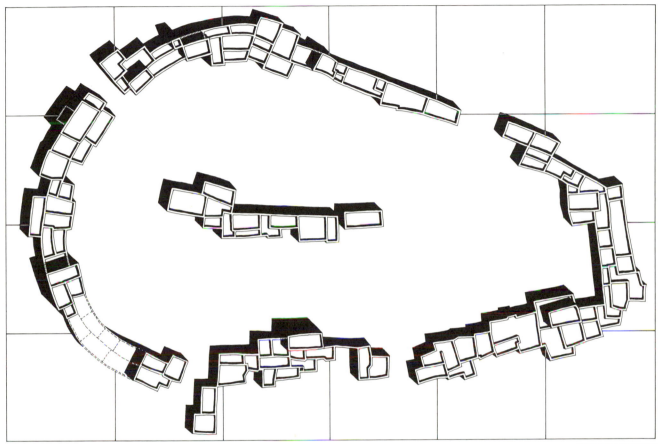

pleted, the residents returned to the main pueblo for the winter, leaving the village deserted until the following spring.

When Victor Mindeleff (1989) visited Lower Pescado, it continued to be abandoned seasonally. During the 1880s the villagers began to remain in Lower Pescado throughout the year. The settlement lies approximately 15 miles (24 kilometers) east of Zuni Pueblo and seems to have contained more or less 110 ground-floor rooms at the time of Mindeleff's visit.

Much larger than Nutria, Lower Pescado measures overall roughly 385 by 570 feet (117 by 174 meters). Its dimensions are nearly the same as those of Kin Tiel, the large Zuni pueblo built around the time of the ancient predecessor of Lower Pescado. Also like Kin Tiel, Lower Pescado has distinctive curvilinear exterior walls.

Mindeleff speculated that the perimeter rooms were the first to be built, probably on the top of earlier walls. The interior room block and corral fences appear to have been added in the plaza later. No structures were built beyond the perimeter, thus preserving the compact, uncluttered character of the village plan.

Several sections of Lower Pescado's north wall exhibit unusually well laid masonry, implying prehistoric origin. One or more rows of rooms may have continued the southwest curve of the perimeter wall, as indicated by the dashed lines in the reconstructed plan. This would suggest four entries into the plaza, two to the north and two to the south.

Mostly one story high, Lower Pescado's comparatively large rooms appear to have had one or more rows of interior posts supporting roof beams. The large compartments lend a barn-like character to the pueblo, reflecting its functions as a farming community. At several points masonry staircases lead up to rooftops, which could facilitate food processing, such as drying meat or vegetables in the sun.

NUTRIA
Zuni

One of four historic Zuni farming communities, Nutria is located at the head of the Nutria Valley about 21 miles (33 kilometers) northeast of Zuni Pueblo in west-central New Mexico. In this area running streams furnish abundant water for crop irrigation. In Spanish nutria means "otter," a likely reference to the well-watered site (Woodbury 1979b:481).

Situated at an altitude of 6,820 feet (2,079 meters) above sea level, the site is surrounded by plains grasslands. Juniper and piñon woodlands cover near-by mesas. Sandstone outcrops abound on the site, and spring-fed Nutria River passes perhaps 330 feet (100 meters) northwest of the site.

The reconstruction presented here depicts the site as Victor Mindeleff (1979:94–95, plates LXVII, LXVIII) recorded it in the 1880s. Beneath the historic village, however, lie the remains of a prehistoric settlement occupying roughly the same area. Ancient stone foundations probably support many of Nutria's major walls.

Ceramics collected from the remains of the prehistoric pueblo confirm occupation between possibly A.D. 1275 and 1325. Keith W. Kintigh (1985:45) tentatively estimates that ancient Nutria had perhaps 120 or so ground-floor rooms, twice the number Mindeleff recorded. Assuming that half the rooms had second floors, the total number of rooms for the prehistoric pueblo would be 180.

Established in the latter nineteenth century after Ojo Caliente and before Lower Pescado, the historic village of Nutria at first was occupied only during the planting and harvesting seasons. In winter the residents returned

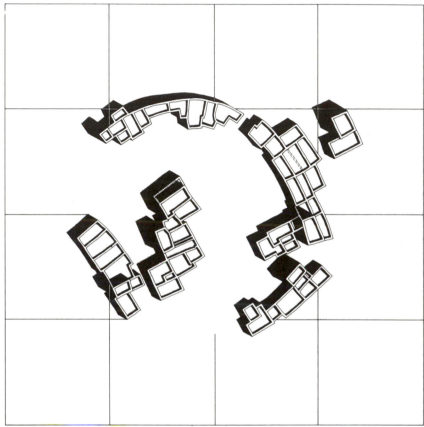

NUTRIA

to Zuni, leaving the settlement deserted until the following spring. In the 1880s Nutria became a year-round community containing at most fifty-six ground-floor rooms. Today the site has been abandoned almost completely, and original wall configurations are difficult to discern.

In plan Nutria consists essentially of a curving C-shaped arc of perimeter buildings to the north, east, and south with two irregular room blocks to the southwest. In some respects the plan recalls the disposition of elements at the Zuni pueblos of Kin Tiel and Lower Pescado. The latter also was

built on top of a prehistoric ruin. In size, however, Nutria is much smaller than Lower Pescado; it measures at most only 225 by 275 feet (69 by 84 meters).

Omitted from this reconstruction are four houses with two or three rooms each found more or less 200 feet (60 meters) east of the compact main group. Also recorded by Mindeleff (1979) in the 1880s, the more recent additions did nothing to enhance the plan of the main group. Mostly one story high, Nutria appears to contain neither a kiva nor a ceremonial room.

WALPI
Hopi

Situated on the south tip of First Mesa at an altitude of 6,200 feet (1,890 meters), Walpi was relocated from the valley plain to its present site shortly after the Pueblo Revolt in 1680. Still inhabited today, the pueblo extends for some 640 feet (192 meters) along the narrow mesa top, which is at most 150 feet (46 meters) wide. The community is contained almost entirely in a single highly irregular building mass ranging from 18 to 90 feet (5.5 to 27.4 meters) in width and from one to three stories in height.

Strung out along First Mesa northeast of Walpi are Sichomovi and Hano. From Hano a steep trail originally led down to the canyon floor; today a narrow paved road provides access to the summit. Parallel to First Mesa and about 7 miles (11 kilometers) to the northwest lies the rugged ridge of Second Mesa, and nearly an equal distance beyond is Third Mesa. The three rocky mesas extend southwest from Black Mesa in northeastern Arizona. Together they constitute the heartland of the Hopi people.

The mother village of First Mesa, Walpi occupies the highest level in the complex Hopi social organization. Sichomovi fills the secondary position, a colonial dependency supporting the village hierarchy. At the lowest level is Hano, also called Tewa. The village has the responsibility of guarding the approach road and protecting the mesa from intruders (Connelly 1979).

Walpi manages to retain an underlying architectural discipline while coping with exceptional physical adversities. Rock outcroppings too large

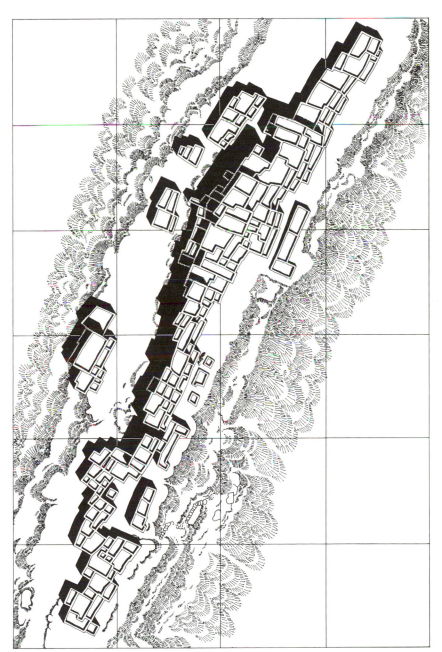

WALPI

to remove are incorporated into building masses, floor levels often vary from room to room to accommodate the uneven terrain, and kivas are chiseled into sandstone depressions along the craggy southeastern edge of the mesa. Even though few walls form right angles in typical room plans, a sense of order is maintained by placing longer walls parallel to the mesa's longitudinal axis and shorter walls as nearly as possible transversely.

The people of Walpi overcame substantial difficulties in adapting themselves to the mesa-top environment. Originally situated on the plain below where water is readily available, the pueblo was relocated to the rugged summit in anticipation of Spanish reprisal following the reconquest of the Southwest. Steep stone stairs and footholds carved into sheer cliff faces provide vertical accessways for women carrying water to the summit in earthenware pots strapped to their backs.

To a large extent the narrow confines of the mesa determine the village plan. For example, Walpi lacks a major plaza, a familiar feature of other Hopi pueblos; large gatherings on special occasions are accommodated in the main plaza of neighboring Sichomovi. The reconstructed plan shown here is based primarily on Victor Mindeleff's (1989: plate XX) survey, photographs, and description recorded in the 1880s. Mindeleff apparently observed somewhat higher building masses and more ground-floor rooms than those recorded by Stanley A. Stubbs (1950) seven decades later.

Like other Hopi pueblo dwellers, the people of Walpi are skilled farmers who use effective systems of agriculture. The only prehistoric coal miners in the Southwest, the Hopi in ancient times extracted coal from surface outcroppings for use in cooking, heating, and firing pottery and as a pigment for paints. The use of coal diminished in historic times for reasons that are not clearly understood (Brew 1979).

More than a century ago Mindeleff observed that the people of Walpi tenaciously cling to their traditional ways: water, provisions, fuel, crops, and supplies of every kind must be transported by hand laboriously up steep trails, sometimes from miles away. Today some Hopi have moved to more accessible locations near the foot of the mesa or in scattered house sites on the canyon floor. Nevertheless, the present-day Hopi live perhaps closer to their aboriginal way of life than do any other group of Native Americans.

SICHOMOVI
Hopi

The Hopi pueblo of Sichomovi is the last of the three villages built on First Mesa. Shortly after the Pueblo Revolt in 1680 the people of Walpi relocated from the valley floor to the mesa top, and the guardian village of Hano was built about 1700. Not until perhaps 1750 did a group from Walpi and a few people from the Rio Grande area construct Sichomovi, probably to accommodate the surplus population of Walpi (Connelly 1979).

The reconstruction presented here shows Sichomovi as it appeared at the time of Victor Mindeleff's survey in 1882 (1989:62, plate XVIII). Apparently more than a century ago the village retained several characteristics of ancient Hopi architecture, which were no longer evident during my visit in 1991. The three original villages of First Mesa presently appear as more or less a single entity, and relatively few buildings exceed a single story in height.

Constructed of uncoursed stone masonry, the reconstructed pueblo of Sichomovi measures at most 170 by 360 feet (52 by 110 meters) in plan. Like Hano, Sichomovi consists of several room blocks clustered around a central plaza on the level mesa top. The largest room block is a somewhat irregular row extending about 280 feet (85 meters) along the southeast edge of the mesa.

An L-shaped cluster of rooms defines the west corner of the 100-foot (30-meter) square plaza, and a short row of rooms encloses the northwest side of the central open space. The block forming the northeast side of the plaza contains two rectangular kivas side by side; they probably are recessed into a natural depression in the surface of the stone summit. Unlike Hano and Walpi, Sichomovi originally had no buildings exceeding two stories in height. The rooftops of the two-story buildings are surprisingly level (Mindeleff 1989: plate XIX).

Most of the room blocks terrace down toward the southeast instead of toward the central plaza, the customary architectural arrangement for Eastern Pueblos. Another distinctive architectural characteristic of Sichomovi is the use of roof hatches and ladders for access to second-story

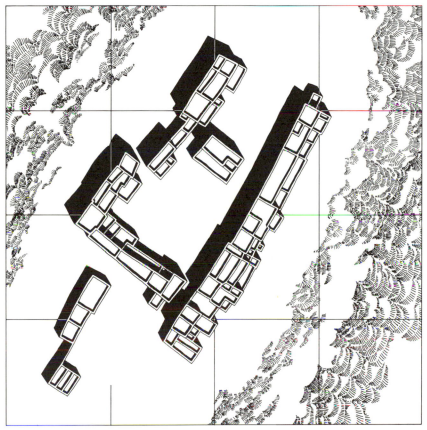

SICHOMOVI

HANO
Hopi

The guardian village of First Mesa is the historic settlement of Hano, also known as Tewa, the language spoken by the residents. The pueblo lies northeast of Sichomovi and Walpi on a narrow finger-like mesa top projecting into the Painted Desert about 85 miles (136 kilometers) northeast of Flagstaff. Hano was founded around 1700 by Los Tanos, a group of Tewa Indians who moved from the Rio Grande area to the Hopi country following the Pueblo Revolt.

The reconstruction presented here is based primarily on the plan and description of Hano recorded by Victor Mindeleff (1989:61, plate XVI) in 1882 and on the scale map published by Stanley A. Stubbs (1950, fig. 23). At the time of Mindeleff's visit Hano and Sichomovi retained their visually separate identities, and most of Hano's room blocks were two or three stories high. These architectural characteristics no longer existed at the time I visited First Mesa in 1991.

Hano is located strategically at a point where the narrow mesa top is barely 200 feet (60 meters) wide. According to Hopi custom, Walpi, the mother village of First Mesa, required the Tewa people to serve as guardians along the main trail approaching Walpi before the founding of Sichomovi. Hano thus was physically separated from Walpi and was relegated to the socially undistinguished position of warriors (Connelly 1979).

The first room block constructed at Hano probably was the north building. The partially three-story structure has rooms of irregular shapes and sizes ranging in area from dwellings of 450 square feet (42 square meters)

rooms, a familiar trait of Zuni architecture. Due to its easterly location, First Mesa may have been exposed to architectural influences unknown on Second Mesa and Third Mesa.

Sichomovi is a satellite community of Walpi and is protected from intrusion by the Tewa-speaking people of Hano. Like the residents of Walpi, those of Sichomovi speak a Shoshonean dialect. In common with Hopi people elsewhere, the inhabitants of First Mesa have consistently resisted Catholic missionary influence since 1680. Among the most conservative of the pueblo people, the Hope tenaciously preserve their ancient architectural and cultural traditions.

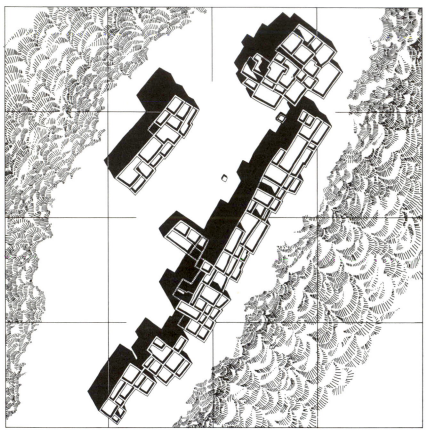

HANO

to store rooms containing perhaps 60 square feet (5.6 square meters). The north building measures possibly 85 feet (26 meters) square and is shaped somewhat like a pyramid, recalling the massing of such pueblos as Taos and Zuni.

Hano grew apparently as the need for space arose rather than according to a predetermined plan. The largest room blocks are two and three stories high; they extend approximately 350 feet (107 meters) along the southeast edge of the mesa and provide the majority of rooms for the pueblo. Unlike the pyramidal north building, the linear room blocks closely resemble those of Walpi and other Hopi villages.

Hano's plaza measures no more than 100 by 135 feet (30 by 41 meters). A century ago the open space contained what appears to be a small stone shrine in its southeast corner. Mindeleff found two rectangular kivas in the pueblo, one in a room block and the other near the mesa's edge along the trail to the northeast. Hano's ground-floor rooms were used for storage; they were entered by way of ladders and roof hatches.

Some Hano people speak not only Tewa and Hopi but also English, Spanish, Navajo, and Apache. The Hano have enhanced their positions as guardians of First Mesa by emphasizing their roles as interpreters for the Hopi. Today many former residents have relocated from the narrow mesa top to homesteads on the valley plain below from which they return periodically to participate in traditional ceremonies.

SHONGOPAVI

Hopi

The mother village of Second Mesa, Shongopavi is a relatively well ordered Hopi pueblo located approximately 2 miles (3 kilometers) west of Shipaulovi and Mishongnovi. Unlike the other inhabited villages of First Mesa and Second Mesa, Shongopavi is situated near the middle of a large, level mesa. The site lies at least 200 feet (60 meters) from the closest edge of the mesa.

The Hopi who built Shongopavi moved up to the mesa top from a site on the canyon floor shortly after the Pueblo Revolt in 1680. Between 1690 and 1730 large numbers of people moved from the Rio Grande Valley to the Hopi Mesa area in fear of Spanish reprisals after the reconquest of the Southwest. Oral traditions say that some of the people of the mother village built Shipaulovi at this time as a place of refuge in case the Spanish returned and threatened Shongopavi (Connelly 1979).

The reconstructed plan shows the inhabited village as Victor Mindeleff (1989:plate XXXIV) recorded it in 1882. In plan Shongopavi consists of three parallel rows of rooms generally two and three stories high and ranging from perhaps 365 to 415 feet (111 to 126 meters) in length. The plan of the pueblo is oriented from more or less northeast to southwest. The room blocks terrace down toward the southeast.

The northwest walls of the room block appear to be tall and unbroken for the most part. The street-like east plaza is about 50 feet (15 meters) wide. A small block of rooms at the southwest corner of the plaza interconnects the east and center rows,

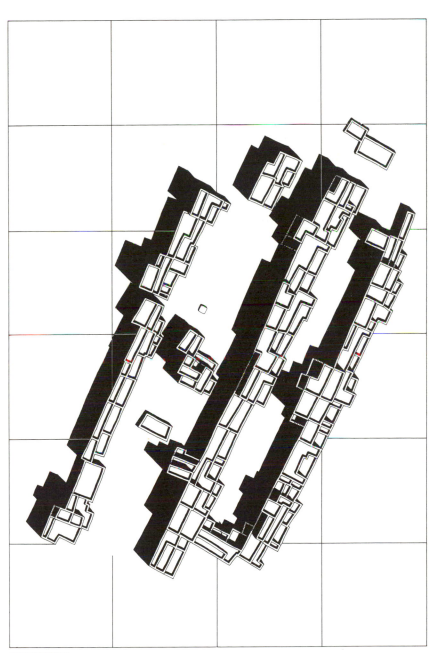

SHONGOPAVI

forming in effect a single large house. The detached rectangular chambers at the north end of the center building are subterranean kivas; a third underground kiva lies about 200 feet (60 meters) to the east near the edge of the mesa.

The northwest room block defines the west plaza with a width of 80 feet (24 meters) or more. Toward the south end of the linear plaza is Shongopavi's fourth rectangular kiva; the chamber is recessed only partially into the rocky surface. A small room block appears near the center of the west plaza, and a second freestanding structure occupies the plaza's north end.

A small shrine recalling the one in Shipaulovi is situated toward the north end of the west plaza. Compared to other Hopi pueblos, Shongopavi is neat and orderly. Most of its walls are plastered and some are whitewashed, rendering a sense of newness to the pueblo. Although Shongopavi is less isolated than Oraibi, the village has no nearby neighbors.

The carefully laid stone walls of Shongopavi are among the finest examples of Hopi masonry. The orderly, street-like plazas of the village recall similar architectural arrangements in such pueblos as Santo Domingo and Acoma. A consistent architectural discipline seems to pervade the urban plan and structural components of Shongopavi.

SHIPAULOVI
Hopi

The smallest of the Hopi pueblos, Shipaulovi is situated on Second Mesa a short distance north of Mishongnovi and about 2 miles (3.2 kilometers) east of Shongopavi. The village is a compact arrangement of relatively standardized units grouped around a central plaza. Somewhat irregular in plan, the plaza measures at most some 60 by 140 feet (18 by 43 meters) and conforms to the northwest to southeast orientation of the rocky mesa top.

Also spelled Shipolovi and Shupaulovi, Shipaulovi has a physical plan that directly reflects the natural terrain of its site. From a distance the pueblo's rectangular walls recall the vertical lines of natural fissures in the cliff edges and the horizontal planes established by the mesa top. The architectural color scheme results from the site's geological composition; the walls are built of indigenous stones covered with adobe made of materials taken from the site.

The close visual harmony between the walls of Shipaulovi and the natural terrain renders it difficult to judge the age of architectural features. The pueblo seems on the one hand to be growing from the site and on the other hand to be returning to it. The reconstruction shown here is based primarily on Victor Mindeleff's (1989: plate XXX) account of the site recorded in the early 1880s.

Most of Shipaulovi's buildings are two stories high, terracing down to single stories around the plaza. Three covered passageways provide convenient access from the pueblo to steep paths and stairs leading from the summit down to surrounding agricultural plots. Shipaulovi maintains a distinctive architectural presence on its mesa-top site.

Near the center of the plaza and close to its northeast side is a small shrine measuring about 2 feet (60 meters) square in plan. The cube-like structure of stone and adobe is a repository for sacred plume sticks and other ceremonial offerings. Similar shrines are found at Mishongnovi, Shongopavi, and Hano.

A second plaza apparently began to develop at the southeast end of Shipaulovi, but space limitations on the crowded summit precluded further additions. The pueblo's southeasternmost structure is a rectangular kiva sunken partly below grade. At its north end the approximately 12-by-25-foot (3.7-by-7.6-meter) chamber is entirely subterranean, but at its south end the rocky terrain falls away exposing upper portions of the kiva's walls.

About 80 feet (24 meters) farther south and 30 feet (9 meters) downslope is Shipaulovi's second kiva, almost entirely subterranean and about half the size of the upper kiva. Several rectangular outbuildings southwest of the pueblo are in a poor state of repair. The rectangular additions around the perimeter of Shipaulovi are not original features; they appear to be used for storage rather than for habitation.

An aerial photograph of the site taken by Stanley A. Stubbs (1950: plate XXII) some sixty years after Mindeleff's visit records changes in Shipaulovi's architectural massing and wall alignments, but the compact arrangement and distinctive central plaza remain essentially unchanged. A third kiva is built on the mesa top to the southwest, and many of the

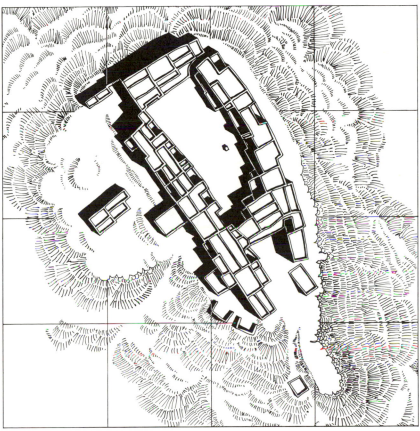

SHIPAULOVI

second-story rooms have disappeared. A characteristic of traditional architecture in the Southwest seems to be constant change: additions, repairs, and alterations appear to be endless.

Shipaulovi was founded about 1700, perhaps by people from the vicinity of Winslow, Arizona. The plaza arrangement of Shipaulovi bears a striking resemblance to that of Homolobi Number 2, a prehistoric site about 9 miles (14 kilometers) south of Winslow (Fewkes 1904). The town plan of Shipaulovi also resembles closely the east, and earliest, plaza group of Mishongnovi.

MISHONGNOVI
Hopi

The compact Second Mesa pueblo of Mishongnovi covers almost all of its rocky mesa-top site. Also spelled Mashongnavi (Mindeleff 1989), Mishongnovi is situated a short distance southeast of Shipaulovi and approximately 2 miles (3 kilometers) east of Shongopavi, the mother village of Second Mesa. The community is located in the Hopi Indian Reservation possibly 80 miles (128 kilometers) north of Flagstaff.

The guardian village of Second Mesa, Mishongnovi was founded around 1700, about the time Hano was established on First Mesa. According to a Hopi legend, the village was built after the Pueblo Revolt of

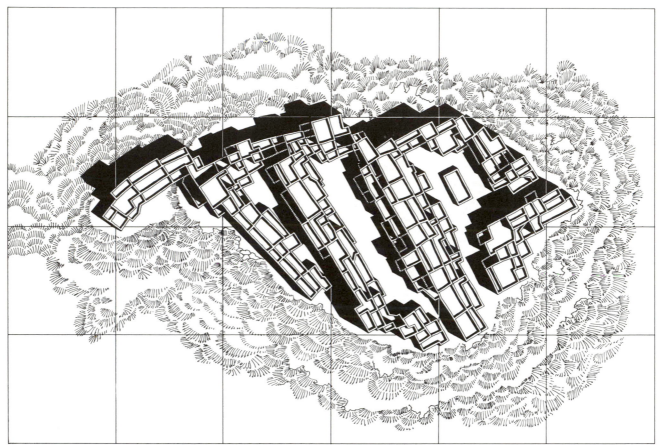

MISHONGNOVI

1680 by settlers who came from the vicinity of the San Francisco Peaks near Flagstaff (Stubbs 1950). The Second Mesa leaders assigned a site for Mishongnovi near Corn Rock, a shrine of Shongopavi, and required the new villagers to protect Second Mesa from intruders.

The reconstruction proposed here is based primarily on the plan and description by Victor Mindeleff (1989: plate XXVI), who recorded Mishongnovi in 1882. The irregular village plan appears to have originated in the vicinity of the relatively well formed

plaza to the east, near the tip of the mesa and closest to the village's farm plots on the canyon floor. The partially subterranean kiva in the center of the roughly 50-by-80-foot (15-by-24-meter) plaza appears to be located in a natural depression of the rocky summit.

The stone masonry rooms of Mishongnovi rise from one to three stories in height and generally terrace down toward the plaza. A high straight wall more or less 215 feet (66 meters) long originally formed the west side of the pueblo. As the popu-

lation increased, a second plaza was created, and eventually one- and two-story rooms were constructed along the original wall. The second plaza is more street-like in character and is estimated to measure 30 by 155 feet (9 by 47 meters).

Mishongnovi continued to grow toward the west, presumably in response to increasing requirements for space. A third plaza was created, and finally a small room block was added on the west end of the mesa top. A single rectangular kiva was recorded in 1882, but in 1950 three additional community rooms were noted on the south slope of the mesa, two to the east and one toward the west (Stubbs 1950: fig. 24). The reconstruction omits the latter three kivas.

Today Mishongnovi retains much of the "tumble-down appearance" noted by Mindeleff (1989:73) more than a century ago. In recent decades scattered houses have appeared in various locations around the mesa. Mishongnovi's pattern of growth by accretion contrasts sharply with the orderly expansion of such pueblos as Kin Tiel or Pueblo Bonito, which increased in size over time without losing their earlier disciplined characters.

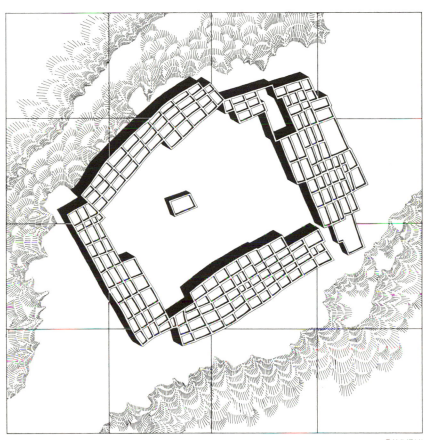

PAYUPKI

PAYUPKI
Hopi

The historic Hopi village of Payupki occupies the inaccessible summit of a bold promontory on Second Mesa about 2 miles (3 kilometers) northwest of Shipaulovi. The steep sides of the sandstone outcropping descend abruptly to the canyon floor below, interrupted only by an encircling ledge 12 to 15 feet (3.7 to 4.6 meters) below the summit. Like Hano, Payupki is said to have been built by refugees from the Rio Grande area shortly after the Pueblo Revolt in 1680.

The reconstruction presented here is based on information recorded by Victor Mindeleff (1989: plate XIII) in 1882. The well-ordered pueblo measures overall perhaps 210 by 270 feet (64 by 82 meters). Four room blocks are arranged almost symmetrically around the rectangular central plaza, which measures at most 120 by 180 feet (37 by 55 meters). A partly underground kiva lies near the center of the plaza. A second rectangular kiva is reported in the south corner of Payupki.

The ruins of the abandoned pueblo contain possibly 188 ground-floor rooms and once may have had a number of second-floor rooms. The walls are built of sandstone slabs of various sizes, some unusually large but all taken from the immediate vicinity of the site. Although the masonry exhibits a high degree of craftsmanship, the walls appear to have been erected somewhat hastily.

An oral tradition, difficult to confirm, suggests that Payupki was built by refugees from Sandia Pueblo, which is found some 15 miles (24 kilometers) north of Albuquerque in the Rio Grande Valley (Brandt 1979: 345). Following the Pueblo Revolt the people of Sandía fled to the Hopi area, probably between 1682 and 1688. Together with other refugees from the

Rio Grande, the Sandia people constructed and occupied the highly ordered pueblo for sixty years or so.

As fear of Spanish reprisals diminished during the eighteenth century, refugees began to return to the Rio Grande area. Sandia Pueblo is known to have been reoccupied in 1748, more or less the time Payupki was abandoned. The relatively brief period of occupancy at Payupki is an example of the displacements and unrest associated with the Pueblo Revolt and its aftermath in the Southwest.

ACOMA
Rio Grande

Also known as Sky City, Acoma is perched dramatically on top of a steep-sided sandstone mesa about 60 miles (97 kilometers) west of Albuquerque. From an altitude of approximately 6,600 feet (2,012 meters) above sea level, the free-standing plateau towers above the surrounding valley floor some 370 feet (113 meters) below. One of the oldest continuously occupied communities in the United States, Acoma bridges both architecturally and culturally between the Eastern and Western pueblos of the Anasazi world.

The site of the spectacular pueblo is the 17-acre (6.9-hectare) summit of an isolated sandstone mesa. Acoma consists primarily of three parallel rows of compact room blocks forming two streets ranging from roughly 10 to 35 feet (3 to 10.7 meters) in width. The room blocks are composed mostly of multistory houses set side by side, with rooftop terraces stepping down toward the south-southeast. The orientation affords maximum warmth from the winter sun and protection from north and west winds.

The reconstruction presented here is based on plans documented in 1934 for the Historic American Building Survey (Nabokov 1986). A north-south concourse divides the community into east and west halves. Altogether, Acoma's original three rows of room blocks measure at most 300 by 800 feet (91 by 244 meters). Not shown in this reconstruction are a church, cemetery, and cloister built probably in the 1630s south of the present-day room blocks. In recent decades additional houses have been constructed between the original pueblo and the religious precinct and in scattered locations along the mesa edges. Unfortunately, some of the more recent structures are located in places that tend to obscure the clarity and integrity of the original plan.

Acoma's seven active kivas are rectangular surface chambers entered by means of roof hatches and ladders like those of the Zunis and Hopis to the west. The communal rooms are incorporated into the room blocks, another characteristic of Western Pueblos. By contrast, the kivas of Rio Grande pueblos usually are circular, often are free-standing, and frequently are subterranean at least in part.

A typical row house for a family in Acoma would have a width of 15 feet or so between east and west masonry-bearing walls. Party walls, which divide adjoining houses, range in thickness up to 2 feet (60 centimeters) and bear on foundation layers of fieldstone. Walls usually are built of adobe bricks or stone with finish coats of adobe plaster on both sides.

The ground-floor plan of a typical town house might consist of five contiguous storage rooms, each measuring possibly 8 by 15 feet (2.4 to 4.6 meters). Larger houses frequently are three to four stories high, their upper-floor rooms used variously for cooking, living, and sleeping. Windowless rooms often serve for storage, and rooftop terraces are used for such activities as drying meats and vegetables on racks and storing firewood.

For their water supply the residents of Acoma seem to depend on cisterns in the rocky mesa top or a spring at the base of the mesa. During my visit to the pueblo in 1990, I saw water standing in three natural basins on the summit and was told that two of them provided water for washing clothes, making adobe, and other nonpotable uses. The third reservoir, located more than 100 feet (30 meters) north of the closest house, appeared to be a source of drinking water. The largest cistern on the mesa top lies well to the south of the church.

The earliest settlers in the vicinity of Acoma apparently began to live in cave shelters and pit houses sometime between A.D. 500 and 700. From 700 to 900 the inhabitants tended to live in single-room structures, occasionally in scattered groups, on hillslopes or elevated terraces. Around 900 the people began to move up to mesa tops or into valleys, where they built houses with contiguous rooms (Garcia-Mason 1979).

Four migrations are believed to account for the ancestral groups of Acoma. They include the original settlers, two migrations from the Zuni area, and one from Mesa Verde. About 1050 the first inhabitants of Acoma began to build rows of rooms using adobe masonry. By perhaps 1200 a second group of immigrants arrived, and distinctive pottery began to be produced.

During the thirteenth century, including the period of the Great Drought between 1276 and 1299, several groups of settlers migrated to Acoma, and around 1300 Mesa Verdeans arrived in the pueblo. Stone masonry began to replace adobe as the predominant building system. All of the building materials for the growing community, not to mention all of the food, fuel, and other daily necessities for the residents, had to be carried up to the rocky summit by way of steep, narrow trails and stairways.

In 1540 Hernando de Alvarado of the Coronado Expedition visited Acoma. At this time the room blocks of the pueblo most likely were located south of the present-day church. Alvarado recorded finding a village of possibly two hundred men, several water reservoirs, woven cotton fabric, deerskins, buffalo hides, corn, domesticated turkeys, turquoise, jewelry, and hundreds of houses three to four stories high.

In 1599 a Spanish expedition under the command of Don Juan de Oñate reportedly besieged and razed the original pueblo and imprisoned or enslaved more than five hundred residents of Acoma. In 1529 Father Juan Ramírez arrived and undertook the construction of the mission church of San Esteban, the convent, and the cemetery. While the new construction was in progress, the people of Acoma may have lived in temporary shelters at the base of the mesa.

During the late 1980s William J. Robinson (1990) and others obtained fifty-one tree-ring samples from twenty of Acoma's oldest houses in widely varying locations. Surprisingly, the analysis showed that all of the dates lie in the relatively brief period of 1546 to 1552. The analysis suggests the possibility that Ramírez may have departed in the early 1540s, leaving the inhabitants of Acoma free to build their three orderly room blocks along the north edges of the mesa.

The brevity of the construction phase during the sixteenth century may account for Acoma's original uniformity of room sizes, similarities in construction details and house types, and disciplined community plan. Unlike Zuni, Walpi, and other historic pueblos, Acoma originally had the highest degree of architectural standardization in the Southwest. Additions and modifications since 1880 have altered substantially the pueblo's original appearance.

The mountains in the vicinity of Acoma are sources of ponderosa pine, Douglas fir, piñon, juniper, and occasionally oak and aspen. Within 15 miles (24 kilometers) of the mesa are today, as they were in prehistoric times, a number of farming villages with productive fields in the hills and valleys of the San José River. Most of the present-day people of Acoma live in the farming villages of Acomita and McCartys, but on special occasions they return to Acoma where many maintain family residences or clan affiliations.

ACOMA, WEST AREA

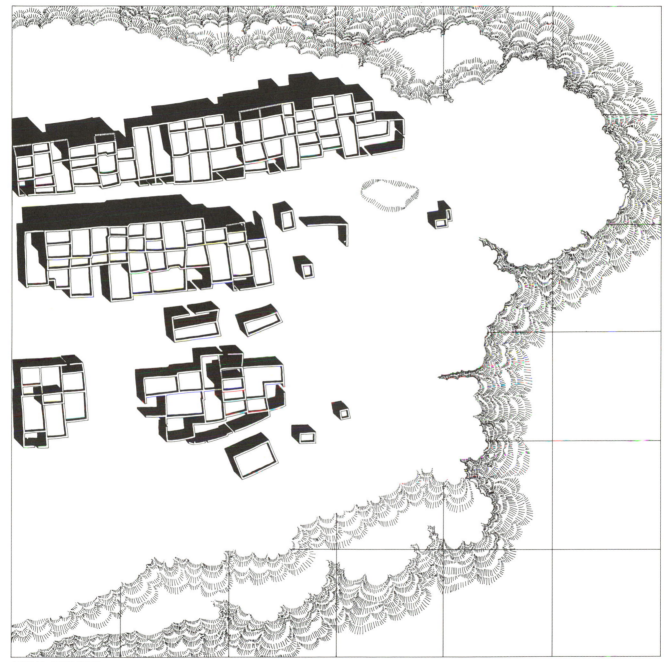

ACOMA, EAST AREA

SANTO DOMINGO, WEST-CENTRAL AREA

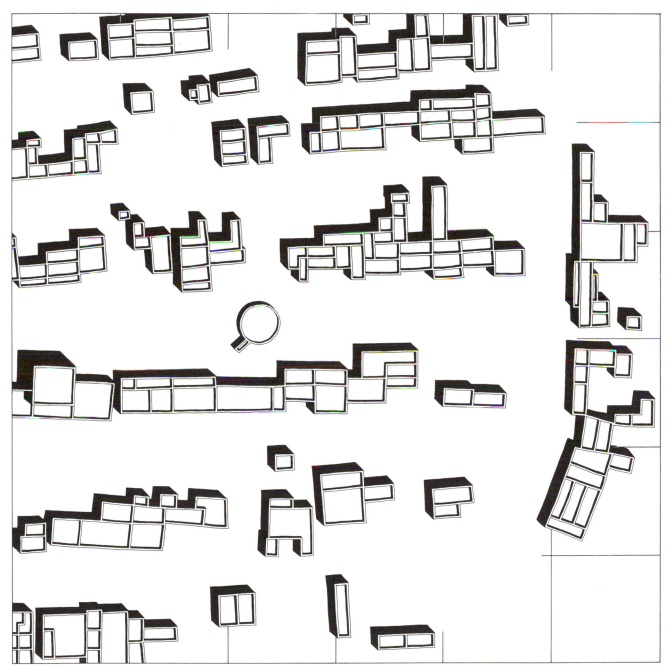

SANTO DOMINGO, EAST-CENTRAL AREA

SANTO DOMINGO
Rio Grande

A prehistoric system of parallel streets organizes the distinctive town plan of present-day Santo Domingo Pueblo. Called Kiua by its residents, the large and populous settlement lies on the east bank of the Rio Grande about 27 miles (43 kilometers) southwest of Santa Fe in north-central New Mexico. A disastrous flood in 1886 washed away most of the old community, but the traditional street arrangement remains unchanged.

Well known for its conservativism, Santo Domingo Pueblo retains its original town plan with buildings lining orderly streets, unlike contemporary pueblos where individual houses often are built in rural sites or on village outskirts. Similar parallel street plans are found in the pueblos of Acoma and Oraibi, two communities laid out long before the Spanish entered the Southwest. However, two north-south streets terminate Santo Domingo's dominant east-west axis and clearly define the town plan, an urban design feature not found in other villages of the ancient Southwest.

The basis of the reconstruction presented here is materials published by Stanley A. Stubbs (1950:fig. 15) and Charles H. Lange (1979:figs. 1, 2). The reconstruction shows six of Santo Domingo's eight parallel east-west streets, each some 1,000 feet (330 meters) long, and the roughly 600-foot- (183-meter-) long end streets oriented from north to south. The 70-to-100-foot- (21-to-30-meter-) wide central street is more ample than the other streets; it serves as a place for community-wide activities, including dances and ceremonies.

The pueblo's two circular kivas are the Turquoise kiva located in the middle of the main street to the east and the Squash kiva in an open space between room blocks on the south side of the main street. The kivas represent opposite colors and seem to symbolize the community's dual organization; both chambers measure around 35 feet (10.7 meters) in diameter. The church and cemetery of Santo Domingo lie a short distance to the east, outside the traditional pueblo.

Communities with parallel street plans are less common in the Southwest than are those grouped around one or more centralized plazas. Closely controlled by tradition, the village plan of Santo Domingo calls for long house blocks arranged along both sides of streets. Many of the houses originally had two or more stories.

Oral traditions say that possibly during the fifteenth century the ancestors of the Santo Domingo people came from somewhere to the north, probably Frijoles Canyon some 17 miles (27 kilometers) or so distant. Well before the Spanish *entrada*, the Kersean-speaking people are said to have divided into the present groups of San Felipe, Cochiti, Santo Domingo, and others (Lange 1979).

In 1597 Don Juan de Oñate gathered the leaders of neighboring pueblos in Santo Domingo, subjected them to a lecture on Spanish politics and religion, which they probably did not comprehend, and required them to pay homage to the king of Spain. While slowly and reluctantly integrating new patterns and ideas with their core values, the people of Santo Domingo have maintained their traditions to a higher degree than many of the other pueblos. Today the distinctive black-on-cream pottery of Santo Domingo, like the pueblo's town plan, continues the bold and conservative design tradition of the centuries-old community.

KEY PLAN OF TAOS PUEBLO

TAOS
Rio Grande

The northernmost and culturally one of the most isolated pueblos of the Rio Grande Valley, Taos straddles a creek named the Rio de Pueblo Taos about 55 miles (88 kilometers) north of Santa Fe in north-central New Mexico. The settlement is situated on a broad, well-watered plateau near the base of the Sangre de Cristo Mountains at an altitude of 7,100 feet (2,164 meters). The area enjoys on the aver-

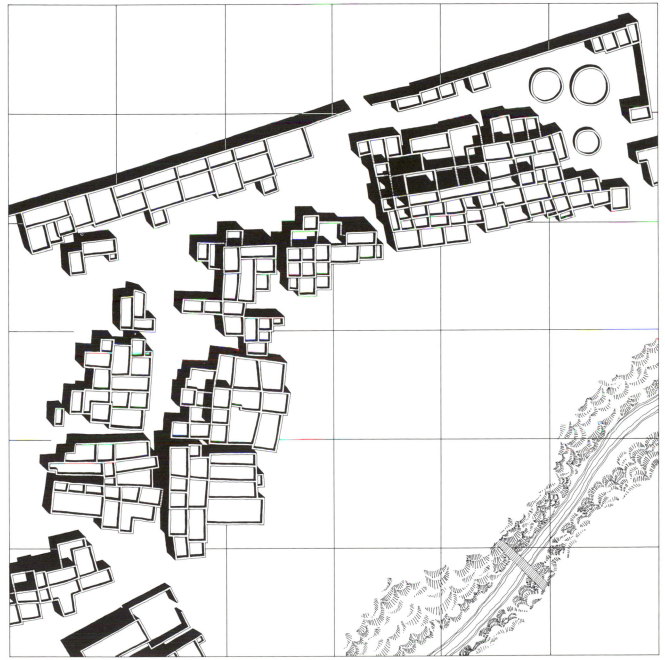

TAOS, NORTH HOUSE

age only a 140-day growing season per annum, not long enough to grow cotton and often insufficient to produce food crops.

The people of Taos necessarily rely more heavily on hunting and gathering than other Rio Grande communities do. Well into historic times the nearby mountains abounded with deer, elk, bear, turkey, grouse, and squirrel, and the sage brush area to the west yielded antelope and rabbits. Hunters from Taos frequently crossed the pass nearby to hunt buffalos on the Great Plains. Like Pecos and Gran Quivira, Taos was for many centuries in contact with such Plains tribes as the Comanches in the 1700s.

Although Taos is less remotely located in the Southwest than Zuni or the Hopi Mesas, the pueblo developed culturally and architecturally to some extent independently from other Rio Grande communities. Between A.D. 1000 and 1200 more than three hundred settlements appeared in the vicinity of Taos; they consisted primarily of pit houses with a few small surface rooms of coursed adobe construction. In time the population increased, and by 1250 larger, multifamily surface room blocks appeared (Bodine 1979).

The growth of Taos may have been augmented by immigrants from the north, possibly from Chimney Rock area or even Chaco Canyon to the west and perhaps occasionally from the Great Plains to the east. The impressive multistoried pueblo on both sides of the watercourse was well established by the time Hernando de Alvarado arrived in 1540. The Spanish explorer observed that the houses of Taos were built very close together and were as high as five or six stories.

The first known aggregated village in the area was called "Cornfield Taos." The early pueblo was built around 1350 about one-quarter of a mile (400 meters) northeast of the present site and probably was abandoned between 1450 and 1500 (Bodine 1979:258). The name Taos may be a Spanish derivation of the native word Tua, meaning in the Tiwa language "house," "houses," or "village." Early in the historic period the Spanish introduced adobe-brick construction involving the use of wood molds to produce bricks of uniform size; adobe subsequently became the standard building material of Taos.

The reconstruction presented here is based on plans and information published by Stanley A. Stubbs (1950: fig. 4) and John J. Bodine (1979: fig. 2) and my observations on the site in 1991. Taos is the only traditional pueblo other than Pecos to be surrounded by a wall, an exceptionally rare feature in Anasazi architecture. The wall serves to formally define the physical limits of the community and continues to be an important visual and symbolic boundary in Taos thought.

The areas within the enclosing wall and the kivas are sacred; areas elsewhere are not. In 1936 some 175 house units and seven kivas, of which one was abandoned, were counted at Taos. The kivas lie along the east side of the pueblo on both sides of the enclosing wall. The overall zone contained within the eroding, five-sided perimeter wall and the kivas measures approximately 800 by 1,100 feet (244 by 335 meters).

The bipartite pueblo of Taos consists of the four-story South House and the five-story North House on both banks of the constantly flowing creek. The South House generally is organized around several loosely defined plazas. The North House is more linear in character; it defines the north and west edges of the large irregular central plaza. On feast days the plaza becomes a stage and the roof terraces serve as bleachers for spectators watching community-wide activities, athletic events, symbolic dances, and ceremonies.

The sections of the room blocks within the perimeter walls form compact units of traditional pueblo architecture, but recently young people began to build individual houses in adjoining fields with no spatial reference to the traditional plan. A century ago families entered the pueblo by means of ladders and roof hatches; today doors and windows have been introduced into many walls. Electricity, however, continues to be banned within the traditional pueblo.

The reconstruction presented here illustrates a 600-foot (183-meter) square area of Taos showing the North House, sections of north and east perimeter walls, and three kivas in a sacred precinct east of the largest room block. The kivas of Taos are the only underground chambers presently known to be used in the Rio Grande Valley. Unusual wood fences surround the roof hatches providing access into the kivas. The fences impart a sense of separateness and provide visual privacy for the kiva entries.

Uneven poles project skyward as high as 15 feet (4.6 meters) from the end of the ladder descending through the roof hatch of each kiva. The subterranean chambers measure more or less 20 to 32 feet (6 to 10 meters) in diameter. Other important architectural elements of Taos are a ceremonial racecourse through the central plaza, middens north and south of the enclosing wall, and shrines and pilgrimage sites at various locations in the surrounding valleys and mountains.

The room blocks and large central plaza of Taos differ markedly in arrangement from the parallel street plans of such pueblos as Santo Domingo, Acoma, and Oraibi. In addition to Taos, settlements divided in two by a central watercourse include Paquimé, Kinishba, Grasshopper, Kin Tiel, Crow Canyon, and most likely prehistoric Zuni Pueblo.

A total of 132 examples of ancient architecture in the Southwest have been considered in the foregoing discussion. Systematic analysis of the monuments permits the architecture to speak for itself without foreign comparisons prior to the advent of Europeans in 1540. To the extent possible, the study examines ancient structures in their own terms, rather than perpetuating the tradition of ignoring prehistoric architecture in general and that of North America in particular.

The presentation attempts to minimize the intrusion of personal attitudes and avoids using ancient architecture to suggest personal architectural ideologies. Taken as a whole, the study suggests a number of principles that seem to underlie the ancient architecture of the Southwest. Some of the principles may be summarized as follows.

Broad **diversity** characterizes the architecture without exception, while a number of similarities recur constantly. For example, jacal, caliche, and stones are used to build walls in different places at various times, but the materials invariably are natural and usually are taken from the site itself or from nearby quarries. Wide variations are found in building material, level of sophistication, craftsmanship, scale, extent of preplanning or accretion, room size and number, site configuration, length of occupation, sequences of abandonment and reuse, and many other factors.

A unique **sense of place** invariably distinguishes each site. The vastly differing geographical and topographical settings of the Southwest range from mesa tops and desert floors to talus slopes, mountain ridges, south-facing caves in cliff faces, and many other distinctive locations. Each site's response to the precise nature of its special place imparts an integral character to its architecture. For example, the unique character of level desert floors finds expression in the caliche-walled compounds of Hohokam architecture, terraces accommodate the uneven floors of Kayenta and Mesa Verde cliff dwellings, and the masonry structures of Chaco Canyon take maximum advantage of easily worked stone found in nearby quarries.

Nonhierarchical order generally governs the interrelation of architectural elements in southwestern sites. The unifying architectural symbol of each settlement is the community as a whole, frequently represented by a plaza or other community gathering place. Public and private spaces are arranged so that neither one dominates the other. A balanced order relates rooms to buildings, room blocks to plazas, open spaces to enclosures, and dwellings to store rooms. The visual order emphasizes the sense of a unified whole rather than individual elements. Possible exceptions to the architectural principle of nonhierarchical order may appear in Hohokam and Salado platform compounds and a limited number of other sites.

Adaptability to natural environments is another design principle of ancient architecture in the Southwest. The Native American builders incorporate their villages into their existing sites with as little change as possible.

For example, large stones or boulders too difficult to relocate easily are incorporated into lower-story walls and spaces at Wupatki, Casa Malpais, Walpi, and the Gila Cliff Dwellings. Accommodation is preferable to the disruption of existing conditions or natural systems.

Human activities shape buildings in the widespread communities of the ancient Southwest. Suites of store rooms connected to living areas indicate individual family subsistence patterns. Secular functions nearly always are related to plazas, ceremonial rooms, and kivas sometimes big enough to accommodate community gatherings. While plazas and kivas are used for ceremonial purposes periodically, they also are important places for daily activities.

Dynamic cycles of growth and decline, as well as abandonment and reuse, characterize the ancient architecture of the Southwest. Although the reconstructions presented in this discussion show all rooms and architectural elements as though they existed concurrently, very few sites contained all of their components at the same time. Most of the communities grew over a period of years. In time new structures were added while others fell into disrepair and eventually returned to the earth from which their original building materials were taken.

An apt parallel exists between the ancient architecture and the mythology of the Southwest. Traditional southwestern myths and legends do not begin and end within themselves; moreover, they seem to anticipate other stories with which they may be interwoven to form a more elaborate narrative, sometimes of epic proportion. Rather than striving to be complete works of architecture within themselves, southwestern buildings and spaces find meaning only within the context of the greater community as a whole.

A general view emerging from this study is one of a complex and constantly changing architecture reflecting the distinctive character of the people who created it. Although the preferences, values, and experiences of southwestern architects may be different from those of architects elsewhere, their approaches to architecture appear to be no less complex. The analysis of their accomplishments establishes a theoretical basis from which we may explore new possibilities for meaningful architecture in the future.

adobe a brick or building material of sun-dried mud, sometimes mixed with fibers.

Anasazi ancient Pueblo people of the southwestern United States; a Navajo word meaning "ancient enemies" or "ancient ones."

antechamber a small, partially underground room located usually south or east of a pit house and used for access and ventilation; an ancillary surface room attached to the perimeter of a kiva.

arroyo a water-carved gully or channel in an arid region.

Athapaskan (also Athapascan, Athabaskan, or Athabascan) one of several related languages spoken by the North American Indians originating in the inland valleys of central Alaska and northwestern Canada; the language spoken by the Navajo and Apache people; a person who speaks the language.

atlatl a hand-held stick used for throwing a spear or dart before the introduction of bows and arrows.

banded masonry horizontal courses of uniformly colored stones forming a distinctive band in a masonry wall.

banquette a raised seat or shelf around the interior perimeter of a pit house or kiva.

bench a geological terrace elevated above the flood plain of a river or lake; a long seat for two or more persons. *See also* banquette.

buwa yave Tewa-language words used referring to "tissue paper" bread, a Hopi delicacy consisting of many tissue-thin layers of corn bread rolled into a cylinder; found at Poshuouinge.

caliche a calcium carbonate formation below the surface of desert floors, material from which can be combined with sand and water to form durable walls like those of Hohokam buildings and compounds.

cavate a small cave dug into a cliff face and used as a living space or for storage.

Chaco Phenomenon a period of Anasazi cultural efflorescence occurring in the Chaco Canyon area between perhaps A.D. 1050 and 1130.

Chichimeca an ancient people living in northern Mexico whose major trading center was Paquimé; considered by their southern neighbors to be barbarous and sometimes referred to as dog people because they reportedly hunted with dogs.

chinking small stones inserted into adobe mortar during construction to strengthen walls.

Cibola an area of the Southwest associated with the Zuni people in western New Mexico and eastern Arizona.

cimientos foundations or room outlines consisting of one or more closely parallel rows of upright cobbles, serving to inhibit the erosion of wall bases.

cist a storage pit lined with stone slabs.

cliff dwelling a pueblo built against a cliff wall, usually under a natural overhang.

compound a wall-enclosed area containing one or more rooms and courtyards.

copper bell a small bell cast in Mexico and used as a trade item in prehistoric times.

corbel an architectural member projecting from a wall and supporting a load, especially one stepping upward and outward from a vertical surface.

core-veneered wall *see* rubble-cored wall.

coursed masonry stones placed in uniform horizontal layers.

cuesta a hill or ridge having a steep face on one side and a gentle slope on the other.

deflector a vertical stone slab or barrier between a source of fresh air and a fire pit in a pit house or kiva floor.

dendrochronology a method of dating based on the comparative study of growth rings in trees and aged wood.

entrada a Spanish word meaning entrance, a reference to the entry of Spanish explorers under the leadership of Francisco Vásquez de Coronado into the Southwest in 1540.

fire pit a stone- or plaster-lined pit used to contain a fire.

foot drum a masonry vault in the floor of a kiva covered with wood planking.

great kiva a large assembly room sufficient in size to accommodate all or most of the members of a community; in Eastern Pueblos, usually a circular chamber recessed partly or fully into the earth; in Western Pueblos traditionally a rectangular room located on grade.

hamlet a settlement housing fifteen to one hundred people.

Hohokam people associated with a desert and upland farming culture in southern Arizona between about A.D. 300 and 1450; a Tohono O'odham word meaning "those who came before" or "all used up."

iron pyrite a common mineral having a pale brass-yellow and metallic luster; iron pyrite mirrors made in Mesoamerica appear as prehistoric trade items in the Southwest; found at Palo Parado.

jacal a wall or partition consisting of vertical posts interconnected by secondary horizontal members and covered on both sides with mud or adobe plaster containing limited quantities of pebbles or small stones to form a solid wall.

kiva a Hopi word meaning ceremonial room; a small group activity room sufficient in size to accommodate the members of an extended family or clan. *See also* great kiva.

latilla a small wood structural member spanning horizontally between beams or joists supporting a floor or roof.

latte megalithic foundations of prehistoric houses in the Marianna Islands of Micronesia in the Western Pacific Ocean.

lintel a horizontal structural member spanning across the top of door, window, or other wall opening and supporting the wall above it.

macaw a brightly colored parrot raised in Mexico and used as a prehistoric trade item in the Southwest.

mano a Spanish word meaning hand; a hand-held stone used for grinding corn on a *metate*.

mesa a Spanish word meaning table; an isolated hill or extended ridge having steeply sloping sides and a level top. *See also* bench.

mesilla literally, a small or low mesa.

metate a fixed stone often having a concave upper surface used for grinding corn with a *mano*.

midden a rubbish dump, often containing a valuable record of cultural events in chronological order.

Mogollon ancient people living in the mountain valleys and uplands of western New Mexico, central Arizona, and northern Mexico; a mountain range in western New Mexico; the name of a Spanish Colonial governor of New Mexico, Don Juan Ignacio Flores Mogollon, who was appointed in 1712.

Mogollon Rim an east-west ridge in central Arizona separating the tributaries of the Little Colorado River to the north from those of the Salt and Gila rivers in the south.

Montezuma Valley a geographical area of southwestern Colorado and southeastern Utah where an estimated thirty thousand Anasazi lived during the A.D. twelfth century.

olla a Spanish word meaning round earthen pot, also a reference to one of the large clay granaries found in Chihuahua and still used in Veracruz and Tlaxcala; found at Olla Cave.

outlier a satellite settlement, particularly a community in or near the San Juan Basin associated with Chaco Canyon.

pecked masonry stones dressed or shaped by striking or pitting with a hammer stone.

pilaster a column engaged with an adjacent wall.

Pima *see* Tohono O'odham.

pit house a semisubterranean room with a wood-framed roof and upper walls plastered over with mud; a type of residence commonly found throughout the ancient Southwest.

podium an elevated base or platform on which a structure is placed.

portico a porch; a covered colonnade at the entrance of a building.

prehistory a reference to times antedating written history; in the Southwest, before 1540.

puchteca (also pochteca) a group of long-distance traders operating from Mesoamerica whose activities may be related to regionally based systems in the Southwest, such as those of Chaco Canyon or Paquimé.

pueblo a Spanish word meaning a small town or village; in the Southwest, a reference to a multiroom dwelling sometimes several stories high or to a resident of such a dwelling.

pyrite *see* iron pyrite.

ramada a sunshade built of post-and-beam construction and supported by four corner posts; a roofed structure with no walls used as an outside work or storage area.

rancheria a settlement consisting of several detached dwellings occupied by members of an extended or nuclear family.

room block a linear or rectangular structure consisting of multiple rectangular rooms built as a unit.

rubble-cored wall a wall consisting of two parallel masonry facings filled between with small stones, clay, and earth.

saguaro a cactus of the desert Southwest and Mexico having a columnar, sparsely branched trunk up to 60 feet (18.3 meters) high and bearing white flowers, edible fruit, and reed-like ribs sometimes used as a building material.

Salado a cultural group identified along the upper Salt River Valley and the Tonto Basin of Arizona and the Mimbres Valley of New Mexico in the A.D. twelfth to fourteenth centuries.

Sinagua a cultural group identified in the vicinity of Flagstaff and later the Verde Valley of central Arizona between the A.D. seventh and fifteenth centuries.

sipapu a small hole in the floor of a kiva symbolizing the place of emergence of ancient people from the underworld; a hole through which spirits are said to pass from this world to the other.

spall a small fragment or chip of stone.

stone-close a flat stone shaped like a doughnut and fitted into a wall to serve as a portal; found at Kin Tiel.

talus rock debris at the base of a cliff.

Tohono O'odham people living in south-central Arizona who probably are descendants of the ancient Hohokam; previously called Pima.

tower kiva a kiva built on top of an elevated, rubble-filled platform, often more than one story high; found at Kin Kletso, Kin Klizhin, Las Vantanas, Kin Ya'a, and other sites.

tree-ring dating *see* dendrochronology.

trincheras a Spanish word meaning entrenchments; in northern Sonora and southern Arizona a reference to a series of prehistoric walls stepping up a hillside, resembling from a distance a stepped pyramid; found at Cerro Prieto.

tri-wall a circular Anasazi ceremonial structure consisting of three concentric masonry walls surrounding a central room; found at Pueblo del Arroyo and Aztec.

Tusayan a geographical area of northeastern Arizona traditionally associated with the Hopi.

unit house a storage facility, pit house, service yard, and trash deposit arranged along an axis often oriented from northwest to southeast.

ventilator a tunnel leading from the ground surface into pit houses and kivas to provide fresh air.

viga a horizontal wood beam supporting a floor or roof structure.

wash the dry bed of a stream, also called dry wash. *See also* arroyo.

wattle and daub *see* jacal.

wythe a line of stones or bricks in the horizontal plane.

Abajo ah-BAH-ho
Abiquiu AH-bee-cue
Abó ah-BOH
Acequia ah-SAY-kya
Acoma AH-co-mah
Aguatubi AH-gwah-TOO-bee
Alkali AL-kah-lie
Alto AHL-toh
Alvarado AHL-vah-RAH-doh
Anasazi AH-nah-SAH-zee
Ancha AHN-kah
animas AHN-ee-mahs
Antonio ahn-TOH-nee-oh
Apache ah-PATCH-ee
Arroyo ah-ROY-yo
Atanacio ah-tah-NAH-see-oh
Athapascan ATH-ah-PASS-can
Atsinna at-SIN-nah
Aviles ah-VEA-lace
Awatovi ah-wah-TOW-vee
Bacabi bah-COB-ee
baja BAH-hah
bayo BAH-yoh
Bernardo bear-NAHR-doe
Besh Ba Gowah BESH-ba-GO-wah
Betatakin bay-TA-tah-kin
Bineola BIN-ee-OH-lah
blanco BLAHN-coh
bonito bo-KNEE-toh
buwa yave BOO-wah YAH-vay
caliente CAH-lee-AIN-tay
caliche cah-LEE-chay
casa CAH-sah
Casamero CAH-sah-MAY-roe
cavate CAVE-ate
cerro SAY-roe
Chaco CHAH-koh
Chama CHAH-mah
Chelly SHAY
Chetro Ketl CHE-troe KE-tel
Chinle CHIN-lee
Chichimeca CHEE-chee-MAY-kah
Chihuahua chee-WAH-wah
chiquita chee-KEE-tah
Chodistaas cho-DISS-tahs
Chukubi chuck-KOO-bee
Chuska CHUSS-kah

Cibola see-BOW-lah
Cicuye see-KOO-yea
cielo see-ALE-oh
cienega see-AI-nay-gah
ciudad SEE-oo-dahd
Coahuila KOH-ah-WHEE-lah
Cochiti koh-CHEE-tee
Coconino KOH-koh-NEE-noh
Cohonina KOH-hoh-NEE-nah
Comanche ko-MAN-chee
Coronado CORE-oh-NOD-oh
Cristo CREASE-toh
Cristóbal crease-TOH-bahl
cruz KROOS
cuaranta kwah-RAHN-tah
cuesta KWAIS-tah
de DAY
derecho day-RAY-choh
dolores doe-LO-rays
domingo doe-MIN-go
Dominquez doe-MIN-gaze
don DOHN
entrada ain-TRAH-dah
Escalante ais-kah-LAHN-tay
Espejo ais-PAY-hoh
Estancia ais-STAHN-see-ah
Eusebio AY-oo-SAY-bee-oh
Felipe fay-LEE-pay
Francisco frahn-CEASE-koh
frijoles free-HOLE-ace
Galaz gah-LAHZ
Galisteo GAH-liss-TAY-oh
Garabato GAH-rah-BOT-oh
Gila HEE-lah
grande GRAHN-day
Gran Quivira GRAHN kwe-VEE-rah
Guanacos wah-NOC-kohs
Halona hah-LOW-nah
Hano HAH-no
Hawiku hah-WEE-koo
Hernando hair-NAHN-doe
Hohokam HO-ho-KAM
hondo HAWN-doe
horno HOR-noh
Hotevilla HOH-tay-VEE-yah
humanas hoo-MAH-nahs
Hungo Pavi HOON-go PAH-vee

Ibarra ee-BAHR-rah
Ildefonso EEL-day-FAUN-so
Isleta is-LAY-tah
jacal ha-CALL
Jeddito hay-DEE-toh
Jemez HAY-mez
jornada hore-NOD-ah
José hoe-SAY
Juan WHAN
Juárez WHA-rez
Jumanos hoo-MAH-nohs
Kayenta ka-YAIN-tah
Kiet Siel KEET SEAL
Kin KIN
Kinishba kin-ISH-bah
Kino KEE-noh
Kiva KEE-vah
Kletso KLET-so
Klizhin KLI-sin
Kuaua KWAH-wah
latilla laht-TEE-yah
latte LAT-tee
Lazaro lah-ZAH-roe
Lomaki low-MOCK-ee
Lorenzo low-RAIN-zoh
macaw mah-CAHW
madre MOD-ray
Malpais MAHL-pie
mano MAH-noh
Mancos MAHN-cos
Manzanos mahn-ZAH-nos
Marco MARK-oh
Mateo mah-TAY-oh
Mazatzal mah-zaht-ZAHL
Menéndez may-NAIN-dez
mesa MAY-sah
metate may-TOT-tay
mimbres MEEM-brays
Mishognovi MISH-ong-NO-vee
Moenkopi MOH-en-COP-ee
Mogollon MUG-ee-yone
Montezuma MON-tee-ZOO-mah
Morro MORE-roe
Muertos MWER-tos
Navajo NAH-vah-ho
Niza NEE-zah
nueva noo-WAY-vah

Nutria NOO-tree-ah
Nuvaqueotaka NOO-vah-KWAY-oh-TOCK-ah
occidental oh-see-DAINT-ahl
ojo OH-ho
olla OY-yah
Oñate oh-NYEA-tay
Oraibi oh-RYE-bee
Otowi oh-TOE-wee
Paako POCK-oh
Pagosa pah-GO-sah
Pajarito PAH-ha-REE-toh
Palo Parado PAH-low pah-RAH-doe
Papago POP-ah-go
Paquimé pock-ee-MAY
Pasiovi PAH-see-OH-vee
Pasiwvi pah-SEE-vee
Payupki pah-YUP-kee
Pecos PAY-cose
Pedro PAY-droe
Peñasco pain-YAHS-coh
Penutian pay-NOO-tee-ahn
Pescado pays-CAH-doe
Piedra pee-AID-rah
Pima PEEM-ah
Pinal PIE-nahl
Pindi PIN-dee
Pintado peen-TOD-oh
pochteca poach-TAKE-ah
Poshuouinge POH-shu-WING-gay
Potsuwii poht-SOO-wee
Prieto pre-A-toh
puchteca pooch-TAKE-ah
pueblo PWE-blow
Puerco PWAYR-coh
Quarai KWAH-rai
Quemado kay-MOD-oh
Quivira kwee-VEE-rah
ramada rah-MAH-dah
Ramah RAH-mah
rancheria RAHN-chair-REE-ya
rinconada RIN-coh-NAH-dah
rio REE-oh
rito REE-toh
robles ROW-blaze

saguaro sah-WHAH-roe
Salado sah-LAH-doh
Salinas sah-LEE-nahs
Salmon SOHL-mun
Salome sah-LOA-may
San SAHN
Sandia sahn-DEE-ah
sangre SAHN-grey
Santo SAHN-toh
Sapawe sah-POW-ay
Shabik'eschee sha-BICK-esh-she
Shipaulovi SHE-paw-LOW-vee
Shongopavi SHONG-oh-PAH-vee
Shoshoni sho-SHO-nee
Sichomovi SITCH-ah-MO-vee
sierra see-AIR-rah
Silvestre seal-VASE-tray
Sinagua see-NAGH-wah
Sipapu see-POP-pu
Sonora so-NOH-rah
Taos TAH-os
Tecapo tay-KAH-poh
Tewa TAY-wah
Tiel TEEL
Tiwa TEE-wah
Tohatchi tow-HATCH-chee
Toh La Kai toh-lah-KYE
Tohono O'odham tow-HO-no o-ode-HAHM
Tonto TOHN-toh
Tovar TOH-vahr
trinchera treen-CHAY-rah
tsegi SAY-ghee
Tsin Kletzin t'sin KLET-zin
Tsiping T'SIP-ing
Tumayo too-MAH-yoh
Tusayan too-sah-YAHN
Tuzigoot TWO-zee-goot
Tyuonyi chew-OHN-yee
Una Vida OO-nah VEE-dah
Ute YOOT
Vasquez VAHS-kaze
Velez VALE-ace
ventanas vain-TAH-nahs
verde VER-day
Vibora vee-BOR-ah

Vicente vee-SAIN-tay
Viga VEE-gah
Walpi WALL-pea
Wijiji wee-GEE-gee
Wukoki woo-KOH-kee
Wupatki woo-POT-kee
Ya'a YAH-AH
Zuni ZOO-nee

Aleshire, Peter, and Jerry Jacka. 1992. "Unearthing a Culture." *Arizona Highways* 68(3):4–19.

Amsden, Theodore. 1934. "Report on Archaeological Survey at El Morro National Monument, from January 15 to February 15, 1934." On file at the Laboratory of Anthropology, Santa Fe.

Andresen, John M. 1989. "The Casa Grande Group." Essay on file at Casa Grande Ruins National Monument, Coolidge, Ariz.

Anyon, Roger, and Stephen A. LeBlanc. 1980. "The Evolution of Mogollon-Mimbres Ceremonial Structures." *The Kiva* 45(3):253–277.

———. 1984. *The Galaz Ruin: A Mimbres Village in Southwestern New Mexico.* Albuquerque: Maxwell Museum of Anthropology and the University of New Mexico Press.

Anyon, Roger, Patricia A. Gilman, and Stephen A. LeBlanc. 1981. "A Re-Evaluation of the Mimbres-Mogollon Archaeological Sequence." *The Kiva* 46(4):209–225.

Arnold, David L. 1982. "Pueblo Pottery: 2,000 Years of Artistry." *National Geographic.* 162(5):593–605.

Bandelier, Adolph Francis. 1890–1892. *Final Report on Investigations among the Indians of the Southwestern United States, Carried on Mainly in the Years from 1880 to 1885.* 2 vols. Papers of the Archaeological Institute of America, American Series 3 and 4. Cambridge, Mass.

———. 1971. *The Delight Makers.* Orlando: Harcourt Brace Jovanovich.

Bodine, John J. 1979. "Taos Pueblo." In *Handbook of North American Indians, Southwest,* 9:255–267. Washington, D.C.: Smithsonian Institution.

Bostwick, Todd. 1989. *The Preservation and Interpretation of Pueblo Grande.* Interpretative pamphlet accompanying an exhibit opening. Pueblo Grande Museum, Phoenix.

Bradley, Bruce A. 1988. "Wallace Ruin Interim Report." *Southwest Lore* (Colorado Archaeological Society, Denver) 54(2):8–23.

———. 1990. *Planning and Growth at a Prehistoric Pueblo: A Case Study from Southwestern Colorado.* Cortez, Col.: Crow Canyon Archaeological Center.

Brady, J. J. 1984. "Chacoan Art and the Chaco Phenomena." In *New Light on Chaco Canyon,* 13–18. Santa Fe: School of American Research.

Brandt, Elizabeth A. 1979. "Sandia Pueblo." In *Handbook of North American Indians, Southwest,* 9:343–350. Washington, D.C.: Smithsonian Institution.

Brew, John Otis. 1946. *Archaeology of Alkali Ridge, Southeastern Utah, with a Review of the Prehistory of the Mesa Verde Division of the San Juan and Some Observations on Archaeological Systematics.* Papers of the Peabody Museum of American Archaeology and Ethnology, Harvard University. Cambridge, Mass.

———. 1979. "Hopi Prehistory and History to 1850." In *Handbook of North American Indians, Southwest,* 9:514–523. Washington, D.C.: Smithsonian Institution.

Brunson, Judy L. 1989. "The Social Organization of the Los Muertos Hohokam: A Reanalysis of Cushing's Hemenway Expedition Data." Ph.D. dissertation, Arizona State University.

Cable, John S., and David E. Doyel. 1987. "Pioneer Period Village Structure and Settlement Pattern in the Phoenix Basin." In *The Hohokam Village*, edited by David Doyel. Glenwood Springs, Col.: Southwest and Rocky Mountain Division of the American Association for the Advancement of Science.

Canby, Thomas Y. 1982. "The Anasazi: Riddles in the Ruins." *National Geographic.* 162(5):554–592.

Carlson, John B. 1990. "America's Ancient Skywatchers." *National Geographic* 177(3):76–107.

Cather, Willa. 1971. *Death Comes for the Archbishop.* New York: Vintage Books Edition, Random House. [Originally published by Alfred A. Knopf in 1927.]

Ciolek-Torrello, Richard. 1984. "An Alternate Model of Room Function for Grasshopper Pueblo, Arizona." In *Intra Spatial Analysis in Archaeology*, edited by Harold J. Hietaka. New York: Cambridge University Press.

Connelly, John C. 1979. "Hopi Social Organization." In *Handbook of North American Indians, Southwest*, 9:539–553. Washington, D.C.: Smithsonian Institution.

Corbett, John M. 1962. *Aztec Ruins National Monument.* National Park Service Historical Handbook Series 36. Washington, D.C.

Cordell, Linda S. 1979. "Prehistory: Eastern Anasazi." In *Handbook of North American Indians, Southwest*, 9:131–151. Washington, D.C.: Smithsonian Institution.

———. 1984. *Prehistory of the Southwest.* Orlando: Academic Press.

Cordell, Linda S., and George J. Gumerman, eds. 1989. *Dynamics of Southwestern Prehistory.* Washington, D.C.: Smithsonian Institution Press.

Cosgrove, H. S., and C. B. Cosgrove. 1932. *The Swarts Ruin, a Typical Mimbres Site in Southwestern New Mexico.* Papers of the Peabody Museum, Harvard University, 24(2). Cambridge, Mass.

Cummings, Byron. 1940. *Kinishba: A Prehistoric Pueblo of the Great Pueblo Period.* Tucson: Hohokam Museums Association and the University of Arizona.

Current, William, and Vincent Scully. 1971. *Pueblo Architecture of the Southwest.* Austin: University of Texas Press.

Cushing, Frank H. 1890. "Preliminary Notes on the Origin, Working Hypothesis, and Primary Research on the Hemenway Southwestern Archaeological Expedition." In *Proceedings of the 7th International Congress of Americanists*, 151–194. Berlin, 1888.

Dean, Jeffrey S. 1969. *Chronology Analysis of Tsegi Phase Sites in Northeastern Arizona.* Papers of the Laboratory of Anthropology of Tree-Ring Research, no. 3. Tucson.

Di Peso, Charles C. 1956. *The Upper Pima of San Cayentana del Tumacacari: An Archaeohistorical Reconstruction of the Ootam of Primeria Alta.* Amerind Foundation Publication 7. Dratoon, Ariz.

————. 1974. *Casas Grandes: A Fallen Trading Center of the Gran Chichi-meca.* Vols. 1–3. Amerind Foundation Series 9. Dragoon, Ariz.

Downum, Christian E. 1986. "The Cerro Prieto/Pan Quemado Archaeological Site Complex." Presented to Arizona House Committee, National Resources and Agriculture, re: HB 24.

————. 1990. "The Robles Survey: Archaeological Investigations of the Lower Santa Cruz River from Gran Marana to Red Rock, AZ." Submitted for publication to Anthropological Papers of the University of Arizona.

Downum, Christian E., and Todd W. Bostwick. 1993. *Archaeology of the Pueblo Grande Platform Mound and Surrounding Features*, Vol. 1. Phoenix: Pueblo Grande Museum Anthropological Papers, no. 1.

Doyel, David E., ed. 1987. *The Hohokam Village: Site Structure and Organization.* Glenwood Springs, Col.: Southwestern and Rocky Mountain Division of the American Association for the Advancement of Science.

Duncan, Marjorie, Patricia A. Gilman, and Raymond P. Mauldin. 1991. "The Mogollon Village Archaeological Project , 1991, Preliminary Report." Report compiled for the U.S. Forest Service.

Durham, Michael S. 1990. *The Smithsonian Guide to Historic America: The Desert States.* Roger G. Kennedy, editorial director. New York: Stewart, Tabori & Chang.

Eddy, Frank W. 1977. *Archaeological Investigations at Chimney Rock Mesa: 1970–72.* Memoirs of the Colorado Archaeological Society 1. Boulder.

Eggan, Fred. 1979. "Pueblos: Introduction." In *Handbook of North American Indians, Southwest,* 9:224–235. Washington, D.C.: Smithsonian Institution.

Erdoes, Richard, and Alfonso Ortiz, eds. 1984. *American Indian Myths and Legends.* New York: Pantheon Books, Random House.

Ferguson, William M., and Arthur H. Rohn. 1987. *Anasazi Ruins of the Southwest in Color.* 4th printing. Albuquerque: University of New Mexico Press. 1990.

Fewkes, J. Walter. 1891. "Reconnaissance of Ruins in or near the Zuni Reservation." *Journal of American Ethnology and Archaeology* 1:92–132.

————. 1904. "Two Summers' Work in Pueblo Ruins." In *22nd Annual Report of The Bureau of American Ethnology for the years 1900–1901.* pt. 1:3–195. Washington, D.C.

————. 1917. "A Prehistoric Mesa Verde Pueblo and Its People." In *Annual Report of the Smithsonian Institution for 1916,* 461–479. Washington, D.C.

Fish, Paul R. 1989. "The Hohokam: 1000 years of Prehistory in the Sonoran Desert." In *Dynamics of Southern Prehistory,* edited by Linda Cordell and George J. Gummerman, 19–63. Washington, D.C.: Smithsonian Institution Press.

Franstead, Dennis, and Oswald Werner. 1974. "The Ethnogeography of the Chaco Canyon Area." On file, at the Division of Cultural Research, National Park Service, Albuquerque.

Frazier, Kendrick. 1986. *People of Chaco: A Canyon and Its Culture.* New York: W. W. Norton & Company.

Garcia-Mason, Velma. 1979. "Acoma Pueblo." In *Handbook of North American Indians, Southwest*, 9:450–466. Washington, D.C.: Smithsonian Institution.

Germick, Stephen, and Joseph S. Crary. 1989. "Prehistoric Adaptations in the Bajada-Upland Area of Tonto Basin: Examples from the A-Cross Road and Henderson Mesa Surveys." Paper presented at the 62nd Annual Pecos Conference, Bandelier National Monument, N.M.

———. 1990. "Prehistoric Settlement and Adaptations in the East Piedmont of the Mazatzal Mountains." Paper presented at the 63rd Annual Pecos Conference, Blanding, Utah.

Germick, Stephen, and John W. Hohman. 1988. "Community and Ceremonial Rooms at Salado Sites." Research report presented at the 53rd Annual Meeting of the Society for American Archaeology, Phoenix.

Gilman, Patricia Ann. 1983. "Changing Architectural Forms in the Prehistoric Southwest." Ph.D. dissertation, Department of Anthropology, University of New Mexico.

Gilman, Patricia Ann, Raymond P. Mauldin, and Valli S. Powell. 1991. "The Mogollon Village Archaeological Project, 1989." Report compiled for the U.S. Forest Service.

Gladwin, Harold Sterling. 1945. *The Chaco Branch Excavations at White Mound and in the Red Mesa Valley.* Gila Pueblo Medallion Paper 33. Globe, Ariz.

Gladwin, Harold S., Emil W. Haury, Edwin B. Sayles, and Nora Gladwin. 1937. *Excavations at Snaketown I: Material Culture.* Gila Pueblo Medallion Paper 25. Globe, Ariz. Reprinted Tucson: Arizona State Museum, 1965.

Graves, Michael W., and William A. Longacre. 1982. "Aggregation and Abandonment at Grasshopper Pueblo, Arizona." *Journal of Field Archaeology* 9(1): 193–206.

Gregonis, Linda M., and Karl J. Reinhard. 1988. *Hohokam Indians of the Tucson Basin.* 4th printing. Tucson: University of Arizona Press.

Gregory, David A. 1987. "The Morphology of Platform Mounds and the Structure of Classic Period Hohokam Sites." In *The Hohokam Village: Site Structure and Organization*, edited by David E. Doyel. Glenwood Springs, Col.: Southwestern and Rocky Mountain Division of the American Association for the Advancement of Sciences.

Guevara Sánchez, Arturo. 1986. *Arqueologia de area de Las Cuarenta Casas, Chihuahua.* Instituto Nacional de Antropologia e Historia, Colección Científica.

Gumerman, George J., and Jeffery S. Dean. 1989. "Prehistoric Cooperation and Competition in the Western Anasazi Area." In *Dynamics of Southwest Prehistory*, edited by Linda S. Cordell and George J. Gummerman, 19–148. Washington, D.C.: Smithsonian Institution Press.

Gumerman, George J., and Robert C. Euler, eds. 1976. "Black Mesa: Retrospect and Prospect." In *Papers on the Archaeology of Black Mesa, Arizona*, 162–170. Carbondale: Southern Illinois University Press.

Gumerman, George J., and Emil W. Haury. 1979. "Prehistory: Hohokam." In *Handbook of North American Indians, Southwest*, 9:75–90. Washington, D.C.: Smithsonian Institution.

Haury, Emil W. 1936. *The Mogollon Culture of Southwestern New Mexico.* Gila Pueblo Medallion Papers, no. 20. Globe, Ariz.

———. 1945. *The Excavations of Los Muertos and Neighboring Ruins in the Salt River Valley, Southern Arizona.* Papers of the Peabody Museum of American Archaeology and Ethnology, Harvard University. Cambridge, Mass.

———. 1967. "The Hohokam: First Masters of the American Desert." *National Geographic* 131(5):670–695.

———. 1976. *The Hohokam, Desert Farmers, and Craftsmen: Excavations at Snaketown, 1964—1965.* Tucson: University of Arizona Press.

Hawkes, Jaquetta. 1974. *Atlas of Ancient Archaeology.* New York: McGraw-Hill.

Hayes, Alden C., and James A. Lancaster. 1975. *Badger House Community, Mesa Verde National Park.* Washington, D.C.: National Park Service.

Hayes, Alden C., Jon Nathan Young, and A. H. Warren. 1981. *Excavation of Mound 7, Gran Quivira National Monument, New Mexico.* U.S. National Park Service Publications in Archaeology 16. Washington, D.C.

Henry, Jeannette, Vine Deloria, Jr., M. Scott Momaday, Bea Medicine, and Alfonso Ortiz, eds. 1970. *Indian Voices: The First Convocation of American Indian Scholars.* San Francisco: Indian Historian Press.

Hewett, Edgar L. 1938. *Pajarito Plateau and Its Ancient People.* Albuquerque: University of New Mexico Press.

Heyden, Doris, and Paul Gendrop. 1973. *Pre-Columbian Architecture of Mesoamerica.* Translated by Judith Stanton. New York: Harry N. Abrams.

Hibben, Frank C. 1937. *Excavation of the Riana Ruin and Chama Valley Survey.* University of New Mexico Anthropological Series 2(1). Albuquerque.

Hietala, Harold J., ed. 1984. *Intrasite Spatial Analysis in Archaeology.* New York: Cambridge University Press.

Hoard, Dorothy. 1989. *A Guide to Bandelier National Monument.* 3d ed. Los Alamos: Los Alamos Historical Society.

Hohman, John W. 1990. *A Master Stabilization, Development, and Interpretive Plan for the Proposed Casa Malpais Interpretive Archaeological Recreational Area.* Phoenix: Louis Berger & Associates.

Hohman, John W., and Linda B. Kelley. 1988. *Erich F. Schmidt's Investigations of Salado Sites in Central Arizona: The Mrs. W. B. Thompson Archaeological Expedition of the American Museum of Natural History.* Museum of Northern Arizona Bulletin Series 56. Flagstaff.

Hunter-Anderson, Rosalind L. 1978. "An Archaeological Survey of the Yellowhouse Dam Area." On file at the Office of Contract Archaeology, University of New Mexico, Albuquerque.

Hyslop, John. 1990. *Inka Settlement Planning.* Austin: University of Texas Press.

Irwin-Williams, Cynthia, and Phillip H. Shelley, eds. 1980. *Investigations at the Salmon Site: The Structure of Chacoan Society in the Northern Southwest.* Portales: Eastern New Mexico University.

Jeancon, Jean Allard. 1922. *Archaeological Research in the Northeastern San Juan Basin of Colorado during the Summer of 1921.* Edited by Frank H. H. Roberts. Denver: State Historical and Natural History Society of Colorado and the University of Denver.

———. 1923. *Excavations in the Chama Valley, New Mexico.* Bureau of American Ethnology Bulletin 81. Washington, D.C.

Jenkins, Myra Ellen, and Albert H. Shroeder. 1974. *A Brief History of New Mexico.* Albuquerque: University of New Mexico Press.

Jennings, Jesse D. 1974. *Prehistory of North America.* 2d ed. New York: McGraw-Hill.

———. 1983. *Ancient North Americans.* New York: W. H. Freeman & Company.

Jones, Dewitt, and Linda S. Cordell. 1985. *Anasazi World.* Portland: Graphic Arts Center Publishing Company.

Judd, Neil M. 1959. *Pueblo del Arroyo, Chaco Canyon, New Mexico.* Smithsonian Miscellaneous Collections 38(1). Washington, D.C.

———. 1964. *The Architecture of Pueblo Bonito.* Smithsonian Miscellaneous Collections 147(1). Washington, D.C.

Judge, W. James. 1984. "New Light on Chaco Canyon." In *New Light on Chaco Canyon,* 1–12. Santa Fe: School of American Research.

Jung, C. G. 1959. "Archetypes of the Collective Subconscious." In *The Basic Writings of C. G. Jung,* edited by Violet de Laszlo. New York: Modern Library, Random House.

Kane, Allen E. 1989. "Did the Sheep Look Up? Sociopolitical Complexity in Ninth Century Dolores Society." In *The Sociopolitical Structure of Prehistoric Southwestern Societies,* edited by Steadman Upham, Kent G. Lightfoot, and Roberta A. Jewett. Boulder: Westview Press.

Kane, A. E., and C. K. Robinson. 1988. *Dolores Archaeological Program: Anasazi Communities at Dolores: McPhee Village.* Denver: U.S. Bureau of Reclamation, Engineering, and Research Center.

Kennedy, Roger G., ed. dir., with text by Michael S. Durham. 1990. *The Smithsonian Guide to Historic America: The Desert States.* New York: Stewart, Tabori & Chang.

Kidder, Alfred V. 1958. *Pecos, New Mexico: Archaeological Notes.* Papers of the Robert S. Peabody Foundation for Archaeology 5. Andover, Mass.

Kintigh, Keith W. 1985. *Settlement, Subsistence, and Society in Late Zuni Prehistory.* Anthropological Papers of the University of Arizona, no. 44. Tucson: University of Arizona Press.

Klima, Bohuslav. 1954. "Paleolithic Huts at Dolni Vestonice, Czechoslovakia." *Antiquity* 28(109):4–41.

Knowles, Ralph L. 1974. "Part One: Adaptation to the Environment." In *Energy and Form: An Ecological Approach to Urban Growth,* 1–46. Cambridge, Mass.: MIT Press.

Lambert, Marjorie F. 1954. *Paako, Archaeological Chronicle of an Indian Village in North Central New Mexico.* Santa Fe: School of American Research.

Lancaster, James A., Jean M. Pinkley, Philip F. Van Cleave, and Don Watson. 1954. *Archaeological Excavations in Mesa Verde National Park, Colorado, 1950.* U.S. National Park Service Archeological Research Series 2. Washington, D.C.

Lange, Charles H. 1979. "Santo Domingo Pueblo." In *Handbook of North American Indians, Southwest,* 9:379–389. Washington, D.C.: Smithsonian Institution.

Lange, Frederic, Nancy Mahoney, Joe Ben Wheat, and Mark L. Chenault. 1986. *Yellow Jacket: A Four Corners Anasazi Ceremonial Center.* Boulder: Johnson Books.

Leach, Edmund. 1970. *Claude Lévi-Strauss.* Chicago: University of Chicago Press.

LeBlanc, Stephen A. 1976. "Mimbres Archaeological Center: Preliminary Report of the Second Season, 1975." *Journal of New World Archaeology* 1(6).

———. 1983. *The Mimbres People: Ancient Pueblo Potters of the American Southwest.* London: Thames and Hudson.

———. 1989. "Cibola: Shifting Cultural Boundaries." In *Dynamics of Southwest Prehistory,* 337–369. Washington, D.C.: Smithsonian Institution Press.

Le Corbusier, [Charles-Edouard Jeanneret]. 1926. *Vers une architecture.* Paris.

Lekson, Stephen H. 1990. "The Southwest's Remarkable Mimbres People." *Archaeology,* Nov.–Dec., 45–48.

———. 1991. "Settlement Patterns and the Chacoan Region." In *Chaco and Hohokam: Prehistoric Regional Systems in the American Southwest,* edited by Patricia L. Crown and W. James Judge, pp. 31–55. Santa Fe: School of American Research Press.

———, ed. 1983. *The Architecture and Dendrochronology of Chetro Ketl, Chaco Canyon, New Mexico.* Reports of the Chaco Center, no. 6. Albuquerque: Division of Cultural Research, National Park Service.

Lekson, Stephen H., with contributions by William G. Gillespie and Thomas C. Windes. 1987. *Great Pueblo Architecture of Chaco Canyon.* Albuquerque: University of New Mexico Press.

Lekson, Stephen H., and Peter J. McKenna. 1979. "Wall Elevations of Major Chacoan Ruins." On file at the Division of Cultural Research, National Park Service. Washington, D.C.

Lekson, Stephen H., Thomas C. Windes, John R. Stein, and W. James Judge. 1988. "The Chaco Canyon Community." *Scientific American* 256(7): 100–109.

Lévi-Strauss, Claude. 1966. *The Savage Mind.* Translated from *La Pensée sauvage* (Paris, 1962). Chicago: University of Chicago Press.

Lipe, William D., James N. Morris, and Timothy A. Kholer. 1988. *Dolores Archaeological Program: Anasazi Communities at Dolores: Grass Mesa Village.* Denver: U.S. Bureau of Reclamation, Engineering, and Research Center.

Lister, Robert H. 1958. *Archaeological Investigations in the Northern Sierra Madre Occidental, Chihuahua and Sonora, Mexico.* University of Colorado Studies Series in Anthropology, no. 7. Boulder: University of Colorado Press.

———. 1984. "Chaco Canyon Archaeology through Time." In *New Light on Chaco Canyon,* 25–36. Santa Fe: School of American Research.

Lister, Robert H., J. Richard Ambler, Florence C. Lister, Lyndon L. Hargrave, and Christy G. Turner II. 1959–1961. *The Coombs Site, Parts I, II, and III.* University of Utah Anthropological Papers 41, Glen Canyon Series B. Salt Lake City.

Lister, Robert H., and Florence C. Lister. 1981. *Chaco Canyon Archaeology and Archaeologists.* Albuquerque: University of New Mexico Press.

———. 1987. *Aztec Ruins on the Animas: Excavated, Preserved, and Interpreted.* Albuquerque: University of New Mexico Press.

———. 1989. *Those Who Came Before.* Globe, Ariz.: Southwest Parks and Monuments Association.

———. 1990. *Aztec Ruins National Monument: Administrative History of an Archaeological Presence.* Santa Fe: Division of History, National Park Service.

Longacre, William A., and J. Jefferson Reid. 1974. "The University of Arizona Archaeological Field School at Grasshopper: Eleven years of Multidisciplinary Research and Teaching." *The Kiva* 40(1–2): 3–38.

Lowell, Julie C. 1991. *Prehistoric Households at Turkey Creek Pueblo, Arizona.* Anthropological Papers of the University of Arizona Number 54. Tucson: University of Arizona Press.

Lumpkins, William. 1984. "Reflections on Chacoan Architecture." In *New Light on Chaco Canyon,* 19–24. Santa Fe: School of American Research.

Lyneis, Margaret M. 1986. "A Spatial Analysis of Anasazi Architecture, A.D. 950–1150, Moapa Valley, Nevada." *The Kiva* 52: 53–74.

Lyneis, Margaret M., Mary K. Rusco, and Keith Myher. 1989. *Investigations at Adam 2 (26CK2059): A Mesa House Phase Site in the Moapa Valley, Nevada.* Nevada State Museum Anthropological Papers, no. 22. Carson City.

McFarland, Elizabeth Fleming. 1991. *Forever Frontier: The Gila Cliff Dwellings.* 4th printing. Albuquerque: University of New Mexico Press.

McKenna, Peter J. 1988. *Late Bonito Phase Developments at the Aztec Ruins, New Mexico.* Santa Fe: National Park Service, Division of Anthropology.

McKenna, Peter J., and James E. Bradford. 1989. *T J Ruin, Gila Cliff Dwelling National Monument.* Santa Fe: National Park Service.

McNitt, Frank. 1966. *Richard Wetherill: Anasazi.* Albuquerque: University of New Mexico Press. [Reprint of 1957.]

Markovitch, Nicholas D., Wolfgang F. E. Preiser, and Fred G. Strum, eds. 1990. *Pueblo Style and Regional Architecture.* New York: Van Nostrand Reinhold.

Marshall, Michael P., John R. Stein, Richard W. Loose, and Judith E. Novotny. 1979. *Anasazi Communities in the San Juan Basin.* Santa Fe: Public Service Company, Albuquerque, and the Historic Preservation Bureau.

Marshall, Michael, and Henry Walt. 1984. *Rio Abajo: Prehistory and History of a Rio Grande Province.* Santa Fe: State Historic Division.

Martin, Paul S. 1979. "Prehistory: Mogollon." In *Handbook of North American Indians, Southwest,* 9:61–74. Washington, D.C.: Smithsonian Institution.

Martin, Paul S., Lawrence Roys, and Gerhardt von Bonin. 1936. *Lowry Ruin in Southwestern Colorado.* Field Museum of Natural History Publication 356, Anthropological Series 23 (1). Chicago.

Mather, Christine, and Sharon Woods. 1986. *Santa Fe Style.* New York: Rizzoli International Publications.

Miller, Donald E. 1974. "A Synthesis of Excavations at Site 42SA863, Three Kiva Pueblo, Montezuma Canyon, San Juan County, Utah." Masters thesis, Brigham Young University.

Mindeleff, Cosmos. 1897. "The Cliff Ruins of Canyon de Chelly, Arizona." In *16th Annual Report of the Bureau of American Ethnology for the Years 1894–1895,* 79–198. Washington, D.C.: Smithsonian Institution.

———. 1989. "Localization of Tusayan Clans." In *Study of Pueblo Architecture in Tusayan and Cibola,* 635–661. Washington, D.C.: Smithsonian Institution Press. [Originally printed in 1900.]

Mindeleff, Victor. 1896*a*. "Aboriginal Remains in Verde Valley, Arizona." In *13th Annual Report of the Bureau of American Ethnology,* 176–221. Washington, D.C.: Smithsonian Institution Press.

———. 1896*b*. "Casa Grande Ruin." In *13th Annual Report of the Bureau of American Ethnology,* 289–319. Washington, D.C.: Smithsonian Institution.

———. 1898. "Navajo Houses." In *17th Annual Report of the Bureau of American Ethnology,* 469–517. Washington, D.C.: Smithsonian Institution.

———. 1989. *A Study of Pueblo Architecture in Tusayan and Cibola.* Washington, D.C.: Smithsonian Institution Press. [Originally published in 1891.]

Montgomery, R. G., W. Smith, and John O. Brew. 1949. *Franciscan Awatovi: The Excavation and Conjectural Reconstruction of a 17th Century Spanish Mission Establishment at a Hopi Indian Town in Northeastern Arizona.* Papers of the Peabody Museum of American Archaeology and Ethnology, Harvard University. Cambridge, Mass.

Morgan, William N. 1980. *Prehistoric Architecture in the Eastern United States.* Cambridge, Mass.: MIT Press.

———. 1988. *Prehistoric Architecture in Micronesia.* Austin: University of Texas Press.

Morris, Don P. 1986. *Archaeological Investigations at Antelope House.* Washington, D.C.: National Park Service.

Musgrove, John, ed. 1987. *Sir Bannister Fletcher's A History of Architecture, Nineteenth Edition.* London: Butterworth Group.

Nabokov, Peter. 1986. *Architecture of Acoma Pueblo: The 1934 Historic American Buildings Survey Project.* Santa Fe: Ancient City Press.

Nabokov, Peter, and Robert Easton. 1989. *Native American Architecture.* New York: Oxford University Press.

Nelson, Nels C. 1914. *Pueblo Ruins of the Galisteo Basin, New Mexico.* Anthropological Papers of the American Museum of Natural History XV, part 1. New York.

Noble, David Grant. 1981. *Ancient Ruins of the Southwest.* Flagstaff: Northland Press.

———. 1984. *New Light on Chaco Canyon.* Santa Fe: School of American Research Press.

———. 1990. *A Trail Guide to Aztec Ruins National Monument.* N.p.: Southwest Parks and Monuments Association in cooperation with the National Park Service.

———, ed. 1989. *Sante Fe: History of an Ancient City.* Santa Fe: School of American Research Press.

Ortiz, Alfonso, vol. ed. 1979. *Handbook of North American Indians.* Vol. 9, *Southwest.* William C. Sturtevant, general editor. Washington, D.C.: Smithsonian Institution.

Osbourne, Douglas. 1964. "Solving the Riddle of Wetherill Mesa." *National Geographic* 125(2):155–195.

Palkovich, Ann M. 1980. *Pueblo Population and Society: The Arroyo Hondo Skeletal and Mortuary Remains.* Arroyo Hondo Archaeological Series, vol. 3. Santa Fe: School of American Research Press.

Panofsky, Erwin. 1957. *Meaning in the Visual Arts.* Garden City, N.Y.: Doubleday Anchor Books.

Pearce, William N. 1937. "A Study of Arrowhead Ruin." Master of Arts Thesis, Texas Technological College.

Peckham, Stewart L. 1969. "An Archaeological Site Inventory of New Mexico, Part I." On file at the Laboratory of Anthropology, Museum of New Mexico, Santa Fe.

Pilles, Peter J., Jr. 1981. "The Southern Sinagua." *Plateau* (Magazine of the Museum of Northern Arizona, Flagstaff.) 53(1):6–17.

———. 1986. *Elden Pueblo: National Register of Historic Places Inventory-Nomination Form.* Flagstaff: USDA Forest Service, Coconino National Forest.

Plog, Fred. 1979. "Prehistory." In *Handbook of North American Indians, Southwest* 9:108–130. Washington, D.C.: Smithsonian Institution.

———. 1989. "The Sinagua and Their Relations." In *Dynamics of Southwestern Prehistory,* edited by Linda Cordell and George J. Gumerman, 263–292. Washington, D.C.: Smithsonian Institution Press.

Powers, Robert P. 1984. "Outliers and Roads in the Chaco System." In *New Light on Chaco Canyon,* 45–58. Santa Fe: School of American Research Press.

Ravesloot, John C. 1988. *Mortuary Practices and Social Differentiation at Casas Grandes, Chihuahua, Mexico.* Anthropological Papers of the University of Arizona Number 49. Tucson: University of Arizona.

Reid, J. Jefferson. 1974. "Behavioral Archaeology at the Grasshopper Ruin." *The Kiva* 40(1–2).

———. 1989. "A Grasshopper Perspective on the Mogollon of the Arizona Mountains." In *Dynamics of Southwest Prehistory*, 56–97. Washington, D.C.: Smithsonian Institution Press.

Rice, Glen E., and Charles L. Redman. 1992. "Power in the Past." *Native Peoples Magazine* (Media Concepts Group, Phoenix.) 5(4): 18–25.

Roberts, Frank H. H., Jr. 1929. *Shabik'eschee Village: A Late Basketmaker Site in Chaco Canyon, New Mexico.* Bureau of American Ethnology Bulletin 92. Washington, D.C.

———. 1931. *The Ruins at Kaituthlanna, Eastern Arizona.* Bureau of American Ethnology Bulletin 100. Washington, D.C.

———. 1932. *The Village of the Great Kivas on the Zuni Reservation, New Mexico.* Bureau of American Ethnology Bulletin 111. Washington, D.C.

Robinson, William J. 1990. "Tree-Ring Studies of the Pueblo de Acoma." *Historical Archaeology* (Published by the Society for Historical Archaeology) 24(3):96–106.

Rohn, Arthur H. 1971. *Mug House, Mesa Verde National Park.* Washington, D.C.: National Park Service, U.S. Department of the Interior.

———. 1977. *Cultural Change and Continuity on Chapin Mesa.* Lawrence: Regents Press of Kansas.

———. 1989a. *Rock Art of Bandelier National Monument.* Albuquerque: University of New Mexico Press.

———. 1989b. "Northern San Juan Prehistory." In *Dynamics of Southwest Prehistory*, edited by Linda S. Cordell and George J. Gummerman, 149–178. Washington, D.C.: Smithsonian Institution Press.

Rudolph, Paul M. 1983. "Comments on Vernacular Architecture." In *Paul Rudolph, 1983–1984, Recipient of the Plym Distinguished Professorship*, edited by James P. Warfield. Urbana-Champaign: School of Architecture, University of Illinois.

Rykwert, Joseph. 1983. *The First Moderns.* Cambridge, Mass.: MIT Press.

———. 1984. *On Adam's House in Paradise.* 2d ed. Cambridge, Mass.: MIT Press.

Sayles, Edwin B. 1937. "Houses." In *Excavations at Snaketown I: Material Culture*, edited by Harold S. Gladwin et al. 59–90. Gila Pueblo Medallion Paper 25. Globe, Ariz. Reprinted Tucson: Arizona State Museum, 1945.

Schroeder, Albert H. 1979a. "Pecos Pueblo." In *Handbook of North American Indians, Southwest*, 9:430–437. Washington, D.C.: Smithsonian Institution.

———. 1979b. "Prehistory: Hakataya." In *Handbook of North American Indians, Southwest*, 9:100–107. Washington, D.C.: Smithsonian Institution.

———. 1979c. "Pueblos Abandoned in Historic Times." In *Handbook of North American Indians, Southwest*, 9:236–254. Washington, D.C.: Smithsonian Institution.

Schroeder, Albert H., and Homer F. Hastings. 1961. *Montezuma Castle National Monument.* National Park Service Historical Handbook Series, no. 27. Washington, D.C.

Schwartz, Douglas W., and R. W. Lang. 1973. "Archaeological Investigations at the Arroyo Hondo Site: Third Field Report—1972. Santa Fe: School of American Research.

Scully, Vincent. 1989. *Pueblo: Mountain, Village, Dance.* 2d ed. Chicago: University of Chicago Press.

Shafer, Harry J. 1990. "Archaeology at the NAN Ruin: The 1989 Season." *The Artifact* (El Paso Archaeological Society) 29(4):1–43.

Shafer, Harry J., and Anna J. Taylor. 1986. "Mimbres Pueblo Dynamics and Ceramic Style Change." *Journal of Field Archaeology* 3(1):43–68.

Simmons, Marc. 1974. "History of Pueblo-Spanish Relations to 1821." In *Handbook of North American Indians, Southwest,* 9:178–193. Washington, D.C.: Smithsonian Institution.

Smiley, T. L., S. A. Stubbs, and B. Bannister. 1953. *A Foundation for the Dating of Some Late Archaeology in the Rio Grande Area, New Mexico.* Laboratory of Tree-ring Research Bulletin 6, Tucson: University of Arizona.

Smith, Watson. 1972. *Prehistoric Kivas of Antelope Mesa, Northeastern Arizona.* Papers of the Peabody Museum of Archaeology and Ethnology, Harvard University 39(1). Cambridge, Mass.

Smith, Watson, Richard B. Woodbury, and Natalie F. S. Woodbury. 1966. *The Excavation of Hawikuh by Frederick Webb Hodge: Report of the Hendricks-Hodge Expedition, 1917–1923.* Contributions from the Museum of the American Indian, Heye Foundation 20. New York.

Spier, Leslie. 1917. "An Outline for a Chronology of Zuni Ruins." *Anthropological Papers of the American Museum of Natural History* 18:205–331. New York: American Museum of Natural History.

Spreiregen, Paul D. 1987. *The Architecture of William Morgan.* Austin: University of Texas Press.

Stuart, David E. 1989. *The Magic of Bandelier.* Santa Fe: Ancient City Press.

Stuart, David E., and Rory P. Gauthier. 1988. *Prehistoric New Mexico.* Albuquerque: University of New Mexico Press.

Stubbs, Stanley A. 1950. *Bird's Eye View of the Pueblos.* Norman: University of Oklahoma Press.

Stubbs, Stanley A., and W. S. Stallings, Jr. 1953. *The Excavation of Pindi Pueblo, New Mexico.* Monograph of the School of American Research 18. Santa Fe.

Sturtevant, William C., gen. ed. 1979. *Handbook of North American Indians.* Vol. 9, *Southwest,* Alfonso Ortiz, volume editor. Washington, D.C.: Smithsonian Institution.

Swentzell, Rina. 1985. "An Understated Sacredness." *MASS: Journal of the School of Architecture and Planning* (University of New Mexico, Albuquerque), Fall, 24–25.

———. 1988. "Bupingeh: The Pueblo Plaza." *El Palacio,* Winter, 14–19.

———. 1990. "Pueblo Space, Form, and Mythology." In *Pueblo Style and Regional Architecture,* edited by Nicholas C. Markovich, Wolfgang F. E. Preiser, and Fred G. Strum, pp. 23–30. New York: Van Nostrand Reinhold.

Upham, Steadman. 1982. *Politics and Power: An Economic and Political History of the Western Pueblo.* New York: Academic Press.

Upham, Steadman, and Gail M. Bockley. 1989. "The Chronologies of Nuvakwewtaqa: Implications for Social Processes." In *The Sociopolitical Structure of Prehistoric Southwestern Societies,* edited by Steadman Upham,

Kent G. Lightfoot, and Roberta A. Jewett, pp. 447–490. Boulder: Westview Press.

Vargas Zapata y Luxán Ponze de León, Diego de. 1914. "The Reconquest of New Mexico, 1692: Extracts from the Journal of General Don Diego de Vargas Zapata Lujan Ponce de Leon." *Old Santa Fe* 1(4):420–435.

Vivian, R. Gordon. 1989. *Chacoan Prehistory of the San Juan Basin.* New York: Academic Press.

Vivian, R. Gordon, and Tom W. Mathews. 1965. *Kin Kletso, a Pueblo III Community in Chaco Canyon, New Mexico.* Coolidge. Southwestern Monuments Association Technical Series 6 (1).

Warfield, James P., ed. 1983. *Paul Rudolph, 1983–1984, Recipient of the Plym Distinguished Professorship.* Urbana-Champaign: School of Architecture, University of Illinois.

Watson, Patty Jo, Stephen A. LeBlanc, and Charles L. Redman. 1980. "Aspects of Zuni Prehistory: Preliminary Report on Excavations and Survey in the El Morro Valley of New Mexico." *Journal of Field Archaeology* 7:201–218.

Wheat, Joe Ben. 1954. *Crooked Ridge Village (Arizona W: 10: 15).* University of Arizona Bulletin 25(3) Social Science Bulletin 24. Tucson.

Wilcox, David R. 1987. "New Models of Social Structure at the Palo Parado Site." In *The Hohokam Village: Site Structure and Organization,* edited by David E. Doyel, 223–248. Glennwood Springs, Col.: Southwestern and Rocky Mountain Division of the American Association for the Advancement of Science.

———. 1991*a.* "New World Prehistory, The Hohokam Ballgame and the Chacoan State: An Essay on Macroregional Analysis." Manuscript on file at the Museum of Northern Arizona, Flagstaff.

———. 1991*b.* "The Mesoamerican Ballgame in the American Southwest." In *The Mesoamerican Ballgame,* edited by Vernon L. Scarborough and David R. Wilcox. Tucson: University of Arizona Press.

———. 1991*c.* "Hohokam Social Complexity." In *Chaco and Hohokam,* edited by Patricia L. Crown and W. James Judge, 253–276. Santa Fe: School of American Research Press.

Wilcox, David R., Thomas R. McGuire, and Charles Sternberg. 1981. *Snaketown Revisited.* Arizona State Museum Archaeological Series, no. 155. Tucson: University of Arizona.

Wilcox, David R., and Lynette O. Shenk. 1977. *The Architecture of the Casa Grande and Its Interpretation.* Arizona State Museum Archaeological Series, no. 115. Tucson: University of Arizona.

Wilcox, David R., and Charles Sternberg. 1983. *Hohokam Ballcourts and Their Interpretation.* Arizona State Museum Archaeological Series, no. 160. Tucson: University of Arizona.

Windes, Thomas C. 1990. *Investigations of Pueblo Alto Complex: 1988–1990.* Santa Fe: National Park Service.

Wing, Kittridge A. 1961. *Bandelier National Monument.* National Park Service Historical Handbook Series, no. 23. Washington, D.C.

Wood, J. Scott. 1986. "Vale of Tiers, Tonto Basin in the 14th Century." Tonto National Forest Cultural Resources Inventory Report 86–130. On file at the Supervisor's Office, Phoenix.

———. 1989. "Vale of Tiers, Too: Late Classic Period Salado Settlement Patterns and Organizational Models for Tonto Basin." Tonto National Forest Cultural Resources Inventory Report 89-12-280. On file at the Supervisor's Office, Phoenix.

Woodbury, Richard B. 1956. *The Antecedents of Zuni Culture.* Transactions of the New York Academy of Sciences 2d ser., 18(6):557–563. New York.

———. 1979*a*. "Prehistory: Introduction." In *Handbook of North American Indians, Southwest,* 9:22–30. Washington, D.C.: Smithsonian Institution.

———. 1979*b*. "Zuni Prehistory and History to 1850." In *Handbook of North American Indians, Southwest,* 9:467–473. Washington, D.C.: Smithsonian Institution.

Zelik, Michael. 1984. "Archaeoastronomy at Chaco Canyon." In *New Light on Chaco Canyon,* 65–72. Santa Fe: School of American Research.

in the Tonto Basin, 117
in Mesa Verde, 140, 142
in Tsiping, 147
at Acoma, 255
great houses
of Chaco Canyon, 23, 24, 39, 50
of the Northern San Juan, 25, 81–87
of the Hohokam, 107–108, 173–183
great kiva
in the Dolores River Valley, 18
in the San Juan Basin, 24, 64, 66, 67, 68, 69, 70, 71, 73, 75
in the Mimbres Valley, 29, 31, 33
in the Gila River Valley, 36
in Chaco Canyon, 39, 41, 45, 46, 47, 205
in the Northern San Juan area, 80, 81, 85, 87, 143
reconstruction of, 84
in the Mogollon area, 103, 163, 165
in the Zuni area, 118, 120, 239
in the Sinagua area, 129, 204
Guam, Mariana Islands, Micronesia 6

H

Halona (red ant place), New Mexico, 194, 239
ruins underlie Zuni Pueblo, 238
one of six traditional pueblos, 239
description of South Halona, 239
hamlet, xv, xvi, 23
defined by size, 3, 267
of White Mound Village, 4, 10
of Mogollon Village, 7
of Harris, 8
near Lowry, 80
of Chodistaas, 99
near Paquimé, 170
near Besh Ba Gowah, 189
Hano (Tewa), Arizona, 237
relative to Walpi, 245; to Sichomovi, 246; to Shipovlovi, 250; to Mishongnovi, 251; to Payupki, 253
site description of, 247–248
Harrington, Mark Raymond (scholar), 94
Harris, New Mexico, xvi, 3, 4, 5
site description of, 8–10
relative to White Mound Village, 10; to Cameron Creek, 27; to Snaketown, 38; to Palo Parado, 114

Haury, Emil (scholar), 7, 8, 9, 37, 39, 176
Hawiku, New Mexico, 155, 157
site description of, 193–195
one of six traditional Zuni pueblos, 239
Hemenway Expedition of 1887–1888, 175
Hernando de Alvarado. *See* Alvarado, Hernando de
Heshotatzina (marked house). *See* Lower Pescado
Hewett, Edgar Lee (scholar), 47, 207, 209, 211
Heye Foundation, Museum of the American Indian, New York, 94
Hibben, Frank C. (scholar), 216
hierarchy, social or economic
at Snaketown, 38
at Dominguez, 89
at Elden, 129
at Grasshopper, 163
at Paquimé, 171
at Los Muertos, 179
at Salome, 184
at Cline Terrace, 187
at Schoolhouse Point, 189
at Besh Ba Gowah, 191
at Nuvaqueotaka, 201, 205
in the Hopi Mesas, 237, 245
High Bank earthworks, Ohio, 5
highway. *See* roads, prehistoric
Historic American Building Survey, 254
Hogback, New Mexico, 25
site description of, 75–76
Hohman, John (scholar), 165
Hohokam (those who came before) culture, xv, xviii
practice of cremation, 8, 111
pithouses of, 8, 9, 10, 38, 39, 111, 184
achievements of, 23, 265
at Snaketown, 37
descendants of, 39, 155, 175, 269
thirteenth-century sites of, 99, 100
influences of, 101, 118, 130,
contact with Chodistaas, 105
at Pueblo Grande, 107
at Cerro Prieto, 108
at Palo Parado, 111
pithouses compared with Mogollon, 114

compounds compared with Salado, 114, 115, 116, 118, 185, 187, 189, 191
relative to Montezuma Castle, 132; to Paquimé, 156, 170; to Cline Terrace, 185; to the Zuni area, 239
ball court compared with Wupatki's, 138
trade with Kinishba, 163
trade with Grasshopper, 165
at Casa Grande, 173
at Los Muertos, 175
Homolobi, Arizona, 251
Hopewell culture
architectural achievements of, 5, 6
See also High Bank; Marietta; Newark; Oldtown; Seal
Hopi Mesas, Arizona, 155, 235, 262
Antelope Mesa: Awatovi, 198
First Mesa: Walpi, 245; Sichomovi, 246; Hano, 247
Second Mesa: Chukubi, 198; Shongopavi, 249; Shipaulovi, 250; Mishongnovi, 251; Payupki; 253
Third Mesa: Old and New Oraibi, Upper and Lower Moenkopi, Hotevilla, and Bacabi, 195
See also Firehouse
Hopi people, xvi, xvii, xix, 12, 39
ancestors of, 102, 132, 134, 135, 140, 142, 155, 165
place names of, 129, 137, 200, 204
Sinagua relations with, 129, 131, 132
share characteristics with Zuni, 135, 238
in Canyon de Chelly, 137
traditional way of life of, 162, 242, 245, 246
trading sphere of, 163
during the Pueblo Revolt, 235, 236
See also Hopi Mesas
House of Taga, Tinian, Mariana Islands, 160, 238
Houses of Paquimé: of the Macaws, of the Dead, of the Pillars, of the Skulls, of the Well, 171
Hovenweep (deserted valley) Castle, Utah, 144, 145
Hovenweep National Monument, Colorado and Utah, xiii

29, 31, 33
pit house sites in, 4, 8
year-round occupation of, 8
Salado sites in, 100, 114
Mindeleff, Cosmos (scholar), 76, 137
Mindeleff, Victor (scholar)
architectural study by, xix
on Chaco Canyon, 41
on Cibola (Zuni) sites, 192, 194, 239,
242, 244
on Tusayan (Hopi) sites, 195, 198,
200, 246, 247, 249, 250, 251, 253
Mishongnovi, Second Mesa, Arizona,
237
relative to Oraibi, 195; to Chukubi,
198; to Shongopavi, 249; to Shipaulovi, 250
site description of, 251–253
Mitla, Oaxaca, Mexico, 160
Mogollon, Don Ignacio Flores (governor), 7
Mogollon culture, xv, xvi, 3
early sites of, 4, 5, 7, 8, 23, 36
burial practices of, 8, 34
architecture of, 9, 10, 11, 33, 36, 38
traits at Cameron Creek, 27, 28, 29
transition to pueblos, 27, 32
pit houses compared with Hohokam, 38, 114
thirteenth-century sites of, 99, 103,
104, 105
relative to Salado ideas, 114, 116,
118, 188, 191
influence on the Zuni, 121, 238, 239
influence on the Sinagua, 132
later sites of, 155, 156, 160, 163, 165
Jornada, in the Estancia Valley, 230
Mogollon Rim, 99, 129, 158, 201
definition of, 268
Mogollon Village, New Mexico
pit house community of, xv, 3, 4
site description of, 7–8
relative to White Mound Village,
10; to Snaketown, 38; to Palo Parado, 114
moiety (dual social division)
in the Rio Grande Valley, xvii
at Turkey Creek, 99, 103
at Santo Domingo, 260
Monks Mound. See Cahokia
Monte Albán, Oaxaca, 6, 160

Montezuma Castle, Arizona, 101
relative to Elden Pueblo, 129
site description of, 131–132
Montezuma Valley, Colorado and Utah,
25, 53, 268
relative to Canyon de Chelly, 76; to
Mesa Verde, 79
sites in, 88, 90, 99, 102, 142, 144
migrations from, 142
trade network of, 184
Morris, Earl H. (scholar), 81
Mound Bottom earthworks, Tennessee,
103
Mound of the Offerings, Paquimé, 170
Moundville earthworks, Alabama, 160
Mount Royal earthworks, Florida, 238
Muddy River, Nevada, 92
Muddy Water, New Mexico, 25
site description of, 73–74
kiva of, 119
Mummy Cave, Arizona, 102, 132
site description of, 136–137
Mummy Lake. See Far View
mural. See painting, wall
Museum of New Mexico, Santa Fe
Laboratory of Anthropology, 127,
149, 216
work at Kuaua, 207
Museum of Northern Arizona, Flagstaff
kiva murals of Awatovi, 200
Museum of the American Indian, Heye
Foundation, New York, 94

N

Nandauwas, Pohnpei, 160
Nan Madol, Pohnpei, 6, 27, 103, 160
"Venice of the Pacific," 238
NAN Ranch, New Mexico, xvi, 23
relative to Cameron Creek, 28; to
Galaz, 29
site description of, 33–34
National Anthropological Archives,
Washington, D.C., 200
Navajo National Monument, Arizona,
102, 132, 134
Navajo people
arrival in the Southwest, xvii
place names of, 12, 51, 54, 55, 56,
76, 132, 134, 163, 198
in the San Juan Basin, 62, 75

in southeastern Utah, 90
Indian Reservation of, 147
alliance during Pueblo Revolt, 235
language spoken by some Hano, 248
Athapascan language of, 267
Nelson, Nels C. (scholar), 222
New Alto (highland), New Mexico,
24, 50
relative to Kin Kletso and Casa Chiquita, 57
site description of, 58–59
compared with Escalante, 89
Newark earthworks, Ohio, 5
Niza, Fray Marcos de (explorer), 193
Northern San Juan Anasazi. See Anasazi, in the Northern San Juan
area
Nutria (otter), New Mexico, 236
relative to Lower Pescado, 242
site description of, 244
Nutria River, New Mexico, 100, 125,
244
Nuvakwewtaqa. See Nuvaqueotaka
Nuvaqueotaka (snow belt) Arizona,
129, 158
trade with Verde Valley, 131
site description of, 201–205

O

Oaxaca, Mexico, 6, 160
Ocmulgee earthlodge, Macon, Georgia
compared to pit house, 4
Ohio River Valley, 5, 103
Ojo Caliente (hot springs), New Mexico, 242
Oldtown earthworks, Ohio, 5
Olla (round earthen pot) Cave, Chihuahua 156, 268
site description of, 172–173
Oñate, Don Juan de (governor)
colonizer of Gran Quivira, 231
expedition to Acoma, 255
lecture in Santo Domingo, 260
open-sided rooms. See rooms with
three walls
Oraibi, Third Mesa, Arizona, xviii, 158
at the time of the *entrada*, 155, 237
site description of, 195–196
plan comparisons, 198, 237, 260
mesa top location of, 198

principles of Southwestern architecture, 265–266

puchteca. *See* pochteca

Pueblo Alto (high town), New Mexico, 24
   relative to Pueblo Bonito, 45; to Chetro Ketl, 47; to Pueblo del Arroyo, 53; to Tsin Kletzin, 55; to New Alto, 58
   site description of, 49–51

Pueblo Bonito (beautiful town), New Mexico, 24
   scale compared with Eastern United States sites, xx
   relative to other Chacoan great houses, 39–59; to outliers, 59–76; to Aztec, 81; to Salmon, 85; to Squaw Springs, 87; to Wallace, 88; to Casa Vibora, 118; to Village of the Great Kivas, 120; to Paquimé, 170; to Kin Tiel, 192; to Oraibi, 195; to Mishongnovi, 253
   site description of, 43–45

Pueblo del Arroyo (town of the gully), New Mexico, 24
   scale compared with Eastern United States sites, xx
   site description of, 51–53
   relative to Pueblo Alto, 53; to Wijiji, 54; to Kin Kletso, 57; to Pueblo Pintado, 65

Pueblo de los Muertos (town of the dead), New Mexico
   relative to Atsinna, 128

Pueblo Grande (great town), Arizona, xv, 100
   compared with Snaketown, 38
   site description of, 107–108
   relative to Park Creek, 116; to Wupatki, 138; to Cline Terrace, 185

Pueblo Grande de Nevada (great town of the heavy snowfall), 94

Pueblo people
   descendants of the Anasazi, xvi
   languages of, xvii
   See also Rio Grande Valley, Zuni, and Hopi towns built after A.D. 1540

Pueblo Pintado (painted house), New Mexico, 25

relative to Pueblo Alto, 51; to Kin Ya'a, 73; to Casa Vibora, 119
site description of, 65–66

Pueblo Revolt of 1680–1692
   in the Zuni area, 157, 194, 236, 239
   in the Hopi area, 198, 200, 245, 246, 247, 249, 251, 253, 254
   in the Rio Grande area, 226, 231, 235
   events of, 235

Puerco (muddy) River of the Rio Grande, 10

Puye Pueblo, New Mexico, 209

pyrite. *See* iron pyrite

Anasazi, xvi
defined by size, 3
in the Rio Grande Valley, 99
near Besh Ba Gowah, 189
near Acoma, 255
Village of the Great Kivas, New Mexico, 101
brings Anasazi ideas to Zuni, 239
Virgin Anasazi, 26
at Main Ridge, 92, 94
relative to Coombs, 94, 96
relocation to Hopi area, 155, 198

W

Wallace, Colorado, 26
relative to Lowry, 79
site description of, 88
to Escalante, 89
wall construction. *See* masonry, jacal
walls defining architectural order
at Chimney Rock, 91
at Nuvaqueotaka, 201
Walnut Creek, Arizona, 106
Walpi, First Mesa, Arizona, 237
relative to Tsiping, 149; to Grasshopper, 163; to Oraibi, 195; to Chukubi, 198; to Awatovi, 198; to Fire House, 200; to Sichomovi, 246; to Hano, 247; to Acoma, 255
site description of, 245–246
West Mesa. *See* Hopi Mesas, Third Mesa
Wetherill, John (explorer), 134
Wetherill, Richard (explorer), 132, 139, 140
Wetherill Mesa, Colorado, 12, 14, 20
Whirlwind House, New Mexico, 24
site description of, 62–63
White House, Canyon de Chelly, Arizona, 25
site description of, 76–77
compared to Hovenweep Castle, 145; to Crumbled House, 147
White Mound Village, Arizona, xvi
beginning as a hamlet, 3, 4
site description of, 10
relative to Tohatchi Village, 11
Wijiji (black greasewood), New Mexico, 24

site description of, 54–55
relative to Tsin Kletzin, 55, 56; to New Alto, 58; to Wallace, 88
Wilcox, David R. (scholar), 37, 111, 173
Winterville earthworks, Mississippi, 103
Wood, J. Scott (scholar), 188
Wukoki, Arizona, 138
Wupatki (tall house), Arizona, 102
relative to Snaketown, 38; to Kiet Siel, 132
site description of, 137–138

X

Xochicalco, Mexico, 27

Y

Yam-p-hamba (San Cristóbal), 226
Yap Islands, Micronesia, 238
Yaqui Indians, xvi
Yavapai Indians, 131
Yellowhouse, New Mexico, 101
relative to Pescado Canyon, 123; to Ramah Schoolhouse, 127; to Lower Pescado, 242
site description of, 124–126
Yellow Jacket, Colorado. *See* Lowry
Yucatán, architecture of, 27, 103, 160, 238

Z

Zapotec architecture, 6, 160
Zuni people, xvii, 238, 239
agriculture of, 12
of the thirteenth century, 99, 100, 101
ancestors of, 128, 140, 142, 155, 165, 193
ideas at Gran Quivira, 230, 232
alliance during the Pueblo Revolt, 235
farming villages of, 242
late communities of, 242, 244
relative to Acoma, 254, 255
Zuni Pueblo, xvi, xvii, 235, 236
plan compared to Oraibi, 195
site description of, 238–242
relative to Sichomovi, 247; to Hano,

248; to Taos, 262
Zuni River Valley, 100, 155
sites in, 118–128, 192–195, 235, 236, 238–244